PROTECTING PRISONERS

PROTECTING PRISONERS

The Standards of the European Committee for the Prevention of Torture in Context

ROD MORGAN

and

MALCOLM D. EVANS

OXFORD
UNIVERSITY PRESS

OXFORD

UNIVERSITY PRESS

Great Clarendon Street, Oxford OX2 6DP

Oxford University Press is a department of the University of Oxford.
It furthers the University's objective of excellence in research, scholarship,
and education by publishing worldwide in

Oxford New York

Athens Auckland Bangkok Bogotá Buenos Aires Calcutta
Cape Town Chennai Dar es Salaam Delhi Florence Hong Kong Istanbul
Karachi Kuala Lumpur Madrid Melbourne Mexico City Mumbai
Nairobi Paris São Paulo Singapore Taipei Tokyo Toronto Warsaw

with associated companies in Berlin Ibadan

Oxford is a registered trade mark of Oxford University Press
in the UK and in certain other countries

Published in the United States
by Oxford University Press Inc., New York

British Library Cataloguing in Publication Data

Data available

Library of Congress Cataloging in Publication Data

Protecting prisoners: the standards of the European Committee for the Prevention of
Torture in context / [edited by] Rod Morgan and Malcolm Evans.
p. cm.
Includes bibliographical references and index.
1. Prisoners—Legal status, laws, etc.—Europe. 2. Torture—Europe. 3. European
Convention for the Prevention of Torture and Inhuman or Degrading Treatment or
Punishment (1987) I. Morgan, Rodney. II. Evans, Malcolm.
KJC9769 .P76 1999
341.6'5'094—dc21 99-16151
ISBN 0-19-829821-8

1 3 5 7 9 10 8 6 4 2

Typeset in Times
by Best-set Typesetter Ltd., Hong Kong
Printed in Great Britain
on acid-free paper by
Biddles Ltd. Guildford, King's Lynn

Preface

This collection of essays on the work of the European Committee for the Prevention of Torture and Inhuman or Degrading Treatment or Punishment (the CPT) arose out of a seminar held at the University of Bristol in September 1997. The seminar was the culmination of a study of the CPT in which we have been engaged more or less continuously since the foundation of the Committee in 1989 and which, during the period 1994–1997, was greatly assisted by a grant from the Airey Neave Trust. The grant enabled us to travel throughout Europe interviewing officials, parliamentarians, lawyers, and NGO representatives in order to gather their views on the work of the CPT and begin to chart the impact of the Committee on the policies of states party. When we approached the Airey Neave Trustees in 1994 they made it plain that they wanted the results of our study to be as widely disseminated as possible. They hoped that we might make the work of the CPT more widely understood and thereby modestly assist the growth of international human rights law in general and the prevention of torture in particular. The Trustees suggested that towards the end of our project we might use part of our grant to organize a seminar to which persons closely involved with the development of the work of the Committee could be invited. This proposal chimed with our own aspirations. Ever since 1989 we have worked closely with various organizations instrumental in framing the ECPT and promoting its work—the Council of Europe, Amnesty International, the Association for the Prevention of Torture (the APT, formerly the Swiss Committee Against Torture), the International Committee of the Red Cross (the ICRC), and so on. We have written widely on the subject and contributed to many conferences and seminars sponsored by these and other organizations.[1] As a result of these activities we have developed a substantial network of contacts. Thus, as our Airey Neave-financed fieldwork drew to a close in 1997, it seemed logical that in the early autumn we should bring together in Bristol a group of experts on the CPT and CPT-related matters having circulated to our invitees in advance a paper on the 'jurisprudence' of the CPT. The contents of that paper eventually formed part of our book (Chapters Six, Seven, and Eight) on the formation and work of the CPT—*Preventing Torture*—which was published by Oxford University Press in September 1998.

The Bristol seminar proved much more valuable than a mere test bed for our own work. A number of the contributors prepared papers which

---

[1] For a fuller account of these activities see Evans, MD and Morgan, R (1998) *Preventing Torture* (Oxford: Clarendon Press), Preface.

complemented our own and expanded on it. Towards the end of the three days we were agreed that we had between us the core of a book capable of advancing the largely historical account represented by *Preventing Torture*. We put that proposition to John Louth, our editor at Oxford University Press, and he agreed. The result is the present collection which we would explain as follows.

Preventing Torture provides an account of the background to the ECPT and the formation and early development of the CPT. A brief history of torture, including an extended discussion of the phenomenon of torture in the late twentieth century, is followed by an overview of the manner in which the prohibition of torture developed into customary international law. There then follows a review of the *travaux préparatoires* of the ECPT, a survey of the composition and *modus operandi* of the Committee and a review of its 'jurisprudence'—by which we mean the standards promulgated in written reports and applied during inspection visits of the Committee. We conclude with a tentative review of the effectiveness of the Committee and consider the dilemmas confronting its work in the medium-term future. It is a substantial book. Yet despite its length *Preventing Torture* cannot pretend to be a definitive account of the 'jurisprudence' of the CPT—for want of space and time we left several major aspects of custodial policy substantially untouched. Moreover, we had not space to do more than provide an overview of the manner in which the work of the CPT relates to that of other international agencies whose activity also encompasses the prohibition of torture and are designed to prevent and censure its occurrence. Moreover, although we copiously illustrated the jurisprudence and *modus operandi* of the Committee with reference to numerous CPT reports and government responses, we had not the space in which to focus in detail on the overall situation in member states. Finally, any study of a working institution, especially an institution operating within the fast-changing contours of contemporary Europe, is by definition a historical study as soon as the authors cease their data-collecting activities, let alone lay their pens aside. We have not ceased our data-collecting activities, but every study has to have a cut-off point and in the case of *Preventing Torture* it was more or less the end of 1997.

Protecting Prisoners, the collection of essays that follows, aims to achieve the following. In Part One we provide what we believe to be an up-to-date and fairly comprehensive account of the work of the CPT. Chapter One briefly sets the scene by describing the nature of the Convention and the working methods of the CPT. Chapter Two provides a digest of the jurisprudence of the Committee arranged by class of prisoners. That is, we describe how CPT standards and safeguards apply to legal and socio-demographic categories of prisoners—suspects detained by the police, criminal suspects remanded in custody pending trial or sentence, offenders sentenced to imprisonment, administrative detainees (including foreign nationals detained under immigration legislation), the mentally disordered detained under mental health legislation, and so on, cross-cut by the important distinctions between adults and juveniles, men and women, nationals and foreign nationals, prisoners of sound mind and those not of sound mind, the innocuous and the dangerous—each of which categories is more or less distinctive in terms of human need and vulnerability to ill-treatment. We believe this is to be a typological framework which officials and NGOs who consume CPT jurisprudence will find useful. It is a departure from the method we employed in *Preventing Torture*. For this current work our cut-off point has been more or less the end of 1998.

Part Two aims to situate the work of the CPT within the torture prohibiting and preventing framework of international law and human rights activism. In Chapter Three Wolfgang Peukert discusses the relationship between the CPT and the European Commission and Court of Human Rights, a sensitive relationship which preoccupied the framers of the ECPT[2] and which is already becoming rather more complex than the position routinely described in the preface to all initial CPT periodic country inspection reports. It is already apparent that the CPT and ECHR mechanisms exercise a two-way jurisprudential influence on each other. In Chapter Four Jim Murdoch explores the manner in which the CPT's standards have expanded, elaborated, and, arguably, superseded the European Prison Rules, a code to which the CPT makes very little reference. This focus neatly underlines an observation and a question. First, the Committee is very largely preoccupied with general custodial conditions—conditions which may, in the Committee's judgement, constitute *inhuman and degrading treatment or punishment*—rather than the torture which preoccupied the founders and framers of the Convention. Secondly, when thinking about the future should the European Prison Rules be radically updated in light of the CPT's efforts? Or would it now be more realistic for the Council of Europe largely to forget the European Prison Rules and focus instead on the regular production of an evolving digest of CPT standards? Such a project would be more organic than the formulation and revision of the European Prison Rules has ever been, but do the CPT's standards have the same weight and credibility?

In Chapter Five Walter Suntinger relates the CPT's efforts to the various United Nations torture prohibiting and preventing mechanisms. There is a symbiotic relationship here. The prohibition of torture following the Universal Declaration of Human Rights has passed into customary international law but the UN still lacks the routine ability effectively to face down member states who fail to live up to their international obligations

---

[2] Evans and Morgan (1998) *Preventing Torture*, Chapter Four.

to prevent torture. There is not yet under the aegis of the UN, as there is now within Europe in the shape of the CPT, a well-resourced hands-on inspectoral body to which member states are required to give access to their custodial sites. It remains to be seen whether the long-standing effort to create such a body by means of an optional protocol to the UN Convention Against Torture will be agreed, but it currently seems doubtful that even if such a body is created it will have the powers enjoyed by the CPT. Should that prove to be the case then consideration ought arguably to be given to stimulating the development of alternative UN mechanisms. In conclusion to Part Two Eric Prokosch of Amnesty International describes in Chapter Six how human rights NGOs like Amnesty press for, and then feed off, the adoption by intergovernmental bodies of standards. He also points out that for international human rights NGOs like Amnesty, the adoption of highly detailed standards may not always be advantageous: they may not be applicable in culturally varied contexts in which resources also differ hugely. This is an issue which is also touched on by Piet van Reenen in Chapter Ten.

Part Three is devoted to analyses of CPT reports on particular countries and the reaction by governments to those reports and their impact on policy. The accounts illustrate the variety of dialogues in which the CPT is engaged with state parties. In Belgium, as Stephan Parmentier argues in Chapter Seven, the visits and reports of the CPT have stimulated profound questioning of traditional custodial practices in Belgium, but there has so far been fairly entrenched resistance to the adoption of the more structural reforms recommended by the CPT. The French situation, as Roland Bank demonstrates in Chapter Eight, is somewhat different. Though there is evidence that prison conditions in France may have improved partly as a result of CPT strictures, there is also evidence of vacillation on the part of the French authorities with regard to the rights of suspects in police custody and deception with regard to facilities for persons detained under the immigration laws. What is not clear from Roland Bank's account is what part, if any, has been played in these developments by French NGOs, but it is our impression that there are not in France, as there are in The Netherlands and the UK, for example, many effective NGOs actively monitoring custodial conditions. It is the role of one clearly effective NGO in Hungary which makes Agnes Kover's account in Chapter Nine particularly interesting. Here is a situation, unlike that described by Stephen Shaw with respect to the UK in Chapter Twelve, where the CPT appears not to have been particularly well briefed before undertaking the visit and being put right after the event about some of the procedural realities of Hungarian police custody by an NGO which has successfully negotiated access to its own police stations. The Dutch situation described by Piet van Reenan in Chapter Ten provides an interesting contrast to the position in France. It is clear that the Dutch authorities are no more keen on having lawyers in Dutch police stations during the early stages of police custody than are the French authorities. But the Dutch authorities, it appears, handle things differently: they tell the CPT in a straightforward manner that they take pride in the professional integrity of their police officers, do not consider there is any evidence of malpractice against suspects in police custody, and, accordingly, do not intend to accede to a central CPT recommendation, namely, that suspects have right of access to a lawyer from the outset of police custody. The Dutch stance is similar to that of the Belgians, though declared more robustly. There is other evidence of blunt Dutch resistance.

The situation in Turkey, described in Chapter Eleven, is radically different again. Semih Gemalmaz, alone of our contributors, has never seen a CPT report on his country because the Turkish authorities have not authorized their publication and direct knowledge is limited to the two Public Statements which the CPT has itself issued. It follows that he has had to do painstaking detective work, trying to prise information from the shroud of confidentiality which envelops CPT reports and government responses if the government chooses not to reveal what is happening. The CPT has visited Turkey more than any other state party and from his analysis of Turkish press reports and other documents it is clear that the Turkish authorities continue to engage in a dialogue of denial and prevarication about a pattern of human rights abuse which is as well known to the domestic Turkish rights NGOs as it is to the CPT. In this battle of wits it is apparent that a largely cowed and ignorant press is used by the Turkish authorities to distort the few impressions gained by the Turkish populace of CPT activities. In Britain, it would seem, the position is very different. As Stephen Shaw reveals in Chapter Twelve, it was never plausible that the CPT could make known to the UK public more than was already known since the work of several highly professional NGOs which have policing and penal policy as their focus have placed these issues firmly in the public arena. Moreover, the first CPT visit to the UK followed hard on the heels of extensive prison riots in April 1990 which led to the establishment of a judicial inquiry, the report of which was exhaustive in its examination of penal policy. In the UK, therefore, CPT reports have proved to be a useful international voice added to a domestic chorus, but it was unlikely that the CPT would provoke policy initiatives not already in train.

Any collection of this nature involves team working. Most, though not all, of our contributors came to Bristol for those three valuable days in September 1997. We thank them for coming and for revising their papers in the light of the Bristol discussions and developments since. We are also indebted to the Airey Neave Trustees for making the seminar possible. Two of our contributors—Roland Bank and Semih Gemalmaz—did not come to Bristol. We approached them subsequently because we wanted to give

Part Three of this text as wide a reach as possible and thought it important to include essays on France and Turkey since they have been a source of considerable difficulties for the CPT in various ways.

In conclusion we would like to thank John Louth, our editor at Oxford University Press, whose encouragement was vital to the realization of this project. And last but not least, our thanks to Rachel Nee and Pat Hammond, our colleagues in the Faculty of Law at the University of Bristol, whose administrative and word-processing skills kept the ship on course and enabled us to deliver a script which was more tidy and accurate than would otherwise have been the case. We, rather than our contributors, proof-read the whole: responsibility for any remaining blemishes rests with us.

Rod Morgan
Malcolm D. Evans

Faculty of Law, University of Bristol
January 1999

Addendum

This text was finalized as of 31 December 1998. A number of contributions make the point that Turkey was yet to authorize the publication of any CPT report. On 23 February 1999 the report arising from the CPT's second *periodic* visit to Turkey from 5 to 17 October 1997 was published (CPT/Inf 99(2)). This is obviously an important development. The report does not set out any factual material concerning allegations of physical ill-treatment but limits itself to recalling the findings made in previous, unpublished, reports. During this visit the CPT 'focused' its attention on verifying whether recently adopted measures to combat torture and ill-treatment were being properly implemented rather that on gathering additional evidence of the use of such methods (para. 11). In consequence, the Public Statements discussed in this volume remain the chief public source of evidence of ill-treatment found in the course of CPT visits. The report also appears to take a more contextual approach to the implementation of the CPT's procedural safeguards that appears in other reports and this would seem to accord with the suggestions offered at the end of Chapter 1 of this volume.

Other reports published in the early months of 1999 and of direct relevance to this volume are:

1. The Netherlands: Interim report arising from the CPT's second *periodic* visit in November 1997 (published 25 March 1999, CPT/Inf (99) 5).
2. Belgium: Interim report arising from the CPT's second *periodic* visit in September 1997 (published 31 March 1999, CPT/Inf (99) 6).

30 April 1999

Contents

A Note on the Citation of CPT Documents

Reports of visits undertaken by the CPT, the responses of states, and other documentation relevant to the functioning of the Committee is published—when authorized—in a numbered series carrying the prefix 'CPT/Inf', followed by the year of publication and the document number. In this book a simplified system of citation has been adopted. The name of the country concerned will be given, followed by a number indicating whether the document relates to a first, second, third, etc visit to the country in question. Where reference is being made to a state response, this will be indicated following the visit number. Interim reports will be called 'R 1' and follow-up reports 'R 2'. Where only one response was requested (or, in one case, known to have been given) this will appear simply as 'R'. Thus 'UK 1' refers to the CPT report on the first visit to the UK and 'UK 1 R 2' refers to the second UK response to that report. Likewise, the Annual Reports of the CPT are referred to as 'Gen Rep 1', 'Gen Rep 2', etc. A table setting out the full CPT/Inf reference number of all reports cited is set out in Appendix 3.

All published CPT documents are available from the Council of Europe and many are now accessible on the Committee's web-site: www.cpt.coe.fr. The 'Yearbook on the European Convention for the Prevention of Torture' published by the University of Nottingham Human Rights Law Centre also carries these materials.

Abbreviations

AI	Amnesty International
AJIL	American Journal of International Law
ANAP	Motherland Party (Turkey)
APT	Association for the Prevention of Torture
CAT	United Nations Committee Against Torture
CHR	United Nations Commission on Human Rights
CLAHR	Committee on Legal Affairs and Human Rights (Council of Europe)
CM	Committee of Ministers (Council of Europe)
COLPI	Constitutional and Legislative Policy Institute (Hungary)
CPT	Committee for the Prevention of Torture and Inhuman or Degrading Treatment or Punishment
Comm Dec	Decision of the European Commission of Human Rights
Comm Rep	Report of the European Commission of Human Rights
DR	Decisions and Reports (of the European Commission of Human Rights)
DYP	True Path Party (Turkey)
EBI	Evaluatiecommissie Beveiligingsbelied Gevangeniswezen (The Netherlands)
ECHR	European Convention on Human Rights
ECHRYb	Yearbook of the European Convention on Human Rights
ECPT	European Convention for the Prevention of Torture and Inhuman or Degrading Treatment or Punishment
EHRLRev	European Human Rights Law Review
EHRR	European Human Rights Reports
EJIL	European Journal of International Law
ELRev	European Law Review
EPR	European Prison Rules
EuGRZ	Europäische Grundrechte-Zeitschrift
GNAT	Grand National Assembly of Turkey
HRAT	Human Rights Association of Turkey
HRC	Human Rights Committee

HRFT	Human Rights Foundation of Turkey
HRLJ	Human Rights Law Journal
ICCPR	International Covenant on Civil and Political Rights
ICJ	International Committee of Jurists
ICLQ	International and Comparative Law Quarterly
ICRC	International Committee of the Red Cross
ISO	International Standardisation Organisation
MichJIL	Michigan Journal of International Law
NGO	Non-Governmental Organization
NQHR	Netherlands Quarterly on Human Rights
OSCE	Organization on Security and Cooperation in Europe
PS	Public Statement (CPT)
PSD	Public Security Detention (Hungary)
RJD	Reports of Judgments and Decisions (of the European Court of Human Rights)
RP	Welfare Party (Turkey)
Res	Resolution
SCAT	Swiss Committee Against Torture
SMR	United Nations Standard Minimum Rules for the Treatment of Prisoners
SRT	UN Special Rapporteur on Torture
SSC	State Security Court (Turkey)
UDHR	Universal Declaration of Human Rights
UK	United Kingdom
UN	United Nations
UNCAT	United Nations Convention Against Torture and other Cruel, Inhuman or Degrading Treatment or Punishment

About the Contributors

Roland Bank is Research Fellow at the Max-Planck Institute for Comparative Public and International Law.

Malcolm D. Evans is Professor of Public International Law, Faculty of Law, University of Bristol.

Semih Gemalmaz is Professor of Human Rights Law and Public Law at the Faculty of Law, University of Istanbul, Turkey.

Agnes Kover is senior legal adviser and researcher at the Constitutional and Legal Policy Institute, Budapest.

Rod Morgan is Professor of Criminal Justice, Faculty of Law, University of Bristol.

Jim Murdoch is Head of the School of Law at the University of Glasgow. His main research interests lie in the general field of human rights. He is a regular contributor to seminars organized by the Council of Europe in Central and Eastern Europe.

Stephan Parmentier is a Professor of Criminology and Human Rights, Faculty of Law, Catholic University of Leuven.

Wolfgang Peukert is Head of Case-Law and Research Unit at the European Court of Human Rights. The views expressed in his contribution are personal and the author wishes to thank the editors for their editorial assistance.

Eric Prokosch Ph.D., is theme research co-ordinator at Amnesty International and was responsible for co-ordinating AI's second Campaign for the Abolition of Torture in 1984–5.

Piet Van Reenan is Chief Inspector of Law Enforcement in the Dutch Ministry of Justice and Professor at the University of Utrecht.

Stephen Shaw is Director, Prison Reform Trust, UK.

Walter Suntinger is a legal researcher at the Ludwig Boltzmann Institute of Human Rights.

Part I

The CPT

1

The CPT: An Introduction

MALCOLM D. EVANS AND ROD MORGAN

The origins of the European Convention for the Prevention of Torture (ECPT) lie in a proposal, inspired by Jean-Jacques Gautier and the Swiss Committee for the Prevention of Torture (SCAT, now renamed the Association for the Prevention of Torture (APT)),[1] for the adoption of an optional protocol to the United Nations Convention Against Torture (the UNCAT). The so-called 'Costa Rican' draft optional protocol was first presented to the UN Commission on Human Rights (CHR) in 1980 but it was understood from the outset that it would not be considered until after the UN Convention itself had been adopted. This took place in 1984 but it was not until 1991 that a revised draft optional protocol was submitted to the CHR and an open-ended working group is still engaged in the process of agreeing a text to be put forward for adoption.[2]

A reason for the hiatus at the UN level was that the moving spirits behind the draft optional protocol switched the focus of their attentions from the UN to the Council of Europe where, in the course of its review of progress with what became the UNCAT, the Parliamentary Assembly of the Council of Europe was pressing the case for the optional protocol.[3] The idea was taken up within the Council of Europe itself by the Legal Affairs Committee and, following further representations from the ICJ and SCAT, led to adoption of the Berrier Report which contained a draft convention described as a 'supplement' to the ECHR, intended 'better to ensure respect for and observance of Article 3' with respect to detainees.[4] The Committee

---

[1] The first drafts of an instrument providing for such a mechanism had been prepared by the SCAT in 1978. It was Niall McDermott of the International Commission of Jurists who suggested that it be recast as an optional protocol to the UNCAT. For a detailed account of the background see International Commission of Jurists/Swiss Committee Against Torture (1979) *Torture: How to make the International Convention Effective* (Geneva: International Commission of Jurists and Swiss Committee Against Torture).

[2] For the Reports of the Working Group see E/CN.4/1993/28; E/CN.4/1994/25; E/CN.4/1995/38; E/CN.4/1996/28; E/CN.4/1997/33; E/CN.4/1998/42. For an analysis of progress see APT (1996) *Working Group on the Draft Optional Protocol to the Convention against Torture and Other Cruel, Inhuman or Degrading Treatment or Punishment, Analytical Report of the Association for the Prevention of Torture* (Geneva: Association for the Prevention of Torture).

[3] See the Meier Report, AS/Jur (32) 22, 8 Dec 1980 and Recommendation 909 (1981), adopted 26 January 1981.

[4] See Recommendation 971 (1983), adopted 28 September 1983.

of Ministers responded by passing the matter to the Steering Committee on Human Rights which, in conjunction with its Committee of Experts, produced the text of the ECPT which was adopted in June 1987 and opened for signature in September of that year.[5]

1. THE NATURE OF THE CONVENTION SYSTEM

For the time being, the ECPT is unique among international human rights treaties. Rather than set out new—or, indeed, any—normative standards, it establishes a visit-based mechanism the purpose of which is to 'examine the treatment of persons deprived of their liberty with a view to strengthening, if necessary, the protection of such persons from torture and from inhuman or degrading treatment or punishment'.[6] The ECPT is both more and less potent than other human rights treaties currently in force. This apparent contradiction needs explaining.

The means by which the Convention seeks to achieve its aims involves the production of a report which forms the basis for a dialogue between the body established under the Convention, the Committee for the Prevention of Torture (CPT), and the state concerned. Although reporting obligations are commonplace within the family of UN human rights instruments, these normally require a state to submit a report indicating the manner in which it is giving effect to the obligations contained in the relevant instrument. This is followed by an examination of this report in the course of a regular formal meeting of the treaty monitoring body at which representatives of the state present their reports, answer questions, and receive 'concluding observations'. Although NGOs and others can feed material into the discussions, it is a relatively formal process over which the state exercises a considerable degree of control. This, for example, is the method of the Committee Against Torture (CAT) established under the UNCAT.[7]

The ECPT is very different. It is the Committee itself which is responsible for the production of the report upon which its dialogue with the state is conducted. In order to produce these reports 'Each State shall permit visits . . . to any place within its jurisdiction where persons are deprived of their liberty by a public authority'.[8] This is a much more wide-ranging

---

[5] For a detailed examination of the drafting history of the ECPT see Evans, MD and Morgan, R (1998) *Preventing Torture* (Oxford: Clarendon Press), Chapter Four.

[6] ECPT, Article 1.

[7] For an overview of the early work of the CAT see Byrnes, A (1992) 'The Committee against Torture' in Alston, P (1992a) *The United Nations and Human Rights* (Oxford: Clarendon Press) and for its more recent work see Morgan, R (1998) 'Preventing Torture and Protecting Prisoners', 11(4) *Interights Bulletin* 178–180.

[8] ECPT, Article 2.

authority than that exercised by other human rights treaty bodies which can only conduct visits subject to requirements of prior consent or other restrictions, or are limited to the investigation of particular situations of which they are seized.[9] The CPT, by contrast, is free to roam where it pleases and has the right to inspect any part of any place where people are detained by public order without prior warning.[10] For example, the Committee can, and does, turn up without warning at police stations in the middle of the night. Moreover, should the Committee in the course of its visits encounter sufficiently serious situations, 'the Committee may immediately communicate observations to the competent authorities of the Party concerned'.[11] In sum, the burden of responsibility for the effective functioning of the Convention rests on the CPT rather than on the states visited, whose principal task is not to initiate but to facilitate and respond.

On the other hand, and unlike the CAT and Human Rights Committee (HRC) established under the International Covenant on Civil and Political Rights (ICCPR), the CPT has no judicial or quasi-judicial function: there are no procedures by which complaints can be presented to the CPT for investigation and adjudication by either states or individuals. Like the UN procedures flowing from the Charter obligations of member states—the '1503' procedure and its Working Groups and Special Rapporteurs[12]—the ultimate product of the CPT's work is a series of recommendations. A failure to comply with these recommendations carries the risk of a form of sanction—a 'public statement'—which is 'political' rather than 'legal' in nature.[13] This might be seen as a weakness within the UN system since the primary purpose of UN procedures is to address situations in which violations of human rights are taking place[14] and they are, in effect, attempting to enter the vacuum created by the practical or jurisdictional inadequacy

[9] See, eg, UNCAT, Article 20 and the mandate of the UN Special Rapporteur on Torture, most recently renewed for three years in CHR Res 1998/38. See also the mandate of the Special Rapporteur on Prisons and Conditions of Detention in Africa (established by the African Commission on Human Rights in October 1996) and the work of the Inter-American Commission on Human Rights, which are outlined and contrasted, *inter alia*, in APT (1997) *Standard Operating Procedures of International Mechanisms Carrying out Visits to Places of Detention* (Geneva: Association for the Prevention of Torture).

[10] Article 9 of the Convention does permit states, in exceptional circumstances, to make representations against a visit being conducted at a particular time to a particular place on a limited number of grounds but this does not appear to have hampered the work of the Committee to date.

[11] ECPT, Article 8(5).

[12] For an overview see Alston, P (1992b) 'The Commission on Human Rights'.

[13] ECPT, Article 10(2) provides that: 'If the Party fails to co-operate or refuses to improve the situation in the light of the Committee's recommendations, the Committee may decide, after the Party has had an opportunity to make known its views, by a majority of two-thirds of its members to make a public statement on the matter.'

[14] For example, the trigger for the application of the procedures under ECOSOC Res 1503 is the existence of 'gross and reliably attested violations of human rights and fundamental freedoms'.

of judicial or quasi-judicial bodies: the political sanction is either in parallel with, or in default of, the judicial.[15] The CPT, however, is intended to be a *preventive* mechanism and so is not called on to pass comment regarding the compliance of states with their obligations at all. Since the rationale for the Convention lies in the assistance it can offer to states in order to prevent instances of torture and inhuman or degrading treatment or punishment from arising in the first place, it would be inappropriate for it to be vested with a judicial or quasi-judicial function. Although it can do less than other treaty monitoring bodies in this regard, this is not a weakness but a reflection of the Convention's principal purpose.

Moreover, were the Committee to exercise judicial-style functions, it would stray into the spheres of activity of the European Court of Human Rights. The framers of the Convention clearly intended that the work of the CPT should not intrude upon that of the Commission and Court of Human Rights. The Preamble to the Convention draws attention to the ECHR machinery which 'operates in relation to persons who allege that they are victims of violations of Article 3' before proceeding to state the belief that 'the protection of persons deprived of their liberty against torture and inhuman or degrading treatment or punishment could be strengthened by non-judicial means of a preventive character based on visits'. The Explanatory Report to the ECPT again stresses that 'its recommendations will not bind the State concerned and the Committee shall not express any view on the interpretation of legal terms. Its task is a purely preventive one.'[16] The resulting division of competence is officially endorsed by the CPT. In the Committee's first general report, adopted in 1991, in a passage which has since been used as an introductory preface to the first visit reports transmitted to each state party, the CPT emphasizes that 'whereas the Commission's and Court's activities aim at "conflict solution" on the legal level, the CPT's activities aim at "conflict avoidance" on the practical level . . . The CPT's task is not to publicly criticise States, but rather to assist them in finding ways to strengthen the "cordon sanitaire" that separates acceptable and unacceptable treatment or behaviour.'[17]

This division of competence is ultimately conditional upon the rather fanciful fiction that European states do not subject detainees to acts or conditions which violate Article 3 of the ECHR and that the function of the CPT is simply to assist states to ensure that this remains the case. However, since this was not and is not true, the reality is not so simple and the CPT has often encountered evidence of torture or of inhuman or degrading treatment. Faced with such evidence, the Committee has been

---

[15] It must be appreciated that states may often choose to pursue an investigation or seek denunciation through political channels and mechanisms rather than utilize judicial or quasi-judicial avenues even when they are available.

[16] Explanatory Report, para 25.   [17] Gen Rep 1, paras 2 and 3.

unable to refrain from using legal terminology. Whilst it may be true that the Committee is not empowered to interpret legal terms, it is inevitable that others will interpret the CPT's use of them, not least the European Commission and Court of Human Rights.[18] To claim that the CPT exercises a solely preventive function is, then, substantially to understate the extent of its impact. The Committee's observations and recommendations both reflect and feed into the debate concerning the legal parameters of the terminology it employs. Only when this point is fully appreciated do the consequences of the lack of normative content within the ECPT begin to become apparent.

The CPT obviously cannot use legal terminology without having an understanding of what the terms mean. Article 3 of the ECHR provides that 'No one shall be subjected to torture or to inhuman or degrading treatment or punishment': the preamble to the ECPT makes clear that this provides the background to the work of the CPT. Yet, motivated by a desire to insulate the Commission and Court of Human Rights from the potential impact of the CPT, the drafters seem to have freed the Committee from almost all forms of restraint. The Explanatory Report to the ECPT stresses that Article 3 is merely a single reflection of the broader norm prohibiting torture or inhuman or degrading treatment[19] and, by implication, suggests that the CPT is to bear this larger canvas in mind. Of course, this feeds into the observation that 'The case-law of the Court and Commission of Human Rights in Article 3 provides a source of guidance for the Committee' but 'the Committee should not seek to interfere in the interpretation and application of Article 3'.[20] The corollary of this is that the CPT can range beyond the jurisprudence of the ECHR, with the, perhaps unforeseen, result that the jurisprudence of the Commission and Court can be bypassed, rather than insulated. The CPT has summed up the result in the following fashion:

In carrying out its functions the CPT has the right to avail itself of legal standards contained not only in the European Convention on Human Rights but also in a number of other relevant human rights instruments (and the interpretation of them by the human rights organs concerned).

At the same time, it is not bound by the case-law of judicial or quasi-judicial bodies acting in the same field, but may use it as a point of departure or reference when assessing the treatment of persons deprived of their liberty in individual countries.[21]

It is, then, clear that the jurisdictional competence of the CPT is not limited by the terms of Article 3 of the ECHR, or, indeed, of any other

---

[18] The relationship between the two instruments is considered by Wolfgang Peukert in Chapter Four below.

[19] Explanatory Report, para 26.   [20] Ibid, para 27.   [21] Gen Rep 1, para 5.

international instrument. This has a number of important consequences. First, the Committee is free to use the terms found in Article 3 in a manner which is not necessarily consistent with that used by the Court and Commission. It can develop its own autonomous understanding of what these terms mean, provided only that it does not purport to make a 'finding' that Article 3 of the ECHR has been violated. If others choose to make the correlation between the CPT's use of the terminology and Article 3 then, formally speaking, that is of no concern to the Committee. There is, in fact, evidence to suggest that the CPT has adopted a scheme of usage which is somewhat different than that used by the Court. It seems to have reserved use of the term 'torture' for the purposive use of force, almost exclusively as regards those in police custody, whereas the term 'inhuman and degrading' is used only in connection with 'environmental' factors, that is, factors concerning the conditions of detention, rather than forms of physical illtreatment. The Court, however, places all these instances along a single continuum and categorizes them on the basis of their gravity—the severity of suffering.[22] This differential usage will inevitably cause confusion.

Secondly, since the purpose of the Convention is to assist states to prevent violations of Article 3, any matter which might bear upon the position of those detained by public authorities falls within the CPT's mandate. As will be seen in Chapter Two, the bulk of the issues raised by the CPT fall comfortably within the range of what might be expected, such as safeguards for those in police custody and physical conditions of detention. Other issues, however, appear unexceptional to observers of the CPT only because of the long-standing nature of their inclusion in the list of CPT concerns. Examples might include visiting arrangements and facilities. Without wishing to question the importance of these as essential components of a civilized penal system, their at best tangential relevance to the prevention of torture or inhuman or degrading treatment renders them marginal to the CPT's mandate. This is not to say that these issues are *not* within the mandate, merely that their inclusion requires explanation. It is equally true that there are many issues not so far addressed by the CPT and which it might seem absurd for them to examine but which, if they chose to do so, could also find a justification within the preventive mandate: for example, why not consider the fitness for office of Prison Governors—or, indeed, the Director of the Prison Service? Other issues, which arguably have great significance for the prevention of ill-treatment and which are therefore far from absurd—laws of evidence, for example, allowing for the conviction of criminals on the basis of uncorroborated confessions—have also not yet been considered in published reports by the CPT. All that needs to be noted at this point is that the only real limitation on the range of issues bearing on ill-treatment in deten-

---

[22] For a critical appraisal of the practice of the Court see Evans and Morgan (1998), Chapter Three and for the terminological usage of the CPT ibid, Chapter Six.

tion which the CPT is competent to raise is its own willingness to raise them, tempered perhaps by the willingness of states to respond.

If this is true of the range of issues which the CPT can raise, the same can also be said of what the Committee might require of a state with regard to such matters. The Committee is free to draw inspiration from the work of the judicial or quasi-judicial bodies and also from the various international codes of conduct and provisions of domestic law. The CPT might reasonably be expected to have regard to at least the following: the UN Standard Minimum Rules for the Treatment of Prisoners, the Body of Principles for the Protection of All Persons under Any Form of Detention or Imprisonment, the UN Standard Minimum Rules for the Administration of Juvenile Justice, and the European Prison Rules. To this list might also be added the work of the UN Special Rapporteur on Torture and, indeed, the more recently established African Rapporteur.[23] However, no matter how long the list or what it contains, the central point is that these sources remain no more than points of inspiration or comparison: as the CPT itself has said, 'The CPT is not bound by substantive treaty provisions, although it may refer to a number of treaties, other international instruments and the case-law formulated thereunder.'[24]

In conclusion, it can be said that the ECPT has created a body which already has greater legal impact than was originally envisaged. It also created a body which was empowered to embark on a 'preventive' dialogue with member states on an unspecified range of subjects with a bearing on detention and the penal system without setting any limitation on the potential range of the subjects to be addressed or the substance of what might be required of states with regard to them. Ratification of the ECPT was—and remains—a remarkably open-ended commitment. Against this background, the need to probe the work of the CPT in order to gain an understanding of the standards which the Committee seeks to apply becomes clear. Until these standards are understood and are subjected to critical appraisal in the light of other relevant standards which bear upon states, it is difficult, if not impossible, to make a rounded evaluation of the Convention system as a whole.

2. THE CONVENTION SYSTEM AT WORK

If the Convention cannot properly be evaluated without an understanding of the standards it promulgates, it is equally true that those standards are themselves influenced, at least in part, by a number of factors which flow from the more mechanical aspects of the Convention's operation. Some of

---

[23] See above, Note 9.   [24] Gen Rep 1, para 6 (ii).

these are derived from the Convention itself, others result from the Committee's practice and methodology, which reflect its preferences and priorities. This section will accordingly provide an overview of the Convention and the *modus operandi* of the Committee. This will have the twin purposes of introducing the Committee and its work and practice to those not familiar with the Convention system and will also seek to highlight those aspects which, either directly or indirectly, have a bearing on the standards which the CPT seeks to uphold.

(a) Participation

The Convention is now in force for a far greater range of states than was originally envisaged, in terms both of numbers and the nature of the problems which they present. At the time of writing (December 1998) all forty member states of the Council of Europe have both signed and ratified the Convention.[25] When the Convention was opened for signature in 1987 the Council of Europe had only twenty-three members, drawn from Southern, Northern, and Western Europe. The addition of seventeen further members, embracing Central and Eastern Europe and extending to the Russian shores on the Sea of Japan, has radically altered the composition of the Council and, with it, the work of the CPT. When it was being drafted, a part of the Convention's rationale was thought to lie in the example it would set to the rest of the world. Many of the countries for whom that example was being set have now become a party to the ECPT.[26]

At the same time, a note of caution should be sounded. The newly admitted states played no part in the discussions leading up to the adoption of the Convention and membership of the Council of Europe was, for a number of these states, made conditional upon their agreeing to ratify a raft of human rights treaties, including the ECPT, within one year of their admission. Few did so with alacrity. For example, Russia undertook to ratify by February 1997 but failed to do so until a little over a year later. Latvia and Lithuania have displayed an equal lack of enthusiasm for participation.[27] Whilst some of the states of Central and Eastern Europe appear to have

---

[25] Lithuania ratified the Convention on 26 November 1998 and, in accordance with ECPT Article 19(2), the Convention enters into force in relation to it on 1 March 1999.

[26] In consequence, the First Protocol to the ECPT, opened for signature in 1993, has lost much of its impact. This was designed to allow non-member states of the Council of Europe to accede to the ECPT at the invitation of the Committee of Ministers. The Protocol is not yet in force and most of the countries to whom such offers might have been made have already joined the Council and signed the Convention. Nevertheless, should the Committee wish to extend even further the geographical scope of its work and operate beyond the confines of the Council, it might yet be able to do so.

[27] Latvia joined the Council of Europe in February 1995 but did not sign the Convention until October 1997 and ratified in February 1998. Lithuania joined the Council in May 1995 and signed the Convention in September of that year but did not ratify until November 1998.

embraced the spirit of the Convention, it is not yet clear that this is universally the case. Moreover, not all of the original Council members have demonstrated unalloyed enthusiasm for the CPT.

The expanding numbers of states party to the Convention inevitably presents severe practical difficulties for a Committee which functions by conducting visits to member states and subsequently seeks to engage those states in an ongoing dialogue. These problems are exacerbated when the states in question are of the size of the Ukraine and the Russian Federation, the size of whose prison populations dwarfs that of other states.[28] The sheer logistics of organizing and conducting a visit programme that opens up remote and relatively inaccessible detention facilities is immense. This is not the place to dwell on the consequences of the expanding membership but two points of relevance to this study need emphasizing.

First, the range of issues which the CPT is able to explore is likely to be adversely affected. Even if the Committee is able to sustain its current points of focus, it may be difficult for it to expand the range into new areas. Secondly, the standards already developed by the Committee are likely to be applied with varying degrees of rigour, depending upon the situation in the country concerned. It has almost certainly been true that, intentionally or intuitively, this has been the practice of the Committee from the start. Nevertheless, the veneer of equality of treatment which has so far held sway is likely to be broken, rendering explicit what has previously been the implicit truth: that the Committee cannot reasonably expect all member states to achieve the same level of provision within a similar time frame. CPT reports and recommendations are likely increasingly to reflect this. This means that the standards which the Committee articulates must be seen as aspirations, goals to be worked towards. It also makes it all the more important that the standards are well understood and justified. Are they, for example, essential or peripheral components in the overall human rights strategy for prevention of ill-treatment within the state concerned? Should each standard be regarded as an end in its own right, or as a mere means to the end of enhancing a 'cordon sanitaire' which may or may not yet exist? This question will be given further consideration at the end of this chapter.

(b) The members of the CPT

Members are elected by the Committee of Ministers of the Council of Europe, from a list of three names submitted by each state,[29] serve a four-year term of office, and are currently eligible to be re-elected only

---

[28] The Russian Federation and the Ukraine are estimated to have prison populations in excess of one million and a quarter of a million respectively (see Home Office (1998) *Prison Statistics England and Wales 1997*, Cm 4017, London: HMSO, Table 1.16).

[29] ECPT, Article 5(1).

once.[30] From the outset, it has been well understood that the tasks to be undertaken by the Committee need to be reflected in its structure and composition. The original model proposed by the ICJ and SCAT, and modelled on the practice of the International Committee of the Red Cross (ICRC), was that the Committee would be relatively small and the actual task of conducting visits within states undertaken by trained 'delegates' of the Committee who would report back to the Committee. The Committee would then produce a report for submission to the state concerned on the basis of this material. This approach would have made the Committee more of an executive-style body. However, the model ultimately adopted was very different. It was decided that the Committee should itself undertake visits and should comprise as many members as there are states party to the Convention, one member for each.[31]

This change of emphasis obviously had consequences for the type of person suitable for membership of the Committee. The Convention provides that members are to be chosen 'from among persons of high moral character, known for their competence in the field of human rights or having professional experience in the areas covered by this Convention'.[32] The Explanatory Report amplifies this, observing that:[33]

it is not thought desirable to specify in detail the professional fields from which members of the Committee might be drawn. It is clear that they do not have to be lawyers. It would be desirable that the Committee should include medical members who have experience in matters such as prison administration and the various fields relevant to the treatment of persons deprived of their liberty. This will make the dialogue between the Committee and the States more effective and facilitate concrete suggestions from the Committee.

The Committee initially comprised a preponderance of lawyers, but also had from the outset a strong cohort of medics. Over the years, the Committee has called for the election of members making for a better balance in terms of both gender and expertise and this is reflected in its current composition: the thirty-two members[34] include nine medics with a variety

---

[30] ECPT, Article 5(3). The Second Protocol to the ECPT permits members to be re-elected to a third term of office. Although opened for signature in 1993, it has not yet entered into force.

[31] For a full account of the drafting process see Evans and Morgan (1998), Chapter Four. Traces of the earlier schemes are still evident in the Convention text. For example, the requirement that three members of the Committee were to have their initial periods of office reduced to ensure an orderly turnover only made sense in the context of the proposal for a small Committee of seven which was at one point proposed. See Cassese, A (1989) 'A New Approach to Human Rights: The European Convention for the Prevention of Torture', 83 *AJIL* 130 at 146.

[32] ECPT, Article 4(2).   [33] Explanatory Report, para 36.

[34] The Convention is currently in force for thirty-nine states; members have not yet been elected for Albania, Andorra, Latvia, Russia, 'TFYRO' Macedonia, and the Ukraine. The appointment of a new member for Portugal is also outstanding. A member for Lithuania will also need to be elected when the Convention enters into force in relation to it on 1 March 1999.

of expertise, two psychologists, a cleric, a parliamentarian, three with a background in prison management or administration, and a criminologist, in addition to fifteen lawyers with varying backgrounds (including judges, prosecutors, and academics), several of whom have had direct experience of penal administration. Nine of the members are women.

The emphasis on increasing the cohort of medical and penal specialists seems set to continue.[35] Without entering into a debate on the wisdom of this,[36] it does reflect the current working practices of the Committee. For example, the Committee places great store on first-hand evidence of physical ill-treatment gained by the medical examination of detainees. Without such evidence, the Committee is reluctant to conclude that there is a risk of ill-treatment occurring. To the extent that the Committee sees itself as being involved in the task of unearthing evidence of physical abuse, the presence of such specialists as members of the Committee may well be desirable. The point that needs to be made here is that this is very much a product of the Committee's own preferences since it has set its own priorities and 'rules of evidence'. When this is fed back into the composition of the Committee, it has a reinforcing effect which makes it even less likely that the Committee will depart from previous practice. The situations which the Committee chooses to address, the issues which it seeks to raise, and the standards it applies are reflected in the composition of the Committee and of visiting delegations. Thus medical expertise is prominently deployed in countries where there is a suspicion of serious physical abuse. On the other hand, the relative absence of apparent interest in allegations of ill-treatment in military establishments is mirrored by the lack of any known interest in securing the services of members with a military background. The absence of members with apparent particular expertise in dealing with immigrants and asylum seekers is also rather surprising, given that this is beginning to feature prominently in the Committee's work, though it did not previously receive the same degree of attention as other, arguably less problematic, matters. The evolving pattern of expertise within the membership of the Committee can, at least in part, be seen as an indicator of the areas in which it is seeking to concentrate and develop its work and standards.

[35] See, for example, Council of Europe, Parliamentary Assembly, Committee on Legal Affairs and Human Rights (1997) *Report on strengthening the machinery of the European Convention for the Prevention of Torture and Inhuman or Degrading Treatment or Punishment*, Parl Ass Doc 7784, 26 March 1997 (hereafter CLAHR Report), para 47, which calls for 'a more balanced composition with regard to professional background, gender and age' with greater participation of 'prison specialists and medical doctors with relevant experience, including forensic medicine'. This was endorsed by the Parliamentary Assembly in Recommendation 1323, 21 April 1997 and Order No 530 and echoed by the CPT in Gen Rep 7, para 19 and Gen Rep 8, para 17.

[36] For a critical appraisal of this approach see Evans and Morgan (1998), 368–371.

What expertise the Committee lacks among its membership it picks up through the *ad hoc* use of expert advisers as members of visiting delegations. The Convention provides that the Committee may 'if it considers it necessary, be assisted by experts and interpreters'.[37] The Explanatory Report explains that the underlying idea was to:

supplement the experience of the Committee by the assistance, for example, of persons who have special training or experience of humanitarian missions, who have a medical background or possess a special competence in the treatment of detainees or in prison regimes, and, when appropriate, as regards young persons.[38]

In its first General Report, the Committee explained that experts could be used when the relevant expertise was unavailable from within the Committee. In fact, the use of experts is far from exceptional: indeed, it is the norm. By the end of 1997, thirty-seven experts had accompanied a total of 120 missions, and some delegations have included as many as four experts. Moreover, some experts have been used extensively—five on more than ten occasions—and have built up far greater experience than a considerable number of Committee members.[39] The Legal Affairs Committee of the Parliamentary Assembly has argued that: 'Were all CPT members to possess the necessary knowledge and experience, the need to resort to outside experts would be far less than at present.'[40] One might doubt whether this is so. It must often be difficult to construct a well-balanced delegation from within the Committee, given the differing fields of expertise, the varying degrees of experience, the need to ensure that the delegation can function in a common language and ensure the participation of men and women. It is likely that there will be a continual need to have a body of experienced experts who can be called on to 'fill the gaps'. Experts assist the Committee; they do not become a part of it and are not involved in the formal adoption of reports. Once again, this reinforces the need for clear and consistent CPT standards which can be drawn on. Since *ad hoc* experts are not in a position to press (directly) for changes in these standards, the continued use of experts might also be a factor contributing to the comparatively low level of departure from and development of the standards set at the outset of the Committee's work.

(c) The visiting programme

The visiting programme lies at the heart of the CPT's working practices and provides the means by which the Committee is able to test the congruence of state practice with the standards the Committee propounds. Three forms

---

[37] ECPT, Article 7(2).   [38] Explanatory Report, para 51.
[39] For a full discussion see Evans and Morgan (1998), 161–164.
[40] CLAHR Report (1997), para 44.

of visits have emerged. *Periodic* visits are made to all member states from time to time 'as far as possible . . . on an equitable basis'.[41] They typically last up to two weeks, during the course of which the Committee visits a range of institutions—police stations, prisons, psychiatric hospitals, and immigration centres—in a variety of locations. The Committee completed the first round of *periodic* visits to the 'old' member states of the Council of Europe at the end of 1993. By then, the states of Central and Eastern Europe were entering the Convention system and it was decided that all new member states would receive a first *periodic* visit within their first year of membership. In consequence, second *periodic* visits to the more long-standing states party have been delayed and the original aspiration that each member state should receive a *periodic* visit every other year has been abandoned for a four-yearly cycle which might itself prove over-optimistic.[42]

The lengthening gap between *periodic* visits has focused even more attention on the generally shorter *ad hoc* visits which are 'required in the circumstances'[43] and which can be triggered by a range of factors, underlying which is a concern that the situation in a particular institution or locality requires more immediate attention. *Follow-up* visits represent a hybrid form and involve the Committee returning to an institution or institutions previously visited in a *periodic* or *ad hoc* visit. Once the first round of *periodic* visits was complete the Committee decided to devote more of its time to these shorter visits, but the growth in membership, and the need to conduct a considerable number of *periodic* visits in a relatively short time span inhibited this. Nevertheless, seven such visits were conducted in 1994, five in 1996, and six in 1997. In 1998, however, only one short *ad hoc* visit took place. By the end of 1998 the Committee had conducted a total of 81 visits, 56 *periodic* and 25 *ad hoc* or *follow-up*. Many *periodic* visits include returns to institutions so that the precise classification of a visit is of little practical significance.[44]

The Committee is required to 'notify the Government of the Party concerned of its intention to carry out a visit', after which it may 'at any time' visit any place where 'persons are deprived of their liberty by a public authority'.[45] This is intended to strike a balance between the need for

[41] Explanatory Report, para 47.

[42] The pattern need not be regular and a number of countries, including Turkey, Spain, and the UK, have received second *periodic* visits within a swifter timescale.

[43] ECPT, Article 7(1).

[44] The distinction was of some significance in the early years of the Convention when the Committee determined the order of first *periodic* visits by drawing lots. By classifying it as an *ad hoc* visit, the Committee was able to conduct what was, in effect, a *periodic* visit to Turkey earlier than would otherwise have been the case. Visits to Romania in 1995 and Russia in 1998 are technically *ad hoc* since they did not form a part of the pre-announced visits for those years. But for practical purposes they were *periodic* in nature.

[45] ECPT, Article 8(1) and Article 2.

surprise and the need to ensure that adequate preparation for the visit can be made by the state concerned. The CPT has adopted a three-stage notification procedure. Before the start of each calendar year it announces the countries to which it intends to conduct *periodic* visits. The number has risen steadily from four in its first year of operation, 1990, to an average of seven thereafter, with eleven planned for 1999. The timing of visits is not revealed at this stage, but about two weeks before the visit is due to take place a notification is sent. This includes details of the timing and duration of the visit and the composition of the visiting delegation; members, *ad hoc* experts, Secretariat, and interpreters.[46] Finally, a provisional list of places to be visited is sent a few days before the visit commences. The Committee is, of course, free to visit other places than those indicated in advance and invariably does so.

The choice of places to be visited lies with the CPT but it will be guided by the information the Committee obtains from a variety of sources: from states themselves, from NGOs, from general press coverage, and, increasingly, from its own previous visits and researches. The standards which the CPT propounds inevitably find a reflection in the types of places of detention it chooses to visit. Whereas all countries can expect a *periodic* visit to include several police stations and a few prisons for both remand and sentenced prisoners, juveniles and adults, men and women, the choice of other custodial sites is more likely to be dictated by local factors and be the subject of recommendations or comments which owe less to a common 'spreadsheet' of expectations than is the case with the more routinely visited facilities.

Visits are carried out by delegations, the composition of which varies depending on the length of the visit and the size of the country. A *periodic* visit to a medium or large country typically involves five members of the Committee, and two *ad hoc* experts. The delegation generally includes two members of the Secretariat also. The importance of the Secretariat to the functioning of the CPT can hardly be overemphasized. Currently thirteen strong, and set for further growth, the senior members of the Secretariat involved in visits are responsible for the preparation of visits, accompanying and providing members with administrative support, drafting reports arising from visits, clerking all meetings, and implementing decisions regarding the dialogue with member states that arises from visits. There has to date been no turnover among the senior members of the Secretariat, whereas the terms of office of all the founder members of the Committee have now expired. It follows that members of the Secretariat are usually much more experienced in the conduct of visits and are far more familiar

---

[46] This is required by ECPT Article 14 in order to allow the state to exercise its 'exceptional' right to object to the Committee being accompanied by a particular expert. The Convention provides that 'As a general rule, the visits shall be carried out by at least two members of the Committee' (ECPT, Article 7(2)).

with the working practices and jurisprudence of the Committee than are the members. Their influence is profound and reaches to the heart of the mechanism. The stability in the Secretariat is another factor that finds its reflection in the approach taken by the Committee to the standards it promulgates.

(d) Post-visit procedure

Following each visit, the Committee adopts a report which sets out the delegation's findings and makes a series of 'recommendations', 'comments', and 'requests for further information'. These distinctions are significant since the Convention refers only to recommendations. Whilst states are obliged to respond to recommendations, comments and requests have a lesser status and the Committee can merely ask that they be responded to. States do not seem to have found this objectionable and the procedure serves the useful purpose of allowing the Committee to raise questions in a less forceful or confrontational fashion.

Reports are drawn up by the delegation which conducted the visit (based around a draft prepared by the Secretariat) and adopted at plenary meetings of the Committee, now held three times a year. The aim is for reports to be adopted within six months of a visit, but this has proved a difficult target to meet, with eight or nine months being not uncommon. Once adopted, reports are transmitted in confidence to the states concerned and form the basis of subsequent dialogues between them. The term 'dialogue' is somewhat misleading: it implies an ongoing interactive process involving frequent exchange. In fact, it appears that communications are seldom exchanged: long silences seem to be the order of the day. This shortcoming the CPT has fully acknowledged, attributing it to lack of Secretariat resources. Failure of the Committee to monitor the implementation of recommendations and chase progress puts at risk the 'credibility and effectiveness' of the Convention.[47] It means that the 'momentum for change generated by a visit will almost certainly be frittered away'.[48]

The Committee requests states to respond to *periodic* visit reports by submitting an interim response within six months and a follow-up report within twelve months. A single response is now usually requested in the wake of an *ad hoc* or *follow-up* visit. Government responses vary in size, style, and substance: the best respond systematically to each recommendation, comment, and request for information; others are more generalized, perfunctory, and thoroughly unilluminating. Whatever the case, the CPT replies by letter to each response, seeking further clarifications or pressing its case when necessary. Ultimately, the dialogue arising from one visit gets caught up in the preparation for, and dialogue arising out of, the next. This

---

[47] Gen Rep 5, para 10.   [48] CLAHR Report (1997), para 23.

relatively formalized process takes a minimum of eighteen months to complete, and often considerably longer. However, there is nothing to prevent the Committee from injecting other elements into the process, including personal visits by members of the Committee or Secretariat. Although not common, this builds on the procedure outlined in the Convention whereby the Committee 'may immediately communicate observations to the competent authorities of the Party concerned',[49] something which usually takes place at the conclusion of a visit. Nevertheless, the nature of the dialogue tends to reinforce the value of fairly formal standards which can be readily articulated and can form a fixed point in a process that may span several years. It is also worth pointing out that the recipients of CPT reports—civil servants and public administrators—are apt to change posts fairly frequently: this again favours a fairly bureaucratic procedure that is not heavily reliant on the contributions and perceptions of particular personnel.

The hallmark of the ECPT is that material gathered in relation to a visit, and all communication between the Committee and the state arising out of a visit, remains confidential unless the state concerned authorizes publication of the material in question.[50] This might have proved an almost insurmountable barrier to the study of the CPT. At the outset of its work, however, the Committee acknowledged the importance of making sure that its standards and methodology were accessible: in 1991 it set out its approach to aspects of 'police custody and imprisonment' in its second general report[51] and 'health care services in prisons' in its third general report in 1992.[52] This practice then lapsed until the seventh and eighth general reports, in 1997 and 1998, which set out its approach to 'foreign nationals detained under aliens legislation' and 'involuntary placement in psychiatric establishments' respectively.[53]

Whatever the reason for this gap in the Committee's output of statements of relevant standards, it was at least in part compensated for by the steady stream of reports which passed into the public domain. Indeed, it has now become the norm for states to authorize the publication of CPT visit reports and many observers now interpret a failure to do so as an indication of something to hide. In addition, the majority of states have also authorized the publication of at least some elements of the post-visit dialogue. By the end of 1998, 53 visit reports and 69 responses (47 interim or sole responses and 22 follow-up reports) had been published. Although some states have withheld publication of early reports for considerable periods,[54] of those states whose visits have taken place more than two years previously, only Turkey is clearly failing to publish any material at all.

---

[49] ECPT, Article 8(5).   [50] ECPT, Article 11(1) and (2).
[51] Gen Rep 2, paras 35–60.   [52] Gen Rep 3, paras 30–77.
[53] Gen Rep 7, paras 24–36; Gen Rep 8, paras 25–58.
[54] eg Spain, Italy, and Cyprus. See Appendix 2.

There is, however, no mystery surrounding the CPT's work in Turkey, given that the Committee has issued two Public Statements, in December 1992 and 1996, on the situation there. The Convention permits the Committee to issue a Public Statement 'If the Party fails to co-operate or refuses to improve the situation in the light of the Committee's recommendations'.[55] This is the only 'sanction' at the Committee's disposal and its sparing use indicates both the high threshold set for resorting to it and the relative impotence of the Committee when faced with unusually intractable situations where there is overwhelming evidence of serious ill-treatment.

It is the relative accessibility of the CPT's corpus of reports which prompts the questions underlying our examination of the Committee's standards and their reception by state parties. This study is also prompted by the observation that nearly every *periodic* report is now cast in a standard mould and this pattern of near-uniformity might inhibit the Committee's ability to address the most pressing problems within the state in question: the elements of commonality might unwittingly override important local elements. It is, for example, noticeable that the two Public Statements so far issued—freed from the formalism of the report template—carry a greater degree of urgency and relevance. This might be put down to the substance of the statements being that much more dramatic. However, equally or comparably shocking revelations appear in published visit reports on other countries, yet the force of these findings can be lost in the generally more formal presentation of the material. At the same time, the desire to arrive at the most telling points regarding torture or inhuman and degrading treatment can also deflect attention from the examination of the more routine issues concerning, for example, preventive safeguards. Both these factors can have an impact on the reception of the standards set out in the reports in the country in question.

3. PREVENTION, STANDARDS, AND EFFECTIVENESS

This section of the chapter will raise some general issues and questions regarding the CPT's operation and effectiveness, a number of which are subsequently picked up by other contributors to this volume. The first point concerns the manner in which the CPT is perceived and its visit reports received.

The CPT has rapidly achieved considerable credibility with NGOs and officials throughout Europe whose interests and responsibilities intersect with the CPT mandate.[56] The CPT and its Secretariat is generally regarded as a highly professional body whose visit reports are for the most part well

---

[55] ECPT, Article 10(2).   [56] See Evans and Morgan (1998), 352–362.

informed, accurate, and appropriately focused. Because there is now a well-established practice of authorizing publication of CPT reports, considerable importance is attached to the first-hand information which the CPT is able to bring into the public domain. Nevertheless, it is apparent that the *manner* in which CPT reports are read limits how they are understood. This calls into question aspects of their current format and dissemination.

Few readers of CPT reports ever see reports other than those concerning their own country or even institution. During the course of our research across Europe we have encountered remarkably few officials or human rights activists who have read a range of CPT reports. Moreover, a large number of the interested persons with whom we have met have, for one reason or another, never seen a CPT report. CPT visit reports are written in French or English, the two working languages of the Council of Europe: in some countries translations into national or minority languages are not generally made available to the local mass media or NGOs. The consequence is that some reports are not widely known about even within the countries that they concern. Moreover, as Semih Gemalmaz emphasizes in Chapter Eleven of this volume, local translations of international documents cannot always be relied on for accuracy even if they are made available (which is not the case as regards CPT reports in Turkey). This linguistic fact of life is a real problem in those Council of Europe countries in which neither French nor English is widely spoken.

Since CPT reports are consumed parochially, if they are seen at all, it follows that few readers are able easily to interpret or contextualize what the Committee describes having found, the standards the Committee promulgates, and the recommendations it makes. Readers generally have no wider frame of reference on which to draw. For example, most, though not all, CPT visit reports come to a conclusion about the degree to which detainees face a risk of suffering ill-treatment at the hands of the police. We have elsewhere questioned the wisdom and validity of this approach[57] because, as is self-evident, in a visit lasting up to two weeks at best, Committee delegations can only visit a few out of what may be several score or hundred of custodial institutions. Even if the members interview in depth more than one hundred prisoners in the course of a visit, this would constitute only a minute proportion of the custodial population in most countries. To take the most extreme case shortly to be investigated, would it make sense for a CPT delegation returning from Russia to estimate the risk of ill-treatment faced by those in detention in a country where there are more than a million prisoners and several hundred thousand arrestees in literally hundreds of police stations, and to do so on the basis of a visit lasting two or three weeks and which could practically have embraced no

[57] See Evans and Morgan (1998), 351.

more than a few pockets of so geographically vast a land? We think not. But Russia represents only one extreme of the situation that applies to all CPT visits. In Chapter Nine, for example, Agnes Kover is critical of the Committee's decision to confine their attentions during the first *periodic* visit to Hungary to Budapest and its immediate environs. Even if it were possible to visit all places of detention—such as in San Marino, a micro-state with a single small prison, one police station, and one *carabinieri* station[58]—during a single brief visit, the CPT could not talk to more than a small proportion of all the persons taken into custody during the space of four years, the likely minimum interval between *periodic* visits.

Putting on one side the validity of risk assessments, the subtle termino-logical distinctions developed by the CPT regarding the estimated *level* of risk are also problematic. Are such distinctions likely to be understood by readers unfamiliar with the corpus of CPT reports? Are, for example, most readers likely to appreciate that a 'risk not to be discounted' or 'not neg-ligible' is more substantial than a 'small risk' or simply 'a risk', but less substantial than 'a significant risk'? Or that a 'significant risk' appears to indicate a risk less substantial than a 'not inconsiderable risk'? And if these gradations are not comprehensible, should the speculations that they inevitably invite be set in motion?[59] Again, we think not. It would be far better if the Committee simply reported that an approximate number of prisoners had been seen and talked with regarding their experiences in custody, that a certain number of allegations were made, and that evidence was obtained corroborating some of the allegations. This approach has been used in some CPT reports, with each aspect of the account being illustrated in detail.[60] Indeed, if recently published reports are any guide the CPT may have decided to abandon its use of a risk continuum.

The CPT is naturally unwilling in either visit or general reports to make explicit comparisons between jurisdictions. Yet, self-evidently, general esti-mations of risk expressed according to a linguistic continuum are bound to lead to comparisons being made, comparisons that could not be other than invidious. Could it really be said, for example, as a result of a 1991 visit, that there was 'currently little risk of people deprived of their liberty by the police being physically ill-treated' in Germany[61] when, five years later, the Committee received allegations of excessive force being used by the

---

[58] San Marino 1, para 3.

[59] For a full discussion see Evans and Morgan (1998), 222–230.

[60] For example, the first two reports on Spain were carefully nuanced: the nature of the alle-gations and the limited supporting evidence were spelt out, but the Committee advancing no overall risk assessment. Instead, the Committee reported grounds for concern regarding alle-gations of minor physical ill-treatment and argued, cautiously, that it would be 'premature to conclude that the phenomenon of torture and severe ill-treatment had been eradicated'. See Spain 1, paras 17–29 and Spain 2, paras 16–28.

[61] Germany 1, para 20.

German police during apprehension, gathered evidence consistent with allegations in two cases, and reported a German police officer saying that the continued use of force after a suspect had been handcuffed or otherwise immobilized was 'typical'?[62] It is very doubtful that the situation in Germany had greatly changed in the interval: much more likely that the CPT, visiting different parts of Germany during its second *periodic* visit, hit on problems which had not surfaced during the first. It will often be a matter of chance whether the Committee hears fresh allegations and collects corroborating evidence during a short visit to only some parts of a country.

The CPT has made efforts to draw together its *jurisprudence* in its annual general reports, so that officials and others can reasonably anticipate the standards it will apply during the course of a visit. A more recent development has been the practice of arranging seminars within countries in *advance* of first *periodic* visits in which members of the CPT Bureau[63] and Secretariat can address officials and human rights activists on the work of the Committee. This enables all concerned to be better prepared for visits and paves the way for assuring co-operation during the course of the subsequent visit. This practice began in 1996 when a seminar was held in Popowo prior to the first visit to Poland in June 1996.[64] In 1997–1998 such pre-visit educational sessions were held in Kyiv, Prague, Tirana, Chisinău, Skopje, Zagreb,[65] and Moscow.[66] The Committee considers this initiative a success. However, the CPT could and arguably should do more to educate those organizations and agencies who engage with the Committee. For example, and as will become apparent from our far from comprehensive review of the Committee's *jurisprudence* in Chapter Two, the reviews of standards relating to different topics set out in the annual general reports are far from complete. The first, and arguably most important, review of issues relating to police custody and imprisonment presented in the second general report is, for example, relatively short and has been significantly elaborated upon in subsequent visit reports. There is a real need for a comprehensive and authoritative compendium, regularly updated, of the CPT's *jurisprudence* to be published by the Council of Europe as a separate document. The Secretary to the CPT, Trevor Stevens, announced in 1997 that the Committee was contemplating such a move[67] but it has yet to be realized.

---

[62] Germany 2, paras 10–14.

[63] The Bureau comprises three members of the Committee, the President and First and Second Vice-Presidents.

[64] Gen Rep 7, para 5.   [65] Gen Rep 8, para 4.

[66] Personal communication with the Secretariat subsequent to publication of Gen Rep 8 in September 1998.

[67] Speech by Trevor Stevens at an APT/British Institute of Human Rights conference on the work of the CPT, Kings College, London, September 1997.

The need for such a document flows from the CPT's having arrived at detailed judgments in successive visit reports about the acceptability of existing facilities and procedures in custodial institutions and making recommendations to remedy what the Committee considers defective safeguards and provisions. But this does of course beg the question as to whether the CPT was wise to lay down detailed standards in the first place. Or, to take a different viewpoint, whether the Committee should develop its jurisprudence more broadly than it has in order to encompass issues so far little touched on. This is a difficult issue and there are competing arguments which need to be considered carefully.

The first unavoidable issue confronting the CPT, in spite of the injunction 'that the Committee shall not express any view on the interpretation of legal norms',[68] concerns the question as to what is *torture* or *inhuman and degrading* treatment. The Committee may be enjoined not to define these terms but if the Committee was ever to report having found evidence of such phenomena, it could scarcely have avoided developing a view as to what *torture* or *inhuman and degrading* treatment actually is. Even if the CPT has not within the privacy of its plenary meetings developed a coherent view of the matter, which is possible,[69] it was inevitable that the Committee's use of the terms and the standards which it articulates would be pored over by civil servants and academic commentators, as we have done in Chapter Two.

We do not think there was any way round this issue. All states permit force to be employed by the police when necessary—indeed, their monopoly of the use of the legitimate use of force is generally taken to be the defining characteristic of the police.[70] All criminal justice systems allow coercion to be applied to persons reasonably suspected of serious crime (to be detained, questioned, remanded in custody pending trial, and so on) and punishment—deliberately imposed by judicial authority—is generally held to be the just deserts of convicted offenders. It has been the purpose of human rights law to see that the application of force, coercion, and punishment is proportionate, deserved, and kept within what have generally come to be accepted as civilized limits.[71] It follows that the CPT, powerfully invested with the capacity to see for itself what is happening in places of custody, has to decide where the thresholds of acceptable force, coercion,

---

[68] Explanatory Report, para 25.

[69] But cf Cassese, A (1996) *Inhuman States: Imprisonment, Detention and Torture in Europe Today* (Cambridge: Polity Press), originally published in Italian (1994) *Umano-Disumano: Commissariarti en prigioni nell'Europa di oggo* (Roma Bari: Laterza), 47–49, who claims that a common understanding emerged without discussion.

[70] See Reiner, R (1992) *The Politics of the Police* (Hemel Hempstead: Wheatsheaf).

[71] See Ashworth, A (1992) *Sentencing and Criminal Justice* (London: Weidenfeld and Nicholson).

and punishment lay and it would scarcely have assisted those agencies being inspected had the Committee employed the lexical device of speaking generally of ill-treatment. That would only have bred confusion.

Confusion, and resentment, would equally have been the result of the CPT declaring in successive visits that custodial conditions—space to population ratios, degrees of privacy, access to facilities, and so on—were unacceptable, indefensible, deplorable, uncivilized, or any other adjective the Committee chose to apply, without defining what would be acceptable, defensible, commendable or civilized. Prison and police managers would have demanded to know by what standards the Committee made such judgements. If they had not made their standards clear, the CPT could reasonably have been accused of deploying rhetoric and purple prose, thereby depriving their recommendations of foundations.[72]

There is nevertheless a difficulty. Precisely what is the relationship between that which the Committee is mandated to prevent and the standards the CPT has chosen to adopt? In this regard, it is necessary to distinguish between torture and inhuman and degrading treatment, as the CPT has defined the phenomena and which is considered in more detail in Chapter Two. The CPT has defined certain custodial conditions as *inhuman and degrading*—for example, overcrowding (defined according to stated space to population ratios), the period of cellular confinement, and sanitary arrangements. Though the Committee's definition may not be accepted,[73] when the Committee makes this evaluation, the factual basis underpinning it is generally not in dispute. In the case of deliberate physical maltreatment severe enough to fall above the torture threshold, however, the issues are of a different order. In most of the countries that the CPT has visited the Committee has heard no allegations of torture nor found evidence that any is practised. Yet the Committee has nevertheless recommended that a whole raft of preventive safeguards be adopted, and virtually no state party has in place *all* the safeguards which the CPT considers desirable.

In those countries where the Committee has found evidence of torture, the CPT recommends the same raft of safeguards as in those where it has not found evidence of torture. However, just as it is difficult to know from CPT reports why the absence of given safeguards in one country appears not to have resulted in the practice of torture, so it is equally difficult to be confident that the establishment of the same missing safeguards will prove either *necessary* or *sufficient* to prevent torture in another country where it

[72] Such a critique was applied in the UK to Her Majesty's Chief Inspector of Prisons in the 1980s before any clear regime standards began to be formulated. See Morgan, R (1985) 'Her Majesty's Inspectorate of Prisons' in Maguire, M, Vagg, J and Morgan, R (eds) *Accountability and Prisons: Opening Up a Closed World* (London: Tavistock).

[73] For example, the UK Government did not accept that the admittedly unsatisfactory conditions at Brixton, Leeds, and Wandsworth Prisons in 1990 were *inhuman and degrading* (UK 1 R 1, para 6).

is practised. The legal framework in some of the countries in which the CPT has found evidence of torture seems from CPT reports to be relatively indistinguishable from that of other countries in which the Committee has not found such evidence. Indeed, the legal framework in some of the countries in which torture or ill-treatment has been found is closer to the CPT's ideals than in some others where it has not. In short, the case for the proposition that the safeguards routinely pressed on states by the CPT *does* prevent torture remains unproven.

This is reinforced by the degree of divergence within the international community over what precisely torture and ill-treatment comprises and the most appropriate means of combating it. This is the point of departure for Part Two of this volume, in which a number of contributors explore the congruence of the CPT's standards with those found elsewhere. In Chapter Three Wolfgang Peukert looks at its relationship with the ECHR organs and jurisprudence. In Chapter Four Jim Murdoch considers the work of the CPT within the context of the Council of Europe as a whole. In Chapter Five Walter Suntinger turns to the international stage and compares the work of the CPT with that of the UN, represented by the Committee against Torture, the Human Rights Committee, and the UN Special Rapporteur on Torture. Finally, in Chapter Six Eric Prokosch compares the priorities of the CPT with those of an international NGO, Amnesty International. As these chapters show, the CPT does not have a monopoly of insights and its views should not be accepted uncritically.

Even assuming that the standards adopted by the CPT meet with general critical approval, a further question then arises. Rather than simply apply the same raft of safeguards to all countries in a fairly mechanistic fashion, should the Committee adopt a more differentiated diagnostic approach with a view to analysing precisely which factors appear critical for addressing the continuance of torture in the country concerned? Should the Committee prioritize its recommendations so as to provide the authorities concerned with a sharper reformist cutting edge in climates where resources will necessarily be scarce and competition for legislative time and administrative initiatives will be at a premium?

We think it would be misleading to pose this question in either/or terms. Both practical experience and a reading of the literature suggests that there are as many factors that are causally associated with torture which fall outside of the Committee's familiar raft of recommendations as fall within it. For example, the pay, general social status, and working conditions of police officers, together with their training and technological support, is, in our judgement, critical in many jurisdictions to their resort to casual or systematic violence against suspects. Other factors which affect the vulnerability of detainees, particularly members of minority groups, include patterns of racial or religious intolerance in the community in which the police operate, as well as the ethnic composition of the police force itself. It is also widely accepted that in many jurisdictions, and particularly where democracy has shallow roots, traditions of professional integrity and fearless independent judgement are sadly lacking among lawyers and doctors, corruption is widespread, and intimidation is rife. In countries where torture is commonplace it is a regrettable fact that having the right to see, or even being seen by, a doctor or lawyer while in custody is not necessarily a safeguard: on the contrary, such so-called professionals may collude with or even aid the torturers.[74] The same applies to magistrates, judges, and public prosecutors. In the same way that some analysts of the governance of the police have come to the conclusion that there is no constitutional or legal blueprint for achieving police accountability—that police accountability is best defined in terms of outcomes, and that local arrangements must be put together to achieve that outcome[75] in the light of local problems and traditions—might the same not be said regarding the prevention of torture? For example, the degree to which uncorroborated confessional evidence can be used to secure a criminal conviction is arguably at least as important a factor affecting the likelihood of torture occurring as the manner in which police interrogations are conducted and recorded. These thoughts provide the background to Part Three of this volume, in which a number of contributors who are intimate with both the problems posed by ill-treatment within their own domestic systems, and the CPT's Reports and the responses of the governments concerned to those Reports, explore the impact and relevance of the CPT's work, highlighting both positive and negative features, successes and missed opportunities.

4. CONCLUSION

A balance has to be struck. There is a case for the CPT establishing a set of minimum standards which, by general consensus (which will generally involve acknowledgement in international human rights instruments), are accepted as being of paramount importance as safeguards against torture occurring everywhere. It is doubtful whether anyone would quarrel with the

---

[74] See, for example: Raynor, M (1987) *Turning a Blind Eye?: Medical Accountability and the Prevention of Torture in South Africa* (Washington DC: Committee on Scientific Freedom and Responsibility); Servicio Paz y Justicia (1989) *Uruguay: Nunca Más—Human Rights Violations, 1972–1985* (Philadelphia: Temple University Press); Physicians for Human Rights (1996) *Torture in Turkey and Its Unwilling Accomplices: The Scope of State Persecution and the Coercion of Physicians* (Boston: Physicians for Human Rights).

[75] One leading international analyst has, for example, defined an accountable police force as one which employs methods and priorities congruent with the attitudes and concerns of the community it serves (see Bayley, DH (1983) 'Accountability and control of the police: some lessons for Britain', in Bennett, T (ed) *The Future of Policing*, Cropwood Series No 15 (Cambridge: Institute of Criminology).

widely established condemnation of incommunicado detention. The temptation for the police to exploit occasions of incommunicado detention is so self-evident that the case for its prohibition scarcely needs arguing. However, it is much more questionable whether the CPT is well advised to elaborate a large number of precise standards spanning the minutiae of police facilities and procedures, let alone the recruitment, training, and equipment of police personnel, the detail of criminal procedure and the law of evidence, and the infrastructure of inspection, grievance-ventilation, and legal and managerial accountability relating to the governance of the police. This is not to say that some or possibly all of these policy spheres will not be legitimate areas for exploration and recommendations in jurisdictions where the physical ill-treatment of suspects in police custody is commonplace. But we believe that CPT reports would command greater attention, both domestically and internationally, if the Committee's reports established more precisely and on a case by case basis precisely how the adoption of its recommendations would make it less likely that particular forms of ill-treatment would occur in specific, identified contexts. Moreover, given the pressures of time and cost, the CPT should be prepared to prioritize its recommendations in order to assist the state to prepare a useful and realistic plan of action, the response and development of which could be monitored in detail. In short, the CPT should furnish each state party with something more akin to a custom-made programme tailored to its particular circumstances and needs rather than the off-the-peg set of recommendations which are currently made.

This does not mean that we think the CPT should not issue general guidance about issues on which it has so far failed to set out its thinking in an annual general report—for example, concerning accountability structures. However, such guidance should be couched in *general* terms. We are not persuaded that issuing precise *formulae* is wise, for, as has already been the case, once detailed formulae are articulated, there is a danger that they will be universally applied in a mechanical fashion. This safeguards the Committee against the charge of not applying its standards consistently but does not necessarily do much to improve protection against ill-treatment. There is a danger of losing sight of the fact that the CPT's task is *not* to ensure that certain procedural standards are everywhere met, but that ill-treatment is prevented. The standards should not be allowed to become ends in themselves: they are at best means to an end. Since the evidence collected by the CPT suggests that the end—the absence of physical ill-treatment—appears in several countries to have substantially been attained without some of the means being in place, what is the ground for pressing for their universal adoption? We suggest that 'horses for courses' are required.

The CPT is currently facing the most substantial challenge of the Committee's short life. Those state parties that have recently ratified the

Convention include several whose geographical size, economic and governmental turmoil, immensity of their custodial populations, and known prevalence of ill-treatment, present the CPT with problems as intractable as can be imagined. We have argued elsewhere[76] that this challenge will require the Committee radically to review all its working methods—the role of members, the programme of visits and the nature of visits, the manner in which the situation in states party is monitored, and the Committee's relationships with NGOs. So far, the CPT has responded to the challenge posed by consistently promulgating universally applicable standards and by allowing their realization to be achieved over time, depending on the socio-economic resources prevailing locally, an approach we have elsewhere referred to as *variable geometry*.[77] In the light of the material presented in this volume, it would be desirable for the CPT to consider this alternative approach.

REFERENCES

Alston, P (1992b) 'The Commission on Human Rights' in Alston, P (ed) *The United Nations and Human Rights* (Oxford: Clarendon Press)
APT (1996) *Working Group on the Draft Optional Protocol to the Convention against Torture and Other Cruel, Inhuman or Degrading Treatment or Punishment, Analytical Report of the Association for the Prevention of Torture* (Geneva: Association for the Prevention of Torture)
APT (1997) *Standard Operating Procedures of International Mechanisms Carrying out Visits to Places of Detention* (Geneva: Association for the Prevention of Torture)
Ashworth, A (1992) *Sentencing and Criminal Justice* (London: Weidenfeld and Nicholson)
Bayley, DH (1983) 'Accountability and control of the police: some lessons for Britain' in Bennett, T (ed) *The Future of Policing*, Cropwood Series No 15 (Cambridge: Institute of Criminology)
Byrnes, A (1992) 'The Committee against Torture' in Alston, P (ed) *The United Nations and Human Rights* (Oxford: Clarendon Press)
Cassese, A (1989) 'A New Approach to Human Rights: The European Convention for the Prevention of Torture', 83 *AJIL* 130
Cassese, A (1996) *Inhuman States: Imprisonment, Detention and Torture in Europe Today* (Cambridge: Polity Press), originally published in Italian (1994) *Umano-Disumano: Commissariarti en prigioni nell'Europa di oggo* (Roma Bari: Laterza), 47–49
Council of Europe, Parliamentary Assembly, Committee on Legal Affairs and Human Rights (1997) *Report on strengthening the machinery of the European*

---

[76] Evans and Morgan (1998), 363–368.   [77] Ibid, 349.

Convention for the Prevention of Torture and Inhuman or Degrading Treatment or Punishment, Parl Ass Doc 7784, 26 March 1997

Evans, MD and Morgan, R (1998) *Preventing Torture* (Oxford: Clarendon Press)

Home Office (1998) *Prison Statistics England and Wales 1997*, Cm 4017 (London: HMSO)

International Commission of Jurists/Swiss Committee Against Torture (1979) *Torture: How to make the International Convention Effective* (Geneva: International Commission of Jurists and Swiss Committee Against Torture)

Meier Report, AS/Jur (32) 22, 8 Dec 1980 and Recommendation 909 (1981)

Morgan, R (1985) 'Her Majesty's Inspectorate of Prisons' in Maguire, M, Vagg, J and Morgan, R (eds) *Accountability and Prisons: Opening Up a Closed World* (London: Tavistock)

Morgan, R (1998) 'Preventing Torture and Protecting Prisoners', 11(4) *Interights Bulletin* 178–180

Physicians for Human Rights (1996) *Torture in Turkey and Its Unwilling Accomplices: The Scope of State Persecution and the Coercion of Physicians* (Boston: Physicians for Human Rights)

Raynor, M (1987) *Turning a Blind Eye?: Medical Accountability and the Prevention of Torture in South Africa* (Washington DC: Committee on Scientific Freedom and Responsibility)

Reiner, R (1992) *The Politics of the Police* (Hemel Hempstead: Wheatsheaf)

Servicio Paz y Justicia (1989) *Uruguay: Nunca Más—Human Rights Violations, 1972–1985* (Philadelphia: Temple University Press)

2

CPT Standards: An Overview

ROD MORGAN AND MALCOLM D. EVANS

1. LOCATING THE STANDARDS

The CPT produces two categories of documents which are vital for the analysis of its 'jurisprudence': the annual general reports which describe its work during the past year; and the individual country reports arising out of its programme of visits. There have now been eight of the former and, by the end of 1998, over fifty of the latter have been published.

At the outset of its work, the CPT concluded that although there was a 'wealth of material' on custodial conditions, 'no clear guidance can be drawn from it for the purpose of dealing with specific situations encountered by the Committee'.[1] The Committee therefore set about devising some 'working tools' to assist it when carrying out inspections. These aids were related to the various types of institutions regularly visited by the CPT—prisons, police stations, psychiatric hospitals, detention centres for aliens, and so on—described the nature and functioning of the visit mechanism, and, notably, summarized the case law of the European Commission and Court of Human Rights relevant to the work of the Committee.[2] The CPT is not bound by the case law built up under the ECHR, and can seek guidance from a number of 'other relevant human rights instruments'. But it seems probable that the decisions of the Commission and Court have a particular influence on the Committee's work.[3]

Although the CPT's 'working tools' have never been published the Committee has partly realized its early aspiration of gradually 'building up . . . a set [of] general criteria for the treatment of persons deprived of their liberty' and of making these 'general standards' public so as 'to offer national authorities some general guidelines in relation to the treatment of persons deprived of their liberty'.[4] On four occasions, in 1992, 1993, 1997, and 1998, the Committee has used its annual general reports to summarize its views on different aspects of the treatment of detainees or different categories of detainees. In 1992 custody in police stations and prisons was

---

[1] Gen Rep 1, para 95.   [2] Ibid, paras 35–36.
[3] Ibid, para 5; see also Chapter One, pp 6–8.   [4] Ibid, para 96.

dealt with generally.[5] In 1993 the Committee addressed the question of health care in prisons.[6] In 1997 the Committee turned to the issue of 'Foreign Nationals Detained Under Aliens Legislation'.[7] In 1998 the Committee considered issues arising out of the 'Involuntary Placement in Psychiatric Establishments' of patients.[8] The purpose of these exercises, according to the Committee, has been both to give advance warning of the expectations of the Committee and to stimulate discussion about the appropriate treatment of detainees, about which the CPT says it welcomes comment.[9] Though the Committee has emphasized that these standards are non-binding—that they are mere 'guidelines' and that the Committee is not seeking 'to play a legislative role'[10]—some of the standards are nevertheless described as 'fundamental safeguards' to which the Committee 'attaches particular importance'.[11] The Committee routinely insists upon adherence to these safeguards even in countries where there is little or no evidence of ill-treatment of a sort which might have been prevented by their existence.

The statements in the annual general reports do not, however, cover all the issues considered in CPT country reports. Moreover, many of the standards set out in the general reports have been subject to subsequent refinement in the light of the Committee's experiences and the responses of states. It follows that, for the time being, the careful analyst of CPT jurisprudence needs to be familiar with a large number of country reports. This difficulty may soon be removed since, according to Trevor Stevens, the CPT's Secretary, the Committee is considering publishing a comprehensive statement of its standards.[12] At the time of writing the most that the Committee has done in this regard—with respect to 'foreign nationals detained under aliens legislation'—is to publish a compendium of extracts from country reports and government replies.[13]

The CPT's jurisprudence can be analysed from a variety of perspectives: institutionally (in relation to different types of custody), thematically (in relation to physical conditions, procedures, legal or medical services, and so on), chronologically (with respect to the focus of the Committee's work over time), or even geographically (with regard to countries representing different historical traditions or socio-economic advantages and disadvantages). For the present, however, it is most useful to consider the expectations of the Committee in relation to different categories of detainees, since

---

[5] Gen Rep 2, paras 35–60.   [6] Gen Rep 3, paras 30–77.
[7] Gen Rep 7, paras 24–36.   [8] Gen Rep 8, paras 25–58.   [9] Ibid, para 24.
[10] Gen Rep, para 96.   [11] Gen Rep 2, paras 35–36.
[12] Trevor Stevens, Kings College, September 1997.
[13] See CPT/Inf (97) 15, *Foreign nationals detained under alien legislation: statements made by the CPT in published visit reports and replies received from the Governments concerned.*

it is not the case that particular agencies or institutions are exclusively or invariably responsible for particular types of detainees. Moreover, since different groups of detainees pose particular issues it is important to adopt an approach which focuses on the person in detention, rather than upon the agency responsible for them. This approach has the merit of highlighting the point that the detainee should be the principal subject of concern, rather than the system and its proper functioning, within which the detainee is merely an object.

2. THE 'T' AND 'IDT' WORDS

The CPT is not a judicial body and it is not bound by the jurisprudence developed under the ECHR, although it is, of course, able to draw guidance from it. Since it is not the role of the Committee to establish whether there has been a breach of Article 3 of the ECHR the CPT has no need to set out its approach to its key terms—*torture* and *inhuman or degrading.* The Committee is concerned with prevention, with the future rather than the past.

This is the theory. Yet the reality is somewhat different. The reality is that what the majority of readers of CPT reports most want to know is whether the Committee has found there to be torture or inhuman or degrading treatment. It follows from this that readers want to know how the Committee has used those terms: What practices have the Committee discovered which they judge to be torture? What procedures or custodial conditions have they concluded are inhuman or degrading? In asking these questions senior officials are not only mindful of the international reputations of the custodial systems for which they are responsible. If the CPT 'finds' there to be evidence of, or a risk of, torture or of inhuman or degrading treatment, this may result in similarly situated detainees lodging applications under the ECHR in order to test the proposition. This eventuality can never be far from the minds of the CPT and its Secretariat, who work in the same building as houses the Court and its Secretariat. It therefore comes as no surprise to learn that early on (and no doubt at regular intervals since) the CPT Secretariat provided the Committee with information concerning the relevant case law under the ECHR.[14] For, as the Secretary to the CPT has made clear, there is in reality a two-way relationship between the CPT and the Commission and Court: decisions made under the ECHR guide the CPT and the findings of the CPT may both stimulate petitions and on occasion may directly influence the application of Article 3.[15] For these reasons it is important

---

[14] See Note 3.　　[15] See Note 12.

briefly to consider how the CPT has used the words *torture* and *inhuman and degrading*[16] treatment.

(a) Torture

The CPT has used the word 'torture' in relatively few country reports though it has found the incidence of physical ill-treatment, particularly at the hands of the police, either to be relatively commonplace or certainly not rare in a large proportion—about two-fifths—of member states. From the published record it appears that the Committee has not yet found it appropriate to refer to the essentially mental stresses exerted on prisoners which the CPT has found in some jurisdictions as amounting to torture.

What, then, is the threshold which the CPT appears to consider it necessary for physical ill-treatment to have crossed in order for it to be described as torture? We conclude that the CPT has so far reserved the word 'torture' for what are perhaps best described as specialized, or exotic, forms of violence purposefully employed to gain a confession or information or generally intended to intimidate or humiliate.[17] Other forms of violence of the sort frequently reported to, and not infrequently found by, the Committee,[18] such as blows with fists or feet or batons or other weapons, have generally been deemed insufficient to justify use of the terms 'severe ill-treatment' or 'torture', even when such blows have apparently been inflicted either with the intention of causing pain or purposefully with a view to extracting information. Physical ill-treatment has been described as torture when, for example, evidence has been found of the use of specialized techniques (such as the suspension of the victim, beating of the soles of the feet, hosing with pressurized water, the placing of a metal bucket on the head and then striking it with metal or wooden instruments, and so on),[19] the use of specialized instruments (notably electric shock

---

[16] Although Article 3 of the ECHR and the ECPT itself refer to 'inhuman or degrading' treatment or punishment, the CPT uses the expression 'inhuman and degrading'. Whereas the ECHR refers to 'torture or inhuman or degrading treatment or punishment', the ECPT refers to 'torture and inhuman or degrading treatment or punishment'. This might possibly account for the CPT in general considering itself to be dealing with two categories rather than with either three categories or a single concept equally applicable in all sets of circumstances.

[17] Though it should be noted that Cassese has stated that in his opinion torture is 'any form of coercion or violence, whether mental or physical, against a person to extort a confession, information, or to humiliate, punish or intimidate that person' and has suggested that the Committee has adopted this definition (Cassese (1996), 47).

[18] CPT findings are typically presented along two continua: the number of allegations and a finding of risk of ill-treatment based on an assessment of the number, nature, and credibility of allegations (for a full discussion of CPT methodology and conclusions see Evans and Morgan (1998), Chapter Six).

[19] For examples, see: Bulgaria 1, para 27; Cyprus 1, para 15; and Turkey PS 1, para 5.

equipment),[20] or special forms of preparation (such as blindfolding or covering the victim's head with a blanket, or officers' faces being masked, to prevent the victim seeing his or her tormenters).[21]

The positioning of the threshold may have as much to do with problems of evidence as the definition of torture.[22] Blows may be struck in the heat of the moment and injuries from punches or kicks or batons may result from incidents at the time of arrest when force may reasonably have been used, as opposed to incidents in the interrogation room where, generally speaking, it has no legitimate place. There is, by contrast, no defensible reason for officers having in their possession or using a device designed to inflict electric shocks and the presence and use of equipment designed to suspend or strap down a suspect during an interrogation involving physical ill-treatment can scarcely be interpreted in terms other than torture. Yet questions of evidence do not appear to explain where the CPT has drawn the line separating 'mere' ill-treatment from torture in all cases. The point is best illustrated by way of example. In Hungary the Committee heard 'numerous' and 'remarkably consistent' allegations concerning a 'precise form' of ill-treatment at the hands of the police:

In most cases, the persons concerned alleged that, after their hands had been handcuffed behind them (or their ankles attached to an item of furniture), they had been struck with truncheons, punched, slapped or kicked by police officers . . . in a number of cases, the allegations made were supported by medical evidence.[23]

Despite the fact that these allegations concerned preparation for and the purposive infliction of a considerable degree of violence, and although corroborative medical evidence was available, the Committee did not employ the terms 'severe ill-treatment' or 'torture' in its report. In the report on Bulgaria, by contrast, these terms were used. There was a good deal of evidence of prisoners having been kicked, punched, slapped, and stamped on, or being struck with wooden objects or metal or plastic pipes. But the distinguishing practice in Bulgaria appears to have been the use of *falaka*, beating the soles of the feet. This requires some preparation and leaves injuries which cannot be attributed to incidents involving the reasonable use of force.[24] The report on Romania mirrors that on Bulgaria. Once again, numerous allegations of physical ill-treatment were supported by medical evidence and the CPT concluded that there was a far from negligible (*loin d'être négligeable*) risk of 'severe ill-treatment', or 'torture'.[25] The forms of ill-treatment recorded included

[20] eg Austria 1, para 42; Greece 1, para 25; Turkey PS 1, para 5.
[21] eg Cyprus 1, para 15; and Spain 1, para 19.
[22] The problems are fully discussed in Evans and Morgan (1998), Chapter Six.
[23] Hungary 1, para 17.   [24] Bulgaria 1, paras 17–18.
[25] Romania 1, para 22.

falaka, administered whilst the victim was tied to a chair or suspended on a metal bar in a position known as 'the rotisserie'.[26] In the final analysis it is difficult to see why severely beating a prisoner with batons while his hands are handcuffed behind his back during the course of questioning is not torture, whereas beating him on the soles of the feet in similar circumstances is.[27] If the distinction between the Hungarian and the Bulgarian and Romanian cases lies in the quality of the evidence available to the Committee, then this is not made clear in the CPT reports. Yet it is difficult to see what other explanation there can be.[28]

The Committee has encountered few allegations of serious physical ill-treatment in non-police settings,[29] and the reports published to date contain only one example of such ill-treatment as amounting to torture, this being at a prison in Spain.[30] The existence of even this isolated example is, however, sufficient to suggest that the Committee as a whole does not endorse the view, apparently held by some prominent figures whilst they were CPT members, that torture is exclusively a police phenomenon[31] or that custodians in other settings 'never use such cruel methods'.[32]

It appears, therefore, that the CPT considers torture to be the premeditated (as opposed to casual or heat-of-the-moment), purposive infliction of severe pain, generally involving the use of specialized techniques or instruments, with a view to extracting information or confessions or the attainment of other specific ends.

[26] Romania 1, para 16.

[27] Similar questions arise out of the Slovak Report, which concluded that those in police custody faced a 'significant risk' of ill-treatment and, on occasion, severe 'ill-treatment', but no mention of torture was made (Slovakia 1, para 18). The forms of ill-treatment included a case of *falaka* (but not, it seems, on so extensive a basis as in Bulgaria and Romania) and an incident in which three dogs were let loose on a handcuffed man. Possibly, the reason why this did not amount to 'torture' was because it was not in the context of an interrogation (ibid, para 16(v)). In Poland also the CPT heard allegations of, and found medical evidence consistent with, single instances of ill-treatment of the sort—electric shocks and *falaka*—which it has elsewhere described as torture, but on this occasion the word was not used (Poland 1, paras 14–18).

[28] There is another possible explanation. During a symposium on the work of the CPT jointly organized by the APT and COLPI in Budapest in June 1998, the then CPT member for Germany, Professor Gunther Kaiser, who was a member of the delegation that visited Hungary, said, when informed of the disjunction in the use of the term 'torture' in the Hungary and Bulgaria reports, that Hungary was the first of the Eastern European states to be visited by the CPT and there had been 'a desire' as to the degree of criticism made. What precisely he meant by this is not clear, for he later asserted that this did not mean that different standards had been applied.

[29] Even in Turkey, where the Committee has found that use of torture is 'widespread', the Committee has stated that they have not found torture to be a problem in prisons (Turkey PS 1, para 22).

[30] In a prison in Spain 1, para 91.

[31] Sorenson, B (1995) 'Prevention of Torture and Inhuman or Degrading Treatment or Punishment: Medical Views' in APT, 259.

[32] Cassese (1996), 66.

The Committee recognizes that torture may be psychological, involving threats, severe humiliation, or isolation, and it has drawn attention to the evidential difficulties attending alleged use of such techniques.[33] In the case of isolation, there is also the difficulty of deciding whether the isolation was justified, whether there were any other additional restrictions and whether they, in turn, were justifiable, and whether the duration of the isolation was reasonable.

These issues have arisen repeatedly during CPT visits, particularly in Scandinavian countries. In Denmark, Norway, and Sweden it is relatively common for pre-trial prisoners to be subject to restrictions regarding their contacts with fellow prisoners and other persons (whether through visits, telephone calls, or correspondence) and even on watching television, listening to the radio, or reading newspapers and magazines. The justifications given for such restrictions are the need to safeguard evidence and to prevent collusion or intimidation. The restrictions are imposed on the authority of the court and, as a consequence, are to some extent at the discretion of prosecutors and, directly or indirectly, the investigating police. During its visits to Scandinavia the CPT has encountered examples of pre-trial prisoners being subject to restrictions of this nature (though still able to be visited by their lawyers) for prolonged periods and the Committee has found some evidence to support claims that it has had adverse mental health consequences.[34]

The Committee has been unequivocal in its criticism of prolonged isolation but has stopped short of describing specific instances as amounting to 'psychological torture' even though some evidence has been found of such restrictions being used by the police to exert pressure on suspects to co-operate and it being clear from prisoners' testimonies that, whether or not restrictions are partly or wholly designed and applied to achieve that result, this is certainly the consequence.[35] The furthest that the CPT has so far been prepared to go is to say that 'solitary confinement can, in certain circumstances, amount to inhuman and degrading treatment',[36] but the CPT has not yet found it to have done so with regard to the use of pre-trial restrictions in Scandinavia. The Committee has restricted itself to recommending a raft of measures designed to ensure that restrictions are judicially and specifically authorized, that they are justified and reviewed and, where applied, are for as short a time as possible and are ameliorated by prisoner–staff contact and out-of-cell activity.[37]

In one instance, regarding the use of solitary confinement in Spain for sentenced prisoners judged to be 'dangerous or unadapted to an ordinary prison regime', the CPT has described the situation as 'inhuman

---

[33] See Spain 1, para 19; Spain 3, para 30. [34] Denmark 1, para 25; Norway 2, para 29.
[35] Denmark 1, para 60; Norway 2, para 34. [36] Gen Rep 2, para 56.
[37] See, eg, Sweden 2, paras 21–27.

treatment'.[38] This use of terminology moves us away from the purposive infliction of pain and the realm of what the Committee describes as torture or severe ill-treatment and towards the sphere of custodial living conditions, in relation to which the CPT has repeatedly used the other key term—inhuman or degrading—from Article 3 of the ECHR.

(b) Inhuman or degrading treatment or punishment

The CPT has never used the terms 'inhuman' and 'degrading' to refer to physical or psychological ill-treatment. The Committee has so far reserved these terms to describe aspects of custodial living conditions, with the exception of the grey or hybrid area regarding pre-trial isolation discussed above. Moreover, the Committee has adopted a cumulative view of living conditions so that conditions that might not in themselves be deemed inhuman and degrading become so when combined with others.[39] Thus the combination of overcrowding, lack of integral sanitation, almost unallevi-ated cellular confinement, and/or lack of outdoor exercise have on several occasions been judged to amount to inhuman and degrading treatment.[40] However, the Committee has also emphasized that physical overcrowding can be so acute as to amount to inhuman and degrading treatment in its own right[41] and on at least one occasion the Committee has found it to be so.[42] Furthermore, there is a suggestion that breach of the general duty of care which all custodial authorities owe to their charges—a duty to which the Committee attaches particular importance—may combine with physi-cal and social custodial conditions to constitute inhuman and degrading conditions. In a Portuguese prison inter-prisoner violence and intimidation, together with overcrowding, lack of integral sanitation, and an absence of organized out-of-cell regime activities, resulted in this finding.[43]

The Committee has sometimes employed the words 'degrading' or 'inhuman' separately, though it has not always been clear whether this is meant to reflect any significant variation in the degree of environmental ill-treatment encountered. In one instance, however, the Committee has made itself very clear. In its second general report the CPT emphasized that it did 'not like' the practice of 'slopping out',[44] but later hardened this opinion by unequivocally asserting that the practice is 'degrading' not just for the persons having to discharge their human waste in the presence, without

---

[38] Spain 1, paras 110–113.

[39] For an account which may reflect the Committee's thinking see Cassese (1996), 48–49. See also Evans and Morgan (1998), Chapter Six.

[40] See Gen Rep 2, para 50; France 1, paras 93–102; Italy 1, para 77; Portugal 2, para 95; UK 1, para 57; Romania 1, para 69 (re police facilities) and para 105.

[41] Gen Rep 2, para 46.   [42] Spain 2, paras 113–114.   [43] Portugal 2, paras 94–95.

[44] The process by which prisoners, occupying cells lacking integral sanitation, use buckets or other receptacles to meet the calls of nature and are periodically released from their cells in order to empty their buckets at some central facility—see Gen Rep 2, para 49.

privacy, of other prisoners in a confined living space, but is also 'degrading' for other prisoners and for the prison staff who have to supervise the subsequent 'slopping out'.[45] Similar considerations prompted the CPT to describe as 'degrading' the practice encountered at the airport in Zurich of requiring those suspected of 'body packing' (swallowing drug-filled condoms) to defecate on a toilet, known as 'the throne', in the centre of a special room and under direct observation.[46]

Other custodial conditions have been described as 'inhuman', such as some overcrowded, unhygienic, dilapidated, and poorly equipped accommodation,[47] or confinement in very small, dark, and unventilated cells without the possibility of outdoor exercise.[48] It is not clear whether the CPT intended the words 'inhuman' and 'degrading' to have distinct meanings in these contexts.

One further nuance of language emerges from CPT reports. The Committee sometimes says that custodial conditions '*could* be said to amount to inhuman and degrading' treatment or punishment but does not say categorically that they are to be considered as such. The implication is that the conditions lie close to the threshold: *some* of the elements making for a cumulative judgement of inhuman and degrading are present to *some* degree, or the degree to which those elements pertain is contested (prisoners say one thing, staff another).[49] Likewise the Committee has found conditions '*akin* to inhuman and degrading treatment' when describing the accommodation and regime in a psychiatric hospital.[50] Here, it appears, the word *akin* was used because the deficiencies identified by the Committee had to be judged in the light of a particular circumstance, namely the mentally disordered character of the population housed.

(c) Use of the key terms—conclusions

It seems, then, that the CPT uses the terms *torture* and *inhuman and degrading* treatment in what can be described as a branched manner which is in contrast to the linear usage found in the jurisprudence of the ECHR. Whereas the ECHR jurisprudence views inhuman and degrading treatment and torture as different points along a continuum, or in a hierarchy, of severity, the CPT appears to be reserving these terms for different forms of ill-treatment. *Torture* is almost exclusively used to refer to physical ill-treatment employed instrumentally by the police. Moreover, the Committee has set a high threshold for the use of the term, largely, one suspects, for evidential reasons. The terms *inhuman* and *degrading*, used either

---

[45] Ireland 1, para 100; see also Cassese (1996), 49–50.   [46] Switzerland 2, para 56.
[47] Greece 1, para 76.   [48] Bulgaria 1, paras 109–110.
[49] See, eg, the Committee's discussion of the situation at Zagora Prison, Bulgaria (Bulgaria 1, paras 109–110).
[50] Greece 1, paras 202–260.

separately or together, have been reserved for forms of environmental ill-treatment, chiefly concerning the conditions in which groups of prisoners are housed, where the purposive element, at least in terms of a particular individual, is lacking or obscure.

Since the Committee applies only one of the recognized terms in each of these separate categories of ill-treatment, it has had to resort to less familiar terminology when describing forms of ill-treatment which fall beneath its thresholds. When environmental conditions are at issue, the words *inhuman* and *degrading* are sometimes used separately in situations where the ill-treatment appears to fall short of that which is *inhuman and degrading*. Physical ill-treatment falling short of *torture* is not called *inhuman* or *degrading* but is described as *ill-treatment*. Environmental ill-treatment falling short of the *inhuman* or the *degrading*, and well below that which is deemed *inhuman and degrading*, is said to be *unacceptable* or *inadmissible*, or it is said that it *could* be considered to be *inhuman and degrading*, but is not actually said to be so.

3. CATEGORIES OF DETAINEES

(a) Suspects and other persons detained temporarily

In all jurisdictions the police have the power, *de jure* or *de facto*, temporarily to detain persons they reasonably suspect of having committed a crime. The period of detention is generally strictly time limited pending a criminal charge being laid, or a prosecutor being persuaded that there is sufficient evidence to warrant more prolonged detention for the purposes of investigation. Following the laying of a charge, or formal arrest by a prosecutor, there are further time limitations upon the period within which the suspect must be brought before a court which will decide whether he or she should be released or remanded in custody while further investigations are conducted or until the accused is brought to trial. This is seldom the full extent of police powers, however. In many jurisdictions the police also have the power to detain various categories of persons not subject, initially at least, to criminal proceedings for administrative or procedural purposes: witnesses, persons whose identity is uncertain, drunks, persons held for various breaches of public order, and so on. What-ever the reason, all these examples involve the temporary detention of persons by the police without any judicial imprimatur of approval and it is widely acknowledged that this is the period during which detainees are most vulnerable to ill-treatment at the hands of the police[51]—a

---

[51] See Amnesty International (1984) *Torture in the Eighties* (London: Amnesty International).

judgement with which the CPT agrees.[52] During the initial period of custody detainees are often in a state of shock and bewilderment, disoriented and feeling isolated, frightened and easily influenced, unaware of their rights, drunk or under the influence of drugs, or a combination of any of these. Even in the best regulated systems the police are apt to capitalize on this vulnerability in order to press home their advantage: now is the time to get the suspect to talk, to provide information, to confess.

The power to detain temporarily granted to the police is itself a form of coercion judged necessary to combat crime and bring offenders to justice. However, in order that the presumption of innocence be respected, and the police be prevented from using their powers oppressively, it is generally recognized that police powers must be narrowly defined, limited, and accompanied by certain safeguards for suspects. Further, the safeguards must be proportionate to:

— the gravity of the offence of which the detainee is suspected (in many jurisdictions, for example, police powers have been extended when detainees are suspected of particularly heinous offences, such as terrorism);
— the degree to which the suspect's liberty and freedom is interfered with (the greater the police powers to detain, the greater the safeguards that are typically provided);
— the vulnerability of the detainee (juveniles, for example, are often the subject of particular safeguards).

In practice, these safeguards have proved to be the source of some of the most sensitive and difficult exchanges between the CPT and state parties, not least because they are not necessarily endorsed by practice under the ECHR.[53]

All CPT reports arising from *periodic* visits include a statement setting out a series of basic principles. The first version of the statement appeared in the Committee's first country report[54] and was formalized in the second general report.[55] It has been developed over time and in its current form is as follows:

---

[52] See Gen Rep 6, para 15: 'The CPT wishes to stress that, in its experience, the period immediately following deprivation of liberty is when the risk of intimidation and physical ill-treatment is greatest.' This statement has been repeated in many country reports.

[53] See, for example, the trenchant criticisms of the CPT's advocacy of the right of access to a lawyer and to a doctor of one's own choice from the outset of custody, which drew upon the Court of Human Rights' judgment in *John Murray v UK* and on the *travaux préparatoires* of the proposed protocol to the ECHR on the rights of those deprived of their liberty in Switzerland 2 R 1, 101 and 103.

[54] Austria 1, para 60.   [55] Gen Rep 2, para 36.

The CPT attaches particular importance to three rights for persons deprived of their liberty by the police:

— the right of those concerned to inform a close relative or another third party of their choice of their situation,
— the right of access to a lawyer,
— the right to request a medical examination by a doctor of their choice.

The CPT considers that these three rights are fundamental safeguards against the ill-treatment of persons deprived of their liberty, which should apply from the very outset of custody (that is, from the moment when those concerned are obliged to remain with the police). Furthermore, in the view of the CPT, persons taken into police custody should be immediately informed of all their rights, including those referred to above.[56]

Though the general thrust of these standards has generally been endorsed, their detailed prescription by the CPT has encountered greater open resistance from state parties than almost all other CPT standards, not least because the Committee has repeatedly insisted on their binding nature, their bureaucratic implementation, and their universal application. The rights should be expressly guaranteed by law. The Committee recognizes that third party notification and access to a lawyer might be delayed 'in order to protect the interests of justice' but any such limitations must be 'clearly defined and their application strictly limited in time'.[57] Moreover, exercise of any power to delay notification or access should also be subject to safeguards: the reasons should be recorded in writing and the decision approved by a senior police officer, the prosecutor, or by the judicial authorities.[58] Access to a lawyer means access from the very first moment when the person is obliged to remain with the police and includes 'the right to contact and to be visited by the lawyer (in both cases under conditions guaranteeing the confidentiality of their discussions) as well as, in principle, the right of the person concerned to have the lawyer present during interrogation'.[59] Further, though access to a particular lawyer might be denied 'in the interests of justice' there can be no justification for totally denying access to a lawyer: it should always be possible to arrange access to an independent lawyer 'who can be trusted not to jeopardise the legitimate interests of the police investigation'.[60] To make this feasible the Committee commends the provision of lists of lawyers being made

---

[56] Bulgaria 1, paras 80–81. The wording of the statement varies somewhat from report to report but has remained more or less stable since 1992. In this version, for example, the right is to 'request' a medical examination by a doctor of the detainee's choice. It is normally stated unequivocally as a right 'to a medical examination' by a doctor of the detainee's choice, in addition to any medical examination carried out by a doctor called by the police authorities (see, eg, Malta 2, para 25).

[57] Gen Rep 2, para 37.   [58] See, eg, Portugal 1, para 41; Belgium 1, para 40.
[59] Gen Rep 2, para 38.   [60] See, eg, Greece 1, para 40; France 3, para 39.

available to detainees[61] and, even more importantly, the operation of schemes whereby detainees unable to pay for legal services can be assisted.[62]

With regard to medical examinations, it is evident that the Committee is concerned to ensure that doctors maintain their independence and are not pressurized. All medical 'examinations should be conducted out of the hearing, and preferably out of the sight, of police officers. Further, the results of every examination, as well as relevant statements by the detainee and the doctor's conclusions, should be formally recorded by the doctor and made available to the detainee and his lawyer.'[63]

The CPT takes the logical view that there is little point in detainees having rights if they are not informed about them. And since the three fundamental rights should be available from the outset of custody, then information regarding them must also be communicated to detainees at the outset of custody. The Committee recommends that a 'form setting out these rights be given systematically',[64] and that the form should employ language which detainees will understand[65] and be available in languages spoken by detainees.[66] To make it absolutely clear that detainees have been told their rights the Committee recommends that they be asked to sign a statement saying that they have been so informed, the argument being that this process protects both the interests of detainees and the police, who might subsequently be accused of not having informed their charges.[67]

Resistance to the detailed application of some of these recommendations has been inspired by a variety of very different considerations. In countries in North-West Europe, for example, where the CPT has found little evidence of ill-treatment at the hands of the police, aspects of the standards are clearly considered unnecessary. The CPT, concerned with conditions in Europe as a whole, has a different perspective to that of the civil servants and legal advisers with whom the Committee deals on behalf of governments. The CPT is concerned with preventing ill-treatment and sees the three fundamental safeguards outlined above as potent devices which contribute to that end. In countries where physical ill-treatment at the hands of the police is not a significant problem, however, the safeguards are probably seen in a different light. Third party notification may be thought of as something which normally happens and that there is no need for elaborate procedures or hard-and-fast rules because initial custody is brief and because it is thought that the police must be given a discretion not to notify persons who they suspect might subvert investigations or

---

[61] See, eg, Ireland 1, para 44.   [62] See, eg, Germany 1, para 35.
[63] Gen Rep 2, para 38.   [64] See, eg, Sweden 1, para 29.
[65] See, eg, Portugal 1, para 47 and Italy 1, para 48.
[66] See, eg, Finland 1, para 48; Slovakia 1, para 47.
[67] See, eg, Germany 1, paras 41 and 45.

destroy evidence. Access to a lawyer may be thought of simply in terms of enabling suspects to prepare for their defence, in which case it will appear irrelevant for those who are detained by the police but not accused of crimes, such as the various classes of administrative detainees. Moreover, in countries where statements made to the police before the prosecutor is involved in the investigation are of little evidential value, or where a premium is placed on oral statements made in court, little importance may be attached to ensuring that suspects have access to lawyers during their initial police custody. Similarly, in such countries the right to have a medical examination by a doctor of one's choice may be seen as fanciful; something which is not objected to, but is unlikely to be realized in practice, largely superfluous, and scarcely worth routine elaboration in order to ensure that the detainee knows that he or she enjoys such a right. For example, in response to the CPT's embrace of the principle of 'normalization' regarding health care,[68] several countries have pointed out that their medical services are organized in such a fashion that individuals enjoying their liberty either do not have a personal general medical practitioner or, when urgently requiring medical assistance, 'must accept attendance by the doctor on duty'.[69]

In other parts of Europe, the CPT's fundamental safeguards may be seen as a serious interference with the autonomy of the police and their ability to get on with their job, particularly with regard to serious crime. Several European countries, for example, grant the police power to detain certain categories of suspects for additional periods, during which third party notification or access to a lawyer may be circumscribed, delayed, or denied, in order to combat the organized threat posed by groups allegedly engaged in terrorism, drug trafficking, and the like. In this context the CPT's safeguards might be considered to undermine the capacity of the police to 'lean' on suspects.

This leads naturally into the closely allied question of the CPT's standards concerning the conduct of interrogations. This was addressed in the second general report, which said that there should be a code of practice governing the conduct of interrogations in every jurisdiction and the code should:

address inter alia the following matters: the systematic informing of the detainee of the identity (name and/or number) of those present at the interview; the permissible length of an interrogation; rest periods between interviews and breaks during an interrogation; places in which interrogations may take place; whether the detainee may be required to stand while being questioned; the questioning of

---

[68] See Gen Rep 3, para 31: 'That prisoners are entitled to the same level of medical care as persons living in the community at large'. For broader discussions of the principle see King, RD and Morgan, R (1980) *The Future of the Prison System* (Farnborough: Gower), 34–37.

[69] See, eg, Iceland 1 R 1, 8. See also below p. 68.

persons who are under the influence of drugs, alcohol, medicine, or who are in a state of shock . . . The position of particularly vulnerable persons (for example, the young, those who are mentally disabled or mentally ill) should be the subject of specific safeguards.[70]

The CPT has also begun to sketch out a framework for the public accountability of police actions relating to custody. This framework is as yet poorly developed, though there is reason to believe that the Committee intends to develop this aspect of its work.[71]

From almost the outset of its work the Committee took the view that the:

fundamental safeguards granted to persons in custody would be reinforced (and the work of police officers quite possibly facilitated) if a single and comprehensive custody record were to exist for each person detained, on which would be recorded all aspects of his custody and action taken regarding them (when deprived of liberty and reasons for that measure; when told of rights; signs of injuries, mental illness, etc; when next of kin/consulate and lawyer contacted and when visited by them; when offered food; when interrogated; when transferred or released, etc). For various matters (for example, items in the person's possession, the fact of being told of one's rights and of invoking or waiving them), the signature of the detainee would be obtained and, if necessary, the absence of a signature explained. Further, the detainee's lawyer would have access to such a custody record.[72]

Moreover, the recommended code for the conduct of interviews with suspects incorporates the expectation that:

It should also be required that a record be systematically kept of the time at which interrogations start and end, of the persons present during the interrogation and of any request made by a detainee during the interrogation.[73]

At the outset the Committee also *recommended* that states 'explore the possibility' of making electronic recordings of interviews with suspects,[74] and went so far as to commend a method for doing so—'one tape to be sealed in the presence of the detainee, the other used as a working copy',[75] a method which the Committee found to be in use in England and Wales and which it seemed to the CPT 'offered all appropriate safeguards'.[76] A *recommendation* that authorities '*explore the possibility*' of electronic

---

[70] Gen Rep 2, para 39.

[71] This was indicated by Trevor Stevens, Secretary to the CPT, in answer to a question following an address on the work of the CPT given at Kings College, London, in September 1997. See Note 12. It is notable, moreover, that the visit to the UK undertaken at about the same time concentrated, *inter alia*, on the 'efficacity [*sic*] of existing legal remedies in cases involving allegations of ill-treatment by police officers'. Among the persons met by the delegation during this fourth visit to the UK was the Director of Public Prosecutions and the Deputy Chairman of the Police Complaints Authority (see Press Release Ref 534a97).

[72] Gen Rep 2, para 40.   [73] Ibid, para 39.   [74] Austria 1, para 67.
[75] Sweden 1, para 34.   [76] UK 1, para 221.

recording is possibly the weakest of CPT formulations and in recent reports has been weakened further by merely 'inviting' the authorities 'to consider' it,[77] a clear downgrading. It is not surprising, therefore, that several reports have made no reference to the desirability of electronically recording interviews.[78] As far as we are aware, England and Wales is the only jurisdiction in Europe where all police interviews are routinely electronically recorded, and the introduction of such a system is relatively costly. It would appear that the CPT suggests the idea whenever they think the authorities might be receptive to it, but do not press the matter strongly. Thus, for example, electronic recording of police interviews was suggested to the Cypriot authorities in 1992[79] (on which occasion the delegation found evidence of severe ill-treatment/torture, allegations which were subsequently the subject of a judicial inquiry) and when the CPT returned to Cyprus in 1996 they appear to have been informed that the Cypriot authorities either had considered, or were considering, the possibility of introducing electronic recording: the Committee asked to be informed of the outcome of these deliberations.[80] Or, to take another example, in Bulgaria in 1995 the CPT delegation noted that the 'Bulgarian Code of Criminal Procedure makes express and detailed provision for the audio-video recording of interviews, at the request of the person concerned or on the initiative of the magistrate responsible for the preliminary investigation'. The CPT welcomed this provision, noted that it had not yet been implemented, and recommended that the Bulgarian authorities consider ways of doing so.[81] On this issue the Committee appears to push harder whenever they judge the door to be slightly ajar. Thus in Northern Ireland, in 1993, the Committee was concerned to learn that though interviews with criminal suspects generally were recorded, those with persons suspected of terrorism and detained under the Prevention of Terrorism Act were not.[82] The Northern Ireland authorities were asked to reconsider the issue and to employ audio and/or video recording.[83]

Two aspects of these early recommendations, which have been reproduced with no substantive alteration in almost all published country reports, are noteworthy. First, is the proposition that accountability measures of this nature assist the police by establishing and/or buttressing the legitimacy of

---

[77] See, eg, Hungary 1, para 52; Netherlands Aruba 1, para 226; Slovenia 1, para 40; Slovakia 1, para 50.

[78] eg Portugal 1 (though the possibility was raised in Portugal 2, para 61); San Marino 1; The Netherlands 1; and Italy 1.

[79] Cyprus 1, para 61.   [80] Cyprus 2, para 45.   [81] Bulgaria 1, para 95.

[82] The practice was not adopted on the grounds that it could not be guaranteed that 'such a recording could not later come to be seen or heard by someone who had a punitive motive' (UK 2 R 1, para 18).

[83] UK 2, paras 82–90.

their work. There is an implicit suggestion that this works in two ways: by providing detailed accounts of their decision making the police will demonstrate their commitment to safeguarding the interests of detainees, and by getting detainees to sign these accounts the police will better be able to defend themselves against unwarranted allegations.

Secondly, since no other international body or set of principles for the protection of detainees has stressed the merits of having a single comprehensive custody record (or electronically recording interviews),[84] it is difficult to escape the conclusion that the CPT was inspired to do so by the practice in England and Wales[85] where this is required by the Police and Criminal Evidence Act 1984.[86] It would not have escaped the Committee's attention (particularly its English-trained secretary lawyer) that the English statute was prompted by scandal regarding ill-treatment at the hands of the police at a time when police custody in England and Wales was little regulated and record keeping was minimal. From CPT country reports it appears that although almost all countries record the principal aspects of custody, such as the time of arrest, time of arrival at the police station, and start and finish times of formal interviews, these accounts are generally recorded in different documents, which makes them relatively difficult to collate, and many potentially important procedures, such as the provision of exercise or food, generally go unrecorded.[87]

There are some indications that the CPT may be becoming less insistent that custody records take a particular bureaucratic form, possibly because the Committee considers it unwise to impose the heavy burden of new procedures and extensive paperwork on systems short of resources and struggling with other changes which are arguably more important. Recent reports on Eastern European countries, for example, have discussed the proposition that there be comprehensive custody records in terms of a *comment* rather than a *recommendation*.[88]

---

[84] See Evans and Morgan (1998), Chapter Seven.

[85] Which the CPT visited first in July 1990.

[86] For discussion, see Morgan, R (1996) 'Custody in the Police Station: How do England and Wales Measure up in Europe?', 17(1) *Policy Studies* 55–72.

[87] In Germany, for example, the Committee found that the 'relevant information on the detention of one individual might well be spread over several registers' (Germany 1, para 44— see also the changes noted in Germany 2, para 39). Likewise in Portugal the CPT delegation found that 'certain aspects of a person's custody were not systematically recorded and that the information which was recorded tended to be spread over a variety of registers and documents' (Portugal 2, para 62).

[88] See Slovenia 1, para 41; Slovakia 1, para 52; Bulgaria 1, para 97; Romania 1, para 48. This may be being carried back into Western Europe. Following its visit to Belgium in September 1997, the Committee recalled its previous recommendation to this effect, but no longer refers to it as a recommendation (Belgium 2, para 41). This might be contrasted with the Committee's approach to the elaboration of a code of conduct for interrogations, which retains its status as a recommendation (see Belgium 2, para 39). Cf Italy 2, para 60 where, in 1995, this also retained the status of a recommendation when reiterated in a second periodic visit.

In conclusion, with regard to police accountability, the CPT has stressed that 'regular and unannounced visits by the prosecuting/judicial authorities to places where persons are detained by the police can have a significant effect in terms of preventing ill-treatment'[89] and 'the existence of an independent mechanism for examining complaints about treatment while in police custody is an essential safeguard'.[90]

As far as physical conditions for suspects and other persons held initially in custody are concerned, the CPT has laid down general expectations in its second general report. The Committee initially took the view that in places of detention intended for short-term custody the 'physical conditions . . . cannot be expected to be as good . . . as in other places where persons may be held for lengthy periods'.[91] Nevertheless, 'certain elementary requirements' had to be met:

All police cells should be of a reasonable size for the number of persons they are used to accommodate, and have adequate lighting (i.e. sufficient to read by, sleeping periods excluded) and ventilation; preferably, cells should enjoy natural light. Further, cells should be equipped with a means of rest (e.g. a fixed chair or bench), and persons obliged to stay overnight in custody should be provided with a clean mattress and blankets.

Persons in custody should be allowed to comply with the needs of nature when necessary in clean and decent conditions, and be offered adequate washing facilities. They should be given food at appropriate times, including at least one full meal (i.e. something more substantial than a sandwich) every day.[92]

That the CPT was dealing with very short-term custody when giving this advice is evident from the fact that there was no mention of daily exercise or access to washing facilities, issues to which the Committee has always attached great importance.[93] In consequence, the CPT has encountered conditions of detention in police stations which it is prepared to accept, provided the facilities are not used for periods of more than one or two days.[94] As will be seen, however, it soon became apparent that simply because a police station was designed and equipped for short-term custody this did not necessarily mean that it was only used for such purposes. The Committee was soon drawn into criticizing police accommodation which, had it been used only for the initial detention of suspects and other persons, would no doubt have been considered acceptable.

Whilst confessing that it was 'a difficult question', the Committee did, however, at the outset of its work express an opinion on what it considered to be a reasonable size for a police cell 'intended for single occupancy for

---

[89] This view has been expressed in many country reports. See, eg, France 1, para 53; Italy 1, para 54; Finland 1, para 51; Switzerland 2, para 54.
[90] Gen Rep 2, para 41.   [91] Ibid, para 42.   [92] Gen Rep 2, para 42.
[93] Ibid, paras 48–49.   [94] eg Switzerland 2, paras 23, 28.

stays in excess of a few hours'. In early 1992 their answer was that it should be of the 'order of 7 square metres, 2 metres or more between walls, 2.5 metres between floor and ceiling'[95] and the Committee has subsequently made cross-reference to this statement.[96] This standard has proved difficult to apply in conditions of long-term penal custody let alone short-term police custody and the Committee has subsequently accepted that cells substantially smaller than this are acceptable. In the past, the CPT's threshold of acceptability has appeared to lie between 4 and 4.5 square metres for overnight stays[97] with cells smaller than 4 square metres being acceptable only for detainees waiting for a 'few' hours.[98] However, it has recently said that cells of 4.5 square metres are not acceptable for overnight stays.[99] Waiting cells of 2 square metres or less have been judged totally unacceptable for even the shortest of periods and the CPT routinely recommends that they be taken out of service immediately.[100] Finally, when suspects are being detained, the CPT is of the view that premises must be permanently staffed, day and night: it is not sufficient that detainees have access to call systems enabling them to summon assistance from other facilities or police patrols.[101]

(b) Immigration detainees

The CPT has from the beginning emphasized that it is concerned, *inter alia*, with the administrative detention of persons held under immigration regulations. These include:

persons refused entry to the country concerned; persons who have entered the country illegally and have subsequently been identified by the authorities; persons whose authorisation to stay in the country has expired; asylum seekers whose detention is considered necessary by the authorities; etc.[102]

One of the agencies which the Committee established early contact with was the United Nations High Commissioner for Refugees[103] and from the outset of its work it has visited airport holding centres, irrespective of whether they are controlled by the police, in those countries where there is no separate immigration department, or by the immigration authorities.[104] Moreover, the Committee has expressed its satisfaction with the judgment

---

[95] Ibid, para 43.   [96] See Switzerland 2, para 19.
[97] See, eg, Belgium 1, para 26; Belgium 2, paras 21, 25; Spain 1, para 36.
[98] See, eg, Spain 1, para 38; Italy 1, para 33; Belgium 1, para 26; Belgium 2, para 26.
[99] Belgium 2, para 22.
[100] See, eg, Sweden 1, para 18; Belgium 1, para 29; Belgium 2, para 25; France 2, para 25; Romania 1, paras 57 and 73.
[101] Switzerland 2, paras 27–28.   [102] Gen Rep 7, para 24.   [103] Gen Rep 1, para 42.
[104] See Austria 1, paras 89–93; Denmark 1, para 121.

of the European Court in *Amuur v France*,[105] which confirmed the view of
the CPT, 'that a stay in a transit or "international" zone can, depending on
the circumstances, amount to a deprivation of liberty within the meaning
of Article 5(1)(f) [of the ECHR]'.[106] The Committee felt *vindicated*[107]
because 'on more than one occasion' it had been 'confronted with the
argument that such persons are not "deprived of their liberty" '—and thus
lie outside the CPT's mandate—on the grounds that 'they are free to leave
the zone at any moment by taking any international flight of their choice'.[108]
Nevertheless, it is probably true to say that during the first years of its life
the Committee did not give a high priority to the administrative custody of
aliens. There are signs that it is now doing so. In 1996 the CPT reported
that it was paying increasing attention to holding facilities for foreigners
and signalled its intention of setting out some of the issues involved in the
detention of foreigners in a future annual general report.[109] In 1997 the
Committee did so.[110]

Immigration detainees are often held for very short periods indeed. For
example, persons stopped and refused entry by the immigration authorities
at a port of entry because of some procedural defect (such as an invalid
passport, no valid visa, or not having enough money to be self-sufficient
for the duration of stay they say they are intending to make) may be
required to leave by the next available plane, train, ferry, or bus going to
the destination from whence they came. This can often be achieved within
an hour or two. It follows that at most ports of entry there are holding areas
where the person refused entry may stay if the general international departure hall is deemed an unsuitable place for them to wait. The problem,
however, is that speedy exits are not always feasible and persons refused
entry may have to wait for some time at the port of entry and the holding
facilities are often, in the CPT's judgement, quite inadequate for extended
stays.[111] The Committee insists that the same standards as apply in other
custodial situations should apply for persons forced to stay at ports of entry:

---

[105] *Amuur v France*, Judgment of 25 June 1996, *RJD* 1996-III, 827, paras 38–49.
[106] Gen Rep 7, para 25.   [107] Ibid. See also Stevens, notes 12, 71.
[108] Gen Rep 7, para 25. Perhaps not surprisingly, the CPT did not draw attention to the
Report of the Commission which had endorsed this view as regards asylum seekers. See *Amuur
v France*, Report of 10 January 1996, paras 44–50. Nor did the CPT draw attention to the distinction drawn by the Court between 'restrictions' on liberty and 'deprivations' of liberty
(*Amuur v France*, Judgment of 25 June 1996, *RJD* 1996-III, 827, para 43). Since 'restrictions'
of liberty might mature into deprivations of liberty, it is not clear whether such a distinction
has any practical relevance for the scope of the CPT's mandate.
[109] Gen Rep 6, para 3.
[110] Gen Rep 7, paras 24–37. In the course of its visit to Belgium in September 1997 the CPT
paid particular attention to detention places for foreigners and the report on that visit, published in June 1998, provides a detailed example of the practical application of the principles
set out in the General Report. See Belgium 2, paras 44–79.
[111] See, eg, Greece 2, paras 80–87; Ireland 1, para 173; Spain 1, paras 79–83; UK 3, paras
33–34; Belgium 2, paras 53–54.

It is axiomatic that such persons should be provided with suitable means for sleeping, granted access to their luggage and to suitably equipped sanitary and washing facilities, and allowed to exercise in the open air on a daily basis. Further, access to food and, if necessary, medical care should be guaranteed.[112]

If it is not possible for persons refused entry to leave almost immediately, and if there are not adequate holding facilities for them at the port of entry, they may need to be transferred to another place of custody. These places, which may be suitable for extended stays, may also be used for other categories of immigration detainees, such as asylum seekers whose cases are under investigation and who, for one reason or another, the authorities feel cannot be allowed their liberty, or persons who have outstayed their welcome and whose deportation is pending. In all such cases the CPT insists on the application of another basic custodial principle—that of *separation*. Immigration detainees should not be confined with persons suspected of crimes or convicted or sentenced criminals. They should ideally be accommodated in 'centres specifically designed for that purpose, [places] offering material conditions and a regime appropriate to their legal situation and staffed by suitably-qualified personnel'.[113]

Immigration detainees should not be held in police stations or prisons, which in practice is often the case, although the Committee recognizes that this may *occasionally* be either appropriate or necessary. When an illegal immigrant is first identified, a police station may be the only place available. Prison accommodation may occasionally have to be used because of actual or threatened violence on the part of the person concerned. Alternatively, a prison may be the only place where an immigration detainee can temporarily be held 'in the event of no other secure hospital facility being available'.[114] The guiding principle is, however, that such arrangements should be 'kept to the absolute minimum' and, to the extent that they have to be resorted to, it would be 'indefensible' to oblige immigration detainees to share cellular accommodation with criminal suspects or convicted or sentenced persons. They should be held quite separately.[115]

What should purpose-designed immigration detention centres, which the CPT reports with satisfaction that more and more states party are providing, be like? The Committee says that:

Obviously, such centres should provide accommodation which is adequately furnished, clean and in a good state of repair, and which offers sufficient living space for the numbers involved. Further, care should be taken in the design and layout of the premises to avoid as far as possible any impression of a carceral environment. As regards regime activities, they should include outdoor exercise, access to a

---

[112] Gen Rep 7, para 26.   [113] Ibid, para 29.   [114] Ibid, para 28.
[115] Ibid, paras 27–28.

day room and to radio/television and newspapers/magazines, as well as other appropriate means to recreation (e.g. board games, table tennis). The longer the period for which persons are detained, the more developed should be the activities which are offered to them.[116]

The CPT has also stressed the need for immigration detention centres to be appropriately staffed. The staff should have relevant language skills and cultural awareness and should be sensitive to possible tensions between detainees from different ethnic backgrounds. They should also be equipped to recognize stress reactions among their charges.[117]

The procedural safeguards for immigration detainees which the CPT insists upon are the same as those which apply during the initial phase of police custody, but the particular characteristics of immigration detainees means that certain provisions are given greater emphasis. In particular, immigration detainees should be 'expressly informed, without delay and in a language they understand, of all their rights and of the procedure applicable to them'.[118] Documents explaining the relevant procedures should be available to them and these documents should be in 'the languages most commonly spoken' by immigration detainees in the country concerned. Interpreters should be used.[119] With particular regard to asylum seekers, there should be access to medical care and those providing it should be sensitive to the physical and psychological state of the applicants, 'some of whom may have been tortured or otherwise ill-treated'. Finally, immigration detainees should be 'entitled to maintain contact with the outside world ... in particular to have access to a telephone and to receive visits from relatives and representatives of relevant organisations', by which the CPT no doubt means those NGOs which in many countries provide advice and support for asylum seekers.[120]

Two final issues, arguably lying at the margins of the CPT's mandate, are of concern to the Committee. First, the detention of immigrants often precedes their extradition, expulsion, or deportation. The CPT, possibly following the well-established jurisprudence under the ECHR,[121] is becoming increasingly concerned with the possibility that aliens might be returned to a country where they run the risk of being subjected to torture or to inhuman or degrading treatment or punishment and frequently asks questions during the course of visits about the procedures adopted to ensure that this does not happen.[122] The Committee wishes to satisfy itself, *inter alia*, that 'officials entrusted with handling such cases have been provided with appropriate training and have access to objective and independent information about the human rights situation in other countries'.

---

[116] Gen Rep 7, para 29.   [117] Ibid.   [118] Ibid, para 30.
[119] Ibid.   [120] Ibid, para 31.   [121] See Evans and Morgan (1998), Chapter Seven.
[122] See, eg, Greece 1, para 51; and Netherlands Antilles, para 61; Belgium 2, para 20.

In so far as this concerns both the training and briefing of personnel, this illustrates the almost limitless potential reach of the Committee's preventive mandate and standard setting and reviewing activities. Indeed, it seems that the Committee is uncertain at present as to its role in this regard since, ultimately, evidence of any failure to meet these requirements may not always be found in the country being visited but in the countries to which persons returned in violation of these procedural requirements are now to be found. Given the nature of the issue, the CPT has observed that the ECHR mechanisms are 'better placed than the CPT to examine such allegations and, if appropriate, take preventive action'.[123] This is an interesting inversion, in that the CPT seems to consider that the 'preventive' mechanism developed upon the ECHR's 'judicial' mandate is better placed to achieve a preventive outcome than are the mechanisms it has developed under its own preventive mandate.

Nevertheless, it is apparent that the Committee is currently looking into these issues more closely than hitherto. In June 1998, for example, the Committee conducted a three-day *ad hoc* visit to Frankfurt am Main Airport, Germany. The visit focused 'on the situation of asylum seekers at the . . . Airport during the examination of their request. The Committee also examined the conditions under which their removal orders concerning aliens were enforced.'[124] An *ad hoc* visit to an airport is unprecedented and the background to previous short and focused *ad hoc* visits suggests that it may have been prompted by reports of 'live' cases of ill-treatment[125] or a pattern of ill-treatment requiring urgent investigation.

The second point is that deportation or expulsion may, in the final analysis, have to be achieved coercively if the alien will not depart co-operatively and the Committee has shown concern regarding the means of restraint sometimes allegedly employed.[126]

The force used should be no more than is reasonably necessary. It would, in particular, be entirely unacceptable for persons subject to an expulsion order to be physically assaulted as a form of persuasion to board a means of transport or as punishment for not having done so. Further the Committee must emphasise that to gag a person is a highly dangerous measure.

The CPT also wishes to stress that any provision of medication to persons subject to an expulsion order must be done on the basis of a medical decision and in accordance with medical ethics.[127]

---

[123] Gen Rep 7, para 33.   [124] Council of Europe Press Release 392a98, 3 June 1998.

[125] For example, the three-day visit to Spain in June 1994 was undertaken specifically to interview a number of persons who had recently been detained and who had alleged that they had been tortured (see Spain 3 and Evans and Morgan (1998), 173–174).

[126] 'In particular allegations of beating, binding and gagging, and the administration of tranquillizers against the will of the persons concerned' (Gen Rep 7, para 35).

[127] Ibid, para 36.

(c) Pre-trial detainees

In addition to the period of initial police custody prior to charges being laid and/or suspects being brought before a court, all criminal justice systems provide for the remand in custody of persons awaiting trial. Remands in custody may be for a few days but usually last for several weeks or months and, in some countries, can last for as long as a year or more. It is normal for such custody to be in a prison. The European Prison Rules assume that this is the case[128] and it was probably the assumption that police stations would only be used for short-term custody that influenced the thinking of the CPT when it accepted that police custody would probably involve physical conditions of a lower standard than those to be found in, and expected of, prisons designed for prolonged custody.[129] The problem, as the review of custody of immigration detainees has already indicated, is that police stations, though seldom designed for prolonged custody, are routinely or occasionally used for that purpose in a number of jurisdictions. The CPT has encountered police stations being used to accommodate remand and administrative detainees[130] and might well find them being used for sentenced prisoners.[131] The CPT has repeatedly deplored this practice, since no police station is ever likely to be able to meet the standards of physical conditions and facilities which are required of prisons used for pre-trial custody.

The Committee concedes that because of their more rapid turnover, it is unrealistic to expect remand prisoners to be provided with the 'individualised treatment programmes of the sort that might be aspired to for sentenced prisoners'. Nevertheless, remand prisoners cannot be allowed to 'languish'. They should be provided with a 'satisfactory programme of activities (work, education, sport, etc)' in which they can positively spend their time during the '8 hours or more' of each day that they should be out of their cells.[132] Further, the CPT's requirement that all prisoners be given the opportunity to take outdoor exercise daily for at least one hour applies to remand as well as sentenced prisoners.[133] Similarly, their outdoor exercise facilities should be sufficiently spacious for the prisoners 'to be able

---

[128] The European Prison Rules, which include a section (Rules 91–98) on Untried Prisoners, throughout *assume* that the Rules will be applied by a *prison administration* employing *professional prison staff* (see, eg, Rule 54).

[129] Section 3(a) above and Gen Rep 2, para 42.

[130] See, eg, Hungary 1, para 15; Bulgaria 1, paras 46–64; Finland 1, paras 52–53; UK 3, paras 18–23; Romania 1, para 14.

[131] For example, following a prison officers' industrial dispute in England and Wales, and the emergency passage of the Imprisonment (Temporary Provisions) Act 1980, it became possible for any category of 'Home Office' prisoner (including the convicted and sentenced) to be housed temporarily in police stations designated for the purpose. Throughout the 1980s this was regularly done to a significant degree.

[132] Gen Rep 2, para 47.   [133] Ibid, para 48.

to exert themselves physically'[134] and 'whenever possible offer shelter from inclement weather'.[135] Needless to say, such facilities and programmes are commonly lacking in police stations where prisoners are likely to be idle and confined to their cells almost permanently, with little or no possibility of exercise, outdoor or indoor. Wherever it has encountered such conditions the CPT has emphasized that the use of police stations is not appropriate for long-term custody and has recommended that if the authorities decide that it is unrealistic to provide the appropriate level of facilities and regime activities, the use of police accommodation should cease.[136]

Untried prisoners should also be permitted to wear their own clothes[137] and it is clear that the CPT considers that, to the extent that restrictions are applied, they should have a more generous minimum entitlement to visits than convicted and sentenced prisoners.[138]

A further aspect of pre-trial detention which has concerned the CPT involves restrictions being placed on contacts with fellow prisoners and other persons for purposes such as preserving evidence and preventing collusion or intimidation to subvert the prosecution case.[139] The CPT has implicitly conceded that it may be legitimate for pre-trial prisoners' contacts to be restricted, but maintains that because 'solitary confinement can, in certain circumstances, amount to inhuman and degrading treatment[140] . . . [it should] be as short as possible'.[141] In order to ensure that such restrictions are used parsimoniously the CPT has recommended that the following principles be followed and procedural safeguards adopted:

(1) use and prolongation of solitary confinement should be 'resorted to only in exceptional circumstances', be 'strictly limited to the requirements of the case',[142] and be 'proportional to the needs of the criminal investigation concerned';[143]

(2) that each particular restriction should be authorized by a court, the

[134] This phrase has repeatedly been used by the Committee when confronted with outdoor exercise areas it considers too small. See, for example, Sweden 1, paras 51–52, where 6 by 2.5 metre exercise yards at the Stockholm Remand Prison were judged too cramped; as were concrete-walled enclosures measuring approximately 15 square metres at the Oslo Prison (see Norway 1, paras 61 and 66) and triangular walkways some 14 metres by 4 metres—with central partitions—at Gherla Prison (see Romania 1, para 118).

[135] Gen Rep 2, para 48.

[136] See Finland 1, para 25. See also Romania 1, para 70, where the CPT recommends a complete re-examination of the system of pre-trial detention.

[137] UK 1, para 78.

[138] See section on 'prisoners' contacts with the outside world' below.

[139] See discussion of *inhuman and degrading* treatment in Section 2(b) above.

[140] Psychiatric experts assisting CPT delegations have found evidence of pre-trial prisoners kept more or less isolated for prolonged periods suffering adverse mental health as a consequence of their isolation (see Norway 1, para 64).

[141] Gen Rep 2, para 56.   [142] Denmark 1, para 29.   [143] Sweden 2, para 27.

reasons recorded in writing, and, 'unless the requirements of the investigation dictate otherwise, the prisoner [be] informed of those reasons';[144]

(3) that the imposition of restrictions, and the justification for their continued application, should be regularly reviewed by the court;[145]

(4) 'that prisoners subject to restrictions have an effective right of appeal to a Court or another independent body in respect of particular restrictions applied by a public prosecutor'.[146]

Even if they are legally justified, restrictions of this nature may nevertheless have harmful consequences and the CPT has therefore recommended the adoption of the following safeguard and compensating principle designed to reduce the likelihood of such an outcome:

(1) whenever a prisoner subject to restrictions (or a prison officer on the prisoner's behalf) requests an examination by a medical doctor, that the doctor be called without delay to carry out an examination and the results of that examination, including an account of the prisoner's physical and mental condition as well as, if need be, the foreseeable consequences of prolonged isolation, be set out in a written statement to be forwarded to the competent authorities;[147]

(2) 'any prisoner subject to restrictions for an extended period is offered activities in addition to outside exercise and guaranteed appropriate human contact'.[148]

This means that even though there will be occasions when it will be quite legitimate for pre-trial prisoners to be prevented from having contact with fellow prisoners, and not be allowed to receive visits or telephone calls,[149] they should have human contact with staff in the context of out-of-cell activities which are specially designed to compensate for the fact that

---

[144] That is, they should not be the decisions of police officers or prosecutors (ibid).

[145] It is not clear how frequently the CPT considers it necessary for reviews to take place. In Denmark they must be at least every eight weeks (Denmark 1, Appendix 2, para 11) and in Sweden at least every two weeks (Sweden 2, para 25), neither of which intervals did the CPT criticize or recommend be changed.

[146] In Sweden the use of restrictions is generally authorized by the court but the particular restrictions imposed lie at the discretion of the prosecutor in the particular case (Sweden 2, paras 25–27).

[147] Denmark 1, para 29. Interestingly, this specific recommendation is not included in the general digest of medical standards in prisons in the CPT's 3rd general report. The recommendation is nevertheless repeated the following year in Norway 1, para 65.

[148] Norway 1, para 65; Sweden 2, paras 19–20.

[149] eg France 1, para 135, where, when recommending that a total ban on the use of telephones by pre-trial detainees be reconsidered, it was accepted that some controls may be necessary.

they cannot engage in mainstream inter-prisoner association. Compensating out-of-cell activities should be provided in proportion to the level of restrictions to which prisoners are subject.

4. PRISONERS—GENERALLY

Assuming that prisoners, whether on remand, convicted and awaiting sentence, or sentenced, should normally be held within a prison, the CPT has laid down certain standards which apply to all prisoners in all prisons. These range from basic physical conditions of detention, to aspects of regimes, to accountability mechanisms. Each will be considered in turn.

(a) Living accommodation and crowding

The CPT has attached particular importance to cell size and occupancy rates and, as has been seen,[150] takes the view that certain levels of overcrowding can amount to *inhuman or degrading* treatment either in its own right or in combination with other oppressive aspects of custody. The basic guidance for prison cell space is the same as that for police cells.[151] Single cells of 6 square metres have been described as 'rather small', but acceptable if their occupants can spend a significant portion of the day out of them.[152] Cells of 4 square metres and smaller are considered altogether unacceptable, irrespective of their use.[153] In its second General Report the CPT offered no guidance regarding multiply occupied cells, rooms, or dormitories but has since done so in individual country reports. The Committee appears to have adopted a toleration threshold of approximately 9 square metres for two-person cells. Below this size two-person cells are considered 'cramped'[154] and cells of 7 square metres are said not to be suitable for more than one prisoner.[155] Indeed, cells of 8.5 square metres are said, in principle, to be suitable only for sole occupancy,[156] a formulation which suggests that the Committee recognizes that this is more of an aspiration than a 'measuring rod'. Further guidance on multiple occupation is available in the report on Slovakia where cells of 9–10 square metres contained two prisoners, cells of about 12 square metres three prisoners and cells of 16–17 square metres four prisoners. These cellular arrangements were judged 'restrictive' but acceptable; their more intensive use was considered

---

[150] See Section 2(b) above.   [151] See p. 49 above.   [152] Sweden 1, paras 46 and 73.
[153] Finland 1, para 81; Hungary 1, paras 93 and 97; Romania 1, para 67.
[154] UK 2, para 119. But cf Slovenia 1, para 63, where the dual occupancy of such cells was considered 'cramped' rather than unacceptable.
[155] Hungary 1, para 97; France 3, para 107.   [156] Italy 2, para 115.

'unacceptable'.[157] Likewise, the report on Romania indicated that cells of 10 square metres should not be used for more than two persons, and cells of 16 square metres should be used for no more than four persons for prolonged periods.[158]

Because of the lack of privacy and the increased risk of inter-prisoner predatory behaviour, the CPT generally considers large-scale dormitory accommodation unsatisfactory in prisons, whether it is overcrowded or not.[159] Nevertheless, rooms of 21 square metres have been found acceptable for five prisoners (though four would have been preferable),[160] the Committee has said that rooms of 25 square metres should accommodate no more than six prisoners,[161] and rooms of 35 and 60 square metres have been said to be suitable for no more than seven and twelve prisoners respectively.[162] Elsewhere the Committee has indicated rather lower toleration thresholds. The suggested occupancy levels at a Slovakian prison, where it was accepted that this represented 'a limited amount of living space', were:

cells measuring 11–22 square metres—up to three prisoners; cells measuring 21–29 square metres—six or seven prisoners; cells measuring 25–38 square metres—eight or nine prisoners; cells measuring 31–35 square metres—ten prisoners; cells measuring approximately 40 sq metres—twelve prisoners; and cells measuring 51 square metres—sixteen prisoners.[163]

This suggests that large rooms, in spite of the Committee's general reservations, may be considered acceptable if they provide at least 3 to 3.5 square metres per person.

(b) Hygiene

The CPT pays particular attention to hygiene. It has already been seen that the Committee considers the arrangement of 'slopping out', coupled with overcrowding and the need to discharge human waste without privacy in front of cell mates into a pot or bucket (which invariably precedes 'slopping out'), to be *degrading*.[164] The Committee argues that:

regular access to proper toilet facilities and the maintenance of good standards of hygiene are essential components of a human environment . . . Either a toilet facility should be located in cellular accommodation (preferably in a sanitary annex) or

---

[157] Slovakia 1, para 75.

[158] Romania 1, para 55. See also Belgium 2, para 116, where 9 square metres for two persons and 14 square metres for three persons were on the thresholds of acceptability. In France 3, para 102, 13 square metres was said to be adequate for three but not four prisoners.

[159] Spain 1, para 122.   [160] Greece 1, para 117.   [161] Austria 2, para 66.

[162] Slovenia 1, para 63.

[163] Slovakia 1, para 86. Cf Romania 1, para 56, where 14 female prisoners in 36 square metres were considered less than satisfactory.

[164] See Section 2(b) above.

means should exist enabling prisoners who need to use a toilet facility to be released from their cells without undue delay at all times (including at night).[165]

If there is not a sanitary annexe, lavatories should be screened, for otherwise prisoners 'could be said to be living in a lavatory'.[166] On these grounds the CPT prefers integral sanitation to be provided in cell blocks where it is currently lacking by means of the ' "three cells into two" system of sanitation' (by which the middle cell is in effect converted into two sanitary annexes for the cells on either side) as opposed to the 'so-called "simple sanitation" ' solution (whereby lavatories are placed in each cell).[167] Where there are no lavatories in cells prisoners should not have to wait for more than ten to twenty minutes to gain access to a lavatory elsewhere.[168]

As far as washing is concerned, 'prisoners should have adequate access to shower or bathing facilities. It is desirable for running water to be available within cellular accommodation.'[169] Moreover, the Committee has endorsed the European Prison Rules[170] by stating that 'access to bathing facilities at least once a week is an absolute minimum requirement' and in 'an establishment where prisoners do not have ready access to either toilet facilities or running water, a shower once a week cannot be considered sufficient'.[171] Nor, in especially warm weather, may twice-weekly access to a shower be sufficient,[172] particularly for prisoners engaged in work.[173] The Committee has also expressed the view that particular efforts should be made to ensure that prisoners who are about to appear before a magistrate, or court, are able to present themselves 'in a manner which respects their human dignity'[174]—that is, clean and tidy. In some establishments the Committee has drawn attention to the inadequacy of bathing facilities by pointing to the poor ratio of showers to prisoners.[175] In general, it appears that twice-weekly access for non-working prisoners and daily access for those who are working is considered satisfactory.[176]

Prisoners should be provided with clean bedlinen (sheets and blankets) and with soap and other personal hygiene products (for example, toothbrushes and toothpaste[177]). This means that their bedlinen should regularly be changed and laundered. The Committee has said that a change of bedlinen once a fortnight is inadequate[178] and that if the prison does not launder prisoners' clothes then facilities should be provided to enable

---

[165] Gen Rep 2, para 49.   [166] UK 3, para 80; Portugal 2, para 99.
[167] Denmark 2, para 88; UK 3, para 398.
[168] Sweden 1, para 47; Netherlands 1, para 39.   [169] Gen Rep 2, para 49.
[170] Rule 18.   [171] UK 1, para 74.   [172] France 1, para 112.
[173] Romania 1, para 110.   [174] France 3, para 105.
[175] At Oporto Prison, Portugal the provision of 32 shower heads in the central bathhouse to serve the needs of 1,200 prisoners was described as 'completely inadequate' (Portugal 3, para 17). At Gherla Prison, Romania a single bathhouse served over 2,600 prisoners, creating serious problems (Romania 1, para 110).
[176] Italy 2, para 111.   [177] Austria 2, para 68.   [178] Bulgaria 1, paras 118 and 125.

prisoners to launder their own clothes and dry them.[179] All newly arrived prisoners should be provided with a clean set of blankets and thereafter 'provided with two clean sheets and one or more clean towels each week'.[180] Materials should also be provided to enable prisoners to clean their cells.[181] Oversight of general standards of prison hygiene should lie with prison health care services as part of their preventive health care responsibilities.[182]

In an early report the Committee recommended that prisoners' razors should be sterilized before being issued to them 'or, if they cannot be sterilised (e.g. because they are made of plastic), that each inmate be issued with a new razor'.[183] This topic and recommendation has not appeared since 1990: it is possible that this is because the standard is always met, but this seems rather unlikely.

(c) Lighting, heating, ventilation, and cell facilities

All cells should be equipped with an alarm call system 'preferably linked to a permanently staffed central monitoring point'.[184] It is not sufficient that prisoners be able to attract the attention of staff by calling or banging on their cell doors.[185] In addition to beds and bedding, prisoners should be equipped with 'appropriate furnishings (table, chair and cupboard)'[186] which should be in a good state of repair: in many countries the CPT has found this not to be the case.

The CPT has not stipulated an ideal temperature or temperature range for prisoner accommodation. However, the Committee has made it clear that there should be heating able to cope with wintry conditions and that excessive heating, whether artificial or natural, is also to be avoided. Further, all cells must be adequately ventilated. Thus in Linhó Prison, Sintra, Portugal in January 1992, the delegation observed that the cells in two accommodation blocks had no means of being heated, the glass was missing from 50 per cent of the windows, and the cell temperature in the middle of the day was below 9 °C. The Committee recommended that a high priority be given to reglazing the windows and installing a heating system for use in the winter months.[187] At Basauri Prison, Spain in April 1991, the visiting delegation considered that temperatures of 14 °C and 16 °C in the admissions and accommodation areas respectively were too low and that heating facilities be either reviewed or installed.[188] At Spoleto Prison, Italy

---

[179] Austria 1, para 37.   [180] Spain 1, para 181.
[181] Netherlands Antilles 1, paras 78 and 96; Romania 1, para 71.
[182] Gen Rep 3, para 53.   [183] UK 1, para 76.
[184] Cyprus 1, para 78; see also San Marino 1, para 43.
[185] The situation in Corradino Prison, Malta in 1990 (Malta 1, para 37).
[186] Netherlands Antilles 1, para 96.   [187] Portugal 1, para 84.
[188] Spain 1, para 183.

in October/November 1995, temperatures of 16 °C in cells in the middle of the day were considered inadequate.[189]

All prisoner accommodation should have access to natural light and prisoners should have some control over lighting and ventilation: light switches should be inside cells and prisoners should be able to open and close windows and shutters.[190] Indeed, the Swedish prison authorities were criticized because prisoners in the Stockholm Remand Prison did not have control over the Venetian blinds which screened their windows and 'which added to the sense of oppressiveness' in them.[191] Responsibility for the adequacy of the lighting, heating, and ventilation of prison accommodation should lie with the prison health care services as an important aspect of preventive health care.[192]

(d) Food and drink

The CPT pays close attention to the quantity and quality of prisoners' food. Although it has not stipulated, in the manner of nineteenth-century prison administrators, precise calorific measures of dietary adequacy, it has sometimes commented on the measures laid down by local prison systems[193] and on several occasions has found the quantity of food given to prisoners to be inadequate.[194] The Committee is also concerned with the question of whether food is distributed to prisoners at 'appropriate' times of the day. There should not be too long an interval between meals or drinks. For example, a last meal at 16.00 with nothing further to eat or drink until 07.30 the following day has been judged 'inappropriate'[195] and the CPT has recommended that those in police custody have access to drinking water at all times.[196]

The Committee is also concerned with the manner in which the food is prepared and served. Prison kitchens should be properly ventilated and have separate cooking and storage facilities so as to safeguard culinary hygiene and prevent infestation.[197] Hot food needs to be delivered to accommodation areas in insulated containers which ensure that it arrives hot[198] and distribution needs to be properly supervised by staff to ensure

---

[189] Italy 2, para 118. It appeared that the heating was not due to be turned on until 15 November, shortly after the CPT's visit took place.

[190] Cf Denmark 1, paras 40, 83, and 118. Such developments drew praise from the CPT in France 3, para 83.

[191] Sweden 1, para 44.   [192] Gen Rep 3, para 53.

[193] See Romania 1, paras 75 and 121.

[194] eg Netherlands Antilles 1, para 100; France 3, para 93.

[195] Netherlands Antilles 1, para 87. See also Romania 1, para 77, where intervals of over 24 hours between main meals were noted.

[196] Switzerland 2, para 32.   [197] Netherlands Aruba 1, paras 249–250.

[198] Netherlands Aruba 1, paras 248 and 250; France, Martinique 1, para 49; France 1, para 168; France 3, paras 91–93; Italy 2, para 118.

that all prisoners obtain their fair share. In those prisons where cells lack integral sanitation and where the practice still exists, the CPT considers it 'both unhygienic and uncivilised' that 'slopping out' should take place at the same time as food is distributed.[199] Prisoners should also be provided with plates, cutlery, and cups, since it is not considered ideal that they should eat from the containers used to keep their food hot or have to use their fingers.[200] The Committee also considers that prisoners should be able to wash and dry their eating utensils without using the facilities and equipment used for their personal hygiene and should be provided with bowls and towels to enable them to do so.[201]

The Committee considers dietary matters to be an important aspect of preventive health care. In consequence, it believes that responsibility for the adequacy of prisoners' diets should rest with the prison health care services.[202] This perception has a bearing on the Committee's approach to the provision of special diets for prisoners. Although it has raised this issue from time to time, it is not clear whether the Committee's concern is limited to those who have special *needs* on medical grounds, or whether it also extends to those who have dietary preferences, such as vegetarianism, or whose special needs are based on their religious affiliation.[203]

(e) Regimes

In its second general report the CPT stated that: 'A satisfactory programme of activities (work, education, sport, etc) is of crucial importance for the well-being of prisoners. This holds true for all establishments . . .'[204] The Committee, as has been seen, is particularly concerned about the generally impoverished conditions in which pre-trial prisoners are often held and recommended that such prisoners should spend at least eight hours each day out of their cells 'engaged in purposeful activity of a varied nature'. The Committee added that 'regimes in establishments for sentenced prisoners should be even more favourable'.[205] This means that there must be sufficient places for all prisoners in workshops or educational programmes. The Committee frequently finds that this is not the case and recommends that provision be enhanced.[206]

Where prisoners are serving long-term sentences the regime facilities should be linked to 'individualised custody plans' in order to assist prisoners

---

[199] UK 1, para 75.   [200] Netherlands Antilles, paras 88 and 100.
[201] UK 1, paras 75–76.   [202] Gen Rep 3, para 53.
[203] In Cyprus in 1992, for example, the Committee recorded concerns that provision for 'special diets' was not adequate, but failed to indicate whether these 'special diets' were medical, religious, or preferential in origin (Cyprus 1, para 82).
[204] Gen Rep 2, para 47.   [205] Ibid.
[206] See, eg, Denmark 2, paras 80–81; Finland 1, paras 90–91, 95–96; Greece 1, paras 105–109; Slovakia 1, paras 80–85 and 91–101; France 1, para 108; France 3, paras 89, 106, 107.

'to come to terms with their period of incarceration and to prepare for release'.[207] This is interpreted to mean that educational programmes for long-term prisoners should comprise more than elementary courses: they should cater to both the 'initial and developmental needs' of long-term sentenced prisoners.[208]

Finally, as was seen in relation to pre-trial prisoners, the Committee stresses the importance of exercise: all prisoners, including those under-going cellular confinement as a punishment, should have 'at least one hour of exercise in the open air every day'. Their exercise areas should be 'reasonably spacious' and 'offer shelter from inclement weather':[209] they should also be large enough for prisoners 'to be able to exert themselves physically'.[210]

(f) Prisoners' contact with the outside world, privacy, and confidentiality

The CPT accepts that all contacts between prisoners and the outside world must be controlled. However, the controls should not be disproportionate and arrangements for visits should generally be as 'open' and relaxed as possible.[211] The Committee takes the view that prisoners must be able to safeguard their relationships with their families and close friends and that the guiding principle for prison authorities should be that prisoners' outside contacts are to be promoted and that 'limitations upon such contact [are to be] based exclusively on security concerns of an appreciable nature or resource considerations'.[212] Further, where prisoners are denied visits from certain individuals on security grounds, those prohibitions should be reviewed from time to time in order to assess the continued validity of the prohibition.[213]

The following examples provide some indication of what the CPT considers appropriate. As far as correspondence is concerned, in Aruba the CPT criticized the failure of the prison authorities to provide notepaper, pencils, and stamps so that prisoners could write letters[214] and elsewhere the Committee has emphasized that prisoners' correspondence should be dispatched or distributed promptly.[215] The Committee also considers it preferable that prisoners' letters should 'be examined, rather than read, by prison staff' and if it is necessary to read a prisoner's letter it 'should be done in the presence of the inmate concerned'.[216]

As regards the use of a telephone, in Spain in 1991 and in Malta in 1995

---

[207] Denmark 2, para 91.   [208] Slovenia 1, para 70.   [209] Ibid, para 48.
[210] The CPT has on several occasions found that prisoners subject to disciplinary or security considerations are required to exercise in cages, pens, or yards too small for this criterion to be satisfied (see Note 134).
[211] See, eg, Spain 1, para 169; Slovakia 1, para 129.   [212] eg France 1, para 130.
[213] Spain 1, para 172.   [214] Netherlands Aruba 1, para 258.
[215] Spain 1, para 177; Spain 2, para 141.   [216] Ibid, para 75.

an allowance of one telephone call per month for foreign prisoners was considered inadequate and the authorities were asked to consider increasing the entitlement.[217] In Spain the Committee criticized the inflexibility of a rule that newly admitted prisoners could not make their first telephone call to their family for a period of fifteen days and recommended that they be allowed to call 'as soon as possible after their admission to the establishment'.[218] Where telephone facilities are lacking the Committee has recommended that provision be made for prisoners to receive and make telephone calls.[219] As has already been mentioned, a total ban on the use of telephones by remand prisoners has been the subject of continued criticism by the CPT.[220]

As far as visits are concerned, in France in 1991 the Committee considered the practice of permitting sentenced prisoners to receive one 30-minute visit each week, and remand prisoners three 30-minute visits each week, to be adequate.[221] Elsewhere, visits of half an hour per month for pre-trial prisoners have been judged 'not sufficient to maintain good relations with family and friends' and a recommendation made that the allowance be increased.[222] In Slovakia in 1995 a minimum entitlement, which was largely adhered to, of adult remand prisoners receiving a visit of 30 minutes every month, and of juvenile remand prisoners receiving a visit of 30 minutes every fortnight, was considered inadequate and it was recommended that the entitlement 'be increased substantially'.[223] In Slovenia the entitlement of remand prisoners to a visit of only 15 minutes every week was considered insufficient.[224]

Rules regarding visits and the use of telephones should be applied flexibly in cases where a prisoner's family live some distance away: such prisoners should be able to accumulate visiting entitlements or have the opportunity of using the telephone as a substitute for visits.[225] The CPT has also commended the practice of making special arrangements to assist visitors to travel to the prisons under such circumstances.[226]

Prisoners' visiting rooms should be welcoming[227] and sufficiently quiet and well organized for prisoners to be able to converse with their visitors without having to shout to them (this applies particularly to 'closed' visiting booths, these being rooms in which the prisoner is physically separated from his or her visitor by a glass or plastic screen),[228] there should be seats for everyone taking part,[229] and there should be areas or rooms where prisoners can talk confidentially with their lawyers.[230] It is not

---

[217] Spain 1, paras 175–176; Malta 2, para 76.   [218] Spain 1, paras 175–176.
[219] Bulgaria 1, para 159.   [220] France 1, para 135; France 3, para 149.
[221] France 1, para 131.   [222] Bulgaria 1, para 157.   [223] Slovakia 1, para 49.
[224] Slovenia 1, para 79.
[225] Gen Rep 2, para 51; see also, eg, France 1, para 131; France, Martinique 1, para 78.
[226] See, eg, Finland 1, para 135.   [227] Germany 1, para 171.   [228] Spain 1, para 169.
[229] Portugal 1, para 147.   [230] Greece 1, paras 128–129; Portugal 2, para 144.

considered appropriate, for example, to install listening devices in rooms intended for the use of prisoners to meet with their lawyers.[231]

The Committee has commended the provision of extended 'family' or 'conjugal visits', provided that 'such visits take place in conditions which respect human dignity',[232] something the Committee has not always found to be the case.[233] Such visits should take place in 'home-like conditions, thereby favouring the maintenance of stable relationships between prisoners and their parents, spouse or partner and children'.[234]

Finally, the CPT pays close attention to reception facilities and particularly to the confidentiality of a prisoner's personal information. Reception interviews often concern the nature of the prisoner's offence, possible fears of the prisoner regarding other prisoners, or information concerning medical conditions or medical histories, some aspects of which may be sensitive. Such interviews should be conducted out of the sight and hearing of other prisoners, including not only other new arrivals but other prisoners working as reception orderlies. In addition, staff notes and prisoner files, including medical files,[235] should not be seen by other prisoners. The CPT has found reception arrangements wanting in these respects on a number of occasions.[236] The Committee has also found shortcomings regarding the degree of privacy afforded prisoners during staff searches of their persons or property.[237]

(g) Staffing

The CPT attaches great importance to the training of prison staff in human rights awareness and their being able to carry out their difficult duties without recourse to ill-treatment. The Committee believes that an aptitude for interpersonal communication should be a major factor in staff recruitment.[238] Thus in a number of country reports the CPT has commented critically on: the absence of commitment by staff to entering into 'a constructive dialogue' with prisoners;[239] provocative behaviour by staff towards prisoners;[240] a 'minimalist' approach by staff to their work;[241] the adoption by staff of a 'militaristic' or 'defiant' attitude towards prisoners;[242] and the use of prisoner 'trusties' as a buffer between prisoners and staff.[243] Any

---

[231] Netherlands Antilles 1, para 107.   [232] Portugal 1, para 149.

[233] See, eg, France 1, para 133; in Norway the Committee found the conjugal visit rooms rather too sparsely furnished (Norway 1, para 109); in Spain the rooms for conjugal visits had insufficient heating and showering facilities and the CPT recommended that prisoners and their partners be able to provide their own towels and bed sheets (Spain 1, para 171).

[234] Austria 2, para 134; Belgium 2, para 185.

[235] See also the section on medical care below.

[236] See, eg, UK 1, paras 102–106; Cyprus 1, para 37.   [237] eg Cyprus 2, para 60.

[238] Gen Rep 2, paras 59–60.   [239] Bulgaria 1, para 153.

[240] Netherlands 1, paras 85–88.   [241] Netherlands Aruba 1, para 252.

[242] Ibid; Slovakia 1, para 123.   [243] Netherlands Aruba 1, para 252.

behaviour indicating disrespect for prisoners should be avoided and on at least one occasion the CPT has recommended that drawings or signs in staff offices or general areas connoting disrespect should be removed.[244] Further, the Committee has repeatedly indicated that it favours the employment of female staff in male prisons on the grounds that it 'can improve the general atmosphere in detention areas'.[245]

One aspect of the duty of care owed by prison authorities to prisoners that has concerned the Committee during the course of visits of inspection is the adequacy of staffing levels. The Committee has not set out either an ideal or a minimum staff/prisoner ratio but it has on several occasions criticized staff/prisoner ratios which it considers to be unacceptably low or dangerously inadequate. For example, in Korydallos Prison, Greece, in 1993, the CPT could not see how prisoner control could satisfactorily be assured with three or four officers to a wing which accommodated 350 freely circulating prisoners for most of the day.[246] At Linhó Prison, Portugal, in 1992, the CPT could not see how three officers on duty at night could adequately respond to the needs of 500 prisoners and recommended that staffing provision be reviewed.[247] In Spain, in 1994, the Committee considered inadequate the provision of four prison officers to a wing at the Madrid 1 Prison containing 600 prisoners: it made 'the provision of an acceptable regime of activities well-nigh impossible'.[248] Again in Portugal, on this occasion at Oporto Prison in 1996, the CPT did not think that the provision of three prison officers to a wing housing 400 prisoners during the day, when the prisoners were free to circulate, was sufficient to exert control. The Committee was particularly disturbed by the (arguably understandable) behaviour of the officers, who seldom entered the wing, failed to intervene when trouble erupted, and who employed privileged prisoners to exert authority over fellow prisoners. The arrangements gave strong prisoners a virtually free hand to exploit their fellow prisoners.[249] In Aruba, in 1994, the CPT was concerned by the level of prison officer absenteeism and recommended that a plan be forged to combat it.[250] Concerns were also expressed regarding staffing levels at Gherla Prison in Romania in 1995, where, in a prison housing a total of 2,672 prisoners, the full staff complement amounted to only 252 uniformed officers and 14 civilian personnel.[251]

It is impossible to distil from these varied statements any CPT guidelines for staff/prisoner ratios comparable to, for example, prisoner/space ratios. This is because the examples cited above include two very different statistics. In the case of Gherla Prison, Romania the CPT expressed concern about an overall staffing complement, whereas in the other cases it was

[244] UK 1, para 82.   [245] Bulgaria 1, para 155.   [246] Greece 1, para 107.
[247] Portugal 1, para 100.   [248] Spain 2, para 181.   [249] Portugal 3, para 13.
[250] Netherlands Aruba 1, para 254.
[251] Romania 1, para 101 (21 'officiers' and 231 'sous-officiers').

a staff/prisoner ratio in a particular location at a particular period during the day or night which caused concern. Neither form can easily be converted to the other. A rough rule of thumb is that whatever the overall complement of prison staff for an institution, or police officers for an area, at most a quarter of the staff can be expected to be on duty at any one time. This is because the staff typically have to be assigned to four shifts, three to cover the 24-hour clock, and one of which is on leave. Sickness, training, and other abstractions have also to be provided for. This means that at Gherla Prison the overall staff complement likely provides for approximately 63 staff to be on duty to supervise 2,672 at any one time, a staff/prisoner presence of 1/42.4. This *appears* to provide for a greater staff presence than is implied in the other cases cited, where the officers on duty had anything between 87 and 167 prisoners each to supervise. In fact, however, the overall staff/prisoner ratio at Gherla is at 1/10, an astonishingly low ratio by international standards (in most institutions in Western Europe figures between 1/1 and 1/3 would, depending on the security status of the prison, be typical). It is probable that had the CPT given the overall staff complements in the institutions concerned, they would have been very much more favourable than at Gherla. What is at issue, therefore, is *either* the overall staffing complement, *or* the allocation of staff to particular locations, *or* both the overall complement and the operational allocation of staff, the latter ultimately being constrained by the former. It would appear that the CPT is reluctant to comment on an overall staff/prisoner ratio unless it is so poor that there are manifestly insufficient staff to maintain a secure presence in all situations. The Committee is willing to comment on whether adequate numbers of staff are allocated to particular situations where the safety of prisoners is threatened. The remedy thereafter lies with policy makers: either more staff may be recruited or prisoner numbers reduced, or staff can be more effectively allocated.

Finally, the CPT has on several occasions encountered custodial centres, including prisons, where, contrary to the guidance contained in the European Prison Rules,[252] prison staff have worn firearms while in the presence of prisoners. The Committee considers this practice to be dangerous and undesirable.[253]

(h) Medical care

In its third general report the CPT went into some considerable detail regarding its expectations concerning the medical care of prisoners and has devoted a considerable portion of each country report to such matters ever

---

[252] Rule 63(3).   [253] Finland 1, para 145; Portugal 2, paras 148–149.

since. The Committee applies the principle of 'normalization',[254] though it does not actually use that term. This means that the Committee considers that prison health services should offer medical services and nursing care 'as well as appropriate diets, physiotherapy, rehabilitation or any other necessary special facility, in conditions comparable to those enjoyed by patients in the outside community'.[255] In practice, however, normalization is not an easy principle to interpret. Quite apart from the difficulties (particularly for the CPT) of establishing what are the standards 'enjoyed by patients in the outside community', what happens if the truth is that patients in the outside community 'enjoy' very little or no health care?

On at least one occasion, for example, a government responding to the CPT has pointed out that the level of service recommended by the Committee is not enjoyed in the community. In response to the standard recommendation that persons in police custody be able to consult with a doctor of their choice, the Icelandic Government—representing a country with one of the highest standards of living in Europe—has pointed out that 'there are no police doctors in Iceland' and that when an arrested person needs medical services they are summoned: 'when an Icelandic citizen urgently needs medical assistance he is not entitled to be served by a doctor of his choice, but must accept attendance by the doctor on duty at each particular time'. The Icelandic authorities had no objection to summoning a particular doctor requested by the person in custody, providing 'this is feasible and practicable'. The implication was that it would probably not be feasible or practicable. Similar considerations could well apply to the provision of other medical services, particularly in countries desperately short of resources. The principle of normalization can be a two-edged sword.[256]

The Committee recommends that all newly received prisoners be 'properly interviewed' and 'if necessary, physically examined by a medical doctor as soon as possible after admission' though such medical screening might be carried out by a fully qualified nurse:[257] 'as soon as possible after admission' is interpreted as 'within 24 hours'.[258] Further, while in custody all prisoners should have access to a doctor at any time. Prisoners should be able to consult with medical personnel on a confidential basis and their access to medical personnel should not be screened by prison officers.[259]

[254] See King and Morgan (1980), 34–37. See also European Prison Rule 65(a).

[255] Gen Rep 3, para 38.

[256] Though in Ireland in 1993 it appears that the Director of Prison Medical Services agreed that the time spent by some prison doctors with prisoner patients was poor and unsatisfactory compared, presumably, with the quality of medical services generally delivered in the country. The Committee also noted that some medical functions were being carried out by unqualified staff (Ireland 1, paras 125–127).

[257] Gen Rep 3, para 33.

[258] Bulgaria 1, para 146; Romania 1, para 39 (in relation to those taken into police custody).

[259] Gen Rep 3, para 34.

This applies as much to prisoners subject to security restrictions as prisoners on normal locations.[260]

Medical files should be kept for all prisoners and in the event of transfer the files should be transferred with the prisoners. Further, medical secrecy should be observed in the same way as in the community: responsibility for the confidentiality of medical files should rest with medical doctors.[261] In this regard the Committee has on several occasions criticized the use by prison medical staff of prisoner orderlies who have access to the medical files of their fellow prisoners.[262]

The CPT is particularly concerned with the preservation of prisoners' right of consent: 'Every patient capable of discernment is free to refuse treatment or any other medical intervention. Any derogation from this principle should be based upon law and only relate to clearly and strictly defined exceptional circumstances which are applicable to the population as a whole', the point being that rules regarding, for example, medical intervention in the event of hunger strikes vary from country to country.[263]

In country reports a question frequently arises as to whether staff medical cover is adequate to meet the above standards. Following complaints from prisoners about gaining access to medical personnel, and following a review of their provision, the CPT not infrequently recommends in some detail that medical staff be increased or improved in quality.[264]

(i) Accountability mechanisms

In addition to the keeping of records regarding the use of force in prisons, considered below, the CPT recommends that all prisons have 'effective grievance and inspection procedures'. Grievance ventilation systems should have two aspects, one within the prison system and one outside it. Moreover, the CPT favours systems of independent inspection of prisons by authorities, whether supervisory penal judges or lay bodies like the English Boards of Visitors, which possess 'powers to hear (and if necessary to

---

[260] Netherlands 2, para 76.   [261] Ibid, para 50.   [262] See, eg, Slovakia 1, para 120.
[263] Gen Rep 3, para 47.
[264] In Ireland in 1993, for example, the number of hours that doctors were present at Mountjoy Prison, Dublin, was considered 'manifestly inadequate' for the number of prisoners held (Ireland 1, para 117). In Belgium in 1997 the CPT recorded a whole host of inadequacies spread across all the prisons visited (Belgium 2, paras 135–160). In Austria in 1994 the CPT was highly critical of the absence of adequate medical cover in police gaols (Austria 2, paras 80–87). In Bulgaria in 1995 the CPT judged that health care staffing levels were inadequate at the Pazardjik and Stara Zagora prisons. The Committee made detailed recommendations for the additional employment of nurses, *feldshers* (medical staff who in practice perform the same duties as doctors), and doctors and further recommended that medical staff cover at weekends be reviewed (Bulgaria 1, paras 136–141).

act on) complaints from prisoners and to inspect the establishment's premises'.[265]

Where lay visiting bodies exist the CPT considers it desirable that they should receive appropriate training and that they should be recruited so as to 'reflect the different elements in the community'.[266] In order to enhance and emphasize their independence and impartiality, they should not comprise members of the administration and should ideally be appointed by an authority other than the prison administration.[267] They should also serve for more than a year in order to provide for some continuity of membership.[268] Such bodies should publish an annual report on their activities.[269]

Those responsible for undertaking inspection and grievance ventilation visits should visit regularly—'preferably weekly or at least monthly'[270]— and should make themselves 'visible', that is, they 'must not restrict their contacts to persons who have expressly requested to meet them, but should take the initiative by visiting the prison's detention areas and entering into contact with inmates'. The CPT also considers it essential that such persons be 'authorised to have direct contact with governmental and/or parliamentary authorities. In certain situations, to fulfil [their] functions effectively, [they] must be able to address [themselves] to someone other than just the head of the establishment concerned.'[271]

5. PARTICULAR CATEGORIES OF PRISONERS

The standards considered in the preceding sections set benchmarks which are applicable to all those in custody, to the extent that they are relevant. There are, however, a number of categories of prisoners who have special needs and these have been the subject of special comment by the CPT. Some of these categories are examined below. It must be stressed that these observations supplement the general standards and must be read alongside them. In many instances, there is no need to set out special standards—it is the sympathetic application of the existing general standards in the light of the particular circumstances of the individual prisoner that is called for.

[265] Gen Rep 2, para 54.   [266] Cyprus 1, paras 105–107.
[267] Germany 1, para 166; Netherlands Aruba 1, para 276.
[268] Malta 2, para 79.   [269] Cyprus 1, para 107.
[270] Austria 2, para 93; in Spain in 1991, however, the CPT recommended that supervisory judges visit at least once a week 'irrespective of whether any prisoners have requested to see the judge' (Spain 1, para 189).
[271] Bulgaria 1, para 175; Romania 1, para 143.

(a) Prisoners subject to disciplinary or high-security measures

Prisoners may find themselves subject to a special regime within a prison for a number of reasons, chief of which is the imposition of internal disciplinary sanctions or reasons connected with the offence for which the prisoner has been convicted. In the latter case, this may be a function of the offence itself or it may be needed in order to protect the prisoner from the violence of fellow inmates. This is particularly true of those convicted of sexual offences.

The application of disciplinary measures may often be preceded by the use of a degree of force by prison officers, which may itself blur into a form of disciplinary sanction. Prisoners are ultimately subject to coercive control and the CPT soon signalled its alertness to such 'high-risk' situations as the use of restraints which, in the Committee's judgement, 'call for specific safeguards', these being:

A prisoner against whom any means of force have been used should have the right to be immediately examined and, if necessary, treated by a medical doctor. This examination should be conducted out of the hearing and preferably out of the sight of non-medical staff, and the results of the examination (including any relevant statements by the prisoner and the doctor's conclusions) should be formally recorded and made available to the prisoner. In those rare cases when resort to instruments of physical restraint is required, the prisoner should be kept under constant and adequate supervision. Further, instruments of restraint should be removed at the earliest possible opportunity: they should never be applied, or their application prolonged, as a punishment. Finally, a record should be kept of every instance of the use of force against prisoners.[272]

For these purposes, the use of special cells (variously known as 'strip' or 'silent' cells) which are used for disciplinary or control purposes is included within the definition of a 'use of force', and every instance of their use should be recorded in writing.[273] Another high-risk situation occurs when a prisoner is transferred into disciplinary accommodation and the Committee has had to remind states of the need to ensure that no ill-treatment occurs.[274]

When disciplinary action is taken against a prisoner, the CPT has made it clear that all prison systems should have 'clear disciplinary procedures' which include prisoners having the 'right to be heard on the subject of the offences it is alleged they have committed, and to appeal to high authority against any sanctions imposed'.[275] A right of appeal should be available against all sanctions that can be imposed rather than just the most serious, such as segregation in isolation.[276] The Committee also recommends that, in disciplinary proceedings, prisoners should be able to call witnesses on

---

[272] Gen Rep 2, para 53.   [273] UK 3, para 354.   [274] Belgium 2, paras 87–88.
[275] Gen Rep 2, para 55.   [276] Portugal 1, para 135.

their own behalf and be able to cross-examine evidence given against them. During adjudications prisoners should be able to sit and should have facilities to take notes. The Committee also favours consideration of prisoners having the right to legal representation at adjudications.[277] Further, because prisoners may be segregated from the moment that a charge is laid against them, the Committee considers that cases should be proceeded with promptly (ie within forty-eight hours).[278] Disciplinary segregation unit cells should have call bells and there should always be a member of staff present in such a unit.[279]

The Committee accepts that prisoners may administratively have to be segregated without there being a formal disciplinary hearing (in the interests of 'good order') but these procedures should also be accompanied by safeguards:

The prisoner should be informed of the reasons for the measure taken against him, unless security requirements dictate otherwise, and be given an opportunity to present his views on the matter, and be able to contest the measure before an appropriate authority.[280]

More particularly, the Committee has made it clear that prisoners undergoing disciplinary punishment in segregated conditions should not be kept naked,[281] deprived of a mattress for sleeping at night,[282] nor should they be denied outdoor exercise.[283] They should also be allowed reading materials.[284]

Prisoners subject to such security measures are often labelled 'dangerous' or 'troublesome' and the regimes to which they are subject can be highly restrictive, sometimes amounting to solitary confinement. The CPT considers, as we have seen (see pre-trial custody above), that solitary confinement can amount to 'inhuman and degrading treatment' and that, because it may be harmful, such segregation should always be as short as possible. Further, the Committee recommends that decisions to segregate prisoners should regularly be reviewed (at least every three months) and 'where appropriate on the basis of medico-social opinion'.[285]

As far as the regimes provided for prisoners in segregated conditions or high security units are concerned the CPT again applies the principle of proportionality: a balance must be 'struck between the requirements of the case and the application of a solitary confinement-type regime'.[286] The Committee has extended this principle by reasoning that restrictions should be balanced with compensating privileges. It has already been seen that in

---

[277] Ireland 1, para 148.   [278] Austria 2, para 142.   [279] Greece 1, para 140.
[280] Austria 2, para 142.   [281] See Austria 2, para 147.
[282] See Hungary 1, paras 132–133.   [283] Germany 2, para 159.
[284] Bulgaria 1, paras 162–166; Germany 2, para 160, where the only reading matter available was 'the Bible (in German)'.
[285] Belgium 1, para 99; Bulgaria 1, para 169.   [286] Gen Rep 2, para 56.

the case of pre-trial prisoners the Committee has interpreted this to mean that to the extent that prisoners are not allowed to have contact with their fellow prisoners, then they must have compensating contact with staff instead. Much the same approach has been taken *vis-à-vis* prisoners segregated for control or security reasons:

high security unit prisoners should be able to enjoy a *relatively relaxed regime* (able to mix freely with the relatively small number of prisoners in the unit; allowed to move without restriction within what is likely . . . to be a relatively small physical space; granted a good deal of choice about activities, etc) by way of compensation for their severe custodial situation.[287]

The Committee accepts 'that security considerations may preclude many types of work activities which are found on normal work location', but argues that 'this should not mean that only work of a tedious nature is provided'.[288]

Such units should also be carefully staffed: staff should be 'appropriately trained, possess highly developed communication skills and have a genuine commitment to the exercise of their skills in a more than usually challenging environment' in which the establishment of a positive atmosphere is considered vital.[289]

In The Netherlands this was not found to be the case at the Demersluis Prison high security unit. The regime was unduly restrictive, out-of-cell time was very limited, the available activities were both few in number and unstimulating in nature, and staff–prisoner relations were very poor.[290] The CPT recommended that the regime in the unit be reviewed. The Committee continued to have concerns about Dutch high security units following a return visit in 1997.[291] In Finland in 1992 the CPT found that segregated prisoners spent most of their time alone in their cells with little to occupy them. The Committee regarded this as unacceptable and recommended that the regime be reviewed in order that purposeful activities and appropriate—by which they meant stimulating—human contact be provided to alleviate the consequences of segregation.[292] Similar criticisms were made regarding the section where a small number of life sentence prisoners were housed in the Netherlands Antilles in 1994: in some respects their conditions could be said to be privileged, but the physical space they had was very restrictive, as were their regime facilities. Indeed the Committee thought that the overall situation 'could be considered to be inhuman' in that there was a risk of deterioration in the prisoners' mental state.[293]

In the special units at Peterhead Prison, Scotland in 1994 the Committee

---

[287] Netherlands 1, para 90.   [288] Netherlands 2, para 61.   [289] UK 3, para 330.
[290] Netherlands 1, para 91.   [291] Netherlands 2, paras 58–77.
[292] Finland 1, paras 72–73.   [293] Netherlands Antilles 1, para 92.

also identified shortcomings. In one unit the prisoners were effectively in solitary confinement, a situation that could be considered 'inhuman'. An aggravating ingredient at Peterhead was that the staff wore riot gear in their daily interactions with prisoners: this routine fostered 'confrontational attitudes on the part of both staff and prisoners'.[294] Many of these shortcomings came together in the conditions encountered in Italy where the Committee pointed out that, although it may be necessary to take strict measures in the fight against organized crime, this must not take the form of conditions which might degenerate into inhuman and degrading treatment. The CPT called for the wholesale re-examination of the Italian system of high-security detention, which it described as one of the most harsh it had encountered, combining a lack of procedural safeguards with a lack of regime activities and human contact that amounted to little short of solitary confinement.[295] There was, in addition, evidence of prisoners being transferred between prisons on a frequent basis, a practice which the CPT questioned, drawing attention to the negative consequences this has not only for prisoners' physical and mental well-being but also in terms of maintaining contacts with family and lawyers.[296]

Of course, it is not only dangerous prisoners who pose problems of security. The CPT has made it clear that its mandate is not limited to the ill-treatment of detainees by officials but extends to the duty of care which the authorities owe to all in their custody. This includes the obligation to protect prisoners generally from inter-prisoner violence. This has given cause for concern in a number of countries, and especially with regard to sex offenders, a particularly vulnerable group. Following its 1997 visit to Belgium, the CPT drew attention to alternative strategies of separation and integration and recognized advantages and problems in each: separation usually implied a more restrictive regime, integration implied a real commitment to ensuring no acts of intimidation and inter-prisoner violence occurred. The Committee expressed no preference, believing this to be a decision for the national authorities, but stressed the need for staff to be trained in dealing with this category of detainee.[297]

(b) Women prisoners

The CPT has not systematically set out in a general report a set of standards specifically geared to women prisoners, but it has indicated that the Committee is particularly attentive to their needs[298] and an examination of country reports reveals some recurring themes. Most importantly, the Committee has made it clear that it expects facilities and regime

---

[294] UK 3, para 331.
[295] Italy 2, para 90. See, in general, paras 76–94 and Italy 1, paras 132–148.
[296] Italy 2, para 88.   [297] Belgium 2, paras 93–94.   [298] Gen Rep 2, para 52.

activities available to women to be equitable in relation to, though not necessarily the same as, those provided to male prisoners.[299] This can be illustrated by a number of examples concerning the nature and standard of both accommodation and regime activities.

In the women's section at Korydallos Prison, Athens, the women prisoners were severely overcrowded because one of the units normally assigned to them had been taken over for a small number of high-security male prisoners whose conditions, compared to those of the women, 'bordered on the luxurious'.[300] The Committee recommended that a new high security unit for the men be established elsewhere so that conditions for the women could be improved: it was 'unacceptable . . . that so many should be made to suffer poor conditions of detention for the sake of offering special accommodation to so few'.[301] At Herstedvester Institution (a psychiatric prison), Denmark, the CPT heard that men, but not women, could benefit from being placed in a semi-open regime section: the Committee recommended that the possibility of providing equitable access be explored.[302]

In the Nicosia Central Prison, Cyprus, the CPT noted that women prisoners could not be employed in the prison workshops and, according to the prison authorities, were not interested in educational activities because of their 'low level of education'. As a consequence, the Committee observed, the women only 'undertook activities such as knitting, sewing, embroidery and gardening'. In fact, the delegation received complaints from the women prisoners about their limited regime opportunities, in particular the absence of sporting activities, the absence of educational facilities, and the impossibility of their visiting the library, which was situated in the men's area. The Committee recommended that the Cypriot authorities develop the employment, education, and sporting facilities available to women 'to a level comparable to that offered to male prisoners'.[303]

Equity also guides the CPT with respect to other matters. In Spain, for example, the Committee received complaints that disciplinary measures were applied more frequently to women than to men. The Committee examined the statistics, which they found 'lent credibility' to the allegations and the Spanish authorities were asked for an explanation.[304]

The Committee has also been concerned about a number of specific issues relating to the health and hygiene needs of women prisoners and has, for example, recommended that tampons be provided for all women needing them.[305] Naturally, the relationship between mothers and babies

---

[299] Although it should be noted that the material conditions of detention of women prisoners are often found to be considerably better than those of male prisoners.
[300] Greece 1, para 111.   [301] Ibid, para 113.   [302] Denmark 1, para 86.
[303] Cyprus 1, para 87.   [304] Spain 1, para 196.
[305] Romania 1, para 71 (in the context of police custody).

has given rise to difficult questions. The Committee has noted an alleged incident in which a new-born baby was taken from his mother and placed with foster parents within minutes of his birth. Such a practice would, in the Committee's view, be a 'flagrant example of inhuman and degrading treatment: a mother and child must have the opportunity to stay together for a certain period of time'.[306]

The CPT has not, however, made any clear statement of principle concerning the question of whether women who give birth to children while in prison should be permitted to have their children to live with them and, if so, until what age. But it has set out considerations which should govern policy. The Committee has noted that this is a controversial issue and has said that it does not favour the practice of setting a fixed period of time that mothers are able to keep their children with them.[307] It has also noted that, in the opinion of some commentators, keeping a child in prison beyond the age of two or three years can have negative effects for the child concerned.[308] Nevertheless, the Committee has stipulated that *if* women are allowed to have their children with them, then a 'favourable social and educational environment' should be provided. There should be a distinct mother and baby unit.[309] 'There should be a suitably equipped creche facility, and the assistance of nursery nurses as well as specialised medical care should be guaranteed.'[310] Specialist medical care includes neonatal and infant care.[311] During the period in which the child is with the mother in prison, it is important that the regime permits mothers to spend sufficient time with their babies.[312] Moreover, where women have been permitted to have their infants with them in prison, eventual 'transfer of the child to the outside community and its separation from its mother, should be decided in each individual case, having regard to the child's best interests'.[313]

(c) Juvenile and young prisoners

As with female prisoners, the CPT has not set out in an annual general report standards that it considers appropriate for young or juvenile prisoners. But the Committee has indicated that it pays particular attention to the conditions in which juveniles are kept.[314] Once again, the same basic standards which apply to adults in detention apply with equal force to juveniles[315] but certain themes emerge repeatedly in country reports which build on a statement in the Committee's third general report, namely:

---

[306] Luxembourg 1, para 44.   [307] eg France 1, para 119.   [308] Spain 2, para 136.
[309] Spain 1, para 127.   [310] Greece 1, para 115.
[311] Netherlands Antilles 1, para 152.   [312] Belgium 1, para 108.
[313] Ibid, para 153; France 1, para 120.   [314] Gen Rep 2, para 52.
[315] eg Italy 2, para 157.

Adolescence is a period marked by a certain reorganisation of the personality, requiring a special effort to reduce the risks of long-term social maladjustment. While in custody adolescents should be allowed to stay in a fixed place, surrounded by personal objects and in socially favourable groups. The regime applied to them should be based on intensive activity, including socio-educational meetings, sport, education, vocational training, escorted outings and the availability of appropriate optional activities.[316]

This has been developed somewhat in subsequent country reports, and the Committee has underlined that:

La délégation du CPT a eu la nette impression que le personnel ne s'investissait pas pleinement dans l'organisation d'un régime actif pour les jeunes détenus. A cet égard, il convient de souligner que le personnel affecté dans les établissements pour mineurs devrait être soigneusement sélectionné; plus précisément, il devrait être capable de guider et de motiver les jeunes. Les jeunes détenus devraient bénéficier d'un programme complet d'activités éducatives, de loisirs ainsi que d'autres activités motivantes susceptibles de stimuler leurs potentialités d'insertion/réinsertion sociale et qui leur fassent passer huit heures ou plus hors de leur cellule; l'éducation physique devrait constituer un élément important de ce programme.[317]

Juvenile prisoners should be housed separately from adults ('unless it is clearly in the interest of the young person concerned'),[318] and this includes arrangements when they are being transported or transferred.[319] As has been seen, the staff of juvenile institutions should be carefully chosen: they should be persons 'capable of guiding and motivating young people'.[320] Against this background, the CPT's response to being informed that in the Padre Antonio de Oliveira Re-education Centre, Portugal, 'the administration of a "pedagogic" slap was not entirely unknown'[321] was surprisingly muted. The Committee said that, 'In the interests of the prevention of ill-treatment, the CPT believes that it would be preferable for all forms of physical chastisement of children to be both formally prohibited and avoided in practice.'[322] This could be taken to suggest that the CPT does not consider such forms of chastisement to amount to ill-treatment in their own right, a view that might cause confusion. A more robust approach was adopted in Slovakia, where the use of a ' "Scottish shower" (i.e. 3 to 10 minutes of spraying with water in order to calm [young persons displaying aggressive behaviour] down)' was considered to be 'unacceptable' and it was 'recommended that it be removed from the list of authorized means of coercion'.[323]

---

[316] Gen Rep 3, para 67.　　[317] France 3, para 112.
[318] Slovenia 1, para 76.　　[319] See Finland 1, para 138.
[320] See also, eg, Greece 1, para 116.　　[321] Portugal 2, para 153.
[322] Ibid. See also Italy 2, paras 159–160, where 'pedagogic' slaps were again remarked on, but the Committee did not find itself able to pass comment on whether there was ill-treatment, in the light of the information at its disposal.
[323] Slovakia 1, para 153.

CPT reports on juvenile institutions place great emphasis on the provision of sports facilities since it is judged that physical education should form an important element in programmes of activities.[324] Thus, although the Committee was very impressed with the regime and facilities at the Alexandra Youth Detention Centre, Almelo, Netherlands, it nevertheless regarded the absence of sports provisions (there was no outdoor playing field despite the Unit's extensive grounds and no gymnasium) to be 'a serious shortcoming . . . bearing in mind the age ranges [14 to 16-year-olds] of those detained'.[325] It is equally important that other activities be of a suitably stimulating nature. The Committee was critical of the regime at Feltham Young Offenders Institution and Remand Prison in the UK because, although the 'great majority' of prisoners spent between four and eight hours out of their cells each day, this was 'too often spent on activities such as games and watching television. Further, as regards those inmates who did have an occupational activity, this was not always of a vocational nature.'[326]

It is also clear that the Committee considers that, to the extent that any limitation is imposed, visit entitlements for juveniles should be more generous than those for adults. In Slovakia, where juveniles were already entitled to visits every two weeks compared to monthly visits for adults, the Committee recommended that the entitlements for both categories be 'substantially' improved.[327]

Another matter of particular concern is the use of isolation as a disciplinary sanction for juveniles. Relevant factors concern its duration,[328] the physical conditions in which it is served,[329] the nature of the regime,[330] and the safeguards surrounding its imposition. The following set of recommendations, tailored in this example to the particular circumstances at the Padre Antonio de Oliveira Re-education Centre, Portugal, are illustrative of the CPT's approach. As to the implementation of disciplinary sanctions, the Committee recommended:

— that a minor be guaranteed a right to be heard on the subject of the offence which it is alleged he has committed;
— that there be a formally recognized right of appeal to a high authority against sanctions imposed (for example to the Director of the Centre, as regards sanctions imposed by educators, and

---

[324] eg Italy 2, para 165.   [325] Netherlands 1, para 111.   [326] UK 3, para 148.
[327] Slovakia 1, paras 127–128.
[328] In Italy 2, para 170 the CPT defined a 'prolonged period' as being ten days or more.
[329] See, eg, Slovakia 1, para 157, where isolation rooms of 3.6 square metres, and equipped only with a mattress, were considered too small for overnight use. Perhaps surprisingly, the Committee only thought it 'desirable' that isolation rooms be equipped with a table and a chair, 'if necessary, fixed to the floor'.
[330] See UK 3, paras 132–139.

to the competent judge, as regards sanctions imposed by the Director);

— that a specific register be kept in each Centre, containing full details of all disciplinary sanctions imposed.[331]

As regards the use of sanctions involving isolation of a minor, the CPT recommended:

— that resort to that sanction be regarded as an exceptional measure and made the subject of a notification to the competent judge;
— that it be served in a suitably equipped room (with at least a bed, table, and chair);
— that minors undergoing a measure of isolation as a sanction be provided with reading matter and allowed at least one hour of outdoor exercise every day;
— that the maximum possible duration of such a measure be formally laid down and that the measure never be applied for longer than is strictly necessary.[332]

(d) Vulnerable prisoners with medical and psychiatric conditions

The CPT recommends that information about transmittable diseases (such as hepatitis, AIDS, dermatological infections, and tuberculosis) be regularly circulated to prisoners and staff and, where appropriate, controls over prisoner contacts be exercised.[333] Prisoners with AIDS should be provided with counselling 'before and, if necessary, after any screening test'.[334] The CPT emphasizes that 'there is no medical justification for the segregation of an HIV+ prisoner who is well', and thus prison staff should be trained regarding preventive measures and the need for non-discrimination and confidentiality.[335]

Most prison systems contain prisoners with psychiatric disorders and, in consequence, the CPT recommends that there should be attached to every prison a psychiatrist and that some of the nursing staff should have psychiatric nursing training. The Committee recognizes that there are arguments for and against caring for psychiatrically ill prisoners within prison, as opposed to transferring them to outside psychiatric hospitals. But whichever course is taken transfers should be given the highest priority and the level of care should be adequate, which presumably implies that the quality should be commensurate with that found in the community generally.[336] This undoubtedly represents the most difficult context within

---

[331] Portugal 2, para 163.   [332] Ibid, para 164.   [333] Gen Rep 3, para 54.
[334] Ibid, para 55.   [335] Ibid, paras 55–56.
[336] Ibid, para 43. See the discussion of *normalization* as a principle in Section 4(h) above.

which to interpret the principle of medical 'normalization' since, as a number of CPT reports testify, long-stay psychiatric hospital care is in many countries very poor.[337]

As regards prisoners with 'personality disorders', the CPT recognizes that there is always a 'certain proportion' in prison and that their needs are 'not truly medical': but the Committee considers that 'prison doctors can promote the development of socio-therapeutic programmes for them, in prison units which are organised along community lines'.[338]

Many CPT reports include remarks about suicide prevention, for which medical screening of all newly arrived prisoners is, in the Committee's opinion, particularly important. Further, the Committee recommends that prisoners identified as suicide risks should, for as long as is necessary, be subject to special supervision and should not have easy access to means of killing themselves (cell window bars, broken glass, belts and ties, etc).[339] There should be good communication between prison staff about prisoners identified as suicide risks and 'counselling, support and appropriate association' should be provided.[340] In addition, those at risk should not be stigmatized within the prison.[341] In short, the CPT regularly recommends that prison authorities formulate a suicide prevention programme and the Committee emphasizes that suicide prevention is the responsibility of all prison staff and not just the medical staff.[342]

6. CONCLUSION

The above account is by no means an exhaustive account of what we have termed the CPT's 'jurisprudence'. Nevertheless, it covers the principal fields routinely detailed in CPT country reports and signalled by means of sub-headings in those reports. Though it would be an overstatement to claim that the CPT's jurisprudence was swiftly established and has since become ossified, this is not far from the truth. The templates set out in the second and third general reports have been subject to some minor revisions, but not to any wholesale reappraisal. Some aspects of policy have, however, acquired increased prominence, moving from the periphery of the Committee's work to a more centre stage position—the conditions in which foreigners are detained under aliens legislation, and the manner in which decisions are taken regarding them, provides a clear example of this. Nevertheless, it is largely true that the standards which the Committee

---

[337] See, eg, Greece 1, paras 224–237; Bulgaria 1, paras 178–223; Romania 1, paras 167–182. The shortcomings of care in psychiatric establishments generally are addressed in the CPT's 8th annual General Report and appropriate standards set out (see Gen Rep 8, paras 25–58).
[338] Gen Rep 3, paras 68–69.   [339] Ibid, paras 58–59.   [340] Finland 1, para 109.
[341] See Belgium 2, paras 175–176.   [342] UK 1, para 169.

routinely applies, and the wording that the Committee routinely employs, have changed remarkably little since 1990–1992.

To put the matter another way, significant portions of CPT reports owe more to the Secretariat's computerized memory bank than to country by country drafting. The use of set formulas—familiar and convenient as they are to international organizations working in more than one language—certainly has its advantages, but it does tend to discourage innovation. Changes are likely to be incremental and easily lost on the observer, who may well not credit a subtle alteration with the significance it deserves. By the same token, it also becomes easy to overstate the implications of what might be merely presentational rearrangement. A further consequence is that the work of the Committee can become overly focused on determining which formula is to apply in the light of the facts found in the course of a visit, rather than on responding to the facts in a direct and practical fashion with concrete recommendations.

In the light of all these observations, it is not surprising to find that although there has certainly been some development in the jurisprudence established in the early years of the Committee's work, it amounts to remarkably little. It must, of course, be accepted that the standards reviewed in this chapter might be so well devised as not to be in need of development or revision. The responses to the work of the CPT reviewed in later chapters of this book, however, suggest that that would be too benign a conclusion. Moreover, this would not explain why the CPT has done comparatively little to fill the gaps in its jurisprudence that have been noted not only by others but by the Committee itself. There remains much to be done to perfect and extend the range of the CPT's 'jurisprudence'.

REFERENCES

APT (1995) *The Implementation of the European Convention for the Prevention of Torture and Inhuman or Degrading Treatment or Punishment* (ECPT): *Assessment and Perspectives after Five Years of Activities of the European Committee for the Prevention of Torture and Inhuman or Degrading Treatment or Punishment—Acts of the Seminar of 5 to 7 December 1994, Strasbourg* (Geneva: APT)

Amnesty International (1984) *Torture in the Eighties* (London: Amnesty International)

Cassese, A (1996) *Inhuman States: Imprisonment, Detention and Torture in Europe Today* (Cambridge: Polity Press), originally published in Italian (1994) *Umano-Disumano: Commissariarti en prigioni nell'Europa di oggo* (Roma Bari: Laterza)

Evans, MD and Morgan, R (1998) *Preventing Torture* (Oxford: Clarendon Press)

King, RD and Morgan, R (1980) *The Future of the Prison System* (Farnborough: Gower)

Morgan, R (1996) 'Custody in the Police Station: How do England and Wales Measure up in Europe?', 17(1) *Policy Studies* 55–72

Sorenson, B (1995) 'Prevention of Torture and Inhuman or Degrading Treatment or Punishment: Medical Views' in APT, *The Implementation of the European Convention for the Prevention of Torture and Inhuman or Degrading Treatment or Punishment* (ECPT): *Assessment and Perspectives after Five Years of Activities of the European Committee for the Prevention of Torture and Inhuman or Degrading Treatment or Punishment—Acts of the Seminar of 5 to 7 December 1994, Strasbourg* (Geneva: APT)

Part II

The International Context

3

The European Convention for the Prevention of Torture and the European Convention on Human Rights

WOLFGANG PEUKERT

1. THE AIMS AND MECHANISMS OF THE TWO INSTRUMENTS

The European Convention for the Prevention of Torture (ECPT) and the European Convention on Human Rights (ECHR) are intended to complement each other. The ECPT does not set out any new standards but is designed to reinforce the protection of persons deprived of their liberty from torture or inhuman and degrading punishment or treatment. Whereas the ECHR establishes machinery that responds to complaints from either states or individuals claiming to be the victims of a violation of Article 3 of the ECHR and results in a judicial determination, the ECPT establishes the CPT, which is a non-judicial body whose work is of a preventive nature and is focused upon the production of reports based on visits to Contracting Parties.[1] These reports, and the recommendations they contain, are not meant to condemn states but are intended to help support and reinforce them in their own work of torture prevention.[2] The CPT spells out its view of the relationship between the two instruments in a Preface added to the first periodic report transmitted to a state. This says that:

(1) the Commission and the Court have as their primary goal ascertaining whether breaches of the ECHR have occurred. By contrast, the CPT's task is to prevent abuses, whether physical or mental, of persons deprived of their liberty from occurring; it has its eyes on the future rather than the past.

---

[1] For details see Evans, MD and Morgan, R (1992) 'The ECPT: Operational Practice', 41 *ICLQ* 590; (1994) 'The European Torture Committee: Membership Issues', 5 *EJIL* 249; (1997) 'The ECPT 1992–1997', 46 *ICLQ* 663; (1998) *Preventing Torture* (Oxford: Clarendon Press). See also Machacek, R (1993), 'Supranationaler Schutz vor Folter und Unmenschlicher Behandlung', *Journal für Rechtspolitik* 247; Murdoch, J (1994), 'The Work of the Council of Europe's Torture Committee', 5 *EJIL* 220; (1996) 'The ECPT', 21 *ELRev* 130.

[2] ECPT, Explanatory Report, para 17.

(2) the Commission and Court have substantive treaty provisions to apply and interpret. The CPT is not bound by substantive treaty provisions, although it may refer to a number of treaties, other international instruments, and the case law formulated thereunder.

(3) given the nature of their functions, the Commission and the Court consist of lawyers specializing in the field of human rights. The CPT consists not only of such lawyers but also of medical doctors, experts in penitentiary questions, criminologists, etc.

(4) the Commission and Court only intervene after having been petitioned through applications from individuals or states. The CPT intervenes *ex officio* through periodic or *ad hoc* visits.

(5) the activities of the Commission and the Court culminate in a legally binding finding as to whether a state has breached its obligations under a treaty. The CPT's findings result in a report, and, if necessary, recommendations and other advice, on the basis of which a dialogue can develop; in the event of a state failing to comply with the CPT recommendations, the CPT may issue a public statement on the matter.

The essence of the relationship is put more succinctly elsewhere in each Preface, as being 'whereas the Commission's and Court's activities aim at "conflict solution" on the legal level, the CPT's activities aim at "conflict avoidance" on the practical level'. The views of the Court and Commission on its relationship with the CPT are less well known, but it appears that during the drafting of the ECPT both the Commission and Court were keen to ensure that the CPT did not stray into judicial-style interpretation or determination under Article 3 of the ECHR.[3]

The CPT differs from the ECHR with regard to its underlying purposes and methodology, and to the standards it seeks to uphold. Although the Preamble to the ECPT 'recalls' Article 3 of the ECHR, the text itself does not contain any substantive provision on the question of what constitutes torture or inhuman or degrading treatment. In consequence, when exercising its functions, the CPT can refer not only to the substantive norms contained in the ECHR, but also to other human rights instruments and their interpretation by the competent authorities. It has done so on a number of occasions. For example, it has described a situation as being incompatible with human dignity,[4] thus drawing on terminology found in Article 10(1) of the International Covenant for Civil and Political Rights and in Rule 1 of the European Prison Rules. It has also considered whether Council of Europe Conventions, such as the European Convention for the Transfer of Convicted Persons, are correctly implemented.[5]

---

[3] See generally Evans and Morgan (1998), 118–122.
[4] Switzerland 1, para 149.　　　[5] France 1, para 155.

Of course, since the CPT is not tied to terminology it sometimes describes situations as being, for example, 'deplorable', 'unacceptable', or 'below an acceptable minimum' without further qualification. Even when it has used the terminology employed in other international instruments or codes of conduct, the CPT is not bound by the interpretations which are placed upon those terms by their monitoring or implementation bodies. Thus the interpretation of Article 3 adopted by the organs of the ECHR, or the case law of other judicial or quasi-judicial bodies acting in the same field, may be used as a point of departure or reference when assessing the treatment of persons deprived of their liberty in individual countries, but the CPT can range beyond this.[6]

None of this would be particularly problematic if the relationship between the ECPT and the ECHR was as clearly demarcated as the comments of the CPT suggest. In reality, however, they work in close proximity and inevitably impact upon each other to some degree. In consequence, both of these practices—using unfamiliar terminology and using familiar terminology in an unfamiliar fashion—can create some problems when other bodies, and particularly when the Commission and Court of Human Rights were and are called upon to consider the relevance of the CPT's work for their own, perhaps more closely circumscribed, functions. This is well illustrated by the case of *Aerts v Belgium* before the European Commission and Court of Human Rights, which will be looked at below.

At the same time, there are a number of instances when the CPT must pay very close attention to interpretive work under the ECHR. For example, the Explanatory Report to the ECPT makes it clear that the notion of 'deprivation of liberty', central to the functioning of the CPT, 'is to be understood within the meaning of Article 5 of the ECHR as elucidated by the case-law of the European Commission and Court of Human Rights'.[7] Thus in its seventh general report, the CPT expressly referred to the judgment of the Court in *Amuur v France*[8] as confirming its constant position that a stay in a transit or 'international' zone of an airport can, depending on the circumstances, amount to a deprivation of liberty within the meaning of Article 5(1)(f) ECHR, and that consequently such zones fall within the CPT's mandate.[9] The CPT has also chosen to note on a number of occasions that local police authorities had taken steps to ensure that the legality of police custody was in accordance with Article 5(3) ECHR, that is to say that it was reviewed by a judge shortly after the

---

[6] It should, however, be noted that whilst the CPT can apply more exacting standards, it cannot require less of states than their existing Convention obligations require.

[7] Explanatory Report, para 24.

[8] *Amuur v France*, Judgment of 25 June 1996, *RJD* 1996-III, 827.

[9] Gen Rep 7, para 25. It had, however, failed to draw express attention to the Report of the Commission which had earlier expressed the contrary view.

arrest.[10] The CPT has also referred to Article 8 of the ECHR when considering the detention of asylum seekers, underlining the importance of avoiding splitting up the family unit.[11]

It is, then, clear that there are many points of contact between the CPT and the ECHR. It was always unlikely that either of these two mechanisms—both the creation of the Council of Europe—would be able to conduct their work in a vacuum, unaffected by each other. The passing of time has shown this to be the case and this raises a range of problems which are easier to identify than solve. The purpose of this chapter is to conduct a preliminary exploration of the problems posed by this pattern of reciprocal influence against a background of formal separation.

(a) Points of contact

In addition to the formal points of contact mentioned in the previous section, a number of incidents have arisen which have placed the relationship between the two bodies in sharp relief. Although the European Commission and Court of Human Rights in principle only exercise their control *a posteriori*, it has been established in the case law that extradition and expulsion measures violate Article 3 of the ECHR[12] if the person concerned is threatened with treatment contrary to this provision in the receiving state.[13] In reality, this is a preventive role and, as such, brings the work under the ECHR into very close proximity to that of the CPT, which operates a similar preventive function in such cases. Recognizing this, the CPT has said that:

Any communications addressed to the CPT in Strasbourg by persons alleging that they are to be sent to a country where they run a risk of being subjected to torture or ill-treatment are immediately brought to the attention of the European Commission of Human Rights. The Commission is better placed than the CPT to examine such allegations and, if appropriate, take preventive action.[14]

[10] Netherlands Antilles 1, para 12; Netherlands Aruba 1, para 181.
[11] Denmark 1, para 56.
[12] Expulsion cases may also raise issues under Article 8 of the ECHR if they result in the break-up of a family. See *Mehemi v France*, Judgment of 26 September 1997, *RJD* 1997-VI, 1959.
[13] This was established in *Soering v UK*, Judgment of 7 July 1989, Ser A No 161. Among the more recent examples of such cases *D v UK*, Judgment of 2 May 1997, *RJD* 1997-III, 777 is of particular interest. It should also be noted that the danger needs to be faced in the state to which the person is to be extradited or expelled, but need not necessarily be due to a threat posed by the state or its agents. See *HLR v France*, Judgment of 29 April 1997, where the threat was said to be posed by drugs barons.
[14] Gen Rep 7, para 33. If the CPT encounters a detainee during a visit who claims that they are to be sent to a country where they will face such a risk, the CPT says that 'the visiting delegation will verify that this assertion has been brought to the attention of the relevant national authorities and is being given due consideration. Depending on the circumstances, the delegation might request to be kept informed of the detainee's position and/or inform the detainee

Although this may be true, it should be recalled that whilst under Rule 36 of the Commission's Rules of Procedure a Contracting Party could be requested to suspend a measure of extradition or expulsion, such requests do not have binding effect[15] and the full force of the ECHR's preventive action ultimately depends upon the conclusion of the case.

In proceedings under the ECHR the burden of proof concerning the alleged violations lies, in principle, with the applicant. However, in the inter-state case of *Ireland v UK* the Court did not strictly insist upon this but examined all material before it, whether originating from the Commission, the Parties, or other sources. Indeed, it added that, if necessary, it was prepared to obtain material *proprio motu*. Furthermore, in cases of persons who have sustained serious injuries while in detention and complain of ill-treatment or torture it is for the respondent government to provide an explanation of such injuries.[16] This raises the question of the value attached to CPT reports as evidence in cases brought under the ECHR.

The position seems to be that in proceedings under the Convention the findings of the CPT have probative but not binding value. An early example of a reference to CPT reports is found in the Dissenting Opinion of Judge Pettiti in *Klaas v Germany*,[17] but the first sustained attempt to draw on CPT reports occurred in *Delazarus v UK*[18] and *Raphaie v UK*.[19] In these cases the applicants drew on CPT reports when denouncing the conditions in British prisons. Both applications were declared inadmissible by the Commission, the first as being manifestly ill-founded, the second for non-observance of the six months rule. The CPT had indicated that it considered the combination of overcrowding, the practice of 'slopping out', and the paucity of regime activities to amount to 'inhuman and degrading' treatment.[20] Rather than reject the relevance of the CPT Report for its purposes, the Commission in *Delazarus* acknowledged it in a manner which fell short of an endorsement before distinguishing the circumstances it had described

---

of the possibility of raising the issue with the European Commission of Human Rights (and, in the latter case, verify that he is in a position to submit a petition to the Commission)' (ibid).

[15] See *Cruz Varas v Sweden*, Judgment of 20 March 1991, Ser A No 201.

[16] *Ribitsch v Austria*, Judgment of 4 December 1995, Ser A No 336, para 34.

[17] *Klaas v Germany*, Judgment of 22 September 1993, Ser A No 269. Judge Pettiti argued that, when deciding to support the claim that the applicant had failed to show that she had been the victim of a disproportionate use of force whilst being arrested, the Court 'did not . . . take sufficient account of a number of data that are . . . [o]f great assistance when assessing the facts'. These included '3. The reports of the European Committee for the Prevention of Torture', which 'are fairly damning of several police forces, [and] all are pleas for help to lawyers in the context of the ECHR . . .'. He seems to have believed that these reports could help support the general tenor of the claim, viz that the use of excessive force was common whilst effecting arrests.

[18] *Delazarus v UK*, App No 17525/90, Comm Dec, 16 February 1993 (unpublished).

[19] *Raphaie v UK*, App No 20035/92, Comm Dec, 2 December 1993 (unpublished).

[20] UK 1, para 57.

from those that pertained to the applicant. The Commission observed that it did:

not doubt that the conditions in Wandsworth Prison, involving overcrowding, a lack of activity, a lack of integral sanitation and poor hygiene, were extremely unsatis-factory and that they were in urgent need of improvement. The Government recog-nise this and informed the Commission of a rebuilding scheme to include in-cell sanitation. This is to be welcomed. However, the Commission is only competent to deal with the case it has before it, not the general situation of prisoners at Wandsworth. The applicant in the present case cannot complain of overcrowding because throughout his stay at Wandsworth he was in a single cell. This fact must have reduced the difficulties created by the lack of integral sanitation in the cell. Moreover the poor general conditions are not the basis of the applicant's main com-plaint about his removal from association with other prisoners.[21]

Subsequently, the 1993 CPT report on Greece has been drawn on in the context of a number of applications brought against Greece. In *Tosunoglu v Greece*, the Commission cited passages from the 1993 CPT report when considering conditions of detention at Larissa Prison. The Commission took note of the CPT's opinions in the context of arriving at its own conclusion that, although open to criticism, the conditions complained of did not reach the level of gravity required to amount to a violation of Article 3 of the ECHR and so the application was declared inadmissible.[22] In its report, the CPT had itself not gone quite so far as to say that the conditions were inhuman or degrading but used terms such as 'totally inappropriate' or 'not adequate'.[23] The 1993 CPT report was also very critical of the conditions of detention at the Korydallos prison complex outside Athens, concluding that most inmates were faced with 'a monotonous and purposeless existence [which] is quite inconsistent with the objective of social rehabilitation'.[24] Once again, the CPT stopped short of describing these conditions as inhuman or degrading. However, in May 1998 the Commission did de-clare admissible a complaint concerning the general conditions at the Korydallos prison in Greece and sections of the CPT's report relating to Korydallos were appended to its decision.[25] It remains to be seen whether the Court will go further than the CPT and, if it does, it may raise a ques-tion as to whether the CPT is being too cautious in its approach.

The most acute issues have, however, arisen in cases concerning Turkey. Although it has not authorized the publication of any reports arising out of visits, the gist of the CPT's principal findings in Turkey is known from the

---

[21] *Delazarus v UK*, App No 17525/90, Comm Dec, 16 February 1993, 12 (unpublished).

[22] *Tosunoglu v Greece,* App No 21892/93, Comm Dec, 12 April 1996 (unpublished).

[23] Greece 1, paras 119 and 120. The CPT also recorded that, as far as physical ill-treatment was concerned, Larissa Prison 'had to be considered as a "high risk" establishment from the point of view of ill-treatment occurring' (ibid, para 100).

[24] Ibid, para 108.

[25] *Peers v Greece*, App No 28524/95, Comm Dec, 21 May 1998 (unpublished).

two Public Statements which the Committee issued in 1992 and 1996 and, not surprisingly, these have been drawn to the attention of both the Commission and Court in cases brought before them. For example, in its report in the case of *Aydin v Turkey* the Commission noted that, according to the applicant, findings by the CPT as well as by the UN Committee against Torture, the UN Special Rapporteur, and by various NGOs disclosed 'a consistent pattern of torture in custody and official tolerance on the part of the Turkish authorities . . .'.[26] The Commission itself found that 'the applicant was during her three days in custody blindfolded, beaten, stripped, placed inside a tyre and sprayed with high pressure water, and raped'. In view of the rape the Commission concluded by 26 votes to one that the applicant had been the victim of torture. The Court confirmed this finding by 14 votes to 7 and under the heading of 'International Material' referred, *inter alia*, to the CPT's Public Statements, which expressed the view that the practice of torture and other forms of ill-treatment of those in police custody was 'widespread'.[27] The dissenters on this point considered, however, that the allegations were not proven beyond reasonable doubt, not least because there was no corroborating evidence from any other source of their claims.[28] The precise relevance of the CPT's findings to the conclusion is unclear, but they seem to serve generally to support the thrust of the allegations by indicating a belief that such incidents are indeed widespread.

The case in which the relevance of the CPT's work has so far been most directly at issue is, however, *Aerts v Belgium*. The case related to the detention pending trial of the applicant in the psychiatric wing of Lantin Prison. The applicant claimed that general conditions and lack of regular medical or psychiatric care or attention had resulted in a deterioration in his mental health and that, in sum, his treatment had been inhuman and degrading within the meaning of Article 3 of the ECHR. This wing has been visited by the CPT in the course of its *periodic* visit to Belgium in 1993 and in its subsequent report the CPT denounced the lack of adequate medical care, remarking that 'The standard of care of the patients on the psychiatric wing fell, in every respect, below the minimum acceptable from an ethical and humanitarian point of view.'[29]

The Commission concluded, by a narrow majority of 17 to 14, that the conditions of detention encountered by the applicant did indeed violate Article 3.[30] In reaching their respective conclusions, both the majority and dissenting minority referred to the CPT report, but drew different conclusions from it. Whereas the majority built on the views of the CPT and

---

[26] *Aydin v Turkey*, App No 23178/94, Comm Rep, 7 March 1996, para 183.

[27] *Aydin v Turkey*, Judgment of 27 September 1997, *RJD* 1997-VI, 1866, paras 49–50.

[28] It should be noted that the reversal of the burden of proof found in *Ribitsch v Austria* was not, to their thinking, relevant since the very fact of custody was unproven.

[29] Belgium 1, para 191.

[30] *Aerts v Belgium*, App No 25357/94, Comm Rep, 20 May 1997, paras 66–83, at 81–82.

concluded that conditions were inhuman and degrading, the minority focused on the fact that the report did not describe the conditions in these terms and took this as an indication that they fell short of breaching Article 3. These positions were canvassed again before the Court, which concluded by 7 votes to 2 that there had not been a breach of Article 3. The Court focused on the inability of the applicant to show that he had suffered any serious ill effects from his exposure to these admittedly unsatisfactory general conditions.[31] It did not consider whether the conditions in themselves give rise to a breach of Article 3 and therefore avoided having to translate the observations of the CPT into a finding under the ECHR.

In a sense, the judgment of the Court in *Aerts* indicates that there is still sufficient space between the work of the CPT and the ECHR for them not to come into conflict, even if they do come into contact. In focusing on the conclusions to be drawn from the CPT's use of language in its report, the Commission, arguably, lost sight of the need to determine the effects of the conditions on the applicant, rather than the nature of the conditions. It is the former rather than the latter which is at issue in the context of an individual application and the systemic issues are more appropriately left to the CPT. There is a certain sense of symmetry in concluding this section with the suggestion that the Court may recognize that there are issues which are generally best left to the CPT, given that it opened with the example of the CPT deferring to the ECHR's competence regarding expulsion and extradition cases.

Nevertheless, both the CPT and the ECHR work in a common field and from within a common organization and it remains true that the closer their understanding of the meaning of Article 3 of the ECHR, the less room there will be for such confusions and conflicts in future. The remainder of this chapter will, therefore, sketch out the basic lines of approach adopted by the Court and the CPT to Article 3.

2. THE NOTION OF TORTURE, INHUMAN OR DEGRADING TREATMENT OR PUNISHMENT

Although it is often said that the ECPT does not contain any new substantive norms, but merely introduces a new mechanism, it is sometimes forgotten that the ECHR itself does no more than set out a very basic prohibition. Neither instrument can be said to define what is meant by the prohibition of torture, inhuman or degrading treatment or punishment and so one must turn to the interpretive work of the organs established by them.

---

[31] *Aerts v Belgium*, Judgment, 30 July 1998, para 68.

(a) The CPT

It is beyond the scope of this chapter to consider the work of either body in detail and the approach of the CPT is considered elsewhere.[32] Significantly, the CPT does not describe forms of ill-treatment which, in its view, fall short of torture as being either inhuman or degrading but, rather, describes them as 'ill-treatment'.[33] This makes it difficult to translate all the CPT's findings into the language used by the Commission and Court and this could be a possible source of confusion. This section will, then, commence by giving a flavour of the approach adopted by the CPT in the context of physical ill-treatment of individuals before going on to set out in greater detail the principles which have guided the work of the Commission, in order that a comparison might be made and some general conclusions reached.

The approach of the CPT can be illustrated by referring to its reports on a selection of countries.[34]

(i) Turkey

In its first Public Statement on Turkey in 1992 the CPT was struck by the extremely high number of allegations of torture and other forms of ill-treatment by the police, including:

— suspension by the arms
— suspension by the wrists, which were fastened behind the victim (so-called 'Palestinian hanging')
— electric shocks to sensitive parts of the body (including the genitals)
— squeezing of the testicles
— beating of the soles of the feet (*falaka*)
— hosing with pressurized cold water
— incarceration for lengthy periods in very small and badly ventilated cells
— threats of torture or other serious forms of ill-treatment to the person detained or against others
— severe psychological humiliations

In the light of this, the CPT concluded that the practice of torture and other forms of severe ill-treatment of persons in police custody was widespread in Turkey, with regard both to ordinary criminal suspects and those held

---

[32] See Chapters Two, Four, and Five.
[33] See Evans and Morgan (1998).
[34] The following list is illustrative and does not purport to be a complete account of the instances of findings of torture or ill-treatment by the CPT.

under anti-terrorist provisions.[35] This view was subsequently reaffirmed in the second Public Statement in 1996.[36]

(ii) Spain

In its reports to the Spanish Government on visits to Spain in April 1991 and April and June 1994 the CPT noted that with regard to police and civil guard establishments the following forms of torture and severe ill-treatment were most commonly alleged:

— asphyxiation by the placing of a plastic bag over the head
— electric shocks usually applied to the genitals, mouth, and feet
— immersion of the head in water
— severe beating with truncheons while covered in a blanket
— striking of the head with a heavy book (usually a telephone directory)
— (more rarely) suspension from the wrists or feet
— threats of execution or serious injury to the detainee or others[37]

(iii) Cyprus

The report on visits to Cyprus in November 1992 also contain substantiated allegations describing in detail the same forms of severe ill-treatment inflicted in certain police stations, namely:

— suspension by the legs with the head just a few centimetres above the ground
— the application of electric shocks to various parts of the body (including the penis)
— the placing of a metal bucket on the head and striking it with blows with wooden sticks
— blows struck with truncheons or wooden clubs[38]

---

[35] Turkey PS 1, para 21.

[36] The CPT found 'clear evidence of the practice of torture and other forms of severe ill-treatment by the Turkish police' (ibid, para 2). The cases of seven persons (four women and three men) are related as being 'among the most flagrant examples of torture encountered by CPT delegations in Turkey. To focus only on their allegations of prolonged suspension by the arms, motor function and/or sensation in the upper limbs of all seven persons was found to be impaired—for most of them severely . . . Two of the persons examined had lost the use of both arms; these sequelae could prove irreversible' (ibid, para 3). Once again, the CPT found 'material evidence of resort to ill-treatment, in particular, an instrument adapted in a way which would facilitate the infliction of electric shocks and equipment which could be used to suspend a person by the arms' (ibid). The Turkish authorities are reproached for having 'failed to acknowledge the gravity of the situation' (ibid).

[37] Spain 1, para 19. This was reinforced by the CPT's subsequent visits. See Spain 2, paras 16–21 and Spain 3, paras 12–18.

[38] Cyprus 1, para 15. The Report adds that allegedly, 'the treatment described was inflicted late in the evening, during interrogations which lasted through the night. The officers who were said to have inflicted such treatment had their faces covered. The detainees were said, at a certain stage, to have had their heads covered by a kind of cloth bag and to have been surrounded by people who shouted threats and insults' (ibid, para 16). Several persons 'alleged

Certain persons also claimed to have been struck blows on the soles of the feet with a bar. One person claimed to have had a truncheon introduced into his anus.[39]

(b) The ECHR

As far as the ECHR organs are concerned, the distinction between torture and inhuman or degrading treatment is gradual but from the outset of their work they have found it difficult to mark the precise point of transition. The following sections trace the general approach adopted to this difficult and delicate task.

(i) Torture

As is well known, in *Ireland v UK* five interrogation techniques were called into question: hooding, forcing the person concerned to adopt a wall-standing 'stress position' in rooms where there was a continuous loud and hissing noise, food and drink being reduced to a minimum, and those who fell asleep being immediately woken up and obliged to continue to stand by the wall. The Commission had qualified them as constituting 'torture' on the grounds that their combined application affected the *sensoria* of the persons concerned and put them under severe mental and physical stress. The will to resist or not to give in could not, in such conditions, be formed with any degree of independence.[40] The Court defined torture as 'deliberate inhuman treatment causing very serious and cruel suffering' but concluded that these techniques fell short of this and constituted 'inhuman treatment'.[41]

It is doubtful whether the Court was aware of the dangers which had prompted the Commission to see in these techniques the practice of torture. Modern techniques of interrogation and manipulation no longer need directly to impair corporal integrity. Nevertheless, their effect on the person concerned may be equal to that of 'conventional' torture

---

that they had been hung from metal hooks in the ceiling' and the CPT delegation states that it saw the offices where the criminal investigation department conducted interrogations and there were in fact large metal hooks fixed to the ceiling as described. According to the Report, 'conflicting explanations were given by the police officers for the existence of the hooks' (ibid, para 17).

[39] It should be noted that when the CPT returned to Cyprus in 1996 it heard no allegations of torture or severe ill-treatment by the police directly from detainees, although some allegations continued, and the Committee noted a 'generally positive evolution'. See Cyprus 2, paras 10–13.

[40] *Ireland v UK*, Comm Rep, 25 January 1976, 19 *ECHRYb* 792.

[41] *Ireland v UK*, Judgment, 18 January 1978, Ser A No 25, paras 167–168.

methods.[42] The Commission attributed more importance than the Court to free will. It considered as torture both major interferences with corporal integrity and deprivation of will-power brought about by techniques which, although not directly affecting corporal integrity, nevertheless deprive a person of his will-power by causing severe mental and psychic disturbance. It is significant that these methods were meant to disorientate and deprive the persons concerned of the use of their senses. The Commission under-lined that Article 17(4) of the 1949 Geneva Convention III Relative to the Treatment of Prisoners of War prohibits all physical and mental torture employed to secure information.[43]

This suggests that torture does not necessarily require direct interference with corporal integrity, as the Court seemed to assume. In the *Greek* case the Commission had already considered the possibility of non-physical torture and expressed the view that forms of psychological pressure other than bodily assault which nevertheless created the state of anguish and stress fell under the notion of torture or ill-treatment.[44] Moreover, Article 1 of the UN Convention against Torture and Other Cruel, Inhuman or Degrading Treatment or Punishment expressly extends the term 'torture' to means of psychological pressure.[45]

The Court has been slow to follow the lead of the Commission in con-cluding that torture has occurred but it has now done so in a series of cases involving Turkey, including: severe ill-treatment and rape in *Aydin v Turkey*[46] and 'Palestinian Hanging', in *Aksoy v Turkey*.[47] In *Yağiz v Turkey* the Commission unanimously considered *falaka* to be an act of torture but the Court found that it could not deal with the merits of the case because the ill-treatment complained of had taken place before Turkey had recognized the Court's compulsory jurisdiction.[48] In *Sur v Turkey* the Commission also considered that the applicant had been tortured but the case did

---

[42] Cf the dissenting opinions of Judges Evrigenis and Matscher, ibid, 136, 139; see also O'Boyle, M (1977) 'Torture and Emergency Powers under the European Convention on Human Rights: *Ireland v UK*', 71 *AJIL* 674; Spjut, RJ (1979) 'Torture under the European Convention on Human Rights', 73 *AJIL* 267; Frowein, JA (1990) 'Feiheit von Folter oder grausamer, unmenschlicher oder erniedrigender Behandlung und Strafe nach der Europäi-schen, Menschenrechtskonvention' in Matscher, F (ed), *Folterverbot sowie Religions- und Gewissensfreiheit im Rechtsvergleich*, 69.

[43] *Ireland v UK*, Comm Rep, 25 January 1976, Ser B No 23-I; 19 *ECHRYb* 792.

[44] *Denmark, Norway, Sweden and Netherlands v Greece (Greek* case), App Nos 3321/67, 3322/67, 3344/67, Comm Rep, *12 ECHRYb* 461.

[45] The Commission cited this provision verbatim in *Aydin v Turkey*, App No 23178/94, Comm Rep, 7 March 1996, para 187.

[46] *Aydin v Turkey*, Judgment of 25 September 1997, *RJD* 1997-VI, 1866, paras 80–87.

[47] *Aksoy v Turkey*, Judgment of 18 December 1996, *RJD* 1996-VI, 2260, paras 58–64. The Applicant had also claimed that he had been subjected to electric shocks (made worse by his being doused with water), beatings, slapping, and verbal abuse but the Court took the view that it was unnecessary to consider whether these too amounted to torture, given its findings regarding 'Palestinian Hanging'.

[48] *Yağiz v Turkey*, App No 19092/91, Comm Rep, 16 May 1993; Judgment of 7 August 1996, *RJD* 1996-III, 966.

not have to be decided by the Court as the parties reached a friendly settlement.[49]

Further evidence of the difficulty in determining which side of the line a form of conduct falls is provided by *Tekin v Turkey*. The Commission found it established that the applicant had been 'kept in a cold and dark cell, blindfolded and treated in a way which left wounds and bruises on his body in connection with his interrogation' and that he had complained of torture and ill-treatment which had not been followed up by the authorities.[50] The Commission concluded that he had been subjected to 'at least inhuman and degrading treatment'.[51] In the light of this sign of hesitation it is, perhaps, not surprising that the Court restricted itself to a finding of 'inhuman and degrading treatment', though three of the nine members of the Court felt that even this had not been proved.[52]

(ii) Inhuman treatment

The origins of our understanding of the meaning of 'inhuman treatment' lie in the *Greek* case, in which the Commission said that torture always embraced inhuman and degrading treatment and that inhuman treatment always embraced degrading treatment. It then defined 'inhuman treatment' as being 'at least such treatment as deliberately causes severe suffering, mental or physical, which, in the particular situation, is unjustifiable'.[53] In *Ireland v UK* the Commission went back on this, noting that the term 'unjustifiable' had given rise to some misunderstanding and, in particular, that it did not mean that 'inhuman treatment' could be justified in some circumstances.[54]

When the Court considered the meaning of 'inhuman and degrading' in *Ireland v UK*—the first occasion it was called on to do so—it emphasized

---

[49] *Sur v Turkey*, Judgment of 3 October 1997, *RJD* 1997-VI, 2034.

[50] *Tekin v Turkey*, App No 22496/93, Comm Rep, 17 April 1997, para 214.

[51] Ibid, para 215.   [52] *Tekin v Turkey*, Judgment of 9 June 1998, paras 48–54.

[53] *Greek* case, App Nos 3321/67, 3322/67, 3344/67, Comm Rep, 12 *ECHRYb* 186.

[54] Both Article 15 of the ECHR and Common Article 3 of the Geneva Conventions of 1949 made it clear that no limitation of the prohibition of inhuman treatment was possible, even in emergency or war situations. There existed, therefore, no justification whatsoever for acts of ill-treatment. See *Ireland v UK*, Comm Rep, 25 January 1996, 19 *ECHRYb* 750 ff. However, in *Herczegfalvy v Austria*, Judgment of 24 September 1992, Ser A No 244, the Court, whilst confirming that the treatment of mental patients is subject to control under Article 3, concluded that no violation had occurred even though the applicant had for a certain time been attached with handcuffs to a security bed. This measure was considered to be worrying, but in the Commission's opinion there was not sufficient evidence to disprove the Government's argument that medical necessity justified the treatment at issue. This rather suggests that, in some cases where Article 3 is used, 'justificatory' arguments are not altogether out of the question, albeit in subtle guises. Indeed, it is implicit in decisions such as *Hurtado v Switzerland*, App No 17549/90, Comm Rep, 8 July 1993, that the use of a degree of force may be necessary when effecting an arrest which in other circumstances could have been considered inhuman or degrading. This could easily be seen as a 'justification' for treatment in breach of Article 3. This application resulted in a friendly settlement (see Ser A No 280, 5). Cf also App No 19181/91, Comm Dec, 30 August 1994.

that a certain minimum level of severity had to be attained if a treatment
was to fall within the scope of Article 3 and that the assessment of this
minimum was, in the nature of things, relative, depending on all the circumstances of a given case, in particular the duration of the treatment and
its physical or mental effects as well as, in some cases, the sex, age, and state
of health of the victim.[55] This forms the basis of a formula which is still routinely used and clearly grants great flexibility to the Court in determining
what amounts to a violation.

As has already been mentioned, the Court found the so-called five techniques (referred to above) to constitute inhuman treatment because they
caused intense physical and mental suffering and also led to acute psychiatric disturbance during interrogation[56] whereas, for the Commission, this
would have been sufficient to ground a finding of torture.[57] However, both
the Commission and the Court held in the same case that the practice
employed in certain interrogation centres of subjecting the detainees to violence which resulted in intense suffering and occasionally in substantial
physical injury fell into the category of inhuman treatment.[58] In the inter-
state case of *Cyprus v Turkey*, the Commission considered that rape, physical force resulting in injuries, as well as deprivation of food, drink, and
medical care amounted to inhuman treatment.[59] Following *Aydin v Turkey*,
the rape, at least, would now seem to amount to torture.[60] In *Menteş v
Turkey* the Commission was of the view that a raid by the Turkish army on
a village in south-east Turkey amounted to inhuman and degrading treatment within the meaning of Article 3 but the Court saw in this a violation
of Article 8 of the ECHR (right to respect for home and family life).[61] In
Selçuk & Asker v Turkey, however, both Commission and Court found that
the manner in which the applicants' homes and belongings were destroyed
amounted to inhuman treatment.[62]

---

[55] *Ireland v UK*, Judgment of 18 January 1978, Ser A No 25, para 162.

[56] Ibid, para 167.

[57] But note that the Commission underlined that the five techniques in question violated
Article 3 only when used in combination. When measures such as restriction of sleep or of
food were judged separately, the findings always depended on the circumstances of each case
(*Ireland v UK*, Comm Rep, 19 *ECHRYb* 792–794).

[58] *Ireland v UK*, Judgment of 25 January 1998, Ser A No 25, para 174. Cf *Greek* case, Comm
Rep, 12 *ECHRYb* 501, where it took the view that light beatings did not attain the threshold
level of Article 3. See also *Kamma v The Netherlands*, App No 4771/71, Comm Dec, 21 July
1972, 15 *ECHRYb* 434, where applying pressure on a suspect by suggesting that he would not
be allowed to leave the police station before he had given full information was not considered
to be a violation of Article 3.

[59] *Cyprus v Turkey*, App Nos 6790/71 and 6950/75, Comm Rep, 10 July 1976.

[60] See above, text to Note 27.

[61] *Menteş v Turkey*, App No 23186/94, Comm Rep, 7 March 1996; Judgment of 28 November 1997, *RJD* 1997-VIII, 2689. Cf also the similar case of *Gündem v Turkey*, App No 22275/93,
Comm Rep, 3 September 1996; Judgment, 25 March 1998, in which both the Commission and
the Court considered that a violation of Article 3 was not proven.

[62] *Selçuk & Asker v Turkey*, Judgment of 24 April 1998.

(iii) Degrading treatment or punishment

'Degrading treatment or punishment' is the weakest form of Article 3 violation. Nevertheless, a certain threshold must be reached and it must be distinguished from forms and degrees of violence which may be condemned on moral grounds, or may even amount to an offence under domestic law, but which nevertheless do not attain a sufficient level of severity to constitute degrading treatment in the sense of the Convention. This distinction is illustrated by the *Ireland v UK* case. As has already been mentioned, the 'five interrogation techniques' were considered to be degrading since they were such as to arouse in their victims feelings of fear, anguish, and inferiority capable of humiliating and debasing them and possibly breaking their physical or moral resistance.[63]

Another issue in that case concerned civilian internees who were required, under the supervision of military police, to carry out strenuous physical exercises, including sitting on the floor with the feet outstretched and the knees straight and the arms raised high above their head or kneeling on the floor with head bent down so that the forehead touched the floor and the hands clasped behind their back at waist level. Although it was not established that force was used on those who could not do these tasks, it was clear that they were under a form of compulsion and that even older persons were required to participate. Despite finding that these exercises caused considerable strain and hardship, in particular for elderly persons and those in poor physical condition, the Commission concluded that although the prisoners might feel that such treatment was designed to oppress and degrade them, it was not sufficiently serious as to amount to inhuman or degrading treatment,[64] an opinion shared by the Court.[65]

A further example of the necessity—and difficulty—of determining which side of the line a particular example of a form of treatment capable of giving rise to a violation of Article 3 lies relates to corporal punishment. Judicial corporal punishment applied by police officers was considered degrading within the meaning of the Convention by both the Commission and Court in *Tyrer v UK*.[66] This was subsequently extended to corporal punishment in schools but in *Costello-Roberts v UK* the Court marked the place where forms of corporal punishment in school ceased to fall within the Article 3 concept of 'degrading treatment' when it concluded that three 'whacks' with a rubber-soled gym shoe on the buttocks of a pupil wearing shorts was not sufficiently serious to constitute a violation.[67] Clearly, it is

---

[63] Cf *Ireland v UK*, Judgment of 18 January 1978, Ser A No 25, para 167.

[64] *Ireland v UK*, Comm Rep, 25 January 1976, 19 *ECHRYb* 928 ff.

[65] *Ireland v UK*, Judgment of 18 January 1978, Ser A No 125, para 181.

[66] *Tyrer v UK*, Comm Rep, 14 December 1976; Judgment of 25 April 1978, Ser A No 26. The Court's decision had been taken with 6 votes against one; see the dissenting opinion of Sir Gerald Fitzmaurice, p 22 *et seq.*

[67] *Costello-Roberts v UK*, Judgment of 25 March 1993, Ser A No 247-C, paras 29–32.

necessary to establish the 'entry threshold' into Article 3 by considering what constitutes degrading treatment. Given the nature of the CPT's work, it is unlikely to be faced with many of the *de minimis* problems related to physical ill-treatment considered above.

3. CONCLUSIONS

Comparing the approaches adopted in the findings of the CPT to the classification of what constitutes torture, inhuman, or degrading treatment with the case law of the ECHR organs relating to physical ill-treatment, it seems safe to conclude that no particular discrepancies can be found. What is striking, however, is the fact that CPT reports reveal numerous allegations of severe ill-treatment in places of detention, whilst there are relatively few applications brought under the ECHR in which such alleged violations of Article 3 are presented or, even more significantly, in which Article 3 has been successfully invoked. This may well be due to the fact that Article 26 of the ECHR requires that an individual applicant must have exhausted all domestic remedies before the application can be declared admissible. Some of the alleged victims will obtain reparation on the domestic level but prisoners will often not have either the courage and perseverance or the financial or intellectual capacity to complain effectively about their treatment following their arrest.[68] It is also often quite difficult to furnish the necessary objective evidence in such cases.[69]

Whatever the reasons, this fact alone suggests that the ECPT is a necessary and most effective supplement to the human rights protection afforded by the ECHR. Since the CPT does not decide on whether violations of Article 3 of the ECHR have occurred, but acts with a view to preventing them from occurring, it is not bound by the ECHR organs' interpretations of it. Therefore, it is not vital for its assessment of the situation of those in places of detention to distinguish clearly between situations that might amount to either torture or to less serious but still serious enough violations that take the form of ill- or degrading treatment. Of course, the case law of the Court serves as a point of reference for the CPT. On the other hand, the factual findings of the CPT can serve as evidential material in the

---

[68] Sometimes applicants or their counsel are, in violation of Article 25 of the ECHR, intimidated by domestic authorities when they submit a case to the Strasbourg organs: see *Akdivar v Turkey,* Judgment of 16 September 1996, *RJD* 1996-IV, 1192; *Kurt v Turkey,* Comm Rep, 10 July 1997, Judgment of 25 March 1998; *Assenov v Bulgaria,* App No 24760/94, Comm Rep, 10 July 1997, 167–178, Judgment of 28 October 1998.

[69] Cf *Klaas v Germany,* Judgment of 22 September 1993, Ser A No 269, paras 30–31 in which the Court, contrary to the opinion of the Commission, agreed with the findings of the domestic courts, that despite the applicant's injuries there was insufficient evidence that the police used excessive force in the course of her arrest.

proceedings before the Court. However, it should be stressed that, to date, CPT findings, although referred to, have not been a decisive element for the Court when determining whether a violation of Article 3 of the ECHR has occurred.

Proceedings under the ECHR can lead to the finding of a violation. In such cases the judgments handed down by the Court have not indicated to the respondent states concrete measures of reparation and means of preventing future violations.[70] Rather, they are limited to affording just satisfaction under Article 50 of the ECHR. Nevertheless, the respondent state as well as any other state resorting to similar practices that are found to be in violation of the ECHR is obliged under Article 53 of the ECHR 'to abide by the decision of the Court'. The CPT, on the other hand, does not give any 'judgments' but formulates recommendations which are not binding on the Contracting States. However, a state which does not take these recommendations seriously into account leaves itself open to the risk of being accused by way of an interstate or individual application under the ECHR of violating Article 3 of the ECHR or of being pilloried by a public statement under Article 10(2) of the ECPT. Therefore, as well as having their own individual potency, both instruments can combine to provide enhanced effect for the protection of detained persons against all forms of ill-treatment both on a procedural and a normative level.

Above all else, the development of the ECHR case law shows that terms such as 'torture', 'inhuman', and 'degrading' cannot be interpreted in a static manner, but have to be understood and interpreted in the light of the existing standards in European public order. Nevertheless, it is clear that perceptions do not only shift over time, but that there can exist within the ECHR mechanisms themselves significant variations of opinion even at the same point in time. What this illustrates is that Article 3 is ever-changing and that such developments can often arise out of the creative tension between competing understandings of what the Article 3 prohibition entails. There is no reason why the work of the CPT should not be seen in the same light; as a helpful, constructive contribution to an ongoing process of debate and development.

REFERENCES

Evans, MD and Morgan, R (1992) 'The ECPT: Operational Practice', 41 *ICLQ* 590
Evans, MD and Morgan, R (1994) 'The European Torture Committee: Membership Issues', 5 *EJIL* 249
Evans, MD and Morgan, R (1997) 'The ECPT 1992–1997', 46 *ICLQ* 663

[70] eg *Hauschildt v Denmark*, Judgment of 24 May 1989, Ser A No 154, para 54.

Evans, MD and Morgan, R (1998) *Preventing Torture* (Oxford: Clarendon Press)

Frowein, JA (1990) 'Feiheit von Folter oder grausamer, unmenschlicher oder erniedrigender Behandlung und Strafe nach der Europäischen, Menschenrechtskonvention' in Matscher, F (ed) *Folterverbot sowie Religions- und Gewissensfreiheit im Rechtsvergleich*, 69

Machacek, R (1993) 'Supranationaler Schutz vor Folter und Unmenschlicher Behandlung', *Journal für Rechtspolitik* 247

Matscher, F (ed) (1993) *Folterverbot sowie Religions- und Gewissensfreiheit im Rechtsvergleich*

Murdoch, J (1994) 'The Work of the Council of Europe's Torture Committee', 5 *EJIL* 220

Murdoch, J (1996) 'The ECPT', 21 *ELRev* 130

O'Boyle, M (1977) 'Torture and Emergency Powers under the European Convention on Human Rights: *Ireland v the United Kingdom*', 71 *AJIL* 674

Spjut, RJ (1979) 'Torture under the European Convention on Human Rights', 73 *AJIL* 267

4

CPT Standards within the Context of the Council of Europe

JIM MURDOCH

1. INTRODUCTION

Any assessment of criminal justice involves more than scrutiny of efficiency and effectiveness. At the close of a century in which human dignity and physical integrity have scarcely been adequately respected, there is at least now an acceptance that the exercise of state authority must be balanced with respect for fundamental values. Symbolism is now important. 'Criminal justice ... is concerned with social order not exclusively or even primarily in an instrumental, straightforwardly empirical sense, but rather with social order in a symbolic sense: with a society's sense of itself as a cohesive, viable, and ethical entity.'[1] Such values have been accorded expression through judicial concerns with 'fair trial' to help counterbalance the discretion inherent in the criminal justice process and through concern for the physical and mental well-being of detainees. Enhanced procedural fairness has been followed by the development of administrative and legal controls seeking to provide complaints and inspection machinery in the closed worlds of places of detention. But such developments have not occurred without some tension between values and ends. Exclusionary rules of evidence may result in a particular case in the 'guilty' walking free but may also in the long term discourage inappropriate police interrogation practices. There can also be debate over means. If rights now do not stop at the prison gate, is protection better achieved through inspection and control or through the courts?

Structural shortcomings inherent in judicial processes prevent further advances in safeguarding individual rights in particular areas,[2] and a growing awareness of the limits of traditional legal intervention has prompted introduction of new machinery. Thus the European Convention for the Prevention of Torture and Inhuman and Degrading Treatment or

---

[1] Lacey, N (1995) *Criminal Justice* (Oxford: Oxford University Press), 28.

[2] For discussion of the efficacy of enforcement mechanisms, see Dimitrijevi (1993) 'The Monitoring of Human Rights and the Prevention of Human Rights Violations through Reporting Procedures' in Bloed, A, Leicht, L, Nowak, M and Rosas, A (eds) *Monitoring Human Rights in Europe* (Dordrecht: Martinus Nijhoff), 1–24.

Punishment recognizes that the protection of persons deprived of their
liberty often may be more effectively served by directing attention 'more
to the root causes of human rights violations than just to seek redress for
the symptoms'.[3] This again emphasizes the tension between means and
ends. In advancing concern for detainees the CPT has embarked upon a
process which may well have a substantial impact not only upon domestic
legal systems and administrative practices but also upon existing European
standards promoted through other Council of Europe initiatives. The birth
of a new European institution has not prompted conflict as yet: but the new-
comer is certainly stealing increasing amounts of the limelight normally
reserved for its siblings.

Some rivalry is inevitable, not only on account of the overlap with other
initiatives in the fields of criminal justice, prison detention, and mental
health. Two key decisions have ensured that the Torture Convention
will have a higher profile than perhaps originally envisaged: first, the decision of the framers of the treaty to insert a provision into the Convention
permitting states to authorize (or 'request') publication of the reports
and responses; and second, that of the CPT to develop its own set of standards. These two decisions themselves reflect fundamental values and need
not be considered inappropriate because symbolism also plays a part here—
open government on the one hand,[4] and objectivity and fairness on the
other.[5] However, their combined practical effect has been to pose a more
serious challenge to other existing European norms than needed to have
been the case. While the development of the CPT's 'measuring rods' was
perceived to be of importance for its programme of visits and subsequent
reports to countries, the general willingness of states to authorize publication of country reports has resulted in this 'corpus of standards' achieving
a general importance perhaps not contemplated. It may now be possible to
speak of the gradual emergence of a new European prison code of practice
and of a common European criminal procedure, in each case on account of
the public exercise of the quasi-legislative authority the CPT has assumed.
In turn, exercise of this power raises several questions as to the methods of
standard setting selected, the extent to which CPT standards compare with
existing European norms (and in particular with the European Prison Rules

---

[3] Nowak, M (1989) 'The European Convention on Human Rights and its Control System',
7 *NQHR* 98, 104.
[4] The first reports published were those in relation to Austria and Denmark. The Austrian
Government requested publication to try to correct 'leaks' which had appeared in the press,
while the Danish tradition of open government certainly explains the decision to authorize
release of this report.
[5] The actual justification given for the development of a 'corpus of standards' was the CPT's
perception that existing European and international instruments and case law often lacked
clear guidance when applied to specific situations. See Gen Rep 1, paras 95–96.

and with the ECHR), and whether emerging CPT standards are likely to have any long-term impact upon other Council of Europe initiatives.

CPT standard setting is not without difficulty: first as regards the manner used, and second in respect of the standards set. Promulgation occurs either through codified statement found in general reports or through comments in country reports which give rise to a 'case-law'-style accumulation of precedent (although the difference may not be immediately apparent since reports now generally follow a standardized 'template' applied as a matter of course in the writing of country reports). A 'codified' approach in the form of a generalized statement of concerns published in a general report is the favoured option. Examples involve the statements found in the second report in 1992 concerning police custody and prison conditions,[6] health care in prisons in the 1993 report,[7] and deprivation of liberty of immigration detainees in the 1997 report.[8] These provide consistent and comprehensive checklists of CPT concerns in particular aspects of criminal justice, penal or mental health policy. Each involves the accumulation through time of multi-disciplinary insights, expertise, and deliberation; but since these consolidated statements appear on an irregular basis and concern only particular aspects of detention policies, large tracts of territory remain uncharted and may remain so for several years. In the circumstances, attention turns from yearly general reports to the welter of country reports which provide some insight into CPT expectations during visits. This is 'case law' rather than 'legislation'.

Recommendations in country reports and 'codified' statements in general reports in turn reflect the development of agenda concerns. Police detention, prison, and mental health hospital conditions were obvious starting points for the CPT in its work. Later reports also contained discussion of immigration control detention, while other aspects of deprivation of liberty such as military and juvenile detention have received but scant attention as yet. There may exist a self-evident standard readily applied, or a gradual working-out of a standard through time as the Committee wrestles with a particular problem from a multi-disciplinary approach, particularly if there is little commonality of approach within Europe. Some of the intellectual effort required in such an exercise is reflected in country reports which chart the movement towards reaching agreement in the Committee as to where the boundary between the generally acceptable and the generally unacceptable lies. The 1992 general report, for example, provided dimensions for police cells as a 'rough guideline' in establishing a 'desirable level rather than a minimum standard'.[9] Only through time have these taken on

---

[6] Gen Rep 2, paras 36–59.   [7] Gen Rep 3, paras 30–77.   [8] Gen Rep 7, paras 24–35.
[9] Gen Rep 2, para 43 (prison cells for single occupancy for more than a few hours).

greater certainty as CPT expectations were clarified in the preparation of published country reports.[10] Standard setting can thus involve a lengthy process of incremental decision making. Yet this is seemingly taking place with little reference to existing standards and norms.

2. COMPATIBILITY OF CPT STANDARDS WITH EXISTING COUNCIL OF EUROPE INITIATIVES

(a) The European Prison Rules and CPT standards

A blueprint for prison services is provided by the European Prison Rules.[11] These standards purport to be 'essential to human conditions and positive treatment in modern and progressive systems' and are designed to 'serve as a stimulus to prison administrations' to further 'good contemporary principles of purpose and equity'.[12] Parts I and IV of the Rules cover certain basic principles and treatment objectives, while Part II deals with management and material conditions of detention. A flavour of the Rules is readily obtained from the principles enunciated. Prisoners must be accommodated in material and moral terms which ensure respect for their dignity and accorded treatment which is non-discriminatory, which recognizes religious beliefs, and which sustains health and self-respect.[13] General treatment objectives should aim to minimize the detrimental effects of incarceration through encouraging family contact, the development of skills, and the provision of recreational and leisure opportunities.[14] Since accommodation affects the morale of inmates and staff alike and the attainment of treatment objectives,[15] it must meet 'the requirements of health and hygiene, due regard being paid to climatic conditions' and offer 'a reasonable amount of space, lighting, heating and ventilation'.[16] Sanitary arrangements should permit inmates 'to comply with the needs of nature where necessary and in clean and decent conditions',[17] while personal hygiene needs require baths or showers to be available 'as frequently as necessary . . . according to season and geographical region, but at least once per week'.[18] All of this is 'designed to reflect a modern philosophy of treatment', but one which has jettisoned rehabilitation in favour of humane containment or 'positive custody'.[19] These principles are designed to

---

[10] Discussed by Evans and Morgan (1998) and Chapter Two above.
[11] Council of Ministers, Recommendation R (87) 3, adopted 12 February 1987, replacing Resolution (73) 5 on the Standard Minimum Rules for the Treatment of Prisoners.
[12] Preamble, clauses a–c.
[13] Rules 1–3.   [14] Rules 65–66, 71–86.
[15] Explanatory Memorandum, para 39.
[16] Rule 15.   [17] Rule 17.   [18] Rule 18.
[19] Cf Hudson, B (1987) *Justice Through Punishment* (Basingstoke: Macmillan), 19, 165 *et seq.*

encourage continual improvement through internal consideration. The Rules have no binding force.[20]

Substantial overlap between CPT standards and the Rules is to be expected. Many examples exist of convergence between 'basic principles' found in the Rules and the approach of the CPT, but with the important proviso that CPT standards—both in the form of consolidated pronouncements in annual general reports, and through individual country reports— tend to be more specific. Thus the CPT expects that the provision of a beneficial regime should involve 'purposeful activities of a varied nature' for at least 'eight hours or more outside their cells' in the form of group association activities, education, sport, work with vocational value.[21] The emphasis upon supervision of penal institutions by inspectorates and boards of visitors in the Rules[22] is mirrored in CPT recommendations.[23] Further parallels exist, and again CPT expectations are more precise. Part II of the European Prison Rules deals with the management of prison systems and considers such matters as reception, accommodation and food, personal hygiene, medical services, and general discipline. The Rules provide that medical services should be 'organised in close relation with the general health administration of the community or nation',[24] with the examination of prisoners 'as soon as possible upon admission and thereafter as necessary'.[25] The CPT's own policy statement on medical services in prisons in the third general report in contrast spells out detailed guidelines reflecting the overriding principle that 'prisoners are entitled to the same level of medical care as persons living in the community at large'. Justification for this detailed checklist comes from the recognition of the contribution health care can make in combating any infliction of ill-treatment and in contributing in a positive way to the quality of life within places of detention: inadequate care can 'lead rapidly to situations falling within the scope of the term "inhuman and degrading treatment"'.[26] It also reflects the contribution of medically-qualified members to the work of the CPT. These standards are examples of concrete 'measuring rods' which allow objectivity in assessment of actual conditions

---

[20] Cf Trechsel, S (1990) Report on 'Human Rights of Persons Deprived of their Liberty', 7th International Colloquy on the ECHR, doc H/Coll (90) 3, 20.

[21] This formulation first appears in early country reports (eg Switzerland 1, para 30; Finland 1, para 96) and continues to feature as a specific recommendation (eg in reports to Central and Eastern European countries as in Slovakia 1).

[22] Rules 4–5.

[23] Again, this is a recurrent theme from earliest reports onwards: eg, Austria 1, para 87 (independent visiting body would improve standards in police gaols); Denmark 1, para 59 (restrictions on access by board of visitors 'surprising'); and para 104 (need for independent body to deal with complaints). It continues to concern the CPT in second periodic visits, and indeed the CPT may find it appropriate to make comments on proposals made and action taken since its first visit: eg Malta 2, para 79 (extension of terms of office for prison visitors recommended).

[24] Rule 26(1).   [25] Rule 29.   [26] Gen Rep 3, paras 30 and 31.

and whose underlying rationale is either explicitly stated or is implicitly self-evident.

On the other hand, the CPT has found it more difficult to develop consistency in approach in certain aspects of material conditions even though physical conditions of detention lie at the heart of any assessment of the treatment of inmates. Here, possibly on account of perceived difficulties in establishing a common line on such matters as acceptable prison cell size[27] or in running the risk of exceeding its mandate by exhorting states to consider reducing the prison population and thus deal with the problems that overcrowding brings,[28] there has been less willingness to insist on concrete expectations and more apparent flexibility in standard setting. It is more difficult for states to rebuild prison cells so as to meet CPT standards as to size; there is more of a challenge in insisting that slogans such as 'prison works', however politically attractive in the long term, lead to unacceptable conditions through cramming prisoners into cells or dormitories. Further, the CPT is probably trying to avoid impinging on policy or resource allocation issues to make certain it retains the necessary credibility to ensure the continuation of its 'dialogue' with states, particularly in countries where penal policy has a strong party political content. In contrast, it may be easier for prison services to regulate regime activities; and more realistic to expect states to improve hygiene standards and sanitation arrangements. If this is understandable, it does not help in promoting domestic application of the Committee's expectations. Local reliance upon CPT standards is hampered by lack of clarity. One example is found in the Scottish Prison Complaints Commission Report for 1996. A question had arisen as to whether a cell of seven square metres should be used to hold two prisoners, one of whom had been diagnosed as having the Hepatitis C virus. Domestic prison rules required cells to be of an 'adequate size', but no guidance as to what this meant was provided. The Complaints Commissioner referred to the views expressed in the CPT's report to Ireland that a cell of nine square metres was 'cramped accommodation for two', and suggested that in the circumstances the CPT would be 'less than impressed' with the size of these Scottish cells.[29] The lack of clear guidance from the CPT itself perhaps helps explain the rejection of the recommendation, a deficiency which is in con-

---

[27] See Chapter Two, pp 57–8.

[28] The CPT has begun to discuss the issue of overcrowding by commenting in reports on second periodic visits to increases in prison populations, and there now appears to be greater willingness to raise questions of judicial and executive policies which result in a deprivation of liberty: eg UK 2, para 79 (policies limiting prison population 'at manageable level' have proved successful elsewhere in Europe).

[29] Scottish Prison Complaints Commission (1997) *Report for 1996*, Cm 3688, para 2.10. The recommendation that cells of this size should only be used for one prisoner was rejected by the chief executive of the prison service since no alternative was available other than to place two prisoners in the same cell. It should perhaps be commented that the Complaints Commissioner involved has himself served as an expert on CPT delegations.

trast to the provision of the 'rough guideline' as to a 'desirable level' (rather than any 'minimum standard') for prison cell accommodation.[30]

How then to assess the work of the CPT in terms of its potential impact upon the Prison Rules? CPT standard setting overcomes two fundamental weaknesses of the European Prison Rules. First, the Rules are merely 'to provide realistic basic criteria' for administrators and inspectors to 'make valid judgments of performance and measure progress towards higher standards'[31] and thus no objective scrutiny by an external and independent agency is involved. Second, precision is rarely promoted through regular use of open language such as 'adequate', 'as far as possible', 'desirable', and the like, thus further weakening any normative value.[32] There was an opportunity for the CPT at the outset of its work to embark upon external peer review of domestic compliance with the Rules and thus to 'flesh out' the interpretation of the Rules, but the CPT deliberately chose the alternative path of developing an entirely new set of standards rather than annotating the Rules by spelling out what was meant by words such as 'desirable' or 'adequate' in particular contexts. This approach would have allowed the Rules to have been used to provide a moral and persuasive foundation upon which to build any CPT 'corpus of standards' (at least in relation to prisons) since the CPT would have been provided with a ready-made agenda of concerns and general principles which states had already accepted. Anchoring CPT standards to these Rules could have helped ensure state co-operation and would have helped enhance CPT recommendations by giving them greater legitimacy. If CPT concerns do indeed mirror those found in the Rules, greater citation in aid of the authority of the European Prison Rules would have conferred added weight upon general policy statements. Particular recommendations would have been perceived as the disinterested *interpretation* of an existing instrument in the drafting of which states had enjoyed some degree of involvement, rather than the development *ab initio* of what is projected as a completely new body of principles and practices by a body operating behind closed doors.

To be sure, references to the Rules do exist in CPT country reports, but these involve selective use of the more narrowly-drawn Rules. Early

---

[30] Gen Rep 2, para 43.

[31] Preamble, clause d, Recommendation No (87) 3, Appendix.

[32] Trechsel (1990), 21–23, places the Rules into four categories: first, vague formulations (in particular, when the principle is qualified by the phrase 'as far as possible'); second, evaluative formulations (when there is to be found a qualification such as 'normal', 'suitable', 'adequate', 'desirable', etc); third, 'references to the conflict of objectives inherent in the execution of custodial sentences' (when reference is made to institutional interests in efficient administration, security, and even financial efficiency); and finally, formulations framed in precise terms (eg the requirements of a minimum of one hour's open-air exercise per day and of one bath or shower per week), often though on the most trivial issues, for 'the more important a matter, the greater its complexity'.

reports, for example, contained citation of Rules referring to the requirement of at least one bath or shower per week,[33] the medical examination of prisoners upon admission,[34] the provision of written information on prison regulations,[35] promotion of contacts with family and friends,[36] use of instruments of physical restraint,[37] and one hour's daily exercise in the open air.[38] Later reports also contain sporadic reference to Rules such as to the carrying of firearms by officers who are in direct control of prisoners.[39] On limited occasions the CPT may also make a comment on the general application of the Rules, for example in urging full compliance in the drafting of a state's own prison rules where domestic standards appear not to meet these international criteria,[40] or in welcoming attempts by states to reflect European Prison Rules' standards in new local provisions.[41] But the most striking feature of CPT reports is that the Rules are virtually ignored.

What also seems not to have been considered by the CPT is the effect of this new body of standards upon the future vitality of the European Prison Rules themselves. Gradually (for the development of this new 'corpus' is essentially an incremental process) the Rules are being superseded by 'enhanced' CPT-promulgated standards. The internal reflection which the European Prison Rules is designed to achieve is being replaced by external assessment of compliance with CPT standards.[42] In time, the Rules will disappear below the horizon, eclipsed by the CPT's 'measuring rods' which have the advantages of clarity and consistency. It will be a matter of congratulation rather than concern that more effective human rights machinery will have been achieved, but the passing of the Rules into history will have occurred ostensibly by accident and without the likelihood of even an obituary. In this vital respect, then, CPT standard setting is likely to have a significant impact. The death knell may be the appearance of a comprehensive and codified statement of standards promulgated by the Committee at some future date, or it may already be sounding simply through the accumulation of reports containing additional or more detailed CPT expectations.

---

[33] eg UK 1, para 74 (Rule 19).   [34] eg Austria 1, para 83 (Rule 29).
[35] eg Sweden 1, para 83 (Rule 41).   [36] Germany 1, para 168 (Rules 43(1) and 65).
[37] Spain 1, para 98 (Rule 5).
[38] Rule 86: eg Austria 1, para 78; Malta 1, para 45; Switzerland 1, paras 22–23. The principle is still causing difficulties in certain country visits: eg UK 3, para 94.
[39] Portugal 2, para 149 (Rule 63(3)).   [40] San Marino 1, para 49.
[41] UK 3, para 77 (incorporation of elements of the EPR in 'Prison Service Operating Standards'). State responses may also accept the validity of a recommendation based upon the EPR: eg Germany 1 R 1, 36.
[42] As discussed above at Note 29, in Scotland the Prison Ombudsman has recently made explicit reference to the failure of the Scottish Prison Service to adhere to CPT standards. It should be noted that the Ombudsman has acted on a number of occasions as an expert member on CPT delegations to other states.

(b) The European Convention on Human Rights and CPT standard setting

The limits inherent in the European Convention on Human Rights provide substantial barriers to its use as an effective means for promoting the rights of persons deprived of their liberty. These include often low levels of awareness amongst individuals and legal advisers of such international remedies; unwillingness to make use of such procedures; technical compliance with admissibility requirements such as exhaustion of domestic remedies and satisfaction of standing as a 'victim' of an alleged violation; and over-lengthy and costly machinery.[43] These also justify the need for an approach such as that adopted by the ECPT in establishing a Committee which can operate free from the dead weight of legal procedures. Further, jurisprudence often recognizes an element of state discretion—a 'margin of appreciation'—when determining the minimum level of state responsibilities under the Convention, and there are limits to judicial competency in shaping any relief which essentially seeks to direct state resource allocation. Comparison of substantive CPT standards with those established by the Commission and Court through case interpretation is likely to be more favourable since prevention will require a more purposeful approach.[44]

Some clashes between Strasbourg case law and CPT standards appear inevitable despite attempts by the drafters of the Torture Convention to minimize any potential for conflict. Some of these attempts concern form rather than substance. The Torture Convention provides that any domestic or international law which provides greater protection for an individual is not prejudiced, and, in particular, that the competence of the Commission and Court is not limited,[45] thus safeguarding CPT intervention against the Human Rights Convention provision which prohibits the Commission from dealing with any matter which 'has already been submitted to another procedure of international investigation'.[46] More particularly, the Explanatory Report to the Torture Convention is at pains to emphasize that the CPT is not a judicial body. The CPT must not 'adjudge that violations of the relevant international instruments have been committed' and also it is to 'refrain from expressing its views on the interpretation of those instruments either *in abstracto* or in relation to concrete facts'.[47]

Another approach is to direct the CPT to follow Court decisions. Thus the Committee is to take account of jurisprudence under Article 5 on the meaning of 'deprivation of liberty' in determining the scope of its

---

[43] Cf Müllerson, R (1993) 'The Efficiency of the Individual Complaint Procedures' in Bloed, A, Leicht, L, Nowak, M and Rosas, A (eds), 25–43.

[44] Cf Gen Rep 1, para 5: the CPT aims 'at a degree of protection which is greater than that upheld by the European Commission and European Court of Human Rights'.

[45] Articles 17(1) and (2).   [46] ECHR, Article 27(1)(b).

[47] Explanatory Report, para 17.

mandate[48] in considering what is meant by 'persons deprived of their liberty'.[49] But this can be at best mere guidance. Expectations that such case law would provide the necessary delineation are misplaced since neither the Commission nor the Court has been able to provide a clear and consistent approach: the boundary between 'deprivation of liberty' and a restriction on movement is erratically drawn.[50] The CPT appears to have largely avoided this aspect of the Explanatory Report by treating *de facto* deprivation of liberty as of the essence. This has allowed consideration of holding conditions for aliens under domestic immigration controls to be considered in country reports and in the seventh general report free from the artificiality of labelling for Article 5 purposes. Thus discussion of holding conditions in transit rooms for aliens has readily featured in many visits without consideration of Strasbourg jurisprudence.[51] In contrast, the Commission and Court have been preoccupied with whether particular facts amount to a 'deprivation of liberty'. The 1996 judgment in *Amuur v France* illustrates the difficulties still being faced in this area. Asylum seekers had been held in an airport's transit zone for twenty days and kept under constant police surveillance, remaining free to return to their country of origin, which had given assurances that they would not be ill-treated. The Commission concluded that no deprivation of liberty had occurred since the degree of physical constraint was not substantial enough. On the other hand, the Court decided that Article 5 did apply and that there was a 'deprivation of liberty'. Any exercise of the legitimate power to hold aliens in a transit zone could not be prolonged excessively by a state since this would convert a mere restriction on liberty into a deprivation of liberty. In addition, the very lack of procedural safeguards became a critical element in the assessment. State authorities in such circumstances must accord effective access to decision-making procedures for determining refugee status and also ensure the availability of speedy review by a court of any need for prolonged holding. In the present case, the length of time that the applicants were held and the lack of legal and social assistance were 'equivalent in practice' to a deprivation of liberty.[52] This decision marks a further advance in the protection accorded by Article 5, but if the Committee follows faithfully the commandment to follow such jurisprudence in determining what is meant by 'deprivation of liberty', it may paradoxically exclude the CPT from most transit areas of airports. Although the facts in *Amuur* involved lengthy stays in such zones, there was substantial doubt as

---

[48] ie in interpreting Articles 1, 2, 8(2) and (3), and 17.

[49] Explanatory Report, para 24.

[50] See also Murdoch, J (1993) 'Safeguarding the Liberty of Person: recent Strasbourg Jurisprudence', 42 *ICLQ* 494, 495–499; and Murdoch, J (1998) 'Recent Caselaw under Article 5 of the European Convention on Human Rights', 23 *ELRev* HR/31.

[51] Early instances are Austria 1, paras 89–93 and Spain 1, paras 79–83. Later examples are found in Belgium 1, paras 58–60 and UK 3, paras 177–195.

[52] *Amuur v France*, Judgment of 25 June 1996, *RJD* 1996-III, 827.

to whether Article 5 even applied. Were the CPT to adhere faithfully to the Explanatory Report, individuals who found themselves in transit zones for shorter periods would also find themselves in a second state of limbo, denied both the protection of the Human Rights Convention and the concern of the CPT.

Such attempts to avoid conflict between the two treaties could thus paradoxically limit the CPT's effectiveness. The CPT appears unwilling to allow its mandate to be restrained. Precluded from adjudicating 'that violations of the relevant international instruments have been committed' and from 'expressing its views on the interpretation of those instruments either *in abstracto* or in relation to concrete facts',[53] the Committee in certain cases appears willing to highlight the questionable practice or policy but in the most circumspect way possible through the making of a neutral observation. For example, in the third report to the United Kingdom (concerning facts found during the visit to Scotland), the CPT noted that 'at least in theory, a person arrested very early on a Friday morning might not be taken before a court until the following Tuesday morning, were the Monday to be a court holiday'.[54] This is relevant both to the quality of accommodation and regime in the light of the time a person could be detained in a police station, and also in considering Article 5(3)'s requirement of 'prompt appearance' before a court, which has been interpreted as permitting a maximum delay of four days.[55] There is certainly a clear violation of the Convention, but the CPT felt itself precluded from passing such a remark. Other practices may emerge which also give rise to questions of compliance with Convention guarantees such as censorship of prisoners' mail[56] which could give rise to challenges under Article 8. Alternatively, the CPT may propose action which will remedy any possible existing shortfall such as the failure to provide automatic review procedures for persons detained under mental health legislation,[57] an issue whether domestic law satisfies 'periodic review' requirements under Article 5(4). Formal protocol rather

---

[53] Explanatory Report, para 17.

[54] UK 3, para 279 (in some courts, the first court appearance could occur on the afternoon of the Tuesday).

[55] The Commission continues to apply a rule of ninety-six hours' maximum detention in a rather mechanistic but at least clear and unambiguous way while the Court invariably arrives at the same conclusion: eg *Sakik & Others v Turkey*, Judgment of 26 November 1997, *RJD* 1997-III, 2609, para 45 (the Court merely noted that the police detentions lasting between twelve and fourteen days each exceeded the four days and six hours which had been condemned as violating the paragraph in an earlier case).

[56] eg Luxembourg 1, para 104; Slovenia 1, para 80; Malta 2, para 75; and Denmark 2, para 60. These recommendations are broadly in line with the respective case law of the Court: eg *Silver and Others v United Kingdom*, Judgment of 25 March 1983, Ser A No 61; *McCallum v United Kingdom*, Judgment of 30 August 1990, Ser A No 183; *Campbell v United Kingdom*, Judgment of 25 March 1992, Ser A No 233.

[57] Cyprus 2, para 141: 'Persons admitted compulsorily [to mental health institutions] should be entitled to an automatic review procedure on a regular basis, to establish whether the placement is still necessary. . . . It [is] understood that such a procedure was envisaged in draft legislation . . . the CPT would like to receive information on this subject'.

than practical effectiveness is promoted by this paragraph in the Explanatory Report: recommendations would have greater immediacy if observations as to possible incompatibility were to be included, and state action
would be more likely if only to prevent the embarrassment of judicial
condemnation.

3. 'TORTURE' AND 'INHUMAN AND DEGRADING TREATMENT'

At the heart of the matter is the interpretation of 'torture' and 'inhuman
or degrading treatment or punishment'. These key phrases are found in
both Conventions and thus the potential for conflict in interpretation is
most acute. The CPT's mandate is to prevent 'torture' or 'inhuman and
degrading treatment or punishment', state action also specifically prohibited under Article 3 of the European Convention on Human Rights. It is
clear that these terms have been accorded different meanings for the
related but distinct purposes of prevention (essentially proactive) and adjudication (involving condemnation of past breaches), and it is in this area
that there is maximum scope for conflict between the two treaties. The
Explanatory Report provides that jurisprudence under Article 3 is to
provide a 'source of guidance' for the CPT, but the Committee is enjoined
not to 'seek to interfere in the interpretation and application of Article 3'.[58]
Again, the problem is with the difference in focus. The thrust of CPT activity is pre-emptive action through the establishment of dialogue and with
the focus on the present. Its multi-disciplinary composition will also gener-
ate wider concerns and produce a more dynamic, critical, and purposeful
approach. On the other hand, the Commission and Court face the task of
judicial interpretation of an absolute prohibition against torture and
inhuman and degrading treatment. Certainly, at first glance the scope
of Article 3 protection seems to be broadly in line with CPT concerns. Both
physical and mental suffering are covered and the type of treatment which
may give rise to Article 3 questions includes the use of force during interrogation or police detention,[59] punishment (corporal[60] and solitary
confinement[61]), conditions of detention,[62] extradition and deportation to

---

[58] Explanatory Report, para 27.

[59] *Tomasi v France*, Judgment of 27 August 1992, Ser A No 241-A; *Sur v Turkey*, Judgment
of 3 October 1997, *RJD* 1997-VI, 2034 (struck out of list after friendly settlement); *Yağiz v
Turkey*, Judgment of 7 August 1996, *RJD* 1996-III, 966.

[60] *Tyrer v United Kingdom*, Judgment of 25 April 1978, Ser A No 26.

[61] *Kröcher and Möller v Switzerland*, App No 8463/78, Comm Dec, 16 December 1982, 34
DR 24.

[62] Cf *Guzzardi v Italy*, Judgment of 6 November 1980, Ser A No 39; *Herczegfalvy v Austria*,
Judgment of 24 September 1992, Ser A No 244.

other states,[63] and discriminatory treatment,[64] all of which mirror aspects of CPT reports. Crucial differences in interpretation and in approach, however, exist.

The general principles of interpretation adopted by the Court have two aspects. First, the physical or mental treatment complained of must achieve a minimum level of severity; and second, if this threshold test is reached, then the differentiation between torture, inhuman treatment or punishment, or degrading treatment or punishment is a matter of degree of intensity of suffering. Whether the minimum level of severity has been reached is considered by reference to all the circumstances of the case, for example, the duration of the treatment, its physical and mental effects, and the sex, age, and health of the victim.[65] If the suffering involved is excessive as considered in the light of prevailing general standards,[66] then this threshold test will have been reached and it then becomes a question of which label will be applied. 'Torture' is 'deliberate inhuman treatment causing very serious and cruel suffering'; 'inhuman treatment or punishment' involves 'intense physical and mental suffering'; and 'degrading' treatment or punishment is 'such as to arouse in the victims feelings of fear, anguish and inferiority capable of humiliating and debasing them and possibly breaking their physical or moral resistance'.[67] The result is again line drawing which often displays suggestions of erratic boundaries, particularly at the outer edges of the guarantee.[68] First, while the Court's purported approach is 'dynamic', this can mean that state action is judged according to the generally accepted standards in other European countries, and Commission and Court seek to 'pull up' laggard states to the level of current achievement rather than attempting to lead any advance on a general front. Where no common standard is found (as possibly with detention conditions), protection is not as

---

[63] *Soering v UK*, Judgment of 7 July 1989, Ser A No 161; *Cruz Varas v Sweden*, Judgment of 20 March 1991, Ser A No 201.

[64] *Abdulaziz, Cabales and Balkandali v UK*, Judgment of 28 May 1985, Ser A No 94.

[65] *Ireland v United Kingdom*, Judgment of 18 January 1978, Ser A No 25, para 162. Cultural relativity may be a factor, but this may suggest that some ill-treatment may be condoned. In the *Greek* case, for example, the Commission found that a 'certain roughness of treatment' of persons detained by state officials was tolerated and taken for granted, so 'underlin[ing] the fact that the point up to which prisoners may accept physical violence as being neither cruel nor excessive, varies between different societies and even between different sections of them' (Comm Rep, 5 November 1969, 12 *ECHRYb* 186 at 501, para 11).

[66] *Tyrer v United Kingdom*, Judgment of 25 April 1978, Ser A No 26, para 38.

[67] *Ireland v United Kingdom*, Judgment of 18 January 1978, Ser A No 25, para 167.

[68] In the case of *Ireland v United Kingdom*, individuals deprived of their liberty under prevention of terrorism powers in Northern Ireland were subjected to the 'five techniques'—hooding, wall-standing, subjection to continuous noise, deprivation of sleep and deprivation of food—during interrogation by members of the security forces leading to at least 'intense physical and mental suffering' and 'acute psychiatric disturbances'. The Commission considered this constituted 'torture'; the Court, however, felt this did not 'occasion suffering of the particular intensity and cruelty implied' by the term, and thus amounted instead to 'inhuman treatment'.

purposeful as it could be so that relatively harsh instances of punishment or treatment may fail to be condemned.[69] The trend of case law is that there must always be 'an inevitable element of suffering or humiliation' in the very nature of punishment. Second, the Court's own threshold test of sufficient seriousness can also be used to rein in any tendency to 'trivialize' Article 3 by seeking to apply it to matters which arguably lack the requisite degree of seriousness which was at the historical heart of the Article.[70] Third, state interests may be considered appropriate factors in any assessment (as with issues concerning the justification for solitary confinement[71]). Public policy considerations thus may moderate the absolute nature of the text.

The consequence is that prisoners are unlikely to be able to rely upon Article 3 for assistance. Although care must be taken in reading decisions of the Commission and Court since much will depend on the circumstances surrounding the individual applicant, even where specific behaviour or treatment is criticized there must be extreme or excessive state action[72] or a failure to take humanitarian measures[73] or a finding of extreme psychological effects of imprisonment in a particular case caused by special holding conditions[74] before there will be a breach of Article 3. Solitary confinement regimes are unlikely to attract criticism. While 'prolonged removal from association with others is undesirable', such must be considered in terms of 'the particular conditions of its application, including its stringency, duration and purpose, as well as its effects on the person concerned'.[75] State interests (such as security considerations or the interests of justice) may even justify solitary confinement involving sensory depriva-

---

[69] Trechsel, S (1986) 'Zum Verhältnis zwischen der Folterschutzkonvention und der Europäischen Menschenrechtskonvention' in *Völkerrecht im Dienste des Menschens: Festschrift für Hans Haug*, 356–357.

[70] Harris, D, O'Boyle, M and Warbrick, C (1995) *Law of the European Convention on Human Rights* (Butterworths, London), 55. Cf *Costello-Roberts v United Kingdom*, Judgment of 25 March 1993, Ser A No 247-C; *Lopez Ostra v Spain*, Judgment of 9 December 1994, Ser A No 303-C (living conditions 'certainly very difficult' but not a violation of Article 3).

[71] eg *Ensslin, Baader & Raspe v Germany*, App Nos 7572/76 and 7586/76, Comm Dec, 8 July 1976, 14 *DR* 64.

[72] eg as in *Ireland v United Kingdom*, Judgment of 18 January 1978, Ser A No 25 (use of sensory deprivation interrogation techniques against terrorist suspects).

[73] eg *McFeely v UK*, App No 8317/78, Comm Dec, 15 May 1980, 20 *DR* 44 (prison authorities to exercise custodial authority in such a way as to safeguard health, etc of all prisoners, even those taking part in unlawful protest involving refusal to wash); *Chartier v Italy*, App No 9044/80, Comm Dec, 8 December 1982, 33 *DR* 41 (prisoner suffering from hereditary obesity unable to assert that failure to release him to permit medical treatment resulted in inhuman treatment since adequate treatment was available in prison: but Commission noted that 'particularly serious' cases may require 'humanitarian remedies'); and *Hurtado v Switzerland*, Judgment of 28 January 1994, Ser A No 280 (left to wear clothing soiled during arrest; case struck off list after friendly settlement).

[74] As in *Soering v United Kingdom*, Judgment of 7 July 1989, Ser A No 161. See Breitenmoser & Wilms (1990) 'Human Rights v Extradition', 11 *MichJIL* 845, and Blumenwitz (1989) 'Fall Soering', 16 *EuGRZ* 314.

[75] *R v Denmark*, App No 10263/83, Comm Dec, 11 March 1985, 41 *DR* 149 at 153.

tion.[76] It has proved equally difficult to bring general detention conditions within the scope of Article 3 protection. The feeling seems to be that there is always 'an inevitable element of suffering or humiliation' in the very nature of legitimate punishment,[77] but even where treatment rather than punishment is strictly in issue, even highly unsatisfactory conditions in prisons and in mental hospitals are likely to escape Article 3 censure.[78] Occasional comments such as national authorities must 'maintain a continuous review of the detention arrangements employed with a view to ensuring the health and well-being of all prisoners with due regard to the ordinary and reasonable requirements of imprisonment'[79] have proved of little practical use to applicants.

The CPT's starting point in country reports is the assessment of the likelihood of ill-treatment at the hands of police or prison officers. The CPT will invariably assess the risk of injury[80] facing detainees and formed after taking into account such issues as the number of allegations heard, official reports, and examination of medical reports and of prisoners.[81] Visits may indeed be made to prisons specifically to speak to prisoners about their treatment while in police stations.[82] Alternatively, a country report may contain a request for further information in order that an assessment may be made.[83] There are three CPT concerns: choice of language to convey the assessment of risk; the recommending of steps to prevent any ill-treatment uncovered; and the subsequent monitoring of their implementation. Wording of assessment of risk seems, however, often to obfuscate rather than clarify. Differences between 'a significant risk of being ill-treated'[84] and a 'serious risk of ill-treatment',[85] and between these and a 'serious risk of

---

[76] *Ensslin, Baader & Raspe v Germany*, App Nos 7572/7 and 7586/76, Comm Dec, 8 July 1978, 14 *DR* 64; *Kröcher & Möller v Switzerland*, App No 8463/78, Comm Dec, 9 July 1981, 26 *DR* 24; *Bonzi v Switzerland*, App No 7854/77, Comm Dec, 12 July 1978, 12 *DR* 185. Cf the 1993 decision of inadmissibility in the case of *Delazarus v United Kingdom*, App No 17525/90, Comm Dec, 16 February 1993 (unpublished) (concerning the segregation of a prisoner from other prisoners for 14 weeks and the conditions in which he was held).

[77] *Ireland v United Kingdom*, Judgment of 18 January 1978, Ser A No 25, para 167.

[78] eg *Y v United Kingdom*, App No 6870/75, Comm Dec, 14 May 1977, 10 *DR* 37; *Cyprus v Turkey*, App Nos 6780/74 and 6950/75, Comm Rep, 10 July 1976, 4 *EHRR* 482, CM Res DH 79 (1) (withholding of medical treatment and food and water); *B v United Kingdom*, App No 6870/75, Comm Rep, 7 October 1981, 32 *DR* 5; *McFeely v UK*, App No 8317/78, Comm Dec, 15 May 1980, 20 *DR* 44.

[79] *Dhoest v Belgium*, App No 10448/83, Comm Dec, 14 May 1987, 55 *DR* 5 at 21 (psychiatric detainee had voluntarily given up work).

[80] eg UK 3, para 281 ('little risk' of ill-treatment by Scottish police officers); Portugal 2, para 27 (ill-treatment still 'relatively common phenomenon' in police stations); Austria 2, para 17 ('serious risk of ill-treatment' in police stations).

[81] eg Slovakia 1, paras 15–17 (consistency of allegations heard concerning police violence; medical records and examinations by CPT delegation doctor; prison service medical examinations upon admission showed 40 cases of physical injuries).

[82] eg UK 3, para 302.

[83] eg Germany 2, para 16 (request for further information on complaints lodged against police officers and sanctions imposed).

[84] eg Bulgaria 1, para 27.   [85] eg Austria 2, para 19.

severe ill-treatment/torture'[86] refer to the probability of serious violence at
the hands of police officers and as to its likely intensity, but the fine distinctions in language can ironically appear to suggest an unwillingness to
provide clear and objective 'measuring rods'. In any case, they also pre-
suppose that states carefully scrutinize other reports and are aware of the
fine distinctions being drawn in English or in French (rather than in the
native language).

In short, problems in standard setting are exacerbated by the judgemen-
tal activity in report writing which has come about on account of state
authorization of publication. Further, choice of descriptor is influenced
by the exhortation to avoid influencing interpretation under Article 3,
which in any case is rather restrictive and often lacking clarity. The result
seems sometimes akin to shadow-boxing. For example, Evans and Morgan
comment that the labelling by the CPT of behaviour as 'torture' or
as 'severe ill-treatment' is highly selective. The authors suggest that
'conventional violence—blows with fists or feet or batons or other
weapons—even when purposefully inflicted with the intention of
causing pain in order to elicit confessions or information, or generally
to intimidate' will fail to be stigmatized as 'torture' or 'severe ill-treatment',
terms which are 'generally reserved for the less ambiguous specialised or
exotic forms of violence' such as *falaka*, electric shocks, or suspension
from the wrists or feet even though the resultant injuries to the prisoner
are similar. The fact that the Committee has not described 'severe ill-
treatment' as 'inhuman or degrading treatment' suggests that it has
wished to reserve 'inhuman and degrading' for a different category of ill-
treatment, namely ill-treatment that is not purposive in the sense that
torture is purposive (generally to elicit information or confessions).[87]
This is reinforced by a suggestion from a former Vice-President of the CPT
that the two phenomena are indeed distinct: 'torture'/'severe ill-treatment'
is usually hidden, takes place in police stations, is inflicted to extract information or to intimidate, and is uncovered by medical examination; while
'inhuman and degrading treatment' is open and even acknowledged,
justified by a lack of resources or as inherent in the form of punishment,
and readily found by mere presence in places of detention.[88] If these assessments are correct, then the rejection by the CPT of the Article 3 'spectrum'

---

[86] eg Cyprus 1, para 21.
[87] Evans and Morgan (1998), 240–241; see also Chapter Two, pp 34–40.
[88] Sørensen, B (1995) 'Prevention of Torture and Inhuman or Degrading Treatment or Punishment: Medical Views' in APT, *Implementation of the ECPT, Acts of the Strasbourg Seminar,
Dec 1994* (Geneva: APT), 259–265. Cf Evans and Morgan (1998), 241–242, who argue that
'non-purposive' ill-treatment leading to the labelling of conditions as 'inhuman and degrading' is used 'to describe environmental custodial conditions' and 'in a cumulative manner
[meaning] that conditions or restrictions that might not in themselves be deemed inhuman or
degrading, become so when combined with others'.

approach has clearly been deliberate. The overall effect, however, is to heighten confusion.

As discussed, neither the Commission nor the Court has been able to recognize the crucial importance of accommodation and regime on the wellbeing of individual prisoners. Article 3 seems not to be flexible enough to consider the deleterious effects over the long term of poor prison conditions. Its focus is instead upon individual instances of infliction of specific ill-treatment: the specific physical or psychological treatment rather than the cumulative effect of lengthy deprivation of liberty in unsatisfactory conditions lies at the heart of judicial protection. There is thus a failure to accept that a state has any positive legal duty to minimize the side effects of imprisonment: to the contrary, there is perceived to be an inevitable element of 'humiliation' implicit in the infliction of any punishment. This is in stark contrast to the approach of the CPT, which accepts that 'people are sent to prison as a punishment, not for punishment',[89] and thus by extension that the 'act of depriving a person of liberty entails a correlative duty for the state to safeguard physical and mental welfare until such time as liberty is restored'.[90] The CPT has thus condemned both general holding conditions and specific treatment or practices which would escape Commission or Court criticism. The CPT will in consequence question ill-treatment such as solitary confinement which could lead to 'isolation syndrome',[91] holding in overcrowded and ill-equipped holding conditions,[92] and conditions of juvenile detention.[93]

This more critical attitude reflects the concerns of the CPT to make recommendations to help prevent ill-treatment, an approach which is likely to be broader and less focused than that adopted by judicial bodies in condemning state action or inaction. It also reflects a greater awareness and understanding of the psychological effects of incarceration, an inevitable consequence of having medical expertise available in the CPT. Lawyers and judges have traditionally been reluctant to advance or accept arguments based upon long-term harm; indeed, the limited length of solitary confinement can be used to justify why severe holding conditions do not trigger an Article 3 violation.[94] Only the most obviously unacceptable (that is, to any non-medical specialist) holding conditions will satisfy the Court that there is an Article 3 issue. Ironically, this may allow criticism of non-European holding conditions, reinforcing any tendency to appear blind to

---

[89] UK 1, para 57.   [90] Portugal 2, para 104.

[91] eg Switzerland 1, paras 48–52 (non-voluntary isolation lasting up to seven years without socio-therapeutic stimulation for prisoners); Germany 1, para 72 (solitary confinement should be of minimum duration); Bulgaria 1, paras 109–110 (14-day segregation in dark and unventilated cell of 2 square metres 'inhuman').

[92] eg France 1, paras 92–93; UK 3, paras 331, 343; Portugal 2, para 95; Bulgaria 1, para 113.

[93] France 1, paras 96–97.

[94] eg *Kröcher & Möller v Switzerland*, App No 8463/78, Comm Dec, 9 July 1981, 26 *DR* 24.

defects in 'home' conditions. In *Soering v United Kingdom*, the Court ruled that a state would violate Article 3 if it deported or extradited an individual to another country where 'substantial grounds have been shown for believing that the person concerned . . . faces a real risk of being subjected to torture or to inhuman or degrading treatment or punishment'. The issue concerned the possible extradition of the applicant to Virginia in the United States to face a charge carrying the death penalty. It was established that there was a real risk that Soering would be condemned to death, and thus subject to specific detention conditions while facing execution which through their very nature could result in the imposition of inhuman or degrading treatment (so-called 'death row phenomenon'). The cumulative effect of physical and psychological factors was enough to meet the threshold test of Article 3.[95] The principle applies to deportation or extradition to face more 'straightforward' forms of torture or inhuman or degrading treatment.[96] Detention conditions, then, provide the most crucial area of disagreement between the two treaties. The question is not whether the CPT should take more care in avoiding any conflict, but whether use of CPT reports can prompt review of jurisprudence.

4. FACT FINDING AND THE USE OF CPT REPORTS

Allegations of ill-treatment before the Commission and Court may be answered by a state in one of four ways: first, by outright denial of the application of any ill-treatment; second, by conceding ill-treatment took place but denying state liability; third, by conceding ill-treatment took place but that it did not achieve the necessary minimum threshold test for Article 3; or fourth, by accepting there has been a violation of Article 3 but arguing that the violation is at a lower level of seriousness than that proposed by the applicant. CPT reports will primarily be of use in helping establish the factual basis in the first two situations; in the final two, CPT standards may well have a part to play in encouraging revision of existing case law.

Since factual circumstances are crucial in the determination of both the threshold test and in any subsequent labelling as 'torture', 'inhuman', or 'degrading', fact finding becomes of some importance. Certainly, attempts

[95] *Soering v United Kingdom*, Judgment of 7 July 1989, Ser A No 161, paras 90–91.
[96] eg *Cruz Varas v Sweden*, Judgment of 20 March 1991, Ser A No 201 (deportation after refusal of asylum back to Chile, but not shown that there were substantial grounds for believing there was a real risk of ill-treatment); *Vilvarajah v United Kingdom*, Judgment of 30 October 1991, Ser A No 215 (return of Tamils to Sri Lanka at time of improved situation in country; likelihood of ill-treatment by state officials only 'possibility' and not real risk). In *Cinar v Turkey*, App No 17864/91, Comm Dec, 5 September 1994, 79 *DR* 5, there was no risk of death row phenomenon since the risk of the imposition of the death penalty was merely illusory.

have been made by the Court to help with this task. Establishing the infliction of ill-treatment may be often hindered by the isolation in which the detainee finds himself. In the first instance, where the application of ill-treatment is denied but national authorities are unable to furnish any adequate explanation for injuries sustained while in custody, the facts may not bear any interpretation other than that force has been inflicted upon an individual in custody. As the Court put it in *Ribitsch v Austria*, there is a heavy responsibility upon state officials to justify any injury sustained while an individual is in custody.[97] In *Tomasi v France*, the lack of alternative explanation offered by the government to explain the injuries sustained by the applicant over a period of forty-eight hours while in police custody on a charge of murder connected to terrorist activities was considered significant by the Court when taken along with other evidence such as the applicant's complaints of violence when brought for judicial examination. In all the circumstances, the Court accepted beyond reasonable doubt that the injuries had been inflicted by police officers, and ruled that their severity amounted to ill-treatment.[98] However, this will not apply where alternative and credible explanations for injuries exist, as in *Klass v Germany* where bruising sustained while the applicant was being arrested on a drink-driving offence was attributed by her to the use of excessive police force but by the police to self-infliction of harm. The Court could not hold it established beyond reasonable doubt that state authorities had been responsible.[99]

Nor may national authorities plead that the acts complained of were unauthorized or taken without the knowledge of superior officers. In the *Greek* case, the Commission found it established beyond doubt that members of the Security Police had inflicted torture or ill-treatment as a matter of administrative practice on detainees. In response to the government's contention that a state could only be in breach of its obligations if the state itself had inflicted the treatment, or had at an executive level shown toleration towards the practices complained of, the Commission considered that state responsibility could arise for the acts of any of its organs or agents 'even [at] the lowest level, without express authorisation and even outside or against instructions'. The issue of level of official toleration was indeed relevant in considering exhaustion of domestic remedies, for if it had been established that toleration existed at executive level, 'this fact alone would be a strong indication that the complainant has no possibility of obtaining redress through any national organ, including the courts'.[100]

Similarly, the CPT's general assessment of the likely risk in CPT reports

---

[97] *Ribitsch v Austria*, Judgment of 4 December 1995, Ser A No 336, para 34.
[98] *Tomasi v France*, Judgment of 27 August 1992, Ser A No 241-A.
[99] *Klaas v Germany*, Judgment of 22 September 1993, Ser A No 269.
[100] *Greek* case, 19 *ECHRYb* 512 at 758 and 762. An argument advanced by the respondent state that it was unaware of the conduct of its soldiers was similarly unsuccessful in *Ireland v UK*.

often contains details of physical injuries uncovered in police stations or prisons. Instances of alleged severe ill-treatment of identifiable (but not identified[101]) detainees are detailed.[102] It is not inconceivable that an individual could have his case examined both by the CPT and by the Commission since (as noted) CPT involvement does not formally bar any application under the ECHR.[103] There would indeed appear to be no bar to the CPT forwarding allegations of an Article 3 violation to the Commission. Fact finding can involve the Commission in prolonged attempts to obtain evidence, often in difficult situations both for it and for witnesses.[104] Accordingly it may find it helpful to make use of external assessments and CPT reports may be of use to support the applicant's assertions either in a particular case in which CPT findings apply directly to the applicant, or alternatively in a case in which the applicant seeks to use the facts found by the CPT to give weight to his own assertions.

In the first United Kingdom report, the CPT criticized holding conditions in certain English prisons and considered that the cumulative effect of overcrowding, lack of integral sanitation, and inadequate regime activities all amounted to 'inhuman and degrading treatment'.[105] The Government's response to the CPT was that improvement was necessary, but that the assessment was wrong.[106] In *Raphaie v United Kingdom*,[107] the applicant made several complaints about his treatment in two prisons. He had been forced to share a cell designed for single occupancy, and which

---

[101] Cf Article 11(3): '[N]o personal data shall be published without the express consent of the person concerned.'

[102] eg Switzerland 1, para 101 (six cases of assault on prisoners in Geneva police station); France 1, para 85 (five prisoners severely battered, assaulted after a failed escape attempt in Marseilles); Denmark 1, paras 19–20 (serious ill-treatment of a Gambian and a Tanzanian in Copenhagen prisons); Denmark 1, paras 33, 50 and UK 1, para 64 (cases of suicide); UK 1, paras 192–194 (transfer of prisoner 19 times in 18 months); Switzerland 1, para 79 (last-minute cancellation of transfer of prisoner to home state); Germany 1, para 21 (ill-treatment of demonstrators in Munich); Netherlands 1, paras 63–64 (assault on remand prisoner). But cf ECPT Explanatory Report, para 49: '[The CPT] should not be concerned with the investigation of individual complaints (for which provision is already made, eg under the [ECHR]).'

[103] ECHR, Article 27(1)(b) provides that the Commission cannot deal *inter alia* with any matter which 'has already been submitted to another procedure of international investigation'; ECPT, Article 17(2) provides that 'Nothing in this Convention shall be construed as limiting or derogating from the competence of the organs of the European Convention on Human Rights . . .'. Cf Cassese (1989), 135. See, further, van Dijk, P and van Hoof, GJH (1990) *Theory and Practice of the European Convention on Human Rights*, 2nd edn (Deventer: Kluwer), 71–75.

[104] Thus in *Menteş v Turkey*, Judgment of 28 November 1997, *RJD* 1997-VIII, 2689, the Commission held a three-day hearing in Turkey which involved taking evidence from the applicants, public prosecutors, the senior police officer in the province, and neighbours. The application concerned the destruction of homes and property and allegations of physical violence. In view of a finding of breach of Article 8, the Court decided not to examine the Article 3 allegations further.

[105] UK 1, para 57.   [106] UK 1 R 1, preface, para 5.

[107] *Raphaie v UK*, App No 20035/92, Comm Dec, 2 December 1993 (unpublished).

had no integral sanitation, with one or two others; prisoners had to satisfy the needs of nature by using a chamber pot in the presence of other prisoners; the emptying of the chamber pots took place at the same time as the washing of eating utensils; he had been confined to the cell for 23 hours a day; cockroaches and rats had been present in one prison where he was permitted only 45 minutes of daily exercise; and he had been held in the psychiatric wing without having been given a reason for this placement. The Commission eventually declared the application inadmissible under Article 26 as being time barred. However, the Commission appeared willing to use the CPT's report as additional corroboration as to the factual assertions made by the applicant. In the more recent case of *Aerts v Belgium*, a highly-critical CPT report was used to help establish the factual situation in which the applicant had been held when it proved difficult to obtain clear evidence from the appellant himself on account of his mental illness.[108]

5. CHALLENGING EXISTING ECHR NORMS THROUGH THE USE OF CPT REPORTS

Three possible situations now exist: first, where CPT and ECHR standards in interpreting 'torture' and 'inhuman or degrading treatment or punishment' are broadly similar; second, where ECHR standards are higher than those developed by the CPT; and third, where the CPT is more demanding than Commission and Court. Consistency appears confined to the expression of views on 'torture' and to situations involving what Evans and Morgan call 'exotic' violence[109] which certainly would also be considered as 'torture' under Article 3.[110] The second category—where treatment would violate Article 3 but would not be considered by the CPT as 'torture/severe ill-treatment'—includes 'conventional' violence against suspects in police stations or in prisons. The CPT's justification for this approach is simply not clear, and it seems to leave a hole in a crucial aspect of 'standard setting'. The third and final category—where CPT

---

[108] *Aerts v Belgium*, Judgment of 30 July 1998, paras 28–30, to be reported in *RJD* 1998. The case is discussed further below.

[109] Evans and Morgan (1998), 252, eg application of *falaka*, electric shocks, or suspension from the wrists. The two Public Statements made by the CPT report a persistent failure on the part of the Turkish authorities to deal with the routine infliction of torture in police stations. Findings were to the effect that suspects in Turkish police stations are regularly suspended by the arms and wrists, have electric shocks applied to genitals and other sensitive parts of the body, have the soles of their feet beaten, and have their bodily orifices forcibly penetrated with a stick or truncheon: Turkey PS 1, paras 5–8, 15; Turkey PS 2, para 3. The findings relied upon medical expertise amongst the delegation.

[110] *Ireland v United Kingdom*, Judgment of 18 January 1998, Ser A No 25; *Aksoy v Turkey*, Judgment of 18 December 1996, *RJD* 1996-VI, 2260.

labelling contrasts with Commission and Court complacency—essentially concerns detention conditions.

There are some explanations for a narrower approach by judicial bodies. The absolute and legal nature of the prohibition against torture and inhuman or degrading treatment imposes a demanding threshold test before an Article 3 violation can be established. Further, in discussion of material conditions of detention, Commission and Court competencies are not unlimited: judicial bodies have substantial hurdles to face in moving from the arena of civil and political liberties into that of economic and social rights when shaping relief. But could the CPT's standards have as vital an impact upon Article 3 jurisprudence as it has been argued they are likely to have in respect of the European Prison Rules? The suggestion seems anathema to some commentators, and certainly to the drafters of the Convention and its Explanatory Report. Trechsel writing in 1986 suggested that the consequence of any departure by the CPT from established ECHR standards would lead to 'hopeless confusion, legal uncertainty, and ultimately a weakening of faith in the Human Rights Convention machinery'. He argued that the CPT should concentrate on the 'grey area' between irreproachable conditions of detention and those conditions which just fall short of a violation of Article 3, leaving the more serious conditions to be referred to the Commission for deliberation.[111] It could certainly be argued that some of the confusion predicted has indeed resulted; but Trechsel's solution presupposes that the existence of two sets of 'measuring rods' is in the first place unsatisfactory. It may certainly create some difficulty in developing the 'ongoing dialogue' with states. One standard answer to CPT criticism that conditions are 'inhuman and degrading' is to use in return the language of the Commission and Court that the conditions are certainly far from ideal but not 'inhuman'. Failure by the CPT to label 'conventional' police violence as 'torture' may be perceived by a state as less than stringent criticism and even vaguely sympathetic. However, arguably some degree of tension between standard setting by the CPT and under the ECHR is not only to be expected in the nature of the human rights machinery (proactive-preventive as opposed to reactive-judgemental), but is also potentially creative if it is possible to have each institution confronted by the norms and assumptions of the other. If this can be engineered, it may be possible collectively to move towards increased protection of human rights: that is, the two sets of machinery could be seen as *complementary* rather than competitive as suggested by Trechsel, who seems to imply that the integrity of Commission and Court jurisprudence should be paramount.

Any 'creative' tension is likely to be easier for the CPT to trigger. The Committee is well placed to seize the initiative. There is already long-

---

[111] Trechsel (1986), 358–359.

standing dissatisfaction with Article 3 jurisprudence. It should not be overlooked that the Commission's failure to address prison conditions has already provoked some speculation as to whether there should be a new optional protocol to the Human Rights Convention to ensure legally binding protection for prisoners on such matters as accommodation, medical care, disciplinary issues, training, and association rights.[112] Its multidisciplinary approach has produced new insights, self-evident in their validity to CPT members but more novel to lawyers and judges. Many of these insights are provided by informed medical expertise, such as the severe long-term harm caused to prisoners if held in regimes without appropriate mental and physical stimulation,[113] or to mental health patients held in geographically isolated large psychiatric hospitals.[114] Further, the CPT has also clearly signalled that its set of standards are of general validity. Its apparent rejection of any suggestion that its norms would require revision when it embarked upon visits to the newly-emerging democracies of Central and East European countries makes it clear that standards originally developed during consideration of Western regimes apply throughout Europe. There is now no danger of appearing to have 'two weights and two measures', which would have resulted in a weakening of the normative force of CPT recommendations.[115]

There are, however, formidable barriers in the shape of judicial competency issues facing any attempted advance of Article 3 protection into general holding conditions questions. Put simply, the ECHR is concerned primarily with civil and political rights; where economic and social rights are recognized by the treaty, Commission and Court tend to allow a rather wider 'margin of appreciation' or discretion to state authorities. Holding conditions (overcrowded and unhygienic accommodation, lack of

---

[112] Lång, N (1990), Report on 'Human Rights of Persons Deprived of their Liberty', 7th International Colloquy on the ECHR, doc H/Coll (90) 4, 13–14.

[113] eg Bulgaria 1, paras 112–113 (solitary confinement regime for prisoners sentenced to death after entry into force of moratorium on death penalty considered 'inhuman and degrading').

[114] eg Bulgaria 1, para 191 (mediocre environment not conducive to treatment); Cyprus 1, para 119 ('significant risk of institutionalisation').

[115] Some standards refer directly to prevailing material conditions in the country but do so in an objective way (such as the notion that there should be 'equivalence' of health care between prisons and the general community). Most standards are, however, absolute (such as a minimum of eight hours per day of purposeful activity for prisoners, training for police and prison officers, and procedural rights for suspects). Despite early indications that the CPT would recognize the practical difficulties facing countries emerging from totalitarian government (Germany 1, paras 10–11, 69–70, 110–112, 120 (conditions in institutions formerly under the control of East German authorities) and Malta 1, paras 85–86 (progressive introduction of rights to legal advice for inmates, but advances in treatment by police officers of suspects after removal of former regime should not be 'jeopardised by expecting too much too soon')), the CPT now seems unwilling to draw a distinction between Communist and post-Communist ways of doing things, in contrast to the approach taken by the European Commission on Human Rights: cf Gross, AM (1996) 'Reinforcing the New Democracies: the ECHR and the Former Communist Countries—a Study of the Case Law', 7 *EJIL* 89; Murdoch, J (1996) 'European Convention for the Prevention of Torture', 21 *ELRev* HRC/130, 136–137.

worthwhile activities for prisoners, poor health care, etc) fall within this latter category. The practical effect of upholding applications in this area would be the recognition that the Commission and Court would in effect be directing how a state should establish its spending priorities: while relief to the individual applicant may involve the payment of a certain sum of money to compensate for a harsh environment, the capacity such cases would have for generating further applications would mean that a state would have little option other than to divert resources from other projects in order to stem a flood of adverse findings. A judicial body—and an international one at that—would have appropriated the power of appropriation, no matter how narrowly the relief in any one particular case is drawn. Furthermore, Commission and Court would be seen to be expressing a willingness to place prison detention conditions on their agendas. This would attract a deluge of applications which in turn could swamp available resources and place an impossible burden on the new Court which, as with the former Commission, is ill-suited to such fact finding and investigation. In any case, these bodies would be embarking upon a process of disjointed and thus incremental policy making.[116]

This is not, however, to argue that the need to bring about a dramatic improvement in the material holding conditions for probably countless tens of thousands (and probably hundreds of thousands in the emerging democracies) is not one worthy of judicial attention. The long-standing failure in many countries of each branch of government to tackle obvious defects in prison conditions is deep-rooted; within the judicial branch of government, this may be seen as a denial of public values such as equality of treatment and human dignity. Structural reform via the courtroom has been attempted elsewhere, most obviously in the USA. But it has meant the reshaping of concepts of standing, innovations in procedures, and a fundamental review of the nature and form of judicial remedies.[117] All of this is perhaps to throw into sharper relief why a body such as the CPT with the aptitude, perseverance, long-term vision, and organizational abilities is a more efficient and effective device to tackle prison conditions. However, neither these factors nor the Explanatory Report nor the CPT's own efforts at careful use of language will prevent attempts at using CPT reports in domestic proceedings and applications before the Court. At present only a trickle of Strasbourg applicants have sought to use CPT reports in this way, while the number of citations in aid in domestic proceedings (where the Human Rights Convention is now almost invariably part of the domestic legal order) is also likely to be minimal at this time. As knowledge of the CPT spreads this will certainly change: and with it will come an impact upon existing jurispru-

[116] Cf Horowitz, DL (1977) *The Courts and Social Policy* (Washington: Brookings Institute), 6–9, 34–45.
[117] Fiss, OM (1979) 'The Supreme Court 1978 Term', 93 *Harvard Law Rev* 1.

dence. CPT reports have potential use in litigation as an aid to fact finding and in advancing arguments of incompatibility with Human Rights Convention guarantees, both in relation to application of specific ill-treatment and in failure to provide treatment.[118]

Where an applicant can show his detention falls directly into the category of ill-treatment criticized by the CPT, it may be possible to argue that the opinion of the CPT should be given some weight in the Commission or Court or domestic tribunal. In the 1993 Commission decision in *Delazarus v United Kingdom*, a direct answer as to the weight to be given to the CPT findings again concerning the first United Kingdom report was avoided.[119] The Commission accepted—to use the standard euphemism in such cases— that the overcrowding, lack of integral sanitation, and poor hygiene were 'extremely unsatisfactory', but it could only deal with the concrete facts in the particular case and since the applicant had been held in a single cell, this must have reduced any problem of lack of integral sanitation.[120] The key point was that the Commission in *Delazarus* did not exclude use of CPT reports, in contrast to a singular lack of sympathy shown in earlier decisions in which prisoners had unsuccessfully sought to rely upon a failure to observe the European Prison Rules.[121] The door was left open. Ironically, in *S, M & T v Austria*, the first case in which it appears CPT opinions were referred to by the Commission in assessing whether there had been an Article 3 violation, the Commission cited the CPT's views that immigration detainees were being held in acceptable conditions.[122] Two years later, in *LJ v Finland*, the Commission had regard to the CPT's criticisms that the material conditions of detention in an isolation unit were 'poor', and there was insufficient 'mental and physical stimulation'. The Commission also took into account the government's interim and follow-up reports but dismissed the Article 3 point by concluding that the facts 'did not disclose any appearance of a violation'.[123]

---

[118] eg *Tanka v Finland*, App No 23634/94, Comm Dec (unpublished) (the Commission considered that lack of medical facilities in certain circumstances could be Article 3 issue); *D v UK*, Judgment of 2 May 1997, *RJD* 1997-III, 777 (the state would have been in violation of Article 3 if the applicant, who was in the advanced stages of AIDS and with only a short time to live, were to have been removed to his country of origin after his release on licence from prison in circumstances where it was conceded that the lack of medical treatment in his country of origin would have reduced his life expectancy further).

[119] The Article 3 argument of the applicant was originally founded largely upon criticisms made by the national authority's inspector of prisons; when the UK Report was made public, the applicant amended his argument to reflect the additional condemnation of the CPT.

[120] *Delazarus v UK*, App No 17525/90, Comm Dec, 16 February 1993 (unpublished), para 1.

[121] *Eggs v Switzerland*, App No 7341/76, Comm Dec, 11 December 1976, 6 *DR* 170; *X v Germany*, App No 7408/76, Comm Dec, 11 July 1977, 10 *DR* 221.

[122] *S, M and T v Austria*, App No 19066/91, Comm Dec, 5 April 1993, 74 *DR* 179.

[123] *LJ v Finland*, App No 21221/93, Comm Dec, 28 June 1995 (unpublished).

References to CPT reports are now being considered by the Court itself. In the 1996 case of *Amuur v France*, the applicants maintained that transit zone detention facilities did not meet CPT recommendations in support of their complaint of violations of Article 5 guarantees of liberty of person, but while the relevant CPT report[124] was referred to in the factual and legal background, the Court did not rely upon it in its decision.[125] The closest to a breakthrough is found in the Commission's report of 1997 in *Aerts v Belgium*.[126] Both the majority decision and minority dissent are of interest, even though ultimately the Court decided there was no violation of Article 3. The applicant had been detained by a court in a prison psychiatric annexe where he was examined and subjected to further deprivation of liberty under mental health provisions. The relevant tribunal had instructed that he be placed in a named institution rather than continue to be held in a prison. Subsequent attempts through the courts to have him sent to the institution which had been selected on account of its regime were unsuccessful on account of a shortage of places. After failing to be awarded legal aid to challenge prison detention conditions, he made an application to the Commission and relied upon the CPT report, which had been highly critical of the prison during a visit carried out two and a half weeks after he finally secured a transfer to the institution. The CPT's report had concluded that 'in every regard, the level of care of patients held in the annexe was below the minimum acceptable level from the ethical and human point of view'.[127] The CPT's criticisms were of importance in two respects. First, they helped establish that there had been a failure to provide an adequate treatment regime and thus (by 29 votes to 2) the Commission concluded there had been a violation of Article 5(1). Second—and more significantly—the report gave weight to the finding that the conditions in which the applicant had been held constituted inhuman 'or at least degrading' treatment contrary to Article 3. Here the majority (of 17) accepted the criticisms of inadequate treatment regime, over-crowding, and promiscuity contained in the CPT report, but for the minority (of 14), the very failure of the CPT report to condemn the prison by using the term 'inhuman or degrading treatment' was significant and helped to show that the conditions had not reached the level of severity required.[128] The minority report seemed disingenuous: the failure to use the labels of 'inhuman' or 'degrading' should be considered alongside the CPT's unwill-

---

[124] France 1, paras 79–80.

[125] *Amuur v France*, Judgment of 25 June 1996, *RJD* 1996-III, 827.

[126] *Aerts v Belgium*, App No 25357/94, Comm Rep, 20 May 1997. The Report will appear as an annexe when the Court's judgment of 30 July 1998 is reported in *RJD* 1998.

[127] Belgium 1, para 191 (author's translation).

[128] *Aerts v Belgium*, App No 25357/94, Comm Rep, 20 May 1997, paras 39–55; 66–83; and *Opinion Dissidente*, p 28.

ingness to be seen to be formulating 'interpretations of the provisions of the European Convention on Human Rights' as provided for in the Explanatory Report.[129]

The high expectations this Commission report raised were dashed when the Court's judgment appeared just over a year later. The majority of the Court (by 7 votes to 2) disposed of the matter briefly. There was no proof that the appellant's mental health had deteriorated, and the conditions of detention 'do not seem to have had such serious effects on his mental health as would bring them within the scope of Article 3'. The issue was primarily one of proof. 'Even if it is accepted that the applicant's state of anxiety . . . was caused by the conditions of detention in Lantin, and even allowing for the difficulties [he] may have had [as a severely mentally disturbed patient] in describing how these affected him, it has not been conclusively established that the applicant suffered treatment that could be classified as inhuman or degrading.' However, the majority did seem to accept the CPT's conclusions that the care was below the acceptable minimum standard (as the CPT put it) 'from an ethical and humanitarian point of view' and carried an 'undeniable risk of a deterioration of their mental health' if prolonged.[130] The minority opinion differed over whether the available facts met the minimum level of severity. What was of relevance to the dissenting judges was the urgent need of the applicant to receive appropriate treatment, the failure to provide this, and his detention in wholly unsatisfactory conditions for a period in excess of nine months: in these circumstances the state's treatment involved a 'serious risk of an irreversible deterioration of his mental health' and suffering which exceeded the Article 3 threshold.[131]

Yet while the applicant was ultimately unsuccessful on this point, both the majority and minority on the Court (and the majority of the Commission) were prepared to accept that the conditions as described and assessed by the CPT could place patients at real risk of ill-treatment which could be sufficient in certain circumstances to trigger a violation. The CPT's report was relied upon as of particular importance in establishing not only the factual basis of holding conditions but also the seriousness of their shortcomings. The difference was essentially one of proof. For the majority of the Court the applicant simply had not established to its satisfaction that the threshold test had been reached in his particular circumstances. The position adopted by the minority on the Commission was not persuasive, and was rejected by the Court. The crucial point remains: while the CPT may be under some obligation to avoid an overt challenge to Commission

---

[129] Explanatory Report, para 91.
[130] *Aerts v Belgium*, Judgment of 30 July 1998, paras 64–66.
[131] Ibid, partly dissenting opinion of Judges Pekkamen and Jambrek, paras 5–6.

and Court jurisprudence, there is no such duty upon the judicial bodies to ignore CPT standard setting when persuaded with argument or submissions based upon CPT reports.

6. CRIMINAL PROCESS AND FAIR TRIAL: AN EMERGING EUROPEAN CODE OF CRIMINAL PROCEDURE?

The diversity in domestic criminal procedure provision reflects local traditions often deeply embedded within the psyche of a legal order. CPT country reports provide insights into domestic law and practice of member states, although inevitably the Committee may only achieve a rather superficial view of legal rules. Collectively, these reports constitute a remarkable montage of variations in police powers, levels of discretion available to public prosecutors, involvement of judges in supervisory roles, and availability of procedural rights for suspects. Each legal system has developed its own solutions to the question as to how best to achieve a balance between the interests of the public in ensuring effective and efficient administration of justice and those of an accused in obtaining a fair trial. Some compatibility with external norms is expected. Important principles are established by the European Convention on Human Rights, and much of the groundwork for a minimum level of common provision of fair trial throughout Europe has already been laid by the Commission and Court. Thus the sheer volume of Article 5 and 6 jurisprudence provides a rich and varied foundation upon which to construct a European model of criminal procedure. Fundamental principles such as access to justice, the presumption of innocence, and equality of arms provide a solid framework for any legal system; yet it is both difficult and in any case inappropriate for the Commission and Court to go beyond this and to seek to achieve greater standardization in criminal justice. The role of these judicial organs is essentially to test local provision against international standards, and the choice of means of compliance with the Human Rights Convention is left to the state. Further, there are aspects of criminal procedure which appear largely immune from Convention scrutiny. Against this background, the CPT has the opportunity to recommend common provisions for criminal justice systems with a view to minimize the risks of ill-treatment during police custody, and—crucially—in a manner which is unlikely to provoke conflict with the European Convention on Human Rights.

The Human Rights Convention provides significant procedural protection to individuals suspected of crimes or who have otherwise been deprived of their liberty. Article 5 requires domestic law to accord an individual certain safeguards to ensure that any deprivation of liberty is lawful.

Thus under Article 5 detainees may challenge the confinement in inappropriate regimes[132] or the legality of continuing detention.[133] In cases of arrest upon suspicion of involvement in crime, detainees must be brought 'promptly' before a judicial officer when deprived of their liberty[134] and brought to trial if denied bail within a reasonable time.[135] These complement due process guarantees provided by Article 6 such as the right to a fair and public hearing, to the presumption of innocence, and to legal assistance in preparing the defence where the interests of justice so require.[136] These guarantees have been extended to cover disciplinary proceedings which may lead to deprivation of liberty[137] or of substantial remission of sentence.[138] Over the past forty or so years, these two Articles have influenced the criminal procedures of West European states. Of course, these provisions largely reflect values already well established in most legal systems: and the Strasbourg machinery has largely been used to ensure the fine-tuning of domestic procedures. The crucial question for most states has been the extent to which protection for criminal suspects is to be balanced as an interest against the 'competing' state interest in the effective and efficient investigation of crime. But while treaty obligations have been spelt out with some care in the achievement of equality of arms and in 'periodic review' of indeterminate sentences, these concern 'subsequent' rather than 'initial' aspects of a criminal process. Pre-trial procedures are less open to international regulation. Strasbourg's primary concern under Article 5(1) is whether there has been domestic compliance with substantive and procedural provisions, although the guarantee does ultimately require that procedures are 'fair and proper'.[139]

'Fair and proper' procedures include the specific guarantees of Article 5. Paragraph (2) requires that a detainee is adequately informed of the reasons for his detention so as to permit him to judge the lawfulness of

---

[132] eg *Boamar v Belgium*, Judgment of 29 February 1988, Ser A No 129 (confinement of juvenile in adult prison); *Ashingdane v United Kingdom*, Judgment of 28 May 1985, Ser A No 93 (confinement of psychiatric patient in secure rather than in ordinary hospital).

[133] eg *Winterwerp v The Netherlands*, Judgment of 24 October 1979, Ser A No 33 (challenging mental health detention order); *Thynne, Wilson & Gunnell v United Kingdom*, Judgment of 25 October 1990, Ser A No 190 (discretionary life sentences imposed upon sex offenders); *Doran v The Netherlands*, App No 15268/92, Comm Dec, 30 November 1992 (unpublished) (detention centre refused to implement court order instructing release).

[134] Cf *Brogan and Others v United Kingdom*, Judgment of 29 November 1988, Ser A No 145-B.

[135] eg *Bezicheri v Italy*, Judgment of 25 October 1989, Ser A No 164.

[136] Article 6(3)(c).

[137] *Engel v The Netherlands*, Judgment of 8 June 1976, Ser A No 22, paras 81–82.

[138] *Campbell & Fell v United Kingdom*, Judgment of 28 June 1984, Ser A No 80; cf *McFeely v United Kingdom*, App No 8317/78, Comm Dec, 15 May 1980, 20 *DR* 44 (proceedings before a governor who could award up to 28 days' loss of remission not covered by Article 6).

[139] Cf *Winterwerp v The Netherlands*, Judgment of 24 October 1979, Ser A No 33, paras 45–46.

the state action and, if he thinks fit, to challenge it. The legal basis for the
detention, together with the essential facts relevant to the lawfulness of the
decision to arrest, must be given in 'simple, non-technical language' that an
individual can understand.[140] Article 5(3) requires the prompt appearance
of a suspect who has been kept in custody before a judge or other judicial
officer with a view to ensuring an independent assessment of the legality of
loss of liberty, a provision which (for the purposes of pre-trial procedures)
is concerned primarily with imposing a maximum period of detention
before judicial appearance and with compliance with the essentials of judicial independence.[141] These two guarantees are at the heart of pre-trial procedures. But lacunae exist. As discussed, 'deprivation of liberty' for the
purposes of Article 5 may not cover persons who find themselves subject
to questioning in police stations. In many legal systems the giving of reasons
for deprivation of liberty at the time of arrest may indeed be a prerequi-
site of a *lawful* arrest, but the Convention may not be as rigorous in
demanding immediate notification, at least where the detention is otherwise than on suspicion of having committed an offence.[142] Further, while
detainees in police custody must be brought 'promptly' before a judicial
officer when deprived of their liberty, 'promptly' seems to permit an individual to be detained in police custody before being brought to court for
up to a period of four days.[143] More particularly, whole tracts of pre-trial
procedure are left largely uncharted.

There is thus plenty of scope for the CPT to develop recommendations
concerning, in particular, pre-trial procedure while in police detention, free
from the concerns of potential conflict with the Human Rights treaty.
Indeed, since the prevention of ill-treatment in police stations after the
commencement of detention and during interrogation simultaneously
advances both fairness (from the standpoint of Article 6) as well as the
CPT's own mandate, the two European treaties here are properly considered as complementary mechanisms. Here, the CPT's aim is to develop
rights for suspects through the provision of procedural rights which will
provide safeguards against ill-treatment, backed up by a police complaints
system which permits proper review. The content of these rights has been
spelt out with some care, initially in the second general report[144] and there-

---

[140] *Fox, Campbell and Hartley v United Kingdom*, Judgment of 30 August 1990, Ser A No
182, para 40.
[141] eg *Brogan & Others v United Kingdom*, Judgment of 29 November 1988, Ser A No
145-B.
[142] *Fox, Campbell and Hartley v United Kingdom*, Judgment of 30 August 1990, Ser A No
182, para 40.
[143] Cf *Brogan & Others v United Kingdom*, Judgment of 29 November 1988, Ser A No
145-B.
[144] Gen Rep 2, paras 36–37.

after, with some further refinement, in individual country reports.[145] The three rights—notification of custody to a relative or other person; access to a lawyer; and medical examination by a doctor of the individual's own choosing—can be seen as important aspects of pre-trial procedure involving rights which ultimately have a bearing upon fair trial guarantees.

As in domestic law, recognition is made of state interests. However, CPT recommendations attempt to tailor these to as exact a 'fit' as possible. Restrictions on the right of notification to a relation or third party in the interests of the investigation of an offence should be carefully prescribed, and any power to delay notification should be subject to appropriate safeguards such as the approval of a senior police officer or public prosecutor and to an express time limit.[146] Further, if in exceptional cases it is felt desirable to place restrictions upon access to a particular lawyer of the detainee's choice, then unrestricted access should be given to another independent lawyer 'who can be trusted not to jeopardise the legitimate interests of the police investigations'.[147] Perhaps surprisingly, the CPT has not insisted that a detainee be told of the grounds for his deprivation of liberty as is required under Article 5(2) of the ECHR, although this may be implicit in this right of access to a lawyer. Medical examination by a doctor of the detainee's own choice is seen as a fundamental safeguard against ill-treatment at the hands of police authorities. Such a right should be expressly provided for at all stages of police custody,[148] and in particular during prolonged interrogation by police officers, since this permits 'the independent and objective recording, on a regular basis, of medical evidence of injuries sustained by detainees'.[149] A final development in the gradual 'compilation of standards' in the area of pre-trial detention is found in recommendations concerning the conduct of interrogations of suspects by police officers. This aspect of police treatment is largely ignored: only if interrogation methods are inhuman or degrading would any Human Rights Convention issue arise.[150] Domestic provisions could usefully be supplemented by a code of conduct for interrogations, covering such issues as the systematic informing of the detainee of the details of the officers conducting the interrogation, rest periods between and breaks during interrogation, the places where interrogation may take place, the questioning of vulnerable individuals (such as the young or mentally disabled) or individuals under the influence

---

[145] For further discussion, see Evans and Morgan (1998), Chapter Seven.
[146] eg Finland 1, paras 28–30; Italy 1, para 42.
[147] Finland 1, para 32.   [148] Denmark 1, para 128.
[149] UK 2, para 70: to this end, the record of a medical examination should contain any account of relevant statements including allegations of ill-treatment and the individual's description of his state of health; an account of objective medical findings; and the doctor's conclusions.
[150] Cf above, Note 59.

of drugs or who are in a state of shock, whether a suspect may be required to remain standing during the interrogation, and the recording of the conduct of the interview and of any requests made by the detainee during it.[151] The actual conduct of the police interrogations should be recorded electronically[152] using a system which affords all appropriate safeguards (such as the use of two tapes, one of which would be sealed in the presence of the detainee).[153] Further, intimate body searches of suspects should be carried out in conditions affording a measure of privacy, and in the presence of a qualified doctor.[154]

CPT standard setting in relation to pre-trial procedures is thus less controversial. Advancing fair procedures is an explicit goal of the Human Rights treaty and an implicit task of the CPT, and standard CPT recommendations as to the rights of suspects found in country reports tend to dovetail with ECHR guarantees and jurisprudence by dealing with issues largely untouched by the Commission and Court. In this area, then, CPT creativity is free to flourish unhindered by concerns of possible conflict with other European norms. Consequently, it may now be just possible to talk of the emergence of a more complete European *ordre public* in criminal justice.

7. CONCLUSION

Assessment of the work of the CPT involves two aspects: the extent to which the 'ongoing dialogue' is producing actual improvements in detention conditions; and the impact of standard setting upon existing Council of Europe norms. Although discussion has focused on the latter issue, implicit in discussion has been the extent to which the CPT recognizes that there are limits to its standard setting in order to retain the confidence of state parties. Policy and resource allocation appear to be matters which the Committee avoids. Promulgated standards on occasion lack clarity. In any case, the CPT is often acutely aware of lack of awareness of its work on the part of state officials.[155]

The suggestion has been made that CPT standards will quietly supersede the European Prison Rules, but states will receive more explicit guidance of European expectations in the process. CPT standards will also begin to

---

[151] Iceland 1, para 39.
[152] eg Austria 1, para 66; Sweden 1, paras 32–34; Germany 1, para 43.
[153] eg Iceland 1, para 40.
[154] eg Italy 1, para 39.
[155] National authorities are often exhorted to ensure all relevant officials are made aware of the Convention (and certainly to ensure that persons in charge of places of detention which have been visited are made aware of the CPT's observations once communicated to the national authorities): cf Gen Rep 5, para 6.

have an impact upon pre-trial procedures. This will occur through encouragement of the development of common provision of rights for accused persons while in police custody. This is a useful addition to the work of the Commission and Court, and unlikely to prompt conflict. The central issue is in the challenge posed by the CPT to Strasbourg jurisprudence. Caution on the part of the CPT in seeking reinterpretation of aspects of Article 3 has, until now, been matched by a distance on the part of the Commission and Court towards condemning general or specific holding conditions as 'inhuman' or 'degrading' under Article 3. The gradual raising of awareness of the work of the CPT amongst lawyers is now producing the type of challenge to that jurisprudence which, if successful, may do as much in a couple of test cases as the CPT is able to achieve in its 'ongoing dialogue' by persuasion. The crux is the self-evident observation that governments are liable to pay more attention to a finding of a violation of the Human Rights Convention than they are to a recommendation in a CPT report. The opportunity now exists for applicants to seek to make more use of CPT reports to encourage change through legal process and thus provoke the direct challenge to case law which the framers of the ECPT were keen to avoid.

REFERENCES

Bloed, A, Leicht, L, Nowak, M and Rosas, A (eds) (1993) *Monitoring Human Rights in Europe* (Dordrecht: Martinus Nijhoff)

Bleitenmoser and Wilms (1990) 'Human Rights v Extradition', 11 *MichJIL* 845

Blumenwitz (1989) 'Fall Soering', 16 *EvGRZ* 314

Cassese, A (1989) 'A New Approach to Human Rights: The European Convention for the Prevention of Torture', 83 *AJIL* 130

Dimitrijevi (1993) 'The Monitoring of Human Rights and the Prevention of Human Rights Violations through Reporting Procedures' in Bloed, A, Leicht, L, Nowak, M and Rosas, A (eds), 1–24

Evans, MD and Morgan, R (1998) *Preventing Torture* (Oxford: Clarendon Press)

Fiss, OM (1979) 'The Supreme Court 1978 Term', 93 *Harvard Law Rev* 1

Gross, AM (1996) 'Reinforcing the New Democracies: the ECHR and the Former Communist Countries—a Study of the Case Law', 7 *EJIL* 89

Harris, D, O'Boyle, M and Warbrick, C (1995) *Law of the European Convention on Human Rights* (London: Butterworths)

Horowitz, DL (1977) *The Courts and Social Policy* (Washington: Brookings Institute)

Hudson, B (1987) *Justice Through Punishment* (Basingstoke: Macmillan)

Lacey, N (1995) *Criminal Justice* (Oxford: Oxford University Press)

Lång (1990), Report on 'Human Rights of Persons Deprived of their Liberty', 7th International Colloquy on the ECHR, doc H/Coll (90)4

Müllerson, R (1993) 'The Efficiency of the Individual Complaint Procedures' in Bloed, A, Leicht, L, Nowak, M and Rosas, A (eds)

Murdoch, J (1993) 'Safeguarding the Liberty of Person: recent Strasbourg Jurisprudence', 42 *ICLQ* 494

Murdoch, J (1998) 'Recent Caselaw under Article 5 of the European Convention on Human Rights', 23 *ELRev* HR/31

Nowak, M (1989) 'The European Convention on Human Rights and its Control System', 7 *NQHR* 98

Scottish Prison Complaints Commission (1997) *Report for 1996*, Cm 3688 (Edinburgh: HMSO)

Sørensen, B (1995) 'Prevention of Torture and Inhuman or Degrading Treatment or Punishment: Medical Views' in APT, *The Implementation of the European Convention for the Prevention of Torture and Inhuman or Degrading Treatment or Punishment (ECPT): Assessment and Perspectives after Five Years of Activities of the European Committee for the Prevention of Torture and Inhuman or Degrading Treatment or Punishment—Acts of the Seminar of 5 to 7 December 1994, Strasbourg* (Geneva: APT)

Trechsel, S (1986) 'Zum Verhältnis zwischen der Folterschutzkonvention und der Europäischen Menschenrechtskonvention', Hangartner, Y and Trechsel, S (eds) in *Völkerrecht im Dienste des Menschens: Festschrift für Hans Haug* (Bern; Stuttgart: Haupt)

Trechsel, S (1990) Report on 'Human Rights of Persons Deprived of their Liberty', 7th International Colloquy on the ECHR, doc H/Coll (90)3

van Dijk, P and van Hoof, GJH (1990) *Theory and Practice of the European Convention on Human Rights*, 2nd edn (Deventer: Kluwer)

5

CPT and Other International Standards
for the Prevention of Torture

WALTER SUNTINGER

1. INTRODUCTION

It has been said of the CPT's procedural safeguards that 'it must be stressed that [they] have not been developed in a vacuum'.[1] This observation is true for all CPT standards, and the purpose of this chapter is to examine the manner in which the preventive standards applied by the CPT relate to the broader, comprehensive web of international obligations, norms, and standards of which they form a part.

(a) The concept of prevention

What is prevention of torture or mistreatment?[2] When describing its preventive role in its first general report, the CPT said:

it must ascertain whether . . . there are general or specific conditions or circumstances that are likely to *degenerate into* torture or inhuman or degrading treatment or punishment, or are at any rate *conducive to* such inadmissible acts or practices.[3]

Thus there are certain conditions which may become or degenerate into ill-treatment and certain circumstances which carry within them a risk of abuse or are conducive to abuse. Furthermore, the operation of a preventive mandate entails forming an understanding of what is to be prevented and what are the appropriate responses to acts or incidents of torture/mistreatment. According to this view, the prevention of torture/mistreatment involves a comprehensive approach incorporating four elements:

---

[1] Evans, MD and Morgan, R (1998) *Preventing Torture* (Oxford: Clarendon Press), 258.

[2] The term 'mistreatment' is used as an umbrella concept comprising cruel, inhuman or degrading treatment or punishment, which is not yet considered to be torture. This terminology is adopted because the CPT has chosen to use the more familiar term 'ill-treatment' in a narrower sense, that is, with respect to physical ill-treatment, and not with regard to prison conditions, for which use of the term 'inhuman and degrading treatment' is reserved.

[3] Gen Rep 1, para 45.

(1) that which is to be prevented (the concept of torture and other forms of mistreatment);

(2) the safeguards which must be introduced in order to reduce the risk of such prohibited acts;

(3) the overall conditions necessary for places of detention not to be or become inhuman or degrading;

(4) the reaction to torture/mistreatment in terms of investigation, complaint mechanisms, and sanctions.

The CPT has developed standards in all these fields.[4] So comprehensive an understanding of prevention, including seeing the response to incidents of torture as a preventive tool in its own right, is supported by other relevant international instruments and organs. For example, Articles 2 and 16 of the UNCAT obliges states to take all effective measures to prevent torture and mistreatment. This basic obligation can be regarded as the basis upon which the other Convention provisions dealing with prevention are founded. The former Special Rapporteur on Torture, Peter Kooijmans, considered torture to be the final link in a long chain which begins where human dignity is taken lightly.[5] Prevention involves identifying the links in this chain and breaking it before the end is reached.[6] Again, this suggests that we start with a look at what is to be prevented and then proceed to shed light on the path towards human dignity. Bearing in mind that the concept of human dignity is the basis of all human rights,[7] this approach stresses the relationship between the right to freedom from torture and other human rights and thus the interdependence of all human rights.

(b) The international normative web

The development of international human rights standards at both the universal and the regional levels has been a dynamic process stretching over the last fifty years. Detailed standards relevant to torture prevention can be found in an impressive list of international instruments, ranging from treaties laying down substantive standards to soft law documents, and in the work of international mechanisms which have been established.[8] Further-

---

[4] Cf the classification in Evans and Morgan (1998), Chapters Seven and Eight, but with standards of reaction now taken as a separate issue.

[5] Report of the UN Special Rapporteur on Torture, UN Doc E/CN.4/1993/26, para 582.

[6] Nowak, M and Suntinger, W (1993) 'International mechanisms for the prevention of torture' in Bloed, A, Leicht, L, Nowak, M and Rosas, A (eds) *Monitoring Human Rights in Europe* (Dordrecht: Martinus Nijhoff), 146.

[7] Meron, T (1993) 'Human dignity as a normative concept', 77 *AJIL* 848; Zajadlo, J (1997) 'Human dignity and human rights' in Hanski, R and Suksi, M (eds) (1997) *An Introduction to the International Protection of Human Rights* (Turku: Institute for Human Rights, Abo Akademi University), 15.

[8] This process continues: for example, the then comprehensive list of instruments containing provisions related to torture, drawn up by the UN Special Rapporteur in 1986 (Report of

more, the prohibition of torture is considered to be a norm recognized by international law (both as customary law and as general principle of law) and to constitute a norm of *ius cogens*.[9]

(c) The structure of this analysis

Section Two of this chapter will provide a brief description of the structures and processes within which preventive standards are set or developed. Section Three—the heart of this chapter—then examines the pertinent standards found in international human rights instruments relating to the four aspects of torture prevention identified above. This is then followed by three short sections: Section Four presents an overview of the resulting normative web of mutually influencing standards; Section Five draws on the experience of Austria to offer some thoughts on the factors which influence the domestic impact of international standards; and Section Six offers some concluding suggestions. In a chapter of this nature, it is impossible to examine all issues relating to torture prevention in detail. The focus will be on the prevention of torture in police settings rather than in prisons. Furthermore, the principle of non-refoulement is not dealt with.[10] Equally, only those standards applicable to European countries are mentioned, and standards developed under other regional systems, in particular the

the UN Special Rapporteur, E/CN.4/1986/15, para 26 *et seq*), has expanded considerably. General human rights treaties setting forth substantive standards include: the International Covenant on Civil and Political Rights, the European Convention on Human Rights, the American Convention on Human Rights, the African Charter on Human and Peoples' Rights, and the Convention on the Rights of the Child. The specific anti-torture treaties laying down substantive standards are the UN Convention against Torture and the Inter-American Convention for the Prevention and Punishment of Torture. International mechanisms within the framework of which substantive standards have been developed include: the European Convention for the Prevention of Torture and the UN Special Rapporteur on Torture. Declarations and Resolutions laying down substantive standards include: the Universal Declaration of Human Rights, Minimum Standards for the Treatment of Prisoners, Body of Principles for the Protection of all Persons under Any Form of Detention or Imprisonment, UN Standard Minimum Rules for the Administration of Juvenile Justice ('The Beijing Rules'), Code of Conduct for Law Enforcement Officials, Basic Principles on the Use of Force and Firearms by Law Enforcement Officials, Basic Principles on the Role of Lawyers, Principles of Medical Ethics relevant to the Role of Health Personnel, particularly Physicians, in the Protection of Prisoners and Detainees against Torture and Other Cruel, Inhuman or Degrading Treatment or Punishment, European Prison Rules, and Human Dimension Documents of the OSCE, especially the Moscow Document. See United Nations (1993) *United Nations, Human Rights— A compilation of international instruments* (Geneva: United Nations).

[9] Cf HRC, General Comment 24/52, 12 November 1994, § 8 and 10; UN Special Rapporteur on Torture, UN Doc E/CN.4/1986/15, para 3 (referring to the *Barcelona Traction, Light and Power Company, Limited*, Second Phase, Judgment, ICJ Reports 1970, 3, paras 33–34).

[10] Indeed, its relationship with the CPT's mandate is problematic: for a comparative analysis of the interpretation of the principle of non-refoulement under the CAT and the ECHR, see Suntinger, W (1995) 'The principle of non-refoulement: Looking rather to Geneva than to Strasbourg?', 49 *Austrian Journal of Public and International Law*, 203.

Inter-American system for the protection of human rights, have not been examined.

2. STANDARD SETTING

International human rights standards[11] are set and developed in a variety of procedural and institutional settings which differ considerably in nature. As these differences have a bearing on their output, this section provides a brief overview of the organs and procedures within which such standard-setting takes place.

(a) The International Covenant on Civil and Political Rights (ICCPR)

While most articles of the ICCPR can be seen as having a degree of relevance to torture prevention, especially in the context of prison conditions, there are some Covenant provisions which are of special importance, particularly—and most obviously—Articles 7 (torture) and 10 (accused and convicted persons),[12] but also Articles 9 (personal liberty), 14 (fair trial), and 17 (right to private and family life). Moreover, Article 2, the general obligation to respect and ensure the rights contained in the ICCPR and to guarantee an effective remedy, is of great importance. The Human Rights Committee[13] has developed its normative understanding of these provisions within both its reporting and individual complaints mechanisms. The reporting procedure facilitates a comprehensive examination of the legal, admin-

---

[11] The term 'standards' as used here covers a broad range of prescriptions emanating from different sources of international law.

[12] Article 7 provides: 'No one shall be subjected to torture or to cruel, inhuman or degrading treatment or punishment. In particular, no one shall be subjected without his free consent to medical or scientific experimentation.' Article 10 provides:

1. All persons deprived of their liberty shall be treated with humanity and with respect for the inherent dignity of the human person.
2. (a) Accused persons shall, save in exceptional circumstances, be segregated from convicted persons and shall be subject to separate treatment appropriate to their status as unconvicted persons;
   (b) Accused juvenile persons shall be separated from adults and brought as speedily as possible for adjudication.
3. The penitentiary system shall comprise treatment of prisoners the essential aim of which shall be their reformation and social rehabilitation. Juvenile offenders shall be segregated from adults and be accorded treatment appropriate to their age and legal status.

[13] See McGoldrick, D (1991) *The Human Rights Committee, Its role in the development of the International Covenant on Civil and Political Rights* (Oxford: Clarendon Press); Nowak, M (1993) *CCPR Commentary* (Strasbourg/Kehl/Arlington: HN Engels); Opsahl, T (1992) 'The Human Rights Committee' in Alston, P (ed) *The UN and Human Rights* (Oxford: Clarendon Press), 369.

istrative, and political framework surrounding human rights implementation whilst the individual complaint procedure provides guidance on what constitutes a violation of the provisions of the ICCPR in concrete cases and in a quasi-judicial context.[14] Perhaps the most important contribution to standard setting has been the Committee's General Comments on Articles 7 and 10.[15] Neither the decisions of the HRC on individual complaints nor the results of the reporting procedures are legally binding on states. However, decisions on individual cases and consensus statements by the Committee, including its General Comments, can be considered as authoritative interpretations of the content and scope of the Covenant's provisions.[16]

(b) The European Convention on Human Rights (ECHR)

As with the ICCPR, most of the Convention's articles have relevance for torture prevention. Most fundamentally, Article 3 provides that 'No one shall be subjected to torture or to inhuman or degrading treatment or punishment', and this is buttressed by Articles 5 (the right to liberty and security), 6 (the right to a fair trial), and 8 (the right to respect for private and family life and the right to an effective remedy), all of which have special relevance. The European Commission and Court have developed and clarified the scope of these provisions in many decisions on interstate and individual complaints.[17] The enforcement mechanisms of the Convention system are directed towards determining whether violations of convention obligations have occurred in concrete situations, resulting in legally binding judgments from the European Court of Human Rights. However, judgments of the Court can be regarded as having a broader quasi-binding effect in the sense that they determine the normative content of the treaty provisions.[18]

(c) The UN Convention Against Torture (UNCAT)

The drafters of the UNCAT were able to draw on the experiences of the above-mentioned bodies. The Convention lays down far-reaching

[14] As to the discussions concerning the nature of the HRC, see McGoldrick (1991), 53 *et seq.*

[15] HRC, General Comment 20/44, General Comment 21/44.

[16] See Nowak (1993), 576.

[17] See generally van Dijk, P and van Hoof, GJH (1990) *Theory and Practice of the European Convention on Human Rights* (Deventer: Kluwer); Harris, DJ, O'Boyle, M and Warbrick, C (1995) *Law of the European Convention on Human Rights* (London: Butterworths).

[18] Cf Merrills, JG (1992) *The development of international law by the European Court of Human Rights*, 2nd edn (Manchester: Manchester University Press), 9; as regards international courts in general, see Fastenrath, U (1991) *Lücken im Völkerrecht* (Berlin: Dunker and Humbolt), 122.

obligations which were the result of political bargaining between states, under the influence of a number of NGOs. It contains a definition of torture, prohibits torture in absolute terms, and requires states to punish torture by appropriate penalties. It establishes the principle of universal jurisdiction allowing for the prosecution of perpetrators of torture in all states parties, regardless of the nationality of the victim or the perpetrator and of the place where the act of torture was committed. Furthermore, it explicitly obliges states to investigate all acts of torture and to guarantee an effective complaints procedure.[19] Articles 2 and 16 are particularly important. They oblige states to take 'effective legislative, administrative, judicial or other measures to prevent' torture and mistreatment. All of the other provisions can be regarded as an elaboration of this general obligation, which is 'the main aim and purpose of the Convention'.[20] In other words, states are required to take all steps to eradicate torture.

This leads to the question: What are effective preventive measures, and who judges their effectiveness? Although some measures and resulting standards can be identified at the international level by the anti-torture organs, their effectiveness arguably depends, at least in part, on the national context.[21] The effectiveness of the measures taken can be assessed by other states and, more importantly, by the Committee against Torture (CAT).[22]

The CAT has contributed to the clarification of the UNCAT provisions through the reporting procedure, the individual complaints procedure, and the investigation mechanism under Article 20. It should be noted that the Committee considers itself to be 'not an appellate, a quasi-judicial or an administrative body, but rather a monitoring body created by the States Parties themselves with declaratory powers only'.[23] So far, the CAT does not seem to have fully used—or had the chance to use—its potential to lend further detail and clarity to the general norms set out in the UNCAT,

---

[19] See eg Burgers, J and Danelius, H (1988) *The United Nations Convention against Torture* (Dordrecht: Martinus Nijhoff); Byrnes, A (1992) 'The United Nations Committee Against Torture' in Alston, P (ed) *United Nations and Human Rights* (Oxford: Clarendon Press).

[20] *Alan v Switzerland*, CAT Comm No 21/1995 (8 May 1996) A/51/44, Annex V, para 11.5.

[21] Peter Kooijmans stresses this in the context of country visits by the Special Rapporteur on Torture: 'Most importantly, the recommendations contained in the report of such a country-visit are directly focused on the situation in that country and therefore can be very concrete. . . . they [the recommendations] suggest the steps to be taken to eradicate torture and to prevent its reoccurrence in light of the human rights situation in that specific country'. Kooijmans, P (1991) 'The Role and Action of the UN Special Rapporteur on Torture' in Cassese, A (ed) *The International Fight Against Torture/La Lutte international contre la torture* (Baden-Baden: Nomos), 66. With respect to Austria, see Suntinger, W (1997a) 'International and national dimensions of the fight against torture: The Austrian experience' in Haenni, C (ed) *20 ans consacrés a la réalisation d'une idée* (Geneva: Association for the Prevention of Torture), 257.

[22] Boulesbaa, A (1990) 'The Nature of Obligations Incurred by States under Article 2 of the Convention against Torture', 2 *Human Rights Quarterly* 66.

[23] CAT General Comment on Article 3 CAT, para 9 (a). Annual Report of the CAT Committee, UN Doc A/53/44, Annex IX.

with the commendable exception of its approach to the principle of non-refoulement under Article 3.[24] The questions and criticisms raised during the reporting procedure, and the Committee's conclusions, are generally insufficiently systematic to allow clear conclusions to be drawn concerning the CAT's approach to certain key issues.

(d) The European Convention for the Prevention of Torture (ECPT)

The ECPT does not lay down any substantive standards. However, the Committee established by the Convention (the CPT) has developed standards informed by its experiences when conducting visits since, according to the CPT, pre-existing standards were not always found to be adequate.[25] Developing standards against the background of on-site inspection has the advantage of ensuring practicality. However, the CPT does not seem to address less visible issues and the pertinent standards related to them with similar thoroughness, even though they are also of importance. Its non-judicial and preventive mandate allows the CPT to recommend standards which may go well beyond established human rights norms: its non-legally binding recommendations need not be founded on strict legal reasoning, but can comprise quite pragmatic proposals.

(e) The UN Special Rapporteur on Torture (SRT)

The SRT was established in 1985 by the UN Commission on Human Rights as a thematic procedure, based on ECOSOC Resolution 1235 (XLII). The office has a mandate to examine questions relevant to torture and to report on the occurrence and extent of its practice. In order to fulfil this task, the SRT is to seek and receive credible and reliable information from a variety of sources, including governments and non-governmental organizations, and respond effectively to that information.[26] Although, or perhaps because, the mandate is limited to torture and does not include other forms of mistreatment, the SRT has nevertheless dealt with 'the grey area'[27] between torture and mistreatment. Furthermore, and this is particularly important for current purposes, the SRT has made general recommendations of a preventive character, thereby creating standards which, though echoing in part those found in UN instruments, occasionally go beyond them. If, as has been argued, effective prevention of torture needs to be based on an analysis which sees torture as the final link in a chain, or as the 'ultimate result of a deficient system',[28] then the SRT views the phenomenon from a global

---

[24] The majority of the individual complaints submitted concern Article 3 and the only General Comment so far issued has concerned this Article.
[25] Gen Rep 1, paras 95–96.   [26] See Kooijmans (1991), 56.
[27] E/CN.4/1986/15, paras 22–23.   [28] Kooijmans (1991), 67.

perspective. The SRT's 1995 report contains a helpful compilation of recommendations which have been made and standards which have emerged
over the first decade of the mandate.[29]

(f) Standard setting by political organs

The political organs of the United Nations (the UN Commission on Human
Rights, the UN Congress on Crime Prevention, and the UN General Assembly), the Council of Europe (the Committee of Ministers), and the diplomatic conferences of the Organization for Security and Co-operation in
Europe (OSCE) have developed a range of instruments which contain
detailed standards applicable to the field of the prevention of torture and
mistreatment. These standards are the product of political and diplomatic
processes between states, generally heavily influenced by NGOs. The fact
that these instruments are, formally speaking, not legally binding, and are
sometimes regarded as unimportant by the diplomatic representatives who
create them,[30] appears to facilitate the inclusion of higher standards than
those contained in binding treaties.

3. THE FOUR FIELDS OF TORTURE PREVENTION—A COMPARATIVE ANALYSIS OF STANDARDS

(a) What is to be prevented? The concept of torture and ill-treatment

The CPT uses the terms 'torture' or 'ill-treatment' with respect to acts of
physical violence and the expression 'inhuman or degrading treatment' with
regard to conditions of detention.[31] This terminology is related to the two
aspects of prevention identified by the CPT. In order to know what to
prevent in the future it must look into past and present situations. This
involves an element of fact finding and the labelling of certain situations.
This labelling, however, is not a juridical assessment: rather, it could be
described as the establishment of a basis on which to issue recommendations of a preventive nature. As such, the CPT's work must be viewed in a
different light from the judicial and quasi-judicial organs which are guided
by the terms of their constituting instruments and their own jurisprudence.[32]

[29] E/CN.4/1995/34, para 926.
[30] Cf Professor Arangio-Ruiz: 'states often don't meaningfully support what a resolution
says and they almost always do not mean that the resolution is law'. Quoted in Higgins, R
(1994) *Problems and Process: International Law and How We Use It* (Oxford: Clarendon
Press), 27.
[31] See Evans and Morgan (1998), Chapter Six.
[32] See Burgers and Danelius (1988); Cassese, A (1993) 'The Prohibition of Torture and
Inhuman or Degrading Treatment or Punishment' in St J Macdonald, R, Matscher, F and
Petzold, H (eds) (1993) *The European System for the Protection of Human Rights* (Dordrecht:
Martinus Nijhoff), 248; Nowak (1993), 129 *et seq.*

The experience of applying these concepts in concrete situations has resulted in the clarification of the thresholds between mistreatment and torture and between (still) permitted and (already) prohibited treatment. While the absolute character of the prohibition is beyond question,[33] the setting of these thresholds—particularly the minimum standard—is, to an extent, relative. This is seen most clearly in the work of the European Commission and Court of Human Rights, although the other international organs have implicitly applied similar criteria. The European organs have shown that there are three aspects to be considered:

(i) The individual aspect

To some extent, the impact of a form of treatment depends on the characteristics of the particular individual concerned. This is reflected in the standard formula which provides that:

Ill-treatment must attain a certain minimum level of severity if it is to fall within the scope of Article 3. The assessment of this minimum is, in the nature of things, relative; it depends on all the circumstances of the case, such as the duration of the treatment, its physical or mental effects and, in some cases, the sex, age and state of health of the victim, etc.[34]

(ii) The societal aspect

The acceptability of forms of treatment depends also, to an extent, on societal factors susceptible to change. The European Commission recognized this in the *Greek* case, albeit leaving too much room for relativity, when it said that:

It appears from the testimony that a certain roughness of treatment of both police and military authorities is tolerated by most detainees and even taken for granted ... This underlines the fact that the point up to which prisoners and the public may accept physical violence as being neither cruel nor excessive, varies between different societies and even between different sections of them.[35]

Furthermore, it was correctly stressed by the Court in the *Tyrer* case that:

The Convention is a living instrument which ... must be interpreted in the light of present-day conditions. ... The Court cannot but be influenced by the development and commonly accepted standards in the penal policy of the member States.[36]

On the other hand, the HRC has stressed that 'treating all persons ... with humanity and with respect for their dignity is a fundamental and

---

[33] See eg UNCAT, Article 2(2); HRC, General Comment 21/44, para 3; *Aksoy v Turkey*, Judgment of 18 December 1996, *RJD* 1996-VI, 2260, para 62.

[34] eg *Ireland v UK*, Judgment of 18 January 1978, Ser A No 25, para 162.

[35] *Greek* case, Comm Rep, 5 November 1969 (1969) 12 *ECHRYb* 501. For criticism see, eg, Cassese (1993), 254.

[36] *Tyrer v UK*, Judgment of 25 February 1978, Ser A No 26, para 31.

universally applicable rule' whose application 'cannot be dependent on the material resources available'.[37]

(iii) The aspect of weighing competing interests

When it comes to determining the lower threshold the principle of proportionality is of particular importance. The Court has emphasized that:

> ... in respect of a person deprived of his liberty, any recourse to physical force which has not been made strictly necessary by his own conduct diminishes human dignity and is in principle an infringement of the right set forth in Article 3 of the Convention. It reiterates that the requirements of an investigation and the undeniable difficulties inherent in the fight against crime cannot justify placing limits on the protection to be afforded in respect of the physical integrity of individuals.[38]

How this is done must be considered on a case by case basis. In cases of solitary confinement, for example, security interests have been weighed against those of detained persons, and the balance has been struck in a rather restrictive manner.[39]

As regards the threshold between torture and other forms of mistreatment, the European Court pitched this very high in its judgment concerning the use of the 'five interrogation techniques' in Northern Ireland, stressing the element of severity.[40] Articles 1 and 16 of the UNCAT requires the CAT to have regard to the severity, purpose, or intention of the treatment when making this critical distinction and, likewise, the HRC's General Comment on ICCPR Article 7 provides that 'The distinction (of the different kinds of punishment or treatment) depends on the nature, purpose and severity of the treatment.'[41] However, the CAT has recently taken a less restrictive view than that adopted by the European Court in *Ireland v UK* when finding the interrogation methods used in Israel to constitute torture in the sense of UNCAT Article 1.[42]

---

[37] HRC, General Comment 21/44, para 4.

[38] *Ribitsch v Austria*, Judgment of 4 December 1995, Ser A No 336, para 38. The Austrian Constitutional Court has also developed this into an accurate method of drawing the borderline. See Zellenberg, U (1997) 'Der grundrechtliche Schutz vor Folter, unmenschlicher oder erniedrigender Strafe oder Behandlung' in Machacek, R, Pahr, W and Stadler, G, *Grund-und Menschenrechte in Österreich*, Vol III (Strasbourg/Kehl/Arlington: HN Engels), 459 *et seq*.

[39] *Kröcher and Möller v Switzerland*, Comm Dec, 16 December 1982, 34 *DR* 25, para 24.

[40] *Ireland v UK*, Judgment of 18 January 1978, Ser A No 25, para 162.

[41] HRC, General Comment 20/44, para 4, reprinted in Nowak (1993), 872.

[42] CAT/C/SR.297/Add.1, para 2, B.5: 'These methods include: (1) restraining in very painful conditions, (2) hooding under special conditions, (3) sounding of loud music for prolonged periods, (4) sleep deprivation for prolonged periods, (5) threats, including death threats, (6) violent shaking, and (7) using cold air to chill; and are in the Committee's view breaches of article 16 and also constitute torture as defined in article 1 of the Convention. This conclusion is particularly evident where such methods of interrogation are used in combination, which appears to be the standard case.' A more thorough analysis of the case law in order to further refine this threshold is beyond the scope of this chapter.

(b) Conditions of detention—the sliding scale

The CPT uses the expression 'conditions of detention' to refer to those factors which can, cumulatively, comprise or degenerate into inhuman or degrading treatment.[43] There is, then, a sliding scale moving from acceptable to unacceptable conditions of detention and, in order to prevent deterioration from occurring, the CPT has to examine existing conditions with care and set out the requirements of humanity in detention. The visit-based methodology of the CPT enables it to do this with a high degree of precision.

The other international organs have dealt with conditions of detention from different perspectives. The judicial and quasi-judicial bodies have taken a quite restrictive approach with regard to conditions of detention. This is particularly true for the European Commission of Human Rights.[44] The HRC is better able to take a more rounded view because of its broader normative basis: Article 10(1) ICCPR expressly stipulates that 'all persons deprived of their liberty shall be treated with humanity and with respect for the inherent dignity of the human person'. This is certainly the most important of the treaty provisions concerning conditions of detention.[45] It is explicitly linked to the Article 7 right to personal integrity. But it is also connected to: the right to privacy, including secrecy of correspondence; the prohibition of discrimination; the right to education; freedom of expression; and freedom of religion.[46] As the HRC stated in its General Comment:

Respect for the dignity of (detained) persons must be guaranteed under the same conditions as that for free persons. Persons deprived of their liberty enjoy all the rights set forth in the Covenant, subject to the restrictions that are unavoidable in a closed environment.[47]

Furthermore, the HRC expressly refers to soft law standards applicable to detention, such as the SMR and the Principles on Detention.[48] In addition to the general obligation contained in Article 10(1), sub-paragraphs (2) and (3) also provide for segregation of unconvicted from convicted prisoners and the separation of juveniles from adults. Article 10 of the ICCPR thus constitutes an effective legal basis for the construction of a 'cordon sanitaire' in the form of a humane environment whilst in detention.

The HRC has dealt with conditions of detention under both Articles 7

---

[43] See Evans and Morgan (1998), Chapter Six and above, Chapter Two.

[44] See Cassese (1993), 237 *et seq.*

[45] Together with the comparable Article 5(2) of the Inter-American Convention on Human Rights. The former UN Special Rapporteur on Torture has stressed the general importance of this provision in the fight against torture. See Kooijmans, P (1993) 'Opening address: Torturers and their Masters' in Crelinst, R and Schmid, A (eds) *The Politics of Pain* (Leiden: Centre for the Study of Social Conflicts), 19.

[46] See Nowak (1993), 184.

[47] HRC, General Comment 21/44, para 3.   [48] Ibid, para 5.

and 10. In many cases concerning Uruguay it found conditions of detention at Libertad Prison to be in violation of Article 10 rather than 7,[49] indicating that the threshold for a finding of inhuman treatment within the meaning of Article 10(1) is lower. The case law, however, is far from consistent.

The CAT raises questions concerning conditions of detention on a regular basis. However, it is difficult to distil any clear standards from its practice. The Committee has described solitary confinement cells measuring approximately 0.6 by $0.8 \, m^2$, without light or ventilation and known as 'coffins', to constitute 'a kind of torture' and Turkey was asked to demolish them immediately.[50] Furthermore, the Committee requested 'that other solitary confinement cells should as soon as possible be brought up to international standards, such as those contained in the SMRs for the Treatment of Prisoners'.[51]

There has been oscillation between various convention articles concerning contact with the outside world. Incommunicado detention is incompatible with both Articles 9 and 10 of the ICCPR[52] and in certain cases with Article 7 as well.[53] Contacts with family members are protected by the right to privacy found in Article 17, but the HRC has also found the rigorous censorship of correspondence to violate Article 10, observing that:

... the degree of restriction (of correspondence) must be consistent with the standard of humane treatment of detained persons required by article 10 (1) of the Covenant. In particular, prisoners should be allowed under necessary supervision to communicate with their family and reputable friends at regular intervals, by correspondence as well as by receiving visits.[54]

A final example, drawing on all three instruments, concerns solitary confinement. The CPT has paid particular attention to this issue, whereas, with the possible exception of the ECHR,[55] the other bodies have given it little detailed attention. Solitary confinement, particularly when prolonged or accompanied by aggravating circumstances such as being held incommunicado, constitutes a violation of Article 10 of the ICCPR[56] and the HRC has indicated that it may also violate Article 7.[57] The CAT also

---

[49] Nowak (1993), 187. [50] A/48/44/Add.1, para 52.

[51] Ibid. The CAT has referred to the SMR, which contain the most detailed standards concerning conditions of detention accepted at a global level, on many other occasions.

[52] See the references in Nowak (1993), 187.

[53] eg *El-Megreisi v Libya*, Comm No 440/1990 (23 March 1994) A/49/40, Annex IX(T) (for a period of more than three years).

[54] *Estrella v Uruguay*, Comm No 74/1980 (29 March 1983) 2 *SD* 93, para 9.2.

[55] For the very restrictive interpretation of Article 3 with respect to solitary confinement, see Cassese (1993), 237.

[56] See references in Nowak (1993), 187.

[57] See HRC, General Comment 20/44, para 6.

regularly asks questions concerning the conditions and duration of solitary confinement.[58]

As these examples demonstrate, there is still considerable scope for the standards applied by these bodies to be developed and rationalized.

(c) Safeguards

A number of specific measures or safeguards are considered by all the international anti-torture instruments or organs to be particularly useful in reducing the risk of abuse, particularly for those persons detained in police custody. The CPT places particular emphasis upon three fundamental rights of detained persons: the right to inform a relative or third party about the fact of custody; the right of access to a lawyer; and the right to medical examination by a doctor of one's choice. A number of subsidiary safeguards—the notification of rights, the keeping of custody records, limits on the duration of police custody, the conduct of interrogation, inadmissibility of evidence obtained as a result of ill-treatment, inspection of police stations, and the training of officials—are also emphasized. While all of these safeguards are found in or dealt with by other instruments, they are given effect in different fashions. As the approach of the CPT is considered in detail in a previous chapter of this book,[59] the following sections will look at the approach taken to these standards in other international instruments and by other international bodies.

(i) The three fundamental rights

The degree to which other instruments and bodies consider the CPT's three basic rights to be important varies. The HRC takes the view that:

[t]he protection of the detainee also requires that prompt and regular access be given to doctors and lawyers and, under appropriate supervision when the investigation so requires, to family members.[60]

However, unlike the CPT, the HRC has not yet specified exactly in which manner these safeguards are to be given effect. Similarly, the CAT has paid increasing importance to these three rights. Committee members have raised questions concerning these rights in connection with Article 2 of the UNCAT, which obliges states to take all effective measures to prevent torture.[61] Furthermore, and more importantly, the implementation of these three safeguards has been addressed by the Committee in its conclusions and recommendations.[62] Since these three rights are considered to be effective preventive measures, the obligation under Articles 2 and 16 of the

---

[58] eg A/45/44, para 73; A/46/46, para 68.　　[59] See above, Chapter Two.
[60] HRC, General Comment 20/44, para 11.
[61] A/46/46, para 124; A/46/46, para 136; A/48/44, para 184.
[62] See, eg, A/50/44, para 60(a); A/50/44, para 101; A/51/44, para 150(e).

UNCAT could be taken to imply that states have an obligation to guarantee these rights. As with the HRC, however, the CAT has, as yet, not studied the detailed implementation of these rights. The Special Rapporteur on Torture has also addressed these issues, and has done so in more depth.[63] The case law under Article 6 and, to a lesser extent, Article 8 of the ECHR is also of relevance. Furthermore, the Moscow Document of Human Dimension of the OSCE provides that any person arrested or detained has the right to notify or to require to be notified 'appropriate persons of his choice of his arrest, detention, imprisonment and whereabouts'.[64] The most detailed provisions in this respect, however, are to be found in the Body of Principles for the Protection of all Persons under Any Form of Detention or Imprisonment (Principles on Detention).

(a) The right to inform a relative or third party

Under the Principles on Detention, a detained or imprisoned person is entitled to notify his family members, or other appropriate persons of his choice, of his detention promptly after his arrest and after each transfer from one place of detention to another, or to require that they be so notified.[65] If the detained person is a foreigner, he must also be promptly informed of his right to communicate with a consular post or diplomatic mission of the state of which he is a national, or with the representative of the competent international organization if he is a refugee.[66] In the case of juveniles, the competent authority must undertake the notification on its own initiative.[67] Any such notification must take place without delay. A notification may, however, be delayed for a reasonable period where exceptional needs of the investigation so require.[68] Similar provisions are contained in the SMR and the EPR, which guarantee the right of immediate notification.[69]

(b) The right of access to and contact with a lawyer

The Principles on Detention provide that every detainee shall be entitled, irrespective of the reason for his arrest, to have the assistance of a legal counsel and to be informed of this right. Detainees must be provided with reasonable facilities for exercising that right. If the interests of justice so require, legal counsel must be assigned to detainees.[70] As regards the time factor, Principle 15 provides that communication with the outside world, including legal counsel, may not be 'denied for more than a matter of days', save in exceptional circumstances.[71] The Basic Principles on the Role of Lawyers are stricter: Principle 7 stipulates that detained persons 'shall have prompt access to a lawyer, and in any case not later than forty-eight

---

[63] E/CN.4/1995/34, para 926(d).   [64] Section 23.1.vi.   [65] Principle 16(1).
[66] Principle 16(2).   [67] Principle 16(3).   [68] Principle 16(4).
[69] SMR Rule 92 in conjunction with Rule 95; EPR Rule 92 in conjunction with Rule 99.
[70] Principle 17.   [71] Principle 18(3).

hours from the time of arrest or detention'. The Special Rapporteur on Torture recommends that access be given to legal counsel within twenty-four hours of detention.[72] Moreover, in *John Murray v UK* the European Court of Human Rights stated that, under certain conditions, the concept of fairness:

requires that an accused has the benefit of the assistance of a lawyer already at the initial stages of police interrogation. To deny access to a lawyer during the first 48 hours of police questioning, in a situation where the rights of the defence may well be irretrievably prejudiced, is—whatever the justification for such denial—incompatible with the rights of the accused under Article 6.[73]

Principle 18 of the Principles on Detention lays down a detainee's right to communicate and consult with his legal counsel, for which adequate time and facilities must be allowed. Interviews between a detainee and his legal adviser can be 'in sight but not within the hearing of the official'. The same provision appears in SMR Rule 93 and EPR Rule 93. The European Court of Human Rights has concluded, with reference to Rule 93 of the EPR, that this right flows from Article 6(3)(c) of the ECHR as being a 'basic requirement of a fair trial in a democratic society'.[74] The CAT has made the same recommendation.[75]

The Principles on Detention also provide that the right of a detainee to be visited by, and to consult and communicate without delay and censorship and in full confidentiality with, his legal counsel may not be restricted save in exceptional circumstances specified by law or lawful regulations. Any such restriction has to be indispensable for the maintenance of security and good order.[76]

(c) Medical examination by a doctor of one's own choice

The Principles on Detention guarantee the right to undergo a proper medical examination 'as promptly as possible'[77] and 'to request . . . a second medical examination or opinion'.[78] The SMR provide that an untried prisoner or other detainee is entitled to 'be visited and treated by his own doctor or dentist if . . . he is able to pay any expenses incurred'.[79] A similar provision is contained in the EPR.[80]

(ii) The right to information concerning one's rights

The CPT stresses the importance of detained persons being informed of their rights without delay.[81] The principal human rights instruments do not

---

[72] Ibid.
[73] *John Murray v UK*, Judgment of 8 February 1996, *RJD* 1996-I, 30, para 66. In this judgment the Court also reiterated the applicability of Article 6 to preliminary investigations (para 62).
[74] *S v Switzerland*, Judgment of 28 November 1991, Ser A No 220, para 48.
[75] A/48/44/Add.1, para 48(c).   [76] Principle 18(3).   [77] Principle 24.
[78] Principle 25.   [79] SMR Rule 91.   [80] Rule 98.
[81] Evans and Morgan (1998), 282–285; above, p 43.

contain such an obligation: they only guarantee the right of anyone who is arrested to be informed of the reason for his arrest and of any charges against him, in a language he understands.[82] The UNCAT does not stipulate such a right at all. However, members of the CAT have raised questions concerning the 'four paramount rights'[83] or 'four basic rights',[84] including the right to be informed of one's rights, although there is a lack of consistency.[85] The Principles on Detention again lay down more extensive rights regarding the furnishing of information. Principle 13 provides that any person must, at the moment of arrest or promptly thereafter, be provided with information on his rights and an explanation of how to avail himself of those rights. The information has to be communicated in a language which the person concerned understands.[86] A similar provision is found in paragraphs 23.1.(ii.) (information on reasons for arrest) and (iii.) (information on the 'rights according to domestic law') of the OSCE Moscow Document.

(iii) The duration of police custody

The CPT has dealt with the duration of police custody in a number of reports.[87] Guarantees concerning the maximum permissible length of police custody are treated as part of the right to personal liberty under the general human rights treaties. Article 9(3) of the ICCPR provides that:

anyone arrested or detained on a criminal charge shall be brought promptly before a judge or other officer authorized by law to exercise judicial power.[88]

Much turns on the interpretation of 'promptly'. In its General Comment on Article 9 the HRC said that 'delays must not exceed a few days'[89] and the keeping of a person incommunicado for five days without being brought before a judge was found to violate this standard.[90] This is in line with ECHR case law under which a period of four days and six hours fell outside the strict time constraints permitted by Article 5(3).[91]

These provisions apply only to persons detained on a criminal charge. However, the Principles on Detention extend the right to be 'given an effec-

---

[82] See ICCPR Article 9(2) and ECHR Article 5(2).
[83] CAT/C/SR.201, para 37.   [84] CAT/C/SR.191, para 46.
[85] See Bank, R (1997) 'Preventive measures against Torture: An analysis of standards set by the CPT, CAT HRC and the Special Rapporteur' in Haenni (ed), 131.
[86] Principle 14.   [87] See above, pp 48–9, 54–5.
[88] A similar provision is found in Article 5(3) of the ECHR.
[89] HRC General Comment 8/16, 27 July 1982, para 2.
[90] *Jijón v Ecuador*, Comm No 277/1988 (26 March 1992), A/47/40, Annex IX-I, para 5.3.
[91] *Brogan v UK*, Judgment of 29 November 1988, Ser A No 145-B, para 62. In emergency situations, however, a longer period can be justified if basic safeguards against abuse are in place. See *Brannigan and MacBride v UK*, Judgment of 26 May 1993, Ser A No 258-B, para 55 *et seq*. See, however, *Aksoy v Turkey*, Judgment of 18 December 1996, *RDJ* 1996-VI, 2260, para 83 *et seq*.

tive opportunity to be heard promptly by judicial or other authority' to all detained persons.[92] The CAT regularly asks reporting states, usually with reference to Article 2 of the UNCAT, about the length of police custody[93] and has recommended the shortening of overly long maximum periods.[94] Precisely what the CAT considers an acceptable maximum period of detention cannot be easily ascertained—although a period of thirty days is obviously too long.[95]

(iv) Habeas corpus

The right to challenge the legality of one's detention is closely linked to limitations on the duration of police custody yet, although many consider this to be an essential safeguard against abuse,[96] it does not figure in the work of the CPT. The right to *habeas corpus* is, however, guaranteed in Article 9(4) of the ICCPR, Article 5(4) of the ECHR, Article 37(d) of the Convention on the Rights of the Child, and Principle 32 of the Principles on Detention. The SRT has given it importance as a preventive measure[97] and the CAT has asked questions relating to it.[98] While it is beyond the scope of this chapter to consider the complex issue of *habeas corpus* in detail,[99] it is worth mentioning that there is a 'very significant trend'[100] in the work of the HRC concerning the non-derogable nature of its guarantee. This understanding is already accepted by the Inter-American Court of Human Rights which considers essential judicial guarantees to be non-derogable.[101] In the European context, the Moscow Document of the OSCE stipulates that 'states will endeavour to ensure that the legal guarantees necessary to uphold the rule of law will remain in force during a state of public emergency'.[102]

(v) Interrogation rules

The question of how interrogations are to be conducted lies at the heart of the prevention of torture. The CPT regularly calls for the drawing up of clear rules or guidelines in this respect and has pressed the case for the electronic recording of police interviews. The Committee also recommends, in principle, that a lawyer be able to be present during an interrogation.[103]

---

[92] Principle 11.   [93] eg A/46/46, para 62.   [94] UN Doc A/46/46, para 290.
[95] A/48/44/Add.1, para 25.
[96] Inter-American Court of Human Rights, Advisory Opinion of 9 May 1986, 13 OAE/Ser.L/III.15, doc.14 (1986): 'It is also an effective means of preventing torture and other physical and psychological abuses.'
[97] E/CN.4/1995/34, para 926(f).   [98] A /46/46, para 242.
[99] See generally, Nowak (1993), 178 *et seq*; Harris, O'Boyle, Warbrick (1995), 145 *et seq*.
[100] Report of the sessional working group on the administration of justice, E/CN.4/Sub.2/1997/21, para 23.
[101] Inter-American Court of Human Rights, Advisory Opinion of 6 October 1987, 13 OAE/Ser.L/III.19, doc. 13 (1987).   [102] Para 28.8.
[103] For details see Evans and Morgan (1998), 273; above, Chapter Two, pp 42–3.

Other international human rights organs have dealt with this issue and the use of physical or psychological pressure to elicit information or confessions is outlawed by their respective provisions relating to torture and ill-treatment.[104] There are two issues which act as something of a preliminary to this prohibition: the first concerns the right to silence, the second concerns the positive obligation of states regarding the conduct of interrogations.

According to Article 14(3)(g) of the ICCPR everyone charged with a criminal offence is entitled 'not to be compelled to testify against himself or to confess guilt'. In its General Comment the HRC puts this right into the preventive context, correctly stating that:

In considering this safeguard the provisions of article 7 and article 10, paragraph 1, should be borne in mind. In order to compel the accused to confess or to testify against himself, frequently methods which violate these provisions are used.[105]

Although not explicitly guaranteed by the ECHR, both the European Commission and Court of Human Rights have inferred 'a right to remain silent under police questioning and the privilege against self-incrimination' from Articles 6(1) and (2).[106]

In addition to this general preventive guarantee, several human rights instruments contain more detailed standards concerning interrogation. Article 11 of the UNCAT provides that states 'shall keep under systematic review interrogation rules, instructions methods and practices'. States are therefore under an explicit obligation to draw up interrogation rules and review them 'with a view to preventing torture'. Unfortunately, the practice of the CAT contains no further indications concerning the interpretation of this obligation. Committee members have, however, stressed that interrogations should be recorded,[107] and the Committee has recommended 'that separation between the authorities responsible for detention, on the one hand, and investigation, on the other hand, should be provided for'.[108] The HRC has incorporated the wording of Article 11 of the UNCAT into its General Comment on Article 7 of the ICCPR. The General Comment also states that the time and place of all interrogations should be recorded, together with the names of all those present, and this information should be available for purposes of judicial or administrative proceedings.[109] Similarly, Principle 23 of the Principles on Detention stipulates that the duration of periods of any interrogation, the intervals between them, and the identity of the officials involved shall be recorded and certified and the

---

[104] See, eg, the criticism of the CAT Committee of Israel, CAT/C/SR.297/Add.1.
[105] HRC, General Comment 13/21, para 14.
[106] *John Murray v UK*, Judgment of 8 February 1996, *RJD* 1996-I, 30, paras 45 and 66.
[107] UN Doc A/47/44, para 321.   [108] Doc A/48/44, para 427.
[109] HRC, General Comment 20/44, para 11.

detained person, or his or her counsel, shall have access to this information. The question of interrogation is also dealt with in the compilation of recommendations of the SRT: each interrogation shall be initiated with the identification of all persons present; all interrogation sessions should be recorded and the identity of all persons present be included in the records; blindfolding and hooding should be forbidden.[110]

(vi) Inadmissibility of evidence

Closely linked to interrogation procedures is the question of the admissibility of evidence obtained by the use of improper methods. The CPT has dealt with this issue only peripherally, reminding states of the provisions of Article 15 of the UNCAT from time to time,[111] but not raising the question systematically. Given the standards of the other international bodies, the CPT should arguably have done so. The fight against torture has produced several provisions concerning the inadmissibility of such evidence, based on the conviction that the spectrum of preventive measures needs to be supplemented by rules which, in the words of the HRC, are conducive to the 'discouragement of violations under Article 7 [of the ICCPR]'.[112]

The only explicit provision is Article 15 of the UNCAT, which stipulates:

Each State Party shall ensure that any statement which is established to have been made as a result of torture shall not be invoked as evidence in any proceedings, except against a person accused of torture as evidence that the statement was made.

During the drafting process it was proposed that this be extended to cover other forms of cruel, inhuman or degrading treatment or punishment, but this was rejected.[113] It is clear from both the wording and the history of Article 15 that it covers both statements of the accused and those of other persons. In its General Comment on Article 7 of the ICCPR the HRC has inferred an obligation on the state to ensure the invalidity of all statements and confessions obtained by torture or other mistreatment[114] and has inferred from the Article 14(3)(g) prohibition on self-incrimination[115] that:

The law should require that evidence provided by means of such methods or any other form of compulsion is wholly unacceptable.[116]

In view of the link between compulsion to self-incrimination and torture, this is a commendable approach.

[110] E/CN.4/1995/34, para 926(d).
[111] eg Portugal 1, para 52; Spain 1, para 22.
[112] HRC, General Comment 20/44, para 12.
[113] See E/CN.4/1576, para 46.
[114] HRC, General Comment 20/44, para 12: 'It is important for the discouragement of violations under Article 7 that the law must prohibit the use or admissibility in judicial proceedings of statements or confessions through torture or other prohibited treatment.'
[115] See above, Section 3(c)(v).
[116] HRC, General Comment 13/21, para 14, reprinted in Nowak (1993), 860.

The European Commission and Court have also read a privilege against self-incrimination into Article 6 of the ECHR[117] and found that the use of self-incriminating materials obtained under compulsion violates that Article.[118] Provisions which in some respects are more far-reaching, but in others are more limited, are found in the Principles on Detention. Principle 27 provides:

Non-compliance with these principles in obtaining evidence shall be taken into account in determining the admissibility of such evidence against a detained or imprisoned person.

The SRT has recommended that 'evidence from non-recorded interrogations should be excluded from court proceedings'.[119] There is, then, a rich normative web which seeks to make inadmissible evidence obtained under duress or in a manner lacking transparency.

A resulting question concerns the standard of proof. Article 15 of the UNCAT refers to the inadmissibility of a statement 'established to have been made as a result of torture'. This was raised in *Halimi-Nedzibi v Austria*, in which expert opinion was divided on the causes of an eye injury allegedly suffered by the complainant whilst in police custody. The CAT was unable to conclude that 'the allegations of ill-treatment have been sustained' and, in consequence, did not find a violation of Article 15.[120] The CAT did not elaborate further on the question of proof. It may be that the approach developed by the European Commission and Court could usefully be applied in this context.[121]

(vii) Inspection

The CPT regularly calls for the establishment of inspection procedures for police premises.[122] Article 11 of the UNCAT obliges states to keep 'arrangements for the custody and treatment of persons subjected to any form of arrest, detention or imprisonment' under systematic review 'with a view to preventing' torture and ill-treatment. The same positive obligation can be found in the HRC's General Comment on Article 7 of the ICCPR. The CAT has on several occasions asked that mechanisms for the inspection of prisons and other places of detention be established, thus indicating its belief that such arrangements would indicate compliance with the obligation to prevent torture.[123] The SRT has stressed that the regular inspection

---

[117] See above, Section 3(c)(v).

[118] *Saunders v UK*, Judgment of 17 December 1996, *RJD* 1996-VI, 2044, para 67 *et seq.*

[119] E/CN.4/1995/34, para 926(d).

[120] *Halimi-Nedzibi v Austria,* Comm No 8/1991 (18 November 1993) A/49/44. Annex V-A, para 13.1–4.

[121] See below, Section 3(d)(ii).

[122] Evans and Morgan (1998), 291–293.

[123] 'Independent governmental bodies consisting of persons of high moral standing should

of places of detention is one of the most important and effective measures against torture.[124]

(viii) Training

The importance of training those who come into contact with persons deprived of their liberty is stressed by all organs dealing with the prevention of torture.[125] Article 10 of the UNCAT contains an express obligation:

> to ensure that education and information regarding the prohibition of torture are fully included in the training of law enforcement personnel, civil or military, medical personnel, public officials and other persons [involved].

Furthermore, the prohibition of torture and other forms of mistreatment must be included in rules and instructions setting out the functions and duties of law enforcement personnel. The CAT regularly raises questions relating to Article 10 in the course of its examination of state reports.

(d) The reaction to incidents of torture or cases of mistreatment

If a comprehensive approach to the prevention of torture incorporates the response to cases of torture or mistreatment, this raises a number of issues: What avenues of complaint exist? How should the state investigate alleged violations? How should the victim be protected against defamation? What standard of proof applies? Must the state punish the perpetrator? What amounts to adequate reparation for victims?

The CPT regularly deals with at least some of these questions but its approach is unclear and, perhaps as a consequence, they receive comparatively little attention in the more comprehensive surveys of CPT standards.[126] Although the contribution of the CPT should not be underestimated, the Committee does not normally distinguish between the different issues which arise, and the other international instruments and bodies are more expansive.

(i) The investigation of allegations and the punishment of the perpetrator(s)

Articles 12 and 13 of the UNCAT provide a detailed set of rules concerning the legal protection of victims of torture and mistreatment. According to Article 12 states must ensure that the competent authorities proceed to

---

be appointed to take over the inspection of detention centres and places of imprisonment.' See CAT/C/SR.294/Add.1, para 23, E.4. See also A/46/46, para 220; A/47/44, para 321.

[124] E/CN.4/1995/34, para 926(c).

[125] See, eg, CPT: Ireland 1, para 21; Greece 1, para 27. HRC: General Comment 20/44, para 10.

[126] eg Evans and Morgan (1998) and Chapter Two above.

a prompt and impartial examination, wherever there is reasonable ground to believe that acts of torture or mistreatment have been committed. Article 13 obliges states to ensure that individuals have the right to complain and have their cases promptly and impartially examined. Measures for the protection of complainants and witnesses against intimidation must also be enacted. Furthermore, Article 4 of the UNCAT obliges states to make all acts of torture offences under the criminal law and punishable by appropriate penalties.[127]

In its first decision under the individual complaints procedure, the CAT concluded that a delay of fifteen months before initiating an investigation into allegations of torture was unreasonably long and not in accordance with Article 12.[128] Committee members have spoken of an obligation to carry out an investigation in the wake of the publication of an Amnesty International report raising torture allegations.[129] They have raised concerns concerning rules on defamation considered likely to discourage possible denunciations of torture.[130] They have also addressed the question of whether complaints against the police were dealt with by the police, stating that 'solidarity between police and gendarmerie could stand in the way of the reporting and punishing of such acts'[131] and recommended that a government should establish 'an independent police complaints authority dealing with complaints against members of the Police Department'.[132]

The questions of investigation and complaint mechanisms are also dealt with in the ICCPR and ECHR. There is a comprehensive obligation to combat and prevent torture flowing from Articles 7 and 3 respectively, coupled with the general obligation to respect and ensure those rights and guarantee an effective remedy.[133] The HRC has said that:

Article 7 should be read in conjunction with article 2, paragraph 3, of the Covenant. In their reports, States parties should indicate how their legal system effectively guarantees the immediate termination of all the acts prohibited by article 7 as well as appropriate redress. The right to lodge complaints against maltreatment prohibited by article 7 must be recognized in the domestic law. Complaints must be investigated promptly and impartially by the competent authorities so as to make the remedy effective. The reports of States parties should provide specific information on the remedies available to victims of maltreatment and the procedures that complainants must follow, and statistics on the number of complaints and how they have been dealt with.[134]

---

[127] Committee members have considered maximum penalties of two years in Hungary to be 'extremely light'. See A/48/44, para 345.

[128] *Halimi Nedzibi v Austria*, Comm No 8/1991 (18 November 1993) A/49/44. Annex V-A, p 40, para 13.5.

[129] A/45/44, para 389.   [130] A/47/44, para 322.   [131] A/47/44, para 106.

[132] CAT/SR.294/Add.1, para 23, E.4.

[133] ICCPR Articles 2(1) and (3) and ECHR Articles 1 and 13. See Nowak (1993), 26 *et seq*; Van Dijk and van Hoof (1990), 3 *et seq*, 520 *et seq*.

[134] General Comment 20/44, para 14.

Some recent decisions of the HRC and ECHR organs have added further detail. The HRC has made clear that the right to an effective remedy under Article 2(3) of the ICCPR imposes an obligation to investigate allegations of torture or mistreatment and to prosecute and punish the perpetrator. In the landmark decision in *Rodriguez v Uruguay*, concerning the granting of amnesties for gross violations of human rights, the HRC stated:

The Committee is of the view that [the complainant] is entitled, under article 2, to an effective remedy. It urges the State to take effective measures (a) to carry out an official investigation into the author's allegations of torture, in order to identify the persons responsible for torture and ill-treatment and to enable the author to seek civil redress; (b) to grant appropriate compensation to Mr Rodriguez; and (c) to ensure that similar violations do not occur in the future.[135]

In a subsequent case concerning an enforced disappearance the Committee stated, with respect to punishment:

As the Committee has repeatedly held, the Covenant does not provide a right of individuals to require that the State criminally prosecute another person. The Committee nevertheless considers that the State party is under a duty to investigate thoroughly alleged violations of human rights . . . and to prosecute criminally, try and punish those held responsible for such violations.[136]

In *Aksoy v Turkey* the European Court of Human Rights took a line similar to that of the HRC in *Rodriguez*, saying that:

Accordingly, as regards Article 13, where an individual has an arguable claim that he has been tortured by agents of the State, the notion of an 'effective remedy' entails, in addition to the payment of compensation where appropriate, a thorough and effective investigation capable of leading to the identification and punishment of those responsible and including effective access for the complainant to the investigatory procedure.[137]

The duty to investigate, although not explicitly mentioned, is implicit in the notion of an 'effective remedy'.[138]

(ii) The standard of proof

The issue of the standard of proof in cases of such complaints is closely linked to the question of an effective remedy. The CPT has shown very little interest in this, confining itself to observing that it is difficult to prove ill-treatment.[139] The CAT has raised this issue under the reporting procedure

---

[135] *Rodriguez v Uruguay*, Comm No 322/1988 (19 July 1994) A/49/40. Annex IX-B, para 14.
[136] *Bautista v Colombia*, Comm No 653/1993 (27 October 1995) A/51/40, Vol II, Annex VIII-S, para 8.6.
[137] *Aksoy v Turkey*, Judgment of 18 December 1996, *RJD* 1996-VI, 2260, para 98.
[138] Ibid.
[139] eg Spain 2, para 2. In UK 2, paras 93–94 the CPT asked for comments on proposals to change the standard of proof applied in disciplinary proceedings.

on only a few occasions. It has, however, been dealt with more thoroughly under the ECHR: it has been decided that if it is established that certain injuries were sustained whilst in police custody, the state is under an obligation to provide a plausible explanation for the cause of the injuries. If the state is unable to do so, the version of events given by the complainant will be accepted, assuming that the basic facts are established, usually by medical evidence.[140] This is a commendable approach, given the peculiar vulnerability of persons held in police custody and their difficulty in providing evidence: it can best be described as a 'reversal of the risk of non-persuasion'.[141] Adopting this approach at the national level would enhance the legal protection of victims of mistreatment.[142]

(iii) The right to reparation for torture victims

The UN Sub-Commission on Prevention of Discrimination and Protection of Minorities has developed a set of basic principles and guidelines on the right to reparation for victims of gross violations of human rights and placed this in a preventive perspective:

Reparation shall render justice by removing or redressing the consequences of the wrongful acts and by preventing and deterring violations.[143]

The preventive effect of civil claims for reparation has also been stressed in the USA, it being observed that:

the threat of large civil judgements has led not only to the compensation of victims; it has led to a large number of reforms and to the deterrence of abuse by police and prison officials.[144]

---

[140] See, eg, *Tomasi v France*, Judgment of 27 August 1992, Ser A No 214, paras 108–111; *Ribitsch v Austria*, Judgment of 4 December 1995, Ser A No 336, para 34 *et seq*; *Aksoy v Turkey*, Judgment of 18 December 1996, *RJD* 1996-VI, 2260, para 61.

[141] It seems appropriate to make a distinction between the risk or burden of non-persuasion which lies with the applicant and the burden of proof which, in human rights proceedings, is not on either side. For example, the European Commission and Court have stated that 'where allegations of torture are made under the Convention's protection system the burden of proof does not fall on one or other of the parties, but that it examines all the materials before it'. *Diaz Ruano v Spain*, App No 16988/90, Comm Rep, 31 August 1993, para 58 (1994) 15 *HRLJ* 215. With respect to this problem see Kokott, J (1992) *Beweislastverteilung und Prognoseentscheidungen bei der Inspruchnahme von Grund- und Menschenrechten* (Berlin: Springer), 12 *et seq*; Kriebaum, U (1997) 'Prevention of Human Rights Violations', 1997 (2) *Austrian Review of International Law* 186. Many commentators qualify this phenomenon as a reversal of the burden of proof, see Evans, MD and Morgan, R (1997) 'The European Convention for the Prevention of Torture: 1992–1997', 46 *ICLQ* 670.

[142] At least in Austria it would have important consequences. So far, the human rights protection mechanisms fall short of these standards. In the *Ribitsch* case, the Austrian Constitutional Court had refused to deal with the issue of ill-treatment with the mere reference to the acquittal of the officials in the criminal proceedings. Cf Suntinger, W (1997b) 'Der Fall Ribitsch', 1997/1 *Juridikum* 13 *et seq*.

[143] E/CN.4/Sub.2/1996/17.

[144] Hoffman, P (1996) 'National Efforts to Eradicate Torture', Background paper for International Conference on Torture (unpublished).

The CPT has not yet looked at this issue but it is raised under the UNCAT, the ICCPR, and the ECHR. Article 14 of the UNCAT obliges states to ensure that victims of torture obtain redress and have an enforceable right to fair and adequate compensation, including the means for as full a rehabilitation as possible. This includes compensation for costs of medical or psychological treatment, loss of earnings, and non-material damage. Where a death has resulted, the victim's dependants are entitled to compensation.[145] Although Article 14 is expressly restricted to cases of torture, the CAT has indicated that it also considers compensation to be due in cases of other forms of mistreatment.[146] The HRC has stated that the right to an effective remedy under Article 2 entails a duty 'to grant appropriate compensation'[147] and the European Court of Human Rights has said that 'payment of compensation where appropriate' follows on from Article 13 of the ECHR.[148]

4. THE NORMATIVE 'CORDON SANITAIRE' OF MUTUALLY REINFORCING STANDARDS

What emerges from this analysis of preventive standards is that the international fight against torture has produced an impressive set of standards which, in the words of the CPT, form a 'cordon sanitaire' against torture and mistreatment. The international instruments and organs have helped to clarify particular links in the obnoxious chain leading to torture. But there are differences between the standards that have been developed due in part to the varying legal bases, mandates, and working methods of the international organs concerned.

Recalling the four elements of prevention outlined at the start of this chapter, it is now clear that all the international instruments and organs address the question of what it is that needs to be prevented, the jurisprudence of the European human rights organs being particularly rich in this field. They have also looked at conditions of detention which can easily degenerate into inhuman or degrading treatment and developed preventive standards. The CPT has been the principal contributor to this task but the other bodies have not been inactive. All have identified practices which carry a risk of, or are conducive to, abuse and have developed preventive safeguards. The Principles on Detention have been of great importance in this regard and the ICCPR and ECHR provide many pertinent safeguards,

---

[145] See, eg, CAT/C/SR.294/Add.1, para 23, E.7.
[146] Ibid.
[147] *Rodriguez v Uruguay*, Comm No 322/1988 (19 July 1994) A/49/40. Annex IX-B, para 14. See also General Comment 20/44.
[148] *Aksoy v Turkey*, Judgment of 18 December 1996, *RJD* 1996-VI, 2260, para 98.

with the right to personal liberty and the minimum guarantees of a fair trial being of particular importance. The final element, concerning the response to allegations of torture and mistreatment, has been most thoroughly addressed by the HRC and European Convention organs, where new ground has been broken, particularly as regards questions relating to standards of proof. On the other hand, the potential offered by the UNCAT has not yet been realized and the CPT has not properly addressed these issues at all.

These various standards, and their differing emphases, influence each other: the European Prison Rules are used by the European Commission and Court of Human Rights, as well as by the CPT; the CPT's emphasis on procedural safeguards has influenced the interpretation of the UNCAT as well as the jurisprudence of the European human rights organs; provisions of the UNCAT are referred to by the CPT, the HRC, and the ECHR organs. This process of mutually influencing standards derived from different sources is a good illustration of the dynamic character of international law and of the phenomenon of relative normativity.[149] There is no clear borderline between hard law and soft law. Treaty provisions are not finished products. Legal concepts are indeterminate and are constantly endowed with new content.[150] It is normally the more detailed soft law provisions which serve to lend substance to the generally more abstract notions of hard law.[151]

5. FACTORS AFFECTING THE DOMESTIC IMPACT OF INTERNATIONAL STANDARDS

The preceding sections have identified the international standards relevant to torture prevention and have indicated the differing ways in which those standards have been created and developed. However, the ultimate touchstone of effectiveness must be the impact of those international standards at the national level. The impact of CPT standards at national level will be explored in subsequent chapters of this book but it seems useful at this juncture to point to a number of factors which affect the prospects of national implementation of the international standards that have been identified, drawing on research done in Austria.

---

[149] Fastenrath, U (1993) 'Relative Normativity in International Law', 4 *EJIL* 310.

[150] Fastenrath (1993), 315; Simma, B (1995), 'International Human Rights and General International Law', *Academy of European Law* (ed), *Collected Courses*, Vol IV, Book 2, 1 (The Hague: Martinus Nijhoff), 188.

[151] The use of EPR Rule 93 by the Court to interpret Article 6(3)(c) of the ECHR is particularly illustrative. See *S v Switzerland*, Judgment of 28 November 1991, Ser A No 220.

First, it is a truism to say that theoretical perspectives influence the outcome of any analysis: the prevalence of a given theory determines its normative strength and thus its practical relevance.[152] Thus, the impact of international standards at the national level is influenced by the attitude towards international law in each particular state. While those who view international law as more of a process than as a set of legal rules do not make much of the difference between hard and soft law, more positivist approaches stress the formal normative status of the standards involved and tend to downgrade the normative relevance of soft law standards, limiting their practical impact.[153]

Secondly, the existence and force of the international mechanisms supervising the implementation of international standards is of relevance for their domestic impact, the judgments of the European Court of Human Rights in particular being accorded high standing and authoritative status by states party to the ECHR. The ECPT is thought to provide a fairly strong system of supervision, whereas other soft law standards are not backed up with an implementation system at all.

Thirdly, there is the question of the formal status of international law in national law. International treaties are sometimes incorporated and made directly applicable in municipal law.[154] When this is the case, courts and administrative authorities are obliged to apply the international standards at the national level. If international treaties are incorporated at the level of constitutional provisions, as is the case of the ECHR in Austria, these standards acquire a higher practical relevance than that accorded to other international treaty standards which, in consequence, tend to be downgraded.

Finally, mention should be made of political and societal factors.[155] These include the stance of government, the human rights awareness of political parties, the existence of national structures dealing with human rights issues, and the strength of non-governmental human rights organizations.

---

[152] Fastenrath (1993), 331.

[153] Austria, with its strong positivist tradition, is a good example of this. An argument that the failure to guarantee that communication between a detainee and his lawyer cannot be overheard violates the international standard set out in Rule 93 of the EPR achieves very little, whereas if it can be shown that the European Court of Human Rights considers such a right to flow from Article 6 of the ECHR, this rule must and will be taken seriously.

[154] The CAT regularly recommends incorporation and the direct applicability of the UNCAT. See, eg, A/48/44, paras 86, 87; A/51/44, para 39. See also Alston's suggestion that the inability to invoke the provisions of ratified treaties before national courts puts into question the satisfaction of the obligation to give effect to the relevant provisions; Alston, P (1997) Background paper on challenges of national implementation, Proceedings of International Seminar for Diplomats, Austrian Federal Ministry for Foreign Affairs, 89.

[155] See Leuprecht, P (1997) Background paper on challenges of national implementation, Proceedings of International Seminar for Diplomats, Austrian Federal Ministry for Foreign Affairs, 91.

6. CONCLUDING SUGGESTIONS

A complex international normative web concerning the prevention of torture exists and is developing, with many standards influencing each other. The challenge is to strengthen this process of mutual influence in order to enhance the relevance of the standards applied. The two specialized anti-torture bodies—the CPT and the CAT—have particular potential for doing so. As the most systematic supervision mechanism, the CPT could draw more heavily on the standards developed by others. This would add extra weight to the CPT's own work, particularly if hard law standards were involved. But it would also have the indirect effect of acting as an additional means of implementing those other standards. Articles 2 and 16 of the UNCAT combine to impose a far-reaching obligation on state parties to take all effective measures with a view to preventing torture and other forms of mistreatment. The CAT could consider what measures are effective to achieve this purpose in a more structured and analytical way and, in the process, could take into account the work of other agencies in this field. Placing soft law preventive standards within the framework of the legally binding UNCAT system would significantly enhance their normative force.

Nevertheless, the domestic impact of international standards depends on the normative quality of the standards and the strength of international supervision and to a considerable extent on domestic factors. It is ultimately the legal, political, and societal influences at work in each particular state which determine which standards have a real possibility of being effectively realized, or at the very least not totally neglected. The challenge is to find out which standards can be applied most successfully in a given context and to build a preventive strategy on the basis of such an analysis.

REFERENCES

Alston, P (ed) (1992) *United Nations and Human Rights* (Oxford: Clarendon Press)
Alston, P (1997) Background paper on challenges of national implementation, Proceedings of International Seminar for Diplomats, Austrian Federal Ministry for Foreign Affairs
Bank, R (1997) 'Preventive measures against Torture: An analysis of standards set by the CPT, CAT HRC and the Special Rapporteur' in Haenni (ed), 131
Bloed, A, Leicht, L, Nowak, M and Rosas, A (eds) (1993) *Monitoring Human Rights in Europe* (Dordrecht: Martinus Nijhoff)
Boulesbaa, A (1990) 'The Nature of Obligations Incurred by States under Article 2 of the Convention against Torture', 2 *Human Rights Quarterly* 66
Burgers, J and Danelius, H (1988) *The United Nations Convention against Torture* (Dordrecht: Martinus Nijhoff)
Byrnes, A (1992) 'The Committee Against Torture' in Alston, P (ed), 509

Cassese, A (ed) (1991) *The International Fight Against Torture/La Lutte internationale contre la torture* (Baden-Baden: Nomos)

Cassese, A (1993) 'The Prohibition of Torture and Inhuman or Degrading Treatment or Punishment' in St J Macdonald, R, Matscher, F and Petzold, H (eds), 248

Crelinst, R and Schmid, A (eds) (1993) *The Politics of Pain* (Leiden: Centre of the Study of Social Conflicts)

Evans, MD and Morgan, R (1997) 'The European Convention for the Prevention of Torture: 1992–1997', 46 *ICLQ* 670

Evans, MD and Morgan, R (1998) *Preventing Torture* (Oxford: Clarendon Press)

Fastenrath, U (1991) *Lücken im Völkerrecht* (Berlin: Dunker and Humbolt), 122

Fastenrath, U (1993) 'Relative Normativity in International Law', 4 *EJIL* 310

Haenni, C (ed) (1997) *20 ans consacrés a la réalisation d'une idée* (Geneva: Association for the Prevention of Torture)

Hanski, R and Suksi, M (eds) (1997) *An Introduction to the International Protection of human rights* (Turku: Institute for Human Rights, Abo Akademi University)

Harris, DJ, O'Boyle, M and Warbrick, C (1995) *Law of the European Convention on Human Rights* (London: Butterworths)

Higgins, R (1994) *Problems and Process: International Law and How We Use It* (Oxford: Clarendon Press), 27

Hoffman, P (1996) 'National Efforts to Eradicate Torture', Background paper for International Conference on Torture (unpublished)

Kokott, J (1992) *Beweislastverteilung und Prognoseentscheidungen bei der Inspruchnahme von Grund- und Menschenrechten* (Berlin: Springer)

Kooijmans, P (1991) 'The Role and Action of the UN Special Rapporteur on Torture' in Cassese, A (ed), 66

Kooijmans, P (1993) 'Opening address: Torturers and their Masters' in Crelinst, R and Schmid, A (eds), 19

Kriebaum, U (1997) 'Prevention of Human Rights Violations', 1997 (2) *Austrian Review of International Law* 186

Leuprecht, P (1997) Background paper on challenges of national implementation, Proceedings of International Seminar for Diplomats, Austrian Federal Ministry for Foreign Affairs, 91

McGoldrick, D (1991) *The Human Rights Committee, Its role in the development of the International Covenant on Civil and Political Rights* (Oxford: Clarendon Press)

Machacek, R, Pahr, W and Stadler, G, *Grund-und Menschenrechte in Österreich*, Vol III (Strasbourg/Kehl/Arlington: HN Engels)

Meron, T (1993) 'Human dignity as a normative concept', 77 *AJIL* 848

Merrills, JG (1992) *The development of international law by the European Court of Human Rights*, 2nd edn (Manchester: Manchester University Press)

Nowak, M (1993) *CCPR Commentary* (Strasbourg/Kehl/Arlington: HN Engels)

Nowak, M and Suntinger, W (1993) 'International mechanisms for the prevention of torture' in Bloed, A, Leicht, L, Nowak, M and Rosas, A (eds), 146

Opsahl, T (1992) 'The Human Rights Committee' in Alston, P (ed), 369

Simma, B (1995) 'International Human Rights and General International Law', *Academy of European Law* (ed), *Collected Courses*, Vol IV, Book 2, 1 (The Hague: Martinus Nijhoff)

St J Macdonald, R, Matscher, F and Petzold, H (eds) (1993) *The European System for the Protection of Human Rights* (Dordrecht: Martinus Nijhoff)

Suntinger, W (1995) 'The principle of non-refoulement: Looking rather to Geneva than to Strasbourg?', 49 *Austrian Journal of Public and International Law* 203

Suntinger, W (1997a) 'International and national dimensions of the fight against torture: The Austrian experience' in Haenni, C (ed), 257

Suntinger, W (1997b) 'Der Fall Ribitsch', 1997/1 *Juridikum* 13

United Nations (1993) *United Nations, Human Rights—A compilation of international instruments* (Geneva: United Nations)

van Dijk, P and van Hoof, GJH (1990) *Theory and Practice of the European Convention on Human Rights* (Deventer: Kluwer)

Zajadlo, J (1997) 'Human dignity and human rights' in Hanski and Suksi (eds), 15

Zellenberg, U (1997) 'Der grundrechtliche Schutz vor Folter, unmenschlicher oder erniedrigender Strafe oder Behandlung' in Machacek, R, Pahr, W and Stadler, G, 459

6

Amnesty International's 12-Point Programme for the Prevention of Torture: An Example of NGO Standard Setting

ERIC PROKOSCH

The setting of international standards on human rights is a complex affair. Various entities may set a standard—international or regional; political, expert, or treaty-monitoring bodies; individual experts or officials of an intergovernmental organization. Various processes involving various actors may lead to the setting of a standard. Once set, a standard should be implemented, and its implementation may give rise to the adoption of further standards.

In common with other NGOs working for human rights, Amnesty International (AI) has found itself closely involved in the use and development of standards for the prevention of torture. AI is at once a consumer, a promoter, and a developer of international standards.

- As a *consumer*, AI bases its work on human rights norms as enshrined in the Universal Declaration of Human Rights and other international instruments.
- It *promotes* international standards by making them known and calling on governments to respect them.
- In the course of its work in the areas in which it specializes, AI *develops* its own, more detailed standards for the prevention of human rights violations. If they are of general application, AI tries to win their acceptance by intergovernmental organizations.

In 1983 AI published a 12-Point Programme for the Prevention of Torture. The evolution of the Programme illustrates AI's roles as consumer, promoter, and developer of standards. The story of AI's 12-Point Programme provides an example of NGO standard setting in human rights.

1. EARLY WORK AGAINST TORTURE;
AI'S FIRST CAMPAIGN (1973)

AI began in 1961 as a campaign to draw attention to the plight of prisoners of conscience around the world. Torture was an early concern: the torture of prisoners of conscience was cited in the opening sentence of the public appeal which launched Amnesty in 1961.[1]

Torture as such was not mentioned in Amnesty's first Statute, but the Statute of Amnesty International adopted in 1968 set forth the object of securing throughout the world 'the observance of the provisions of Article 5 . . . of the Universal Declaration of Human Rights' in pursuance of the object of ensuring for every person 'the right freely to hold and to express his convictions'. This meant, by implication, that AI would oppose the torture of prisoners of conscience. An international standard—Article 5 (prohibition of torture) of the Universal Declaration of Human Rights—was being used in this instance to define the scope of an NGO's work.

The 1968 Statute also established the organization's roles of standard setting and promotion by stating that, in pursuit of the objects set forth therein, AI would 'promote as appears appropriate the adoption of constitutions, conventions, treaties and other measures which guarantee the rights contained in the provisions' set forth in the Statute, and that AI would 'support and publicise the activities of and co-operate with international organisations and agencies which work for the implementation of the aforesaid provisions'.

In 1974 AI amended its Statute to state that the organization would oppose 'by all appropriate means the imposition and infliction of . . . torture or other cruel, inhuman or degrading treatment or punishment of prisoners or other detained or restricted persons whether or not they have used or advocated violence'. As in 1968, AI was relying heavily on an international standard as the basis for its own work: the phrase 'torture or other cruel, inhuman or degrading treatment or punishment' was taken almost verbatim from Article 5 of the Universal Declaration of Human Rights.

In the previous year AI had carried out its first worldwide Campaign for the Abolition of Torture. The campaign was launched on 10 December 1972 (Human Rights Day) and culminated with the presentation to the United Nations of a petition with more than a million signatures calling on the UN General Assembly 'to outlaw immediately the torture of prisoners throughout the world'. AI's International Conference for the Abolition of Torture, held in Paris on 10 and 11 December 1973, adopted numerous recommendations, including the strengthening of international and national laws on the protection against torture and the formulation of codes of ethics for

---

[1] Benenson, P (1961) 'The Forgotten Prisoners', *Observer*, London, 28 May.

medical, police, and military personnel. Among the specific recommendations were those of bringing detainees before a judge 'in the shortest possible time'; providing access to prisons and detention centres and international inspection of them; evidence extracted under torture not to be used in judicial proceedings; independent investigation of alleged misbehaviour of military, police, and prison personnel; training in human rights and official responsibilities for military and police personnel.

AI's demands and the recommendations of the Paris conference were reflected in important resolutions adopted by the UN General Assembly in 1973 and 1974. In the second of these, resolution 3218 (XXIX), adopted on 6 November 1974 by a vote of 125 to 0 with one abstention, the General Assembly requested the Fifth UN Congress on the Prevention of Crime and the Treatment of Offenders, due to be held the following year, to include, in the elaboration of the UN Standard Minimum Rules for the Treatment of Prisoners, rules for the protection of all prisoners and detainees against torture and ill-treatment; 'to give urgent attention to the question of the development of an international code of ethics for police and related law enforcement agencies'; and to consider principles of medical ethics relevant to the protection of prisoners and detainees against torture and ill-treatment. Meeting in 1975, the Fifth Congress adopted a draft declaration against torture and forwarded it to the General Assembly. The General Assembly adopted the Declaration on the Protection of All Persons from Being Subjected to Torture and Other Cruel, Inhuman or Degrading Treatment or Punishment ('Declaration against Torture') with one amendment on 9 December 1975.[2]

For the purposes of this chapter, the most important elements of the Declaration against Torture were those which provided for:

- All acts of torture to be offences under the criminal law (Article 7)
- Impartial investigation of complaints and reports of torture (Articles 8, 9)
- Criminal proceedings to be brought against alleged torturers (Article 10)
- No use in proceedings of statements made as a result of torture or other cruel, inhuman, or degrading treatment or punishment ('ill-treatment') (Article 12)
- Redress and compensation for victims of torture and ill-treatment (Article 11)
- Prohibition of torture and ill-treatment to be included in the training of law enforcement officials and in general rules and instructions concerning their duties and functions (Article 5)

[2] Rodley, NS (1987) *The Treatment of Prisoners under International Law* (Oxford: Clarendon Press), 27–35.

Professional codes of ethics forbidding torture were adopted by UN bodies in the following years. The Code of Conduct for Law Enforcement Officials was adopted by the General Assembly in 1979, and the Principles of Medical Ethics relevant to the Role of Health Personnel, particularly Physicians, in the Protection of Prisoners and Detainees against Torture and Other Cruel, Inhuman or Degrading Treatment or Punishment were adopted by the General Assembly in 1982.[3] Credit is due to many actors, but it is clear that, as with the Declaration against Torture, pressure from NGOs, including the public interest generated by AI's 1973 campaign, had helped to secure the adoption of UN standards.

2. AI'S SECOND CAMPAIGN FOR THE ABOLITION OF TORTURE (1984–1985); THE 12-POINT PROGRAMME

In 1980 AI's International Council resolved (in its decision 8) to reinforce AI's work against torture 'by dedicating ourselves to the Campaign for the Abolition of Torture on the campaign's 10th anniversary in 1983'. It urged in particular members and groups to proceed, 'in the legal aspect of the struggle against torture, by making widely known *both* the international instruments now under discussion in the UN and elsewhere to outlaw torture, *and* AI's role in their formulation and eventual adoption, and especially by continuing to work for an effective UN Convention against Torture which would include provision for the routine and *ad hoc* international inspection of all places of detention [emphases in original]'. The International Council further resolved 'to provide [AI] members and groups with appropriate material so that they can participate effectively in this campaign . . .' and 'to involve the membership through the groups as actively as possible in this work'.

If a new campaign was needed it was because torture had not stopped. The research capacity built up at AI after the first campaign showed the prevalence of torture and ill-treatment around the world. Since the first campaign AI had developed techniques for tackling torture including medical investigation, the system of Urgent Action appeals, and campaigns focusing on torture and other human rights violations in specific countries. Other NGOs had been formed to fight torture on various fronts. Yet torture persisted. The international standards were being ignored by the governments which had adopted them—starting with Article 3 of the Declaration against Torture, 'No State may permit or tolerate torture or other cruel, inhuman or degrading treatment or punishment . . .'.

---

[3] Cf Rodle (1987), Chapter 12. In 1975 the World Medical Association had adopted the Declaration of Tokyo stating that doctors must not countenance, condone, or participate in torture.

Some international standards are in the form of recommendations; others constitute obligations of governments. If the standards were better known, there might be more pressure to fulfil the obligations. This was one of the ideas behind AI's 12-Point Programme for the Prevention of Torture, one of the first drafts of which was little more than a summary of the UN Declaration. Another, rather different, idea was that it should serve as a plan of action for the campaign. As adopted in October 1983, the 12-Point Programme combined these features and several more.

The 12-Point Programme opens with a preamble, after which are the 12 points—actually some 27 measures grouped under 12 headings. The measures are of several sorts:

- Some are simply restatements of requirements set forth in the Declaration against Torture, which have to do essentially with the repression of torture and with preventive measures to be taken within the criminal justice system. Thus: 'Governments should ensure that acts of torture are punishable offences under the criminal law' (Point 7); cf Declaration against Torture, Article 7: 'Each State shall ensure that all acts of torture as defined in article 1 are offences under its criminal law . . .'.
- Some of the provisions of the Declaration have been reformulated or stated more broadly to make them more comprehensive or more understandable to the public. Thus: 'Those responsible for torture should be brought to justice' (Point 8); cf Declaration, Article 9: 'If an investigation under article 8 or article 9 establishes that an act of torture as defined in article 1 appears to have been committed, criminal proceedings shall be instituted against the alleged offender or offenders in accordance with national law . . .'.
- Some points go beyond the requirements of the Declaration and are thus new standards for repression, prevention, or the protection of detainees which AI through its work against torture had found to be important. Thus the call to bring torturers to justice is followed by a call for universal jurisdiction: 'This principle should apply wherever they happen to be, wherever the crime was committed and whatever the nationality of the perpetrators or victims' (Point 8). This in turn is followed by a sentence aimed at explaining the concept of universal jurisdiction: 'There should be no "safe haven" for torturers.' Other new standards were: bringing all prisoners before a judicial authority promptly after being taken into custody (Point 2); ensuring that relatives, lawyers, and doctors have prompt and regular access to them (Point 2); forbidding secret detention by ensuring that prisoners are held in publicly recognized places (Point 3); ensuring that accurate information about their whereabouts is made available to relatives and lawyers (Point 3); informing prisoners promptly of their rights (Point 4); regular independent visits of

inspection to places of detention (Point 4); separation of authorities responsible for detention from those in charge of investigation (Point 4); instructing officials involved in the custody, interrogation, or treatment of prisoners that they are obliged to refuse to obey an order to torture (Point 9). Some of these new standards were in line with recommendations of UN expert bodies, but they had not been incorporated in UN human rights instruments.[4]

- Point 1 of the Programme calls for political action: 'The highest authorities of every country should demonstrate their total opposition to torture . . .'. It reflects one of the main ideas of the campaign: stopping torture is a matter of political will.[5]
- Some measures in the Programme are to be taken by governments in the international arena, for example ratification of the International Covenant on Civil and Political Rights and its (first) Optional Protocol (Point 12) and intercessions with other governments accused of torture.

One of the most difficult issues that arose in the preparation of the 12-Point Programme was incommunicado detention. An early draft called on governments to adopt 'provisions against incommunicado detention';[6] a later draft presented recommendations for safeguards in detention under the heading 'No incommunicado detention'. In the end, it was decided that AI could not oppose incommunicado detention absolutely because there might be some circumstances where its use was legitimate. AI's concern was not with incommunicado detention itself but with the risk of torture.

Rather than calling for an end to incommunicado detention, AI would propose safeguards providing for access to detainees—bringing them promptly before a judicial authority after being taken into custody and pro-

---

[4] In its General Comment 7, adopted in 1982, the Human Rights Committee set up under the International Covenant on Civil and Political Rights had proposed a series of safeguards against torture and ill-treatment including 'granting, without prejudice to the investigation, persons such as doctors, lawyers and family members access to the detainees' and 'provisions requiring that detainees should be held in places that are publicly recognized'. In resolution 1982/10 of 7 September 1982 the UN Sub-Commission on Prevention of Discrimination and Protection of Minorities had stated that it considered it desirable 'that there should be independent inspections, without prior notice, of places of detention, and interrogation centres'.

[5] As stated in the report produced for the campaign, 'Torture *can* be stopped. The international legal framework for its abolition exists, as do the investigative methods to verify and expose it. What is lacking is the political will of governments to stop torturing people. It is as simple and as difficult as that.' (Amnesty International (1984) *Torture in the Eighties* (London: Amnesty International), 4.) The notion of political will was taken up by the UN Special Rapporteur on Torture in his 1994 report to the Commission on Human Rights. He wrote: 'In the final analysis, the elimination of torture is a matter of political will. Its persistence is testimony to the failure of political will. Where it occurs the absence of safeguards and the prevalence of impunity is the measure of the gap between the commitment to its eradication and the political will required to enforce the commitment.' (Report of the Special Rapporteur, E/CN.4/1994/31, para 670.)

[6] The phrase was borrowed from General Comment 7 of the Human Rights Committee.

viding relatives, lawyers, and doctors with prompt and regular access to them. These measures, set forth in Point 2 of the Programme, are preceded by an evocation of the risk of torture in incommunicado detention, where the victims are 'unable to contact people outside who could help them or find out what is happening to them'—hence the need for access.

Here and elsewhere, the 12-Point Programme was designed to educate the public about the features of institutional settings which facilitate torture and the need for safeguards to remove those features or those settings. The Programme had other functions as well:

- It made existing international standards more understandable, partly by the use of simple language—'prisoners' rather than 'detainees', 'torture' standing for 'torture or other cruel, inhuman or degrading treatment or punishment' (the full term was given in the preamble to the Programme).
- It presented the safeguards as a coherent Programme by grouping them in a logical progression, starting with the most important ones, and including for the most part only safeguards with universal application.
- The Programme was directed at governments, the target of AI's campaigning. (In the preamble, 'concerned individuals and organizations' were invited to join in promoting the Programme.)
- The Programme stood as a yardstick of governmental behaviour. (The preamble put this point politely: 'Amnesty International believes that the implementation of these measures is a positive indication of a government's commitment to abolish torture and to work for its abolition worldwide.')
- As mentioned above, the Programme served to promote new standards which AI considered important. Some of these were already under consideration in draft instruments under discussion at the UN, such as the draft convention against torture.

In line with the 1980 decision of AI's International Council, the AI membership was involved in action based on the 12-Point Programme during the second Campaign for the Abolition of Torture, which was launched in April 1984 and continued to the end of 1985. The campaign itself was designed to bring out some of the key features of the Programme. Many thousands of letters were written by AI members and the public in the course of the campaign, calling on governments accused of torture to take remedial steps in line with the Programme, and particularly to institute impartial investigations into credible allegations of torture documented by AI, as called for in the Declaration against Torture. There was a poster exhibition on the prevention of torture, emphasizing the need to break through the isolation of prisoners in incommunicado detention—the 'access to prisoners' theme.

On 10 December 1984 the Convention against Torture and Other Cruel,

Inhuman or Degrading Treatment or Punishment ('Convention against Torture') was adopted by the UN General Assembly. During the next year AI sections publicized the Convention using a poster which set forth its most important features.

In the years following the adoption of the 12-Point Programme, a number of new standards proposed in it became incorporated in UN treaties and resolutions relating to the prevention of torture and other human rights violations. Thus, the principle of universal jurisdiction was incorporated in the Convention against Torture (Articles 5–8); the principle of bringing detainees promptly before a judicial authority, in the Declaration on the Protection of All Persons From Enforced Disappearance ('Declaration on Enforced Disappearance', 1992, Article 10(1)); improved provisions for access by lawyers, in the Body of Principles for the Protection of All Persons under Any Form of Detention or Imprisonment (1988, Principles 18(3), 19; cf Standard Minimum Rules for the Treatment of Prisoners, rule 93); the principle of holding detainees in publicly recognized places of detention, in the Declaration on Enforced Disappearance (Article 10(1)); the principle of making information about their detention and place of detention available promptly to relatives and lawyers, in the Declaration on Enforced Disappearance (Article 10(2)); the principle of due obedience, in the Principles on the Effective Prevention and Investigation of Extra-legal, Arbitrary and Summary Executions ('Principles on Extra-legal Executions', 1989, principle 3) and the Declaration on Enforced Disappearance (Article 6(1)).

3. 14-POINT PROGRAMMES ON 'DISAPPEARANCES' AND EXTRAJUDICIAL EXECUTIONS

In the early 1990s AI compiled a 14-Point Programme for the Prevention of 'Disappearances' and a 14-Point Programme for the Prevention of Extrajudicial Executions. The two Programmes were issued in December 1992 in preparation for a worldwide campaign to confront these two human rights violations.

Many of the measures contained in the Programmes were the same as those in the 12-Point Programme for the Prevention of Torture, but the language was changed to reflect new ideas and new international instruments—particularly the Declaration on Enforced Disappearance, the Principles on Extra-legal Executions, and the Body of Principles for the Protection of All Persons under Any Form of Detention or Imprisonment. Certain safeguards were tightened by being made to operate faster: people taken into custody were to be brought before a judicial authority 'without delay'; accurate information on arrest and place of detention was to be made available 'promptly' to relatives, lawyers, and the courts. New measures were added: strict chain-of-command control over security forces; non-refoulement of potential victims; and a habeas-corpus-type remedy, available at all times to enable relatives and lawyers to find out immediately where a prisoner is held, to ensure his or her safety, and to obtain the release of anyone arbitrarily detained. The Programmes stated that the prohibition of 'disappearances' and extrajudicial executions 'and the essential safeguards for their prevention' must not be suspended under any circumstances—a reference to the idea of a habeas-corpus-type remedy as a non-derogable right.

4. TOWARDS A FURTHER STRENGTHENING OF STANDARDS: THE REVISION OF THE 12-POINT PROGRAMME

Since 1991 AI has been engaged in a revision of its original 12-Point Programme for the Prevention of Torture. The revised version will be made public in due course.

The revision brings the 1983 text up to date to reflect the changes made when the 14-Point Programmes on 'disappearances' and extrajudicial executions were introduced in 1992. It is also an opportunity for the introduction of new standards, further tightening of the standards previously set forth, changes to reflect developments at the UN (calling for ratification of the Convention against Torture, changing the language on compensation and rehabilitation in point 10 to reflect the draft basic principles and guidelines on the right to reparation drafted by Theo van Boven and currently under discussion at the Commission on Human Rights), and other improvements in wording and arrangement.

Ideas under consideration for possible incorporation in the revised 12-Point Programme include:

- Provision for the judicial supervision of detention. The Programme would state that judges should have the right and duty to supervise effectively the detention of prisoners.
- Calling for lawyers to be present during interrogations.

Still under discussion is what the Programme should say about the prohibition or limitation of incommunicado detention.

In formulating standards in a document of this sort, AI has often had to balance the advantages of specificity against the need for universality. Some measures would be excellent safeguards against torture but cannot be implemented in some parts of the world because of lack of means. For example, detainees should ideally have a medical examination by a doctor of their choice on being taken into custody, but this measure is impractical in countries where basic medical resources are scarce. The absence of a standard from AI's list or the phrasing of a standard in rather general terms does not preclude the recommendation of more specific standards in countries where they can be implemented.

Since 1992 there has been no significant strengthening of standards for the prevention of torture in UN human rights instruments. The effort to create an Optional Protocol to the Convention against Torture which would set up a system of visits of inspection to places of detention has been frustratingly slow. At the same time, UN and regional expert bodies have made recommendations which follow AI's standards and in some places go beyond them. Thus, the UN Special Rapporteur on Torture has called for regular independent visits of inspection to all places of detention; for legislative provisions stipulating that evidence obtained through the use of torture, including confessions, should be excluded from judicial proceedings; for informing a relative of the detainee of the arrest and place of detention within eighteen hours in all circumstances; for medical inspection of detainees at the time of arrest; and for specific safeguards during interrogation. He has also stated that incommunicado detention should be made illegal.[7]

5. CONCLUSIONS

It is well known that UN human rights standards often progress through a sequence from recommendations of expert bodies to resolutions by political bodies to 'hard law' in the form of international conventions. The role of NGOs in pressing for the adoption of specific standards is also relatively well known. What is less understood is the role of standards within the work of NGOs and the interplay between NGO standards and UN standards.

Like the CPT, AI has developed standards largely through practical experience. The safeguards and remedies set forth in Chapter 6 of the AI report *Torture in the Eighties* (1984) were culled from the recommendations which AI had been making to governments accused of torture, and from the recommendations of national commissions and expert bodies. In putting together the 12-Point Programme for the Prevention of Torture, AI relied on its own sense of which measures were most important in practice.[8] This

---

[7] Report of the Special Rapporteur, E/CN.4/1995/34, para 926. Earlier, the CPT had set forth the right of persons detained by the police to have the fact of the detention notified to a third party of their choice, the right of access to a lawyer, and the right to request a medical examination by a doctor of his or her choice, as 'fundamental safeguards' against ill-treatment (see Chapter Two).

[8] Other important standards issued by AI have included the 14-Point Programmes on 'disappearances' and extrajudicial executions, mentioned above; 'Proposed Standards for National Human Rights Commissions' (1993, AI Index: IOR 40/01/93); the 15-Point Programme for

sense also led to decisions on which measures to propose for adoption in UN instruments.

The development of NGO standards continues, but no important standards for protection against torture and related human rights violations have been adopted as UN instruments since the adoption of the Declaration on Enforced Disappearance in 1992. With the present climate at the UN judged by many to be hostile to standard setting,[9] the NGO role in relation to human rights standards may become increasingly important.

REFERENCES

Amnesty International (1984) *Torture in the Eighties* (London: Amnesty International)

Howen, N (1997) 'International Human Rights Law-Making: Keeping the Spirit Alive', 2 *EHRLRev* 566–583

Rodley, NS (1987) *The Treatment of Prisoners under International Law* (Oxford: Clarendon Press)

Implementing Human Rights in International Peace-keeping Operations, reproduced in Appendix VIII of *Amnesty International Report 1995;* and medical standards, including the 1996 Declaration on the Role of Health Professionals in the Exposure of Torture and Ill-treatment and the 1996 Principles for the Medical Investigation of Torture and Other Cruel, Inhuman or Degrading Treatment (reproduced in *Amnesty International Report 1997*, London, Amnesty International, appendices VII and VIII respectively).

[9] See Howen, N (1997) 'International Human Rights Law-Making: Keeping the Spirit Alive', 2 *EHRLRev* 566–583.

Part III
The National Context

7

The Validity and Impact of CPT Standards with Regard to Belgium

STEPHAN PARMENTIER

1. INTRODUCTION

Between 14 and 23 November 1993 the CPT visited Belgium for the first time, making Belgium the last of the first-wave countries to ratify the Convention to receive a *periodic* visit. Nevertheless, it would have been difficult for the CPT to have come earlier: Belgium was the last of the member states of the then Council of Europe to ratify the ECPT, namely in June 1991.[1]

During this first visit the CPT delegation inspected three types of institutions: several police stations, particularly in the Brussels area and at the national airport; three prisons in different parts of the country (Bruges in Flanders, Lantin in Wollonie, and Sint-Gillis in the Brussels capital region); and two sites where asylum seekers were detained, one in Walem and the other at the national airport. Though the CPT transmitted its report on the visit to the Belgian Government in June 1994, the Government did not authorize publication of it until October 1994, almost a year after the visit. This delay was due to two factors. The report (in French) had to be translated into Dutch, the other official language of Belgium. Secondly, it was apparently appropriate for the Minister to let the local elections of October 1994 pass before the critical CPT report was made public.[2] The published report was accompanied by a six-page press release which contained provisional replies by the three ministers responsible for the institutions which were the subject of the CPT's findings and recommendations. As is customary, the CPT requested a formal response within six months, that is, by the end of 1994. The Government's response was sent to Strasbourg in May 1995. This resulted in a knock-on delay in the submission of the Government's final response, which was transmitted to Strasbourg in February 1996.

[1] For an overview of the legislative process see Parmentier, S (1992) 'Kijken achier tralies. België en de Europese Conventic voor de Preventie van Foltering en Onmenselijke en Vernederende Behandeling' ('Looking Behind Bars. Belgium and the European Convention for the Prevention of Torture and Inhuman and Degrading Treatment'), 13 *Panopticon*, 468–499.

[2] See the answer of the Minister of Justice to a parliamentary question: *Vragen en Antwoorden*, Senate, 1994–1995, 17 November 1994 (Vr nr 876, Pataer).

The CPT paid a second *periodic* visit to Belgium in autumn 1997 and adopted its subsequent report in April 1998. The Committee visited the same type of institutions as on the first occasion and followed up its visits to the prisons at Lantin and Sint-Gillis. The Committee also visited the cells at the Brussels *Palais de Justice* and two mental hospitals in Wollonie. There was less delay over translation on this occasion. The CPT's second report was published in June 1998, again accompanied by a six-page press release.

The importance of these CPT reports can scarcely be overestimated. This was the first occasion that an international body had examined detention conditions in Belgium and the CPT reports were critical of the Belgium authorities. In the space available it is not possible to examine all the issues addressed by the CPT: I shall adopt a more limited objective. In what follows I shall consider the validity of the CPT in a Belgian context and the impact of the Committee's recommendations on Belgian policy. I shall consider both questions in relation to three issues: first, the indicia of torture and ill-treatment; secondly, custodial standards; and, thirdly, safeguards against ill-treatment.

2. TORTURE AND ILL-TREATMENT

As is its custom, the CPT addressed two issues: allegations of ill-treatment and the risk of ill-treatment. During its first visit (during which the Committee visited community police stations in Bruges, Brussels, and Liège and the gendarmerie in Brussels and at the national airport[3]) the Committee heard no allegations of serious ill-treatment which might be considered torture or as coming close to torture. The Committee did receive allegations of ill-treatment, however. Beating and kicking during police questioning was alleged on a couple of occasions, as was similar treatment during transfer between prisons. Allegations of ill-treatment were also received regarding the forced repatriation of Africans by the gendarmerie at Brussels Airport: disproportionate use of handcuffs and sedatives was said to have been used while they were being escorted.

---

[3] Belgium had until recently three types of police forces: the community police (*police communale*) under the command of the local mayor; the national police (gendarmerie) operating nationally under the supervision of its joint staff of generals; and the judicial police (*police judiciaire*) under the command of the Public Prosecutor in the geographical territory under his supervision. The first two were ultimately the responsibility of the Minister of the Interior and the third the responsibility of the Minister of Justice. Following the Parliamentary Commission of Inquiry into the functioning of the police forces and the judicial authorities in dealing with the paedophile scandals of recent years (better known as the Dutroux Commission), the Government decided in May 1998 to merge all three forces into a unified police force.

This information formed the basis of the Committee's estimation that there was a risk of detainees being ill-treated while in police detention.[4] The Committee requested more information: how many complaints had been made against the police in recent years and how many disciplinary and criminal prosecutions had been taken and sanctions imposed? The Committee recommended that senior police commanders unequivocally inform their subordinates that the ill-treatment of detainees is intolerable and would be punished severely.

In its responses the Belgium Government provided statistics regarding ill-treatment at the hands of the police. But the data were not specific. In the interim report of May 1995 the authorities acknowledged that they were unable to provide figures regarding the number of complaints made against the police, or the number of disciplinary proceedings taken. It was for this reason that a survey of all 584 community police corps in Belgium was conducted, and the results incorporated in the follow-up report of February 1996.[5] Of the 86 complaints lodged with the administrative and judicial authorities in 1992–1993 the vast majority were dismissed, a small number were under review, and four had given rise to a light sanction such as a reprimand or a short suspension. The raw figures do not allow for any further interpretation. The data regarding complaints against the gendarmerie for the use of force tell a different story. According to the Inspector General of the gendarmerie there were only seven such complaints in 1992 (out of a total of 137) and nine in 1993 (out of a total of 244). Further information from the Inspectorate, however, led these figures to be significantly adjusted, with resulting uncertainty.[6]

The manner in which these data were presented is illuminating. They confirm a pattern characteristic of Belgian governance in recent decades, namely, the absence of statistical information adequate for policy formation. This is true not only of the police: it applies to the administration of civil and criminal justice generally and has repeatedly been highlighted in academic and other writings. Thus the gendarmerie, the largest police force in the country, has lacked transparency. The authorities are left in the dark about the number of complaints made and their consequences. This gives rise to the suspicion that only the tip of the complaints iceberg is visible.

The second CPT *periodic* visit in 1997 seemed to confirm this interpretation. The Committee again heard allegations of ill-treatment at the hands of the police from foreigners and nationals, both during transportation and in police stations. Allegations were also made again regarding the treatment of foreigners during expulsion procedures and these were confirmed by the

---

[4] Belgium 1, para 22.   [5] Belgium 1 R 2, 3–4.   [6] Ibid.

CPT's medical examinations. The delegation met with *Comité P* (the Committee for the Supervision of Police Forces, a national body established in 1993).The annual report of *Comité P* records that 249 complaints were lodged against the police in the period August 1996–June 1997, 52 per cent of which were judged to involve a violation of relevant legal provisions and 44 of which were sent to the judicial or administrative authorities. The actual figure is probably substantially higher since *Comité P* does not deal with all complaints against the police. *Comité P* concluded that the Belgian police forces have shown 'a manifest lack of professionalism, a very relative respect for the rights and freedoms of citizens, a lack of respect for the guidelines and procedures and a negligent and impertinent attitude vis-à-vis the principles of the police law'. This information prompted the CPT to repeat its earlier concern that the Belgian authorities should display greater vigilance and control.[7]

Press coverage of the second CPT report remained meagre, as has the number of allegations of ill-treatment by the police. Indeed the CPT report on Belgium has been more closely studied in The Netherlands than in Belgium.[8] Nevertheless, the judgements of *Comité P* and the CPT were recently given force by a case involving a Nigerian asylum seeker, Semira Adamu, whose application had been rejected and who was to be expelled. After boarding the aeroplane in September 1998 members of the gendarmerie used a cushion to silence Ms Adamu, as a result of which she lost consciousness and died. The public outcry was enormous and three days after the incident the Minister of the Interior resigned. The new Minister appointed a Commission to consider the current guidelines on forced repatriation. The Commission's report was due in January 1999.

3. INSUFFICIENT ACTION AGAINST ILL-TREATMENT

The Belgian Government chose not to address in great depth the CPT's recommendation that senior police officers be more vigorous in their response to police ill-treatment. It limited itself to some general references to the new police law, which was last updated in August 1992.[9] Several provisions in the law emphasize the need for police forces to respect individual rights and freedoms and to make use of force within the boundaries of the law in order to pursue a legitimate objective that cannot otherwise be obtained. The Government also referred to internal instructions of the gen-

---

[7] Belgium 2, para 11.
[8] See, eg, 'Belgische politie slaat enschopt' ('Belgian police beats and kicks'), *Brabants Dagblad*, 19 June 1998.
[9] Belgium 1 R 1, 5–6.

darmerie and to the new charter of the community police, both of which are considered to be in conformity with the police law. It also announced, in rather vague terms, that a code of ethics for police forces would be elaborated on the instructions of the Minister of the Interior. The Government's subsequent follow-up report was silent on all these issues, including the status of the proposed code of ethics. It is not surprising, therefore, that in its second *periodic* report the CPT returned to this issue and insisted on a firmer stance by the Belgian authorities. The Committee recommended that the Minister of the Interior take formal action. Meanwhile work on the code of ethics has progressed slowly. The CPT was informed that a first draft would be ready by autumn 1997. The CPT recommended that completion of the work be given priority but when the Committee's report was authorized for publication the Government's press release made no reference to the code, announcing instead that a draft bill on police disciplinary measures would be issued. The question of use of force by police officers was said now to be dealt with in their training.

The remainder of this section will consider two particular facets of matters concerning physical conditions of detention because of the importance attached to them by the CPT during their Belgian visits.

(a) Overcrowding

Two-thirds of the report arising out of the CPT's first *periodic* visit was devoted to the three prisons visited. The newly opened prison at Bruges seemed to comply best with CPT standards, the delegation being critical only of the compulsory work regime for women.[10] In Lantin Prison the Committee considered that the activities provided for prisoners should be substantially extended and the number of skilled medical personnel increased. The Committee was also critical about the psychiatric annexe: it was judged to be understaffed and lacking in psychiatric therapeutic programmes.[11] But it was on the conditions at Sint-Gilles Prison that the Committee concentrated its critical attention.

The CPT was shocked by the sanitary conditions at Sint-Gillis—the absence of in-cell lavatories, the dirty sheets, the broken windows, the inadequate heating, and the generally deplorable condition of the building. At the time of the visit the population at Sint-Gillis was approaching 50 per cent overcrowded (720 prisoners occupying 500 places). Single cells were being shared by two or three prisoners. Moreover the Committee considered the employment, educational, and recreational activities to be totally

---

[10] Belgium 1, para 136.   [11] Ibid, paras 175–192.

insufficient. Prisoners were confined to their cells for up to twenty-two hours per day. This combination of factors led the Committee to deliver the devastatingly critical judgement that Sint-Gilles exhibited a 'perverse combination of overcrowding, lack of adequate sanitation and an impoverished regime' which, in the CPT's view, amounted to inhuman and degrading treatment.[12] The situation at Sint-Gilles was mitigated by the good staff-prisoner relations and the positive attitude of the director. Nevertheless, the Committee recommended that the Belgian authorities give the highest priority to improving the 'mediaeval' living conditions of the prisoners and reducing the overcrowding.

Close observers of the Belgian prison system could not have been surprised by the CPT findings. The prison riots of September 1987 had already highlighted many of the problems—the small and overcrowded cells, the dirty and inadequate visiting rooms, the lack of running water and sanitary facilities, and the worn out walls and floors. The situation had received widespread criticism from NGOs, parliamentarians, and academics alike.[13] After the riots, the then Minister of Justice had started to take measures to deal with the most salient problems. Some older institutions were refurbished and, more controversially, some new prisons were built to relieve older ones.[14] Legislation was passed, such as the pre-trial detention law of 1990,[15] and other statutes, such as the Vagrancy Act, abolished in an attempt to reduce the prison population. These efforts proved insufficient. By the early 1990s the prison population had again grown substantially.

In its first report the CPT limited itself to mentioning several Belgian government decisions taken in the months preceding transmission of the CPT report.[16] The Minister of Justice had decided to make wider use of existing legal instruments providing for the non-execution of substitute prison sentences and the conditional release of certain categories of detainees in order to reduce the prison population. In March 1994 the Belgian Cabinet opted for a second strategy of expanding prisons' capacity by nearly 25 per cent (from 5,900 to 7,200 places) by building new prisons at Andenne and Saint-Hubert. In the press release issued at the same time as the publication of the CPT report the Government highlighted both strategies in response to the CPT's severe criticism of Belgian prison conditions.

Whether the CPT visit of 1993 had a direct impact on the government

---

[12] Belgium 1, paras 85–86.

[13] See Snacken, S (1988) 'Hoe meer zielen, hoe meer vreugd? Over capaciteitsproblemen in de gevangenissen' (Capacity Problems in Prisons), 9 *Panopticon* 1–7; and (1987) *Het Beleisch zen in Europees perspektief* (The Belgian Prison System in a European Perspective), Proceedings of a Colloquium held at the European Parliament, Brussels, 13 November 1987.

[14] For a critical viewpoint, see: De Wit, J and Van Outrive, L (1988) *Gevang juswezen en abolitionisme* (The Prison System and Abolitionism) (Gent: Liga voor Mensenrechten), 8–53.

[15] See: Declercq, R and Verstraeten, R (eds) (1991) *Voorlopige* hechtenis; *de wet van 20 juli 1990* (Pre-trial Detention: the Law of 20 July 1990) (Leuven: Acco).

[16] Belgium 1, para 26.

initiatives of early 1994 is difficult to tell. Testing the proposition requires closer analysis of the decision making processes involved. It nevertheless seems plausible that the visit, and the comments of the delegation at the close of the visit, gave additional support to the advocates of change within the Government and assisted policy initiatives to move ahead more easily than would otherwise have been the case. What is beyond doubt is that the CPT report exerted substantial influence on several areas of civil society. It relaunched an intensive debate about prisons policy in the press,[17] amongst NGOs,[18] and in academia.[19] The report was closely studied by personnel within or connected to the Belgian Prison Service—the pastors, social workers, and prison officials themselves. The report—the first of its kind from an international and impartial body—provided support for those within the service who were frustrated and it is ironic that the best known Flemish human rights NGO—the *Liga voor de Mensenrechten*—awarded its human rights prize for 1994 to the Director of Sint-Gillis Prison, the institution so fiercely criticized by the CPT.

In its responses to the CPT the Belgian Government stressed that it was simultaneously pursuing three strategies to improve living conditions in the prisons visited. The interim report described renovation work at the institutions concerned.[20] The follow-up report of February 1996 described additions to the capacity of the prison system, including the building of two new prisons. It also announced the transfer of foreigners to newly built detention centres for illegal immigrants,[21] and reiterated that efforts were being made to reduce the prison population through the use of existing alternative sentences. Moreover, the Government alluded to the new law on penal mediation of February 1994 which provided the Public Prosecutor with alternative means of dealing with minor offences. Yet the Government was vague about the actual impact of all these measures which had been adopted two years previously.

This vagueness did not escape the CPT when they visited again in September 1997. The Committee acknowledged the efforts of the Belgian

---

[17] See the extensive comments in the newspapers—eg *De Moreen, De Standaard Gazet van Antwerpen, La Libre Belgique*, and *Le Soir*—of 15–16 October 1994.

[18] See, eg: Geboers, J, Smaers, G and Van Laethem, W (eds) (1995) *Detentie in België. Een kritische analyse van het radport van het Europees Comité ter Preventie van Follering over hun eerste bezoek aan België* (Detention in Belgium. A Critical Analysis of the Report of the European Committee for the Prevention of Torture after its Visit to Belgium) (Gent: Liga voor Mensenrechten).

[19] See, eg: Parmentier, S (1995) 'Het Europees Coniitd voor de Preventie van Foltering op een kruispunt' (The European Committee for the Prevention of Torture at a Crossroads), 2 *Mensenrechten. Jaarboek 1994 van het Interuniversitair Centrum Mensenrechten*, 365–378; Parmentier, S and Peters, T (eds) (forthcoming) *Detentie doorgelicht. De Beleische rapporten van het Europees Comité voor de Preventle van Folterinp, en Onmenseliike en Vemederende Behandeling of Bestraffing* (Detention Studied. The Belgian Reports of the European Committee for the Prevention of Torture) (Leuven: Leuven University Press).

[20] Belgium 1 R 1, 39–40.

[21] Belgium 1 R 2, 9–11.

Government to address prison conditions: they referred to the Minister of Justice's policy paper of June 1996.[22] A couple of months later, however, the scandal surrounding the Dutroux case, and the resulting changes to the judicial system, drastically hampered the implementation of many of the proposed measures. Though the second CPT report showed understanding for these dramatic and unforeseen events, the Committee nevertheless insisted on further efforts and more rapid changes.[23] In its press release responding to the report the Government mentioned the establishment in early 1997 of a special unit to co-ordinate all 'alternative measures' to detention. The Government also announced an experiment with electronic monitoring to be conducted in Sint-Gillis Prison, the experiment to be evaluated by the University of Leuven. The first results from this experiment are expected in 1999.

(b) Inadequate provisions for asylum seekers

In 1993 the CPT also visited two sites where foreigners were held in detention, the waiting room in the transit area at Brussels Airport and the closed centre in Walem. The legal possibility of detaining foreigners—illegal immigrants and asylum seekers who had exhausted the asylum procedure—was introduced in 1991 and significantly extended in the spring of 1993 their detention pending their repatriation. In 1993 the period of detention was limited to two months, though it has since been extended to eight months.[24]

The CPT was very critical about the material conditions under which foreigners were being held.[25] In Walem asylum seekers were detained in an old fort over one hundred years old, a fire having damaged the centre in which they were formerly held. The fort lacked all basic provisions regarding lighting, heating, maintenance and hygiene. The situation was slightly better in the transit area of the airport, but the facilities were nevertheless considered too rudimentary and cramped. The CPT found the accommodation in both places unacceptable and argued that in some respects it involved 'inhuman and degrading treatment' which risked the physical integrity of the detainees. The recommendations were crystal clear. The Government was requested to take urgent measures to improve the situation. In fact, during the course of its visit the CPT was informed that two new detention centres for asylum seekers were shortly to be opened and that the one at Walem would be closed.

[22] De Clercq, S (1996) *Orientatienota: Strafbeleid en tenuitvoerleednp, van straffen* (Policy Paper: Penal Policy and the Execution of Sanctions) (Brussel: Ministerie van Justitie).
[23] Belgium 2, paras 80–85.
[24] See Snacken, S and De Mesmaeker, K (1998) 'Vrijheidsberoving van illegalen' (Deprivation of Liberty of Illegal Immigrants), 4 *Mensenrechten Jaarboek 1996/97 van het Interuniversitair Centrum Mensenrechten*, 199–224.
[25] Belgium 1, paras 56–72.

The CPT was not the only body critical of the situation of asylum seekers. Several NGOs had expressed their indignation about the poor material conditions at Walem. Moreover, just two months prior to the CPT's first visit the *Brussels Tribunal de Première Instance* had judged that the treatment of a group of Somali asylum seekers detained at Brussels Airport had all the characteristics of inhuman and degrading treatment and had ordered the authorities to improve the facilities for persons staying in these premises. This judgment was cited in the CPT report.[26]

In its press release of November 1994 the Government asserted that the CPT criticisms regarding Walem were now redundant: the centre had been closed the previous March. The residents had been transferred to two other centres with adequate facilities in the neighbourhood of the airport, one for asylum seekers awaiting a decision on admissibility (centre '127'), and one for those declared inadmissible (centre '127bis'). More interesting, however, is the fact that the Government disputed the CPT's competence to draw conclusions and to issue recommendations regarding the situation of persons in the transit zone at the airport. It was argued that persons held in the transit zone were not deprived of their liberty. Foreigners arriving without the necessary documents were said not to be detained: they were merely refused access to Belgian territory.[27] The same arguments were made in the Government's interim response to the CPT. In the follow-up report of February 1996, the Government provided more information about the functioning of the new centres for asylum seekers.[28] The problem at the airport appeared to have been solved by the construction of a completely new building, which included a special room for persons refused entry. The Minister of the Interior had also given permission to a number of NGOs to visit the other detention centres in order to check the conditions. During its 1997 visit the CPT followed up its 1993 visits and also went to other places of detention for asylum seekers. On this occasion the Committee's appraisal proved to be quite positive. The Committee limited itself to recommending slight changes to make the stay of detained persons more agreeable.[29]

4. LEGAL SAFEGUARDS FOR PERSONS HELD IN DETENTION

The CPT places great importance on the legal safeguards for persons held in detention,[30] and has been particularly critical of the position in

---

[26] Ibid, para 58.
[27] For a critical view, see: Verschueren, F (1995) 'De gesloten centra voor asielzoekers en illegale vreemdelingen' (The Closed Centres for Asylum Seekers and Illegal Foreigners) in Geboers, Smaers and Van Laethem, 108–117.
[28] Belgium 1 R 2, 6–8.   [29] Belgium 2, paras 53–70.   [30] See Chapter Two.

Belgium, both with regard to arrestees held in police custody and prisoners in prisons.

(a) The absence of adequate legal safeguards for persons held in police custody

As a result of its first visit, the CPT concluded that Belgian provisions did not comply with the safeguards which the Committee considers fundamental for persons held in police custody.[31] In Belgium it appeared that only persons arrested for administrative reasons (for example, for disturbing public order, or by way of preventive arrest) possessed the right to notify a third person of their choice of their arrest and detention. Persons arrested on 'judicial' grounds, that is with the intention of being brought before a judge or on the prior order of a judge, had no such right. The CPT recommended that all persons held in police custody have the right to notify a third person of their choice, and that any restrictions on this right be clearly defined by law. As for access to legal counsel during police custody, Belgian legislation accords such a right only in cases of judicial arrest and, more specifically, when persons are brought before a judge who is to decide about extending the period of custody. In these circumstances the lawyer can be contacted by his client and can visit him, but the lawyer may not attend any interrogations of his client by the police. These provisions were judged defective by the CPT. The Committee recommended that all persons in police custody should have the right of access to legal counsel of their choice from the outset of custody and throughout each phase of the legal procers. This right, the Committee argued, should not be limited to a simple visit by the lawyer, but should include the right to be interrogated in the presence of a lawyer.

Belgian legislation was silent regarding the third element in the CPT's list of fundamental rights—medical examination by a doctor of one's choice, in order to have any signs of ill-treatment assessed by an independent expert. Although the police suggested that in practice arrested persons would always be allowed access to a doctor of their choice, the CPT judged this an insufficient safeguard. The Committee recommended that Belgian legislation be amended to incorporate the right to be examined by a doctor, out of hearing of the police, and that the results of such examinations be made available to the detainee and his or her lawyer. Finally, the CPT recommended that arrested persons have the right to be informed about their rights, and that a code of conduct be agreed to govern interrogations by the police.

It is interesting to note that these criticisms were directed against regu-

---

[31] Belgium 1, paras 35–50.

lations that were the outcome of a fundamental reform in the years immediately preceding the CPT's visit. The new police law of 1992, and the new law on pre-trial detention of 1990, had strengthened the legal position of arrested and detained persons. The new provisions nevertheless fell well short of CPT standards. This is not because the issues highlighted by the CPT had not been discussed. Many had come up during the parliamentary debates on the above laws, but were discarded for want of sufficient political support.[32] For the Belgian political and legal world, the issues seem to have been non-issues. This is reflected in the government press release when the first CPT report was published: it was silent about possible legislative initiatives to extend the legal safeguards for persons held in police custody. The Belgian media and NGOs proved equally weak in bringing these issues to the public agenda.

The years following the first CPT report witnessed no change in the official Belgian position regarding these issues which can best be characterized as indifferent. In their interim report, the Government minimized the importance to be attached to formal legal safeguards in two ways.[33] First, they emphasized that, despite the absence of formal legal rights, police practice is often more liberal, particularly regarding notification of third persons and access to a doctor. The argument was different in relation to access to legal counsel. Here, the Government argued that it was difficult to organize practically, given the brevity of the custody period. They also suggested that access to a lawyer could hamper official investigations. Thus, no indications were given concerning the political will of the Belgian Government to take any concrete legislative actions. In the follow-up report of February 1996, the issue of legal safeguards was limited to one sentence, which simply referred to the previous report.

It was therefore no surprise that the second CPT report was overtly critical of the Government's attitude or, more precisely, the lack of any progress with regard to each of the fundamental safeguards mentioned.[34] The Committee expressed concern about the situation and forcefully re-iterated its earlier recommendations that each of the safeguards be incorporated in legislation *expressis verbis*. The Committee rejected as insufficient any practices in dealing with arrested persons which, however liberal or well intended by the police, had no firm legal basis. Since the Government's subsequent press release remained extremely vague, if not mute, about the CPT's concerns, it seems highly unlikely that there will be any initiatives in this field in the foreseeable future.

[32] See Hutsebaut, F (1995) 'De behandeling van en de waarborgen voor arrestanten' (The Treatment of and Guarantees for Arrested Persons) in Geboers, Smaers and Van Laethem, 36–52.
[33] Belgium 1 R 1, 14–20.   [34] Belgium 2, paras 34–41.

(b) The absence of complaint and inspection procedures for prisoners

During its first visit the CPT also looked into the legal position of sentenced prisoners.[35] Again, its conclusions were critical. The Committee was surprised that no formal complaints procedure existed for prisoners, albeit that in practice they could take several steps to protest against certain aspects of their detention. The second matter concerned inspections. Although, legally speaking, various authorities possessed the competence to inspect prisons or various aspects of the prison regime, a central and independent system of inspection was lacking. The CPT insisted that both a complaints procedure and an inspection system are crucial elements in the prevention of torture and ill-treatment in prisons. This is particularly the case for prisoners judged to be dangerous because they are likely to be subject to special security or disciplinary measures. The CPT recommended that the Belgian authorities should, without delay, establish an effective complaints procedure and further recommended that every detainee receiving a disciplinary sanction be informed in writing about the reasons for the sanction and be provided with an avenue of appeal. The recommendation regarding inspection was somewhat less stringent: the Belgian authorities were asked to explore the possibility of establishing an independent inspection body.

On these issues the official government press release accompanying the first CPT report was laconic. It did not address the issues squarely but almost evasively referred to the negotiations under way within the Council of Europe regarding an additional protocol to the European Convention on Human Rights relating to the rights of detainees. This position illustrated the Government's general attitude *vis-à-vis* complaint procedures and inspection. The interim report said not a word on either issue. In the follow-up report of February 1996 the Government mentioned the recent establishment of an inspection service within the Ministry of Justice, to become operational in the course of the same year.[36]

The critique and recommendations of the CPT went to the heart of the matter by pointing directly to the stunning absence of complaint and inspection procedures in the Belgian prison system. Some commentators went so far as to argue that the CPT underestimated the problem and was too flattering to the Government.[37] They pointed out that collective complaints are prohibited under the prison regulations and that unfounded complaints can give rise to disciplinary measures. As to the inspection procedures already in place, it was emphasized that these are hardly used in practice and certainly do not comply with the criterion of independence. An aca-

---

[35] Belgium 1, paras 226–239 and 244–248.   [36] Belgium 1 R 2, 35–36.
[37] Smaers, G (1995) 'De rechtsbescherming van personen die van hun vrijheid beroofd zijn' (The Legal Protection of Persons Deprived of Their Liberty) in Geboers, Smaers and Van Laethem, 53–63.

demic initiative of early 1996 injected new life into the debate about complaint procedures. The Belgian Association for Criminology devoted its annual meeting to the legal position of detainees.[38] Several speakers explicitly took the CPT recommendations as their point of departure to propose changes in the Belgian legislation.

These developments gained momentum following the events of summer 1996. The Minister of Justice asked Professor Dupont of the University of Leuven to draft the basic principles of a new law that would govern all aspects of prison detention.[39] Chapters were reserved for the issues of complaints, discipline, and inspection. It is noteworthy that the author, when justifying the need for a comprehensive and updated legal position of detainees, explicitly and repeatedly referred to the criticisms and recommendations of the CPT.[40] On completion of his massive task in autumn 1997, a Commission was established under his chairmanship to elaborate a draft law for the purposes of parliamentary debate and decision making. The results of this initiative are expected in October 1999. In its second report the CPT welcomed these developments and again emphasized the need to give priority to the creation of an effective complaints procedure for prisoners.[41]

5. CONCLUSION

Let us return to the two questions raised at the beginning of this chapter: first, whether the standards advanced by the CPT can be considered valid in the Belgian context; and, secondly, whether those standards have had any impact on Belgian policy and practice.

The first question can unequivocally be answered in the affirmative. The CPT has raised a number of important issues, with the consequence that the visibility and credibility of the Committee has been raised in Belgium. The gross overcrowding and inadequate living conditions in some Belgian prisons has been highlighted, as have the poor living conditions in various closed centres for asylum seekers. These problems were not new. They had previously been documented by detainees and their families, by NGOs, by politicians, by academics, and even by prison staff. The CPT added value, however, because the CPT—an international and independent organ—made the position clear and beyond dispute. It lent the argument symbolic weight.

---

[38] Tubex, H and Vanacker, J (eds) (1997) *Rechtspositie en beklagrecht van gedetineerden* (Legal Position and Complaint Right of Detainees) (Brugge: Die Keure).
[39] Dupont, L (ed) (1998) *Op web, naar een beginselenwet gevangeniswezen* (On the Road to a Basic Law on the Prison System) (Leuven: Leuven University Press), 21–229.
[40] Ibid, 122 and 149.   [41] Belgium 2, para 205.

The CPT findings also proved valid in areas of detention that were less conspicuous and probably half-hidden, such as detention by police forces. The Committee took several allegations of ill-treatment seriously and insisted on a clear policy statement from the political and police authorities. As a result, the CPT put such practices on the public agenda: the Committee increased their visibility and made the public aware of them.

Finally, the CPT managed to raise a couple of issues that operated almost under cover, deeply embedded in traditional Belgian practice. The Committee questioned the absence of legal safeguards for persons held in police custody and the lack of prisoner complaint and inspection procedures in prisons. Though neither of these issues has subsequently generated major political or public debates, their validity arguably resides in their preventive importance *vis-à-vis* ill-treatment. The Committee applied its rigid supranational consistency, developed on the basis of comparative practice since 1989. In the Belgian context this application has broken new ground.

Not every Belgian commentator in the field of the administration of justice will necessarily agree with this, essentially academic, judgement. For some observers some of the CPT's interventions will be judged less valid. And that reaction is linked to the second question: whether the CPT standards have had any impact in Belgium.

The question of impact is far more difficult, and can only be assessed adequately by differentiating between different spheres of policy making, and moreover, by looking at policy changes over time. The impact of CPT standards on Belgian public policy has arguably been minimal to date. The striking example of positive impact is the Government's decision to close down certain centres for asylum seekers following the CPT's critical verdict on the living conditions in them. But with this exception it is difficult to find examples that suggest a direct causal relationship between the Committee's findings and government policy. This is not to assert that in all other areas CPT visits and reports have been without influence. As far as the improvement of living conditions in prisons is concerned, for example, the Government has frequently referred to the Committee's recommendations as part of the justification for their decisions. But this is not necessarily evidence that decisions to renovate prisons and to construct new institutions were taken as a direct result of CPT findings. The Government had arguably already made crucial decisions to this effect before the first CPT visit and the Committee's recommendations were integrated with this ongoing government policy. At best, the CPT's findings and recommendations probably provided additional support and leverage for those forces in Government susceptible to change.

Further, it has to be concluded that several issues raised in CPT reports have had little or no impact on official policy. This is arguably the case in the area of ill-treatment by police forces. Policy initiatives designed to prevent ill-treatment have so far been few and vague. It seems that particular incidents, such as the recent case of the asylum seeker who died during the course of repatriation, have far greater impact on government policy than the insistent recommendations of the CPT. Yet the CPT reports are nonetheless important. They provide crucial points of reference and inspiration for any further action that might be undertaken by the Government or on behalf of the private sector. The same argument applies in relation to those issues which have so far received no response from the Belgian Government or, more importantly, where the Government disputes the need for reform. This is particularly the case regarding safeguards for detainees in police custody. In the short run the political will for innovation is lacking but there is no reason to assume that the CPT standards could not serve as a point of reference in the future.

If the examples of direct impact of the CPT on Belgian public policy are few, the Committee's impact on Belgian civil society can hardly be overestimated. The work of the CPT has generated enormous interest among NGOs and practitioners involved in prisons policy, forensic and social affairs, and human rights. This is evidenced by the intensive contacts of several NGOs and persons with the CPT in preparation for the Committee's visits to Belgium. Indeed the quality of the CPT reports on Belgium arguably owes a good deal to the quality of the information received from various sources in the country. Moreover, the mobilization of the 'inner circle' that took place prior to the CPT visits has been matched by the heightened public awareness that followed them. In this respect the mass media played a crucial role and the academic community was vital for deepening the understanding of a more specialized audience. The impact of the second visit appears to have been greater than that of the first, suggesting a cumulative effect. It remains to be seen whether the CPT's standards will continue to serve as a major point of reference for Belgian civil society in its efforts to upgrade the position of detainees.

Finally, a discussion of the impact of CPT standards would be incomplete without mentioning an intriguing area in which public policy and concerns from other sectors of society are coinciding and may provide the basis for cross-fertilization. The best example lies in the work of the ongoing Commission to elaborate a draft law on detention in prisons, of which the issues of complaint and inspection procedures constitute only one part. In his preparatory work Professor Dupont explicitly referred to the CPT recommendations and took them as guiding principles to shape his own proposals, which will be submitted to Parliament. This illustrates very nicely that CPT findings and recommendations, which do not seem to have any direct impact on public policy, may nevertheless serve as points of reference and indirectly shape policy.

REFERENCES

Belgian Colloquium (1987) *Het Beleisch zen in Europees perspektief*, Proceedings of a Colloquium held at the European Parliament (Brussels, 13 November 1987)

Declercq, R and Verstraeten, R (eds) (1991) *Voorlopige hechtenis; de wet van 20 juli 1990* (Leuven: Acco)

De Clercq, S (1996) *Orientatienota: Strafbeleid en tenuitvoerleednp, van straffen* (Brussel: Ministerie van Justitie)

De Wit, J and Van Outrive, L (1988) *Gevang juswezen en abolitionisme* (Gent: Liga voor Mensenrechten)

Dupont, L (ed) (1998) *Op web, naar een beginselenwet gevangeniswezen* (Leuven: Leuven University Press)

Geboers, J, Smaers, G and Van Laethem, W (eds) (1995) *Detentie in België. Een kritische analyse van het radport van het Europees Comité ter Preventie van Follering over hun eerste bezoek aan België* (Gent: Liga voor Mensenrechten)

Hutsebaut, F (1995) 'De behandeling van en de waarborgen voor arrestanten' in Geboers, Smaers and Van Laethem (eds), 36–52

Parmentier, S (1992) 'Kijken achier tralies. België en de Europese Conventic voor de Preventie van Foltering en Onmenselijke en Vernederende Behandeling', 13 *Panopticon* 468–499

Parmentier, S (1995) 'Het Europees Coniitd voor de Preventie van Foltering op een kruispunt', 2 *Mensenrechten Jaarboek 1994 van het Interuniversitair Centrum Mensenrechten*, 365–378

Parmentier, S and Peters, T (eds) (forthcoming) *Detentie doorgelicht. De Beleische rapporten van het Europees Comité voor de Preventle van Folterinp, en Onmenselijke en Vemederende Behandeling of Bestraffing* (Leuven: Leuven University Press)

Smaers, G (1995) 'De rechtsbescherming van personen die van hun vrijheid beroofd zijn' in Geboers, Smaers and Van Laethem (eds), 53–63

Snacken, S (1988) 'Hoe meer zielen, hoe meer vreugd? Over capaciteitsproblemen in de gevangenissen', 9 *Panopticon* 1–7

Snacken, S and De Mesmaeker, K (1998) 'Vrijheidsberoving van illegalen', 4 *Mensenrechten. Jaarboek 1996/97 van het Interuniversitair Centrum Mensenrechten*, 199–224

Tubex, H and Vanacker, J (eds) (1997) *Rechtspositie en beklagrecht van gedetineerden* (Brugge: Die Keure)

Verschueren, F (1995) 'De gesloten centra voor asielzoekers en illegale vreemdelingen' in Geboers, Smaers and Van Laethem (eds), 108–117

8

The CPT in France

ROLAND BANK

The CPT carried out two *periodic* visits of thirteen days each in 1991 and 1996 and one *ad hoc* visit of three days in 1994. A further *ad hoc* visit lasting five days was made in 1994 to the French overseas department of Martinique. Given that the situation in Martinique is not comparable to that in the mother country, the following analysis will be restricted to the inspections of continental French territory.[1]

The first *periodic* visit to France involved an inspection of most of the principal types of detention facilities: police and gendarmerie stations (including the administrative detention of foreigners), prisons, and psychiatric hospitals.[2] Some of these places of detention were revisited in 1996.[3] In addition to these follow-up inspections, the 1996 visit involved several new police and gendarmerie stations and three further prisons, including an institution for young offenders.[4] The 1994 *ad hoc* visit was dedicated entirely to the inspection of six Paris police establishments, in particular the *Dépôt de la Préfecture de Police*. The following analysis will concentrate on the 1991 *periodic* and 1994 *ad hoc* visits and the respective reactions of the

---

[1] In Martinique the Committee mainly criticized custodial conditions in the police station and in the prison whereas those in the gendarmerie station were considered satisfactory. Living conditions in the prison were characterized by: extreme overcrowding; an almost complete absence of occupational activity; material conditions in need of repair; bad hygiene; and insufficient medical resources. By contrast, the CPT found there to be little risk of physical ill-treatment for persons detained by the police or the gendarmerie or in the prison (Martinique 1, paras 88–95).

[2] More specifically, four stations of the police and the gendarmerie (one including several sections and branches), a detention section at the *Palais de Justice* in Paris, three prisons (two *maisons d'arrêt* and one *centre pénitentiare*), five medical or psychiatric establishments, and four centres for the administrative detention of foreigners were visited.

[3] Namely, the *Dépôt de la Préfecture de Police de Paris*, Arenc Administrative Detention Centre in Marseille, the prison of Marseilles-Baumettes, the holding facilities of the *Palais de Justice*, and the health services provided in special units at Monfavet Special Hospital Centre, at the Paris Hôtel-Dieu Hospital, and the *Préfecture de Police de Paris*.

[4] Overall, the 1996 visit included the inspection of twelve police or gendarmerie establishments, two administrative detention centres (run by the police), four prisons, and three health establishments. Although final conclusions as to the main issues of interest to the CPT during the second *periodic* visit can be drawn only after the eventual publication of the report, the increase in the number of police and gendarmerie establishments visited clearly indicates increased interest in this area of custody.

French Government.[5] At the time of writing (April 1998) the CPT report resulting from the 1996 *periodic* visit and the French Government response to it remains unpublished.

1. THE 1991 VISIT

(a) The CPT report

The CPT report arising out of the first *periodic* visit to France is lengthy and contains many highly critical observations. The Committee heard a large number of allegations of police brutality, including beatings, forms of psychological pressure, and deprivation of food and medication. Because of the consistency of these allegations the CPT concluded that persons arrested by the police in France ran a 'non-negligible risk of being ill-treated'.[6] The Committee was also critical of the absence of certain safeguards and recommended a strong reinforcement of safeguards for persons apprehended by the police (in particular, the right to inform a third party about the fact of being detained, the right to immediate access to a lawyer and to a doctor of the detainee's choice), the introduction of guide-lines for and electronic recording of police interviews as well as improvements in the training of police officers.[7] Moreover, the Committee found that conditions of detention in some stations run by the police or the gendarmerie left a great deal to be desired, particularly with regard to bad sanitation, overcrowding, and failure to provide food or an adequate quantity of food.[8]

In the course of its inspection of prisons the CPT received few allegations of ill-treatment. However, one case concerning alleged ill-treatment following an attempt to flee was submitted to the French authorities for examination. Severe criticism was expressed regarding particular practices, such as attaching pregnant female prisoners to their beds in a civil hospital prior to delivery and providing no occupation for prisoners held for twenty-three hours a day in overcrowded cells (the remand prison in Nice), which were designated as 'inhuman treatment'.[9] More generally, the detention conditions in both remand prisons visited were considered to be anything but satisfactory. The CPT recommended measures to reduce the overcrowding, improve the hygiene, increase the occupational activities available to prisoners, and provide access to phone calls.[10] The Committee also recommended that the number of medical personnel be increased in order that the level of medical and psychological care in general be

---

[5] For a discussion of CPT reports on France compared with the CAT and the HRC see Bank, R (1997) 'International Efforts to Combat Torture and Inhuman Treatment: Have the New Mechanisms Improved Protection?', 8 *EJIL* 570, 587–589.

[6] France 1, para 11.   [7] Ibid, paras 12, 40, 42, 44, 48–49.

[8] Ibid, paras 30–35.   [9] Ibid, paras 90, 97.   [10] Ibid, paras 103, 114, 108, 135.

raised and the presence of qualified personnel at night and weekends be guaranteed.[11]

Conditions for the administrative detention of foreigners were acceptable in most of the institutions visited, with the notable exception of the *Dépôt de la Préfecture de Police*. Here, the situation was marked by substandard hygiene and the absence of facilities for detainee occupation and open-air exercise, leading to severe criticism and respective recommendations of the CPT.[12]

The CPT was particularly concerned about the situation in the department for difficult patients at the hospital in Montfavet. The Committee noted the danger of inhuman treatment due to the absence of a therapeutic programme and safeguards with regard to the application of physical restraints and the imposition of solitary confinement. They recommended that: the number of qualified personnel be increased; individualized treatment programmes be put in place; therapeutic facilities be provided; the use of long-term isolation be ended; rules be introduced regarding the use of restraints and isolation; and a complaints system instituted.[13]

(b) Government reactions

In their written response the French Government discussed most of the CPT's report. Only nine (out of 60) recommendations, six (out of 36) comments, and no requests for information (out of 38) were left unanswered. Frequently, however, several individual recommendations were responded to in one complex answer, thereby making it difficult to ascertain the reaction to a specific CPT recommendation.

The Government claimed to have reacted with specific measures to nine CPT recommendations and ten comments. Some of these measures comprised material improvements in custodial conditions arising out of renovation programmes. Others aimed at enhancing prisoner regimes by hiring additional personnel,[14] appealing to personnel sensitivity with regard to the confinement of psychiatric patients, improving the quality and distribution of food, and better protecting prisoner privacy during body searches.[15] Particularly forthright was the reaction of the French Government to the CPT's criticism of the practice of attaching female prisoners to their beds before giving birth in a civil hospital. A special room was to be built for these prisoners and the use of restraints abolished. Moreover, a commission was established with a mandate to eliminate similar practices in other hospitals.[16] Finally, one *immediate observation* from the CPT led to the prompt

---

[11] Ibid, paras 171 ff, 182.   [12] Ibid, para 214.   [13] Ibid, paras 196, 203.
[14] France 1 R 1, para 439.
[15] Ibid, paras 531, 434 ff, 456, 86 respectively. It is noteworthy that the follow-up report is silent regarding these undertakings.
[16] Ibid, para 251 and France 1 R 2, paras 132–146.

removal of certain police cells. Some of the positive answers given by the Government failed to specify what measures had been or were to be taken, however.

Positive measures of a more structural nature included the introduction of some safeguards governing disciplinary procedures,[17] the granting of a right to prisoners to address informal complaints to the President of the CPT, and the granting to prisoners of access to a doctor and of telephones to detainees in a detention centre for foreigners in Paris.[18] Moreover, the French Government claimed already to have initiated many measures independently of the CPT report. Thirty recommendations and eleven comments met with such a response, suggesting that ongoing renovation programmes were adequately addressing many of the material deficiencies criticized by the CPT.[19]

By contrast, the Government proved reluctant to improve the safeguards for persons apprehended by the police. None of the Committee's eleven recommendations regarding this area of policy met with a permanently positive response. The Government initially proposed positive amendments of the *Code de Procédure Pénale* introducing rights: to examination by a doctor of the detainee's choice from a list to be drawn up by the public prosecutor (while, however, limiting this possibility to cases in which neither the public prosecutor nor a police officer has called a doctor);[20] immediate access to a lawyer; and the issue of a brochure setting out detainees' rights. However, these positive responses were largely withdrawn within six months of being inserted in the *Code de Procédure Pénale*. The right to an examination by a doctor of the detainee's choice was abolished, allegedly because of practical problems in drawing up a list of doctors from which the detainee could choose.[21] The right of access to a lawyer was subjected to a delay period of twenty hours (thirty-six hours in 'organized crime' cases) from the time of apprehension.[22] And the suggestions that the police introduce electronic recording of police interviews[23] and individualized custody records[24] were categorically rejected.

Also rejected were the CPT recommendations that there be introduced the possibility to make telephone calls in remand prisons[25] and the provision of first aid around the clock in prisons by guaranteeing the presence of appropriately qualified personnel.[26] The rejections were founded on the

---

[17] The duration of a possible prolongation of detention in connection with disciplinary sentences was regulated (France 1 R 1, para 342).

[18] Ibid, paras 161, 187.   [19] Ibid, paras 31–36, 187 ff, 265 ff, 268–306.

[20] Ibid, paras 124 ff. This condition ran contrary to the preventive aim behind the CPT recommendation. In any critical case this possibility might be excluded by previous action on the part of the authorities.

[21] Ibid, paras 94 ff. However, this argument does not sound convincing given the short time the provision was in force.

[22] Ibid, paras 97 ff, 103.   [23] Ibid, para 133.   [24] Ibid, para 139.

[25] Ibid, para 314.   [26] Ibid, para 454.

presumed sufficiency of the existing provisions (safeguards for police custody), security considerations (electronic recording, telephone opportunities for remand prisoners), excessive costs (electronic recording), and lack of qualified personnel (presence of first-aid personnel in prisons). Without explicitly rejecting a recommendation, the French Government also emphasized the financial limitations on improvements with regard to administrative detention of foreigners.

Four of the CPT's comments were openly rejected by the French Government. In particular, they refused to improve the opportunities to receive visits for detainees undergoing in-patient treatment in a civil hospital by hinting at architectural limitations. The Government also rejected the CPT's suggestion that security and medical personnel in the same hospital be differentiated by wearing distinctive clothing because the doctors responsible for the hospital forbade the wearing of uniforms.[27] In addition, it was said that improved areas for open-air exercise in the Marseille remand prison could not be provided because of security considerations.[28] Finally, contrary to the CPT's opinion, the number of medical personnel in the Nice remand prison was considered sufficient.[29]

The CPT's requests for information were in most cases (30 out of 38 questions overall) answered comprehensively. However, eight of the CPT's questions were only partly answered. Some of the incomplete answers were explained by ongoing investigations into the matter concerned, but others involved a failure to discuss the practical dimension of the CPT's requests. For example, the CPT's question regarding the practical implementation of the judicial authorities' mandate to control police detention was answered by merely claiming that the judiciary is *'la gardienne des libertés individuelles'* without providing any explanation as to how this is achieved practically.[30]

2. THE 1994 FOLLOW-UP VISIT

(a) The CPT report

Any positive impression gained from the French Government's response to the CPT's first visit was cast into doubt by the publication of the CPT

---

[27] Ibid, paras 169 ff. This seems a weak excuse since the appearance of medical and security personnel might be differentiated by means other than security personnel wearing uniforms.

[28] However, it remains unclear why the rejection of the CPT's criticism (lack of space and of horizontal view despite the placement on the 5th floor terrace) may be justified by a former attempt to flee with the help of a helicopter. It is not evident why the possibility of a horizontal view in one way or another would encourage or support comparable attempts (see France 1, para 109 and France 1 R 1, para 316).

[29] Ibid, para 443.   [30] France 1, para 54 and France 1 R 1, paras 148–157.

report on its visit to Paris in 1994. This *ad hoc* visit was designed to review the measures taken by the French authorities in response to the severe criticism the Committee expressed during its first visit with regard to conditions for arrested persons and, in particular, foreigners in administrative detention at the Paris *Dépôt de la Préfecture de Police*. As a result of its follow-up inquiries, the delegation concluded that some small improvements had been made, but that substantial changes had not yet been realized.[31] Moreover, the delegation noted the absence of several measures that had been promised.[32]

Given that the 1994 visit concentrated on police custodial detention conditions it was not possible on this occasion for the Committee to undertake an in-depth evaluation regarding the risk of physical ill-treatment at the hands of the police. Yet, in spite of having received a certain number of allegations, the Committee indicated in its report a slight improvement in the situation compared to that found during the 1991 *periodic* visit.[33]

Some improvement in the custodial conditions for juveniles was noted and the Committee observed slight improvements regarding hygienic conditions for arrested adult males. But many of the problems observed in 1991, particularly regarding overcrowding, continued. The French Government had claimed a more 'harmonic' (rationalized) use of cell capacity in its response to the first CPT report,[34] but obviously without any tangible results.

The detention centre for foreigners at the Paris *Dépôt* was the subject of particularly harsh criticisms by the CPT in 1991. In its response the French Government had hinted at planned renovation and modernization work as part of a country-wide programme approved as early as 1985. Yet the Government appears to have been reluctant to give any priority to compliance with the CPT's recommendations and comments. Hardly any progress had been achieved at the time of the *ad hoc* visit. In particular, there was no improvement in the occupational activities offered and conditions affecting the health of detainees, such as the provision of natural light in the cells.

---

[31] France 2, paras 9, 16 ff.

[32] See France 1 R 1, paras 28–36, 71–74, and 187.

[33] France 2, para 36. This caveat—the absence of an in-depth investigation—seems unhelpful: it leaves open the possible interpretation that the situation may not have improved. It also waters down the strength of the CPT's recommendations by qualifying the level of risk of ill-treatment prevailing. It provides a justification for both inaction (since the situation is already improving there is no need to intensify efforts) and action (there are still problems which have to be tackled). If the Committee admits that it has not been able fully to evaluate a situation, then any evaluation that is none the less offered is less than convincing. The Committee usually analyses the consistency of complaints received alongside a review of the legal safeguards that are in place and their practical functioning, thereby giving a comprehensive picture of the situation. But in the case of this *ad hoc* visit all discussion of legal safeguards was postponed to the time of the CPT's response to the interim and follow-up reports of the French Government (ibid, para 37).

[34] France 1, para 68 and France 2, para 9.

Even a newly built section contained very dark and partly dirty cells. Moreover, the follow-up visit revealed that the promise given by the French Government to guarantee foreign detainees access to medical examinations had not been fulfilled.[35]

Visits in 1994 to other police establishments also provoked the Committee's criticism: cells were too small, hygienic conditions insufficient, and fresh sheets sometimes not distributed. Once again, assurances given by the French Government in response to the first CPT report had not been implemented: a significant number of the detainees interviewed by the CPT delegation had not been provided with food by the police since their arrest up to twenty-four hours previously.[36]

(b) Government reactions

In several respects the French Government reacted positively to the CPT's 1994 findings and recommendations. For example, in response to an *immediate* observation from the CPT delegation the authorities took out of service a cell lacking ventilation. With regard to the Paris *Dépôt* for foreigners the Government again referred to the renovation programme planned for the whole country, but on this occasion announced the closure of the institution in May 1995 in order that the renovation measures be carried out. Assurances were given that the CPT's recommendations regarding the detention unit for arrested men would be reflected in the work to be undertaken. Furthermore, several of the Government's answers—regarding the provision of natural and artificial light in cells, improved orderliness, the distribution of clean mattresses and covers for overnight detainees, and the application of insecticides against mosquitoes —point to measures already carried out with respect to problems identified by the CPT, but it is not clear whether these measures were taken in response to the CPT or were taken anyway.

These answers apart, the overall impression given by the Government's response is one of evasion and obfuscation. The CPT recommendations and comments are not answered point by point. Rather, the renovation measures envisaged are described in general terms often without specifically referring to CPT criticisms or showing how particular identified deficiencies would be overcome. Out of 22 recommendations[37] six remained entirely

---

[35] France 1 R 1, para 187 and France 2, paras 23–26. For further analysis of the present situation in France see Ganoux (1996) 'Prévention des mauvais traitements: Rapport sur les conditions de détention et le traitement des personnes privées de liberté en France', *Les Cahiers de l'Institut des droits de l'homme*, Cahiers No 2, Université Catholique de Lyon, 33–193.

[36] France 2, para 34.

[37] Splitting up the nominally nine recommendations into the different shortcomings to which they refer gives 22 recommendations overall.

unanswered[38] and three more were not squarely addressed.[39] In particular, the French Government reacted to the CPT's request that there be a re-examination of the question of distribution of food to detainees by describing existing instructions which, according to the CPT's findings, were patently not working.[40] This response was particularly surprising because the French Government had undertaken to make changes in their response, outlined above, to the 1991 CPT report. The apparent ignorance of the French authorities with regard to earlier exchanges with the CPT on this question can only be interpreted as an indication of the Government's lack of commitment to abide by undertakings previously given.

Similarly, the CPT's only comment was not taken up in the Government's response. Despite the serious nature of the problems addressed, requests for information on complaints, about lack of access to a doctor, interruptions of medical treatment for illnesses as severe as AIDS or tuberculosis, and gaps in the provision of certain medicines, were responded to with only very brief comments. The Government claimed that everything was satisfactory, apparently without having carried out any investigations regarding the questions raised.[41]

Given the persistence of the problems addressed in the first CPT report, and the reluctance exhibited in the French Government's response to act expeditiously to improve the situation, it is not surprising that the *Dépôt* received a follow-up visit during the course of the second *periodic* visit to France in 1996.

3. FINAL OBSERVATIONS

The CPT produced a detailed and critical report on its first *periodic* visit, to which the French Government responded in a relatively open manner. A high proportion of the CPT's recommendations and comments met with an apparently positive response on the part of the French authorities, reporting on, or at least promising, several improvements. Most of these changes related to simple aspects of material conditions in single establishments, however. There were by contrast few positive reactions to requests for structural changes, a not atypical government response to CPT

---

[38] France 2, paras 21 (with reference to the deficiencies criticized in paras 16–19 concerning open-air exercise and the lack of occupational activities in the *Dépôt*, open-air exercise, lack of natural and artificial light as well as of occupational activities in Vincenne) and 33 (relating to the provision of mattresses and covers to drunk persons detained).

[39] For example, the French authorities reported on rules for the construction of police cells as an answer to the CPT's recommendation that they adopt CPT standards (cf France 2, para 33 and France 2 R 1, 26).

[40] France 2, para 34 and France 2 R 1, 27.

[41] France 2, para 23 and France 2 R 1, 26.

recommendations.[42] Thus the concrete impact of the first CPT visit is to be found in specific improvements in the everyday quality of life of detainees in certain institutions or the abolition of particular practices rather than in modifications to general legal or administrative framework provisions. Moreover, the fact that the French Government did not make clear, in its published response to the CPT 1994 *ad hoc* visit report, to what extent the measures taken had been instigated by the report makes it difficult to estimate how much impact the visit made. The French authorities mainly refer to programmes which had already been scheduled or initiated, thereby suggesting that the CPT intervention played rather a small role in policy development.

Some observations regarding the French Government's responses are particularly perturbing. Following the first CPT visit the position regarding legal safeguards guaranteed to persons apprehended by the police were to be amended in a manner almost fully complying with core CPT recommendations. In contrast to the passivity or resistance which frequently characterize government responses to CPT recommendations of a structural nature the French response initially *appeared* unusually positive. But these propositions were later almost entirely reversed. Secondly, the CPT *ad hoc* visit of 1994 demonstrated that a government's verbal commitment to improve a situation according to CPT recommendations and comments may turn out to be only lip-service. Moreover, this impression was confirmed by the Government's subsequent reaction to the *ad hoc* visit report which clearly did not lead to any additional action regarding, for instance, deficiencies in food distribution. Finally, from an analysis of the Government's response to the *ad hoc* visit report one cannot avoid the conclusion that the Government was not impressed by seeing France subjected to such a visit despite the fact that an *ad hoc* mission expressly indicates the particular concern of the Committee about a certain situation.

REFERENCES

Bank, R (1997) 'International Efforts to Combat Torture and Inhuman Treatment: Have the New Mechanisms Improved Protection?', 8 *EJIL* 570
Evans, MD and Morgan, R (1998) *Preventing Torture* (Oxford: Clarendon Press)
Ganoux (1996) 'Prévention des mauvais traitements: Rapport sur les conditions de détention et le traitement des personnes privées de liberté en France', *Les Cahiers de l'Institut des droits de l'homme*, Cahiers No 2, Université Catholique de Lyon, 33–193

---

[42] See, for example, Bank (1997) and Evans and Morgan (1998), Chapter 9.

9

A Critical Review of the CPT's Visit to Hungary

AGNES KOVER

1. INTRODUCTION

Hungary joined the Council of Europe in November 1990. It ratified the ECHR in November 1992 and the ECPT in November 1993. In accordance with Article 19(2) of the ECPT, that Convention entered into force for Hungary on 1 March 1994 and the CPT undertook its first periodic visit from 1–14 November 1994. The visit report was adopted in mid-June 1995 and transmitted to the Hungarian authorities early in July 1995. The report was published, along with a series of 'Comments' on the report, on 1 February 1996, that is, some fifteen months after the visit.[1] The undated 'Interim Response' was published on 18 April 1996.[2] No further material has yet been made available.

The visit had a considerable impact on the democratic transformation and humanization of the Hungarian criminal justice system, particularly as regards pre-trial detention, imprisonment, and other forms of deprivation of liberty. The purpose of this chapter is critically to review the CPT's report and to offer an assessment of the impact of the report. It also offers some reflections upon the methodology and standards applied by the CPT which seem appropriate in light of the Hungarian experience. It is not the intention to summarize the report, but reference will be made to salient findings as and where necessary. Rather than present a number of general observations relating to the report as a whole, this chapter will focus on aspects of the visit and recommendations concerning policing matters which fall within the responsibility of the Ministry of the Interior and which, generally speaking, pose the greatest problems.[3] It goes without saying that much of the CPT report is of considerable value. Nevertheless, there are

---

[1] Hungary 1.   [2] Hungary 1 R 1.

[3] This is not to minimize the criticism made in other parts of the report. See, for example, the highly critical comments concerning the Kerepestarcsa Community Hostel (an institution under the authority of the Ministry of the Interior) which prompted the CPT to make 'immediate observations' under Article 8(5) of the Convention and which the Hungarian authorities ultimately closed (see Hungary 1, paras 10, 12, and 57–86 and Hungarian Comments, ibid, p 83; Hungary 1 R 1, 50).

weaknesses, the chief of which will be highlighted in the following sections,[4] in which a number of points will be made arising from Section IIA of the CPT's report, concerning establishments under the authority of the Ministry of the Interior. These embrace the general legal framework governing detention, findings of physical ill-treatment, physical conditions of detention, and safeguards against ill-treatment. A preliminary point concerns the choice of places visited.

2. THE CHOICE OF PLACES VISITED

With the exception of the Tokol Prison and Remand Centre for Adolescents and the Kerepestarcsa Community Shelter for immigrants (which is only just outside the Budapest district) the Committee restricted itself to visiting police cells and prisons in Budapest itself. An investigation limited to institutions in Budapest and its environs cannot provide a comprehensive picture since Hungary tends towards over-centralization and there are significant social and economic differences between its various regions: Budapest, as the capital, has priority when funds are distributed among institutions. The conditions of detainees held in the capital are often more favourable than elsewhere. The regions have fewer opportunities to represent themselves and press for their needs and interests to be recognized than does the capital. This has several consequences relevant for current purposes.

In order to present an accurate picture of the situation nationally, the CPT would need to investigate several regions of the country, including both the wealthier counties in the west of the country and the poorer ones in the east and in the south. Recommendations generated by an inspection of Budapest alone may not be as appropriate as those which might have been generated had the CPT been exposed to the situation in the country as a whole.

3. FORMS OF DETENTION[5]

It seems, unfortunately, that the Committee was insufficiently conversant with the Hungarian regulations concerning the various forms of detention which are recognized by law. Although the report mentions the two main

[4] Again, this is not to suggest that there are no weaknesses in parts of the report dealing with establishments under the authority of the Ministry of Justice. For example, it is surprising that the section of the report dealing with suicide and self-mutilation in prisons (Hungary 1, paras 117–120) fails to mention and respond to the Hungarian practice of imposing disciplinary sanctions on those who attempt suicide.

[5] See Hungary 1, para 14.

legal sources of regulations,[6] it does not pay sufficient attention to the complex manner in which arrest and detention is regulated and executed in practice. For example, the CPT cites section 33 (3) of the Police Act, but this is only one of several passages concerning the temporary deprivations of freedom without court supervision. The section cited concerns public security detention (PSD) and provides that:

Police officers may apprehend persons for the purpose of bringing them before the competent authority . . .[7]

However, the Committee failed to note section 33 (2) of the Act, which states that:

any ordinary citizen can be presented before the police authorities in the interest of public security in the following cases: if a person cannot identify him or herself, or refuses to show his/her identity papers; if a person is suspected of having committed a crime; if a person is obliged to subject him/herself to a blood or urine test to determine the level of alcohol in his blood; and if a person continues to commit an offence in violation of the Misdemeanour Code in spite of prior warning.[8]

The length of PSD is eight hours and can be extended for an additional four hours. The extension process is not controlled either legally or administratively, so the maximum length of PSD is in fact twelve hours. There is also a second type of PSD which can last for up to twenty-four hours.[9]

Persons held in PSD are placed in separate cells which are located in a different part of the police building from that in which pre-trial detainees are held. No PSD cells were visited by the CPT, even though they are inside the same police stations where pre-trial detainees are kept. Moreover, there are a significant number of police stations where only PSD cells can be found. The physical conditions of these PSD cells are generally much worse than the police cells where pre-trial detainees are held, and which were visited and considered unsatisfactory.[10] It is likely, therefore, that they would fall well within the definition of what the CPT considers to be 'inhuman and degrading treatment'. It is estimated that several hundred thousand individuals are held annually in these places and, according to police registries, approximately 15–20 persons are held daily in an average district police station in Budapest.

During the period of PSD, several of what the CPT normally considers

---

[6] These being Act 34 of 1994 on the Police and the Act I of 1973 on Criminal Procedure. See also Hungary 1, para 14.

[7] Police Act, section 33(3).   [8] Police Act, section 33(2).

[9] Police Act, section 38(1).

[10] See, for example, Hungary 1, paras 30–33, where conditions were variously described as 'extremely poor' and 'not acceptable for even short-term custody' (8th District police station); 'a cause for concern' (Pest County holding facility); 'far from satisfactory' (police central holding facility, Budapest).

to be basic rights of detained persons are routinely violated. For example, given the relative brevity of such forms of detention, the police do not allow notification of a close relative or third party, in spite of the fact that this is provided for in the Police Act.[11] Moreover, a person held in PSD is not even automatically informed of the reasons for his arrest or of any charge against him. This practice is in accord with the Police Act, which provides that detained persons must be told the reason why they have been detained only if they ask.[12]

The failure of the CPT to recognize the significance of PSD is exacerbated by the unfortunate fact that the supervisory role of the Public Prosecutors does not extend to issues connected with PSD. The CPT needs to examine the regulations with greater thoroughness because the 'devil is in the detail' and during these short periods of custody—to which many citizens are subject, including many who are not suspected of criminal offences—there is a heightened risk of abuse.

4. PROCEDURAL SAFEGUARDS AND POLICE CUSTODY

(a) The time when rights come into force

The problems associated with PSD and administrative detention have already been noted. The principal form of detention is that provided for under section 91 of the Criminal Procedure Act. Such detention can last for up to seventy-two hours and according to the latest regulation (which was introduced after the Committee's visit) cannot be extended without judicial review. Nevertheless, the detained person's basic rights (to notify family or a third party, to have access to a lawyer, to be apprised of his rights, and to be notified of the reason for arrest) do not yet apply since, as with PSD and administrative detention, this form of temporary detention is not classified as a form of criminal detention. Hence, in Hungary, it is legally possible for there to be no judicial control over the first seventy-two hours of detention. The situation is even worse in the case of immigrants, who can spend five days in detention without judicial control.[13] Detention under these circumstances, without the protection of basic legal safeguards, results in such a high level of unnecessary uncertainty that it arguably amounts to 'inhuman and degrading treatment'. The Committee might consider applying the notion of 'inhuman and degrading treatment' to at least the failure

[11] See Police Act, section 18(1).
[12] Police Act, section 33(4). Neither this provision nor this practice accords with ECHR Article 5(2), which states that any person taken into custody must be 'informed promptly, in a language which he understands, of the reasons for his arrest and of any charge against him'.
[13] Act 86 of 1993 on the Entry, Stay in Hungary and Immigration of Foreigners.

to inform detainees promptly of the reasons for their arrest and detention.[14]

(b) Access to legal counsel

Allowing lawyers to visit detainees promptly and on a regular basis acts as a significant external safeguard against the risk of ill-treatment. It enables detainees to give their lawyers information about the facts of their cases and the circumstances of their detention and treatment. The lawyer could then, if necessary, take up these issues with the authorities. In Hungary, however, such possibilities exist largely in theory. In cases where detainees do not have the financial resources to employ a lawyer of their choice (which is fairly common in the socio-economic groups from which most detainees come) and where an official lawyer is appointed for their defence the chance of some form of control over the conditions of their detention is lost, as is their right to legal protection.

In accordance with the Hungarian Constitution, every person charged with a crime is entitled to legal representation. According to international standards, access to counsel must be provided soon after detention in order that that right be effective.[15] Under the European Convention on Human Rights, the European Commission has held that it is not enough for the state to appoint defence counsel for indigent defendants: the state must also provide *effective* counsel. The state is obliged to ensure that counsel fulfil their duties adequately, or replace them.[16] Against this background, it is disappointing that the CPT failed to probe this issue more deeply, for the report does not reflect the reality of the right of access to legal counsel in Hungary.

The CPT consistently maintains that the right to legal assistance must be available *from the outset* of detention and the Committee noted the need to clarify the precise moment at which the right of access to a lawyer becomes effective in Hungary.[17] Unfortunately, and as indicated in the previous subsection, the legal position is not sufficiently clear in this respect, a point which the CPT might have been expected to have identified in advance of, or in the course of, their visit.

This is of secondary importance, however, to the failure of the CPT to grasp the reality of the situation concerning the right to legal defence or access to legal counsel in Hungary even where it does, in theory, exist. Although the law formally secures pre-trial detainees the right to a lawyer

---

[14] ECHR, Article 5(2).   [15] See the ICCPR, Articles 15 (3) (b) and (d).

[16] See App No 9127/80, Comm Dec 6 October 1981 (unpublished). See *Strasbourg Digest of Case Law*, Vol 2, 846 and UN (1994) *Human Rights and Pre-trial Detention* (Geneva: United Nations), 22.

[17] Hungary 1, para 45.

appointed by the state, 80–90 per cent of such defendants do not enjoy representation. There are of course many reasons for this, including: the extremely low fees for appointed counsel (currently 2,000 forints per case, equivalent to $13); long delays in payment; the substantial expense an attorney must incur to obtain copies of official documents; and the fact that many essential costs incurred in the defence of a client—including travel to and from penitentiaries and police stations where pre-trial detainees are held—are not covered at all. As a result, it is virtually impossible for many lawyers to visit pre-trial detention centres and police cells to speak with their clients. These issues are particularly important in Eastern Europe (if not elsewhere), where one of the typical double binds is to legislate rights issues on the highest level, while disregarding implementation costs.

This renders the right of legal defence all but meaningless in a large number of cases. The lawyer typically has no contact with his client in the course of the pre-trial investigation, or even later. The first personal meeting between lawyer and detainee often takes place in court at trial, without the lawyer having spoken to, or even seen, the defendant beforehand. According to data from the Hungarian Supreme Court, only nine out of 139 detainees surveyed in one county had been visited before trial by their appointed lawyers. Surveys carried out since have shown this to be a widespread problem. During the police cell monitoring project (conducted in 1996 by the Constitutional and Legislative Policy Institute (COLPI) and the Hungarian Helsinki Committee), of 483 detainees asked, only 71 reported that they had met with their appointed lawyer before trial.[18] This is a very different picture from that painted in the CPT report, a picture which bears little relationship to reality.[19]

5. FINDINGS OF ILL-TREATMENT

In its report the CPT chronicles a sorry picture of physical ill-treatment in police custody, and concludes that 'persons deprived of their liberty by the police in Budapest run a not inconsiderable risk of ill-treatment'.[20] The

---

[18] COLPI/Hungarian Helsinki Committee (1998) *Punished Before Sentence: Detention and Police Cells in Hungary 1996* (Budapest: COLPI/Hungarian Helsinki Committee), 90–94.

[19] See, for example, Hungary 1, para 44: 'it appears that these provisions [concerning the appointment of counsel] were respected in practice'. It goes on to say that those who needed to do so were 'permitted to select a duty lawyer from a list held by the police' (ibid) but nothing is said about access to that lawyer.

[20] Hungary 1, para 22. In their Comments, published alongside the Report, the Ministry of Interior accepted that 'the Committee may have got hold of information indicating that some detainees suffered bodily harm during police procedures' , but it took the view that 'the Committee's information . . . is not sufficient to make a legally substantiated claim that persons taken into custody by Budapest police are (in general) in danger of physical ill-treatment' (Hungary 1 R 1, 84).

Committee received 'numerous' allegations of physical ill-treatment, both at the time of arrest and during interrogation. The allegations, it seems, were made by detainees interviewed in both police stations and the Budapest Remand Prison and the Tokol Prison and Remand Centre for Adolescents.[21] The allegations were 'remarkably consistent':

In most cases, the persons concerned alleged that, after their hands had been handcuffed behind them (or their ankles attached to an item of furniture), they had been struck with truncheons, punched, slapped or kicked by police officers.[22]

There was considerable supporting medical evidence[23] and the 'sheer number of allegations of ill-treatment by the police and their consistency as regards the precise form of ill-treatment involved are striking'.[24]

Given the wealth of evidence of purposive ill-treatment, why did the CPT reach so mild a conclusion? The finding that persons deprived of their liberty by the police in Budapest 'run a not inconsiderable risk of ill-treatment' might instead have referred to the risk of 'severe ill-treatment/torture', the terminology employed with respect to Bulgaria, where the principal difference seems to be that *falaka* was found.[25] The failure of the Committee to employ the more critical and appropriate terminology is both surprising and disappointing.

6. INVESTIGATIONS OF COMPLAINTS OF ILL-TREATMENT

In the light of its findings the CPT observed that:

Naturally, one of the most effective means of preventing ill-treatment by police officers lies in the diligent examination of complaints of such treatment and, where appropriate, the imposition of suitable disciplinary and penal sanctions.[26]

The Committee requested statistical data concerning the number of complaints lodged relating to alleged incidents of ill-treatment by the police, the number of disciplinary and/or criminal proceedings initiated as a result of those complaints, and an account of the disciplinary/criminal sanctions imposed. This information was subsequently submitted in the Hungarian Government's Interim Response. It indicated that in 1993 there

---

[21] Hungary, 1 para 17. The Report refers to '*the* various police establishments visited' (emphasis added).

[22] Ibid.   [23] Ibid, paras 18–21.   [24] Ibid, para 22.

[25] Ibid, para 27. But cf an alleged incident of dogs being set on a handcuffed detainee in Bratislava which also fell short of the 'severe ill-treatment/torture' threshold. Slovakia 1, paras 16(v) and 18.

[26] Hungary 1, para 26.

were 142 indictments and 22 court decisions, with 58 indictments and 28 court decisions in 1994.[27]

The CPT will be able to judge the seriousness of prosecutors' readiness to investigate and prosecute cases where police ill-treatment is alleged if the Committee compares the figures on the prosecution of the police with those in ordinary cases. The termination of investigations for typical police crimes (ill-treatment during official procedure, forced interrogation, and unlawful detention) is usually above 80 per cent. In 1994, 38.3 per cent of all crime investigations were terminated because the perpetrator could not be identified; in 2 per cent because it could not be proved that the suspect was the person who had committed the crime; and in 6.5 per cent because the act could not be identified as a crime. By contrast, of 952 investigations commenced against police officers for brutality or other abusive behaviour, in 683 cases (or 71.1 per cent) the investigation was terminated on the grounds that the form of police behaviour in question was not a crime. Only 19.7 per cent of the petitions filed against police officers resulted in a prosecution, compared with more than 40 per cent in all other criminal cases.

7. PHYSICAL CONDITIONS OF POLICE CELLS

The CPT found much of the police cellular accommodation which it inspected to be unsatisfactory in nature or condition. At the conclusion of its visit the delegation made an 'immediate observation' under Article 8(5). It was requested that the cells in the Budapest 8th District Police Station be taken out of use forthwith. The request was complied with.[28] A comparison of the CPT's report with those prepared by the Penal Supervision Department of the Chief Public Prosecutor's Office a few years earlier (based on investigations conducted in 1991–1992) shows that considerable progress has been made. The Penal Supervision Department has been in charge of the legal supervision of police cells since 1990, and its inspections have resulted in continuous improvement of both the conditions of cells in particular and of detention in general. Following their first reports, 35 per cent of the cells inspected were deemed unfit for human habitation and closed. A further 25 per cent, though not closed, are not used. This puts the comparatively restrained nature of the CPT's response to the conditions it encountered in perspective: until very recently conditions had been very bad and much progress had already been made.

[27] Hungary 1 R 1, 40–42. The 1993 decisions resulted in two suspended sentences of imprisonment, eight persons fined, two persons reprimanded, four persons placed on probation, and six persons acquitted. In 1994 two suspended sentences of imprisonment were imposed, fourteen persons fined, three persons placed on probation, one person reprimanded, and eight persons acquitted.

[28] Ibid, paras 11–12.

8. THE PLACE AND THE LENGTH OF PRE-TRIAL DETENTION
DURING THE POLICE INVESTIGATION

In contrast to general European practice, the initial phase of pre-trial detention in Hungary, which covers the police investigation, is implemented in police cells and is of unlimited duration. The CPT found 'it was common for persons to be held on remand in police establishments for several months'.[29] This practice is provided for in an exception to the principal rule in the Implementation of Punishments Act, according to which pre-trial detention has to be implemented in a remand prison.[30]

The extent of the practice is apparent from published statistics. In 1994, out of a total of 8,442 pre-trial detainees, 4,398 (52 per cent) were kept in police cells. In 1996, although the number of detainees had fallen, the proportion kept in police cells remained the same: 3,500 out of a total of 6,704. The average duration of detention in police cells is 3–6 months. Approximately 10 per cent of detainees spend 8–12 months in police cells that were designed for much shorter stays.

One of the most significant effects of the CPT's visit has been the acceleration of the preparation of a new law of criminal procedure. It was originally proposed that after the first 72 hours of custody, further periods of pre-trial detention would be in remand prisons. However, the law passed in March 1998 permits pre-trial detainees to be held in police cells for a period of 30 days, and this period can be extended to 60 days in exceptional cases.[31] The CPT's aspirations are clearly not going to be met.[32] Furthermore, there is still no limit to the overall length of pre-trial detention, merely upon the period which can be in police custody.

The CPT is rightly critical of long periods of pre-trial detention. But might not the notion 'inhuman and degrading treatment' reasonably be applied to unreasonably long periods of pre-trial detention?[33]

---

[29] Ibid, para 15.

[30] Act 11 of 1979, section 116(1), as amended by Act 32 of 1993, the exception being provided for in section 116(3).

[31] Draft Law of Criminal Procedure, section 135(2).

[32] See also the views of the Ministry of the Interior to the effect that current practice accords with the law and that major change is unlikely. See Hungary 1, para 85 and Hungary 1 R 1, 44–45.

[33] According to ICCPR Article 9(3), the right to trial within a reasonable time is guaranteed and in reviewing the national legislation of one country, the Committee has implied that a six-month limit on pre-trial detention was incompatible with this obligation (GAOR, A/45/40, vol I, para 47 (Democratic Yemen)). Similarly, when considering the right 'to trial within a reasonable time or to release pending trial' under ECHR Article 5(3) the Court has held that the reasonableness of the length of detention is assessed independently of the reasonableness of the delay before trial, and even if the length of time before trial may be 'reasonable' under Article 6(1) of the Convention, detention before trial for similar periods may not be. See *Neumeister v Austria*, Judgment of 27 June 1968, Ser A No 8, para 4 and *Matznetter v Austria*, Judgment of 10 November 1969, Ser A No 10, para 12.

9. EXTERNAL SUPERVISION

Making conditions of detention subject to inspection, or rather observation, by external organizations is another way of establishing a sense of constant supervision. The CPT report presses the case for this, noting the establishment of the Parliamentary Ombudsman and recommending that 'public prosecutors be encouraged to accord a high priority to on-the-spot supervision of places of detention'.[34] The efficacy of the supervisory role of public prosecutors is open to doubt and experience within the Hungarian Helsinki Committee/COLPI Police Cells Monitoring Project (established in co-operation with the Ministry of the Interior) suggests that this function can appropriately be carried out by NGOs and human rights groups. In the light of this experience, one wonders why the Committee failed to encourage the Hungarian Government to adopt the system of lay visitors to police stations, as outlined in the CPT's second general report.[35]

Local government bodies could also be expected to exercise supervisory powers, as they do in some Western European countries. Both the UN Standard Minimum Rules and the European Prison Rules address the relationship between the detainee and the outside world and provide an acceptable basis for regular observation of the treatment and living conditions of detainees by independent human rights organizations. Such a system could provide a source of continuous information to international organizations as well as ensuring that the most effective use is made of data within the local political context.

Public opinion and the media play an essential part in the work of national NGOs. NGOs regularly inform the relevant authorities and official bodies of the results of their visits and also inform the local and national press. They pass on information to the community about the conditions inside closed institutions and the current status of the enjoyment of basic human rights. The work of international human rights bodies such as the CPT could be supplemented and made more complete were there greater co-operation with local and national organizations regularly involved in visiting programmes with trained professionals who visit police cells and are able to interpret and assess what they see. If the police authorities seek to present a more favourable impression than is actually the case, in the long run the true picture will emerge.

10. WESTERN STANDARDS V EASTERN CONDITIONS

This final section goes beyond the technical criticisms of the CPT report and offers some reflections on the arguments of so-called 'realists' who

---

[34] Hungary 1, para 55.   [35] See Gen Rep 2, para 41.

claim that the general differences in economic wealth and standards of living mean that a different approach must be taken to the application of 'Western standards' to custodial conditions in Central and Eastern Europe. In short, the claim is sometimes made that the pace of change must take account of the cost of change.

(a) Cost v value considerations

The first question to be considered is whether financial or cost criteria have any relevance to custodial issues. At one extreme, it could be argued that if financial considerations were paramount, the most efficient form of punishment would be the death penalty or, in minor cases, forms of physical punishment: a serious beating or mutilation costs the community less than the maintenance of closed institutions, especially if these institutions are managed according to pan-European standards. Once stated, it is easy to see that financial and efficiency considerations cannot be paramount. Even in times of economic hardship, the principal issues are not related to costs but to values. This means that the quality of the penal system, as well as the nature and extent of rights declared and observed, depends fundamentally on value choices. Only after those choices have been made can one address the question of costs. This does not mean that cost considerations are unimportant. On the contrary, they are crucial to a rational approach to institutions and the evaluation of their efficiency. However, a clear distinction has to be made between value and cost considerations.

Value and cost considerations may strengthen or weaken each other. In some countries, particularly in Eastern Europe, the regulatory framework reflects sets of values which do not inform practice because of a shortage of funds. This undermines the authority of both the values themselves and the legal order which generates them. The irrational and inefficient functioning of institutions undermines our conscious choice of values. It also means that those funds which are devoted to the system are misapplied, in that they fail to uphold the sets of values which they were intended to implement and underpin. Whilst cost-oriented analyses are essential, therefore, their validity is restricted by the boundaries defined by choices of values which need not be cost driven.

In fact a cost-based approach can buttress our choice of values. For example, it might facilitate the consideration of community-based sentences as opposed to custodial sentences: even if it is accepted that community-based systems require greater initial investment than maintaining the use of closed institutions (although even this is a myth), if long-term effects and social costs are taken into account, the financial benefits of community-based services become clear. The question then becomes the relevant time frame for analysis.

(b) The rights–cost matrix

The model presented below attempts to demonstrate the ideal typical (in the Max Weber sense) forms of relationship between rights and costs within closed institutions. Costs are represented on the horizontal axis, and rights on the vertical axis. The matrix illustrates the range of possibilities:

- High levels of rights attainment coupled with low costs. This is obviously the ideal situation, but is likely to be difficult to achieve.
- Low levels of rights attainment coupled with low costs. This situation exists in many parts of the world. For example, in many of the poorer countries in Africa the funds available for closed institutions are very limited and the level of rights attainment is also low.
- High levels of rights attainment coupled with high costs. This might be termed the Scandinavian model, where such a situation is common.
- Low levels of rights attainment coupled with high costs. This might be termed the 'totalitarian model'. Costs may be nearly or as high as in the 'Scandinavian model', but there are few rights for those in custody. Dictatorial and military regimes belong to this category. Direct and indirect personnel costs are very high, closed institutions are used in a high proportion of cases, and the system is very rigid. In many cases, the enjoyment of rights is not functionally targeted and the system follows its own inherent interests rather than functional rights-oriented objectives.

The formerly socialist countries of Central and Eastern Europe were close to the 'totalitarian model'. The reason for this was that their systems of closed institutions (principally prisons) traditionally functioned as a part of the political establishment and centralized state bureaucracy and were merely a symbolic but rather a practical and direct extension of state

```
R    High              *Ideal Model           *Scandinavian Model
I         |
G         |
H         |
T         |                *African Model        *Totalitarian Model
S    Low ----------------------------------------------------------High
                              COSTS
```

power.[36] They were also very costly. What is needed, of course, is a move towards the 'ideal model' which is cost-effective in terms of rights attainment. In order to make this possible, it is necessary to know exactly how much closed institutions really cost, what values should guide cost rationalization, and what working alternatives can be offered.

(c) Does poverty preclude the realization of human rights?

Does the economic situation in Central and Eastern Europe preclude the realization of human rights and the implementation of European standards in closed institutions? First, one has to consider whether different standards of achievement may legitimately be expected when they are set against a background of universal international standards and values. Such differentiation is neither expected nor advocated with regard to other financial, economic, or, increasingly, environmental regulation. It is, then, difficult to see the legitimacy of such claims as regards the enjoyment of basic human rights.

The institutional framework of society necessarily reflects the democratic or anti-democratic nature of that society. In many cases the democratic nature of institutions does not require further financial resources: rather, what is required is a rational and systematic reorganization of the whole institutional system, a rethinking of objectives and measures, the (re)definition of certain fundamental values, and a more rational allocation of funds, all in order to reflect and realize the underlying choice of values. Rather than reject the challenge posed by the acceptance of international standards on the grounds of cost, that challenge should be seen as an opportunity critically to examine the existing institutional system from a cost perspective in order to highlight and eliminate those practices which are both financially wasteful and which stand in the way of the realization of the rights themselves. It is possible to square the circle.

11. CONCLUSION

The promulgation and realization of rights plays an important role in the shaping of the community's expectations, duties, and wishes as well as the efficiency of their activities. The presence of these rights acts beneficially deep under the skin of society, out of sight but with a considerable influence upon society as a whole. Since the political transition, the countries of Central and Eastern Europe have made strenuous efforts to incorporate

---

[36] This was often reflected and reinforced by the guards being a unit of the armed forces.

human rights within their legal systems. In many cases, however, this is limited to the promulgation of rights and political rhetoric. The realization of human rights is more difficult and cannot be done without substantial reforms and moves towards more open, transparent, and receptive institutions.

The CPT's reports have had an enormous impact on the domestic legal regulation and daily practice surrounding the deprivation of liberty and have done much to foster these essential prerequisites for the achievement of a higher level of rights attainment within custodial settings. It is precisely for this reason that it is so important that the Committee's remarks be well argued, based on an accurate picture of the domestic situation, and firmly grounded in legal substance. To the extent that reports fall short of these desiderata, the state may feel itself to be confirmed in any undesirable practices, and, indeed, the Committee's findings can stand in the way of the advancement of the very forms of local reform which it wishes to encourage. It is against this background that this comment has emphasized some of the more pertinent shortcomings in the CPT's first report on Hungary.

REFERENCES

COLPI/Hungarian Helsinki Committee (1998) *Punished Before Sentence: Detention and Police Cells in Hungary 1996* (Budapest: COLPI/Hungarian Helsinki Committee)
UN (1994) *Human Rights and Pre-trial Detention* (Geneva: United Nations)

10

Inspection and Quality Control: The CPT in The Netherlands

PIET VAN REENAN

1. INTRODUCTION

From 30 August to 8 September 1992 a delegation of the CPT visited The Netherlands to undertake a *periodic* visit. The report arising from this visit was published on 15 July 1993 and the Dutch Government's response appeared five months later on 20 December 1993.[1] The CPT has since visited the Dutch overseas territories of the Antilles (twice) and Aruba (once)[2] and a second *periodic* visit to The Netherlands was undertaken in November 1997. The report arising from this second visit was published after this chapter was first drafted[3] and will be referred to only briefly. Since the Dutch Antilles and Aruba visits involve issues somewhat different from those in The Netherlands, what follows will focus on the 1992 visit to The Netherlands.

Although the CPT reports on The Netherlands contain no shocking revelations with respect to the Committee's mandate—torture or inhuman or degrading treatment—aspects of the visits and report are nonetheless of note and worthy of discussion. They may provide us with lessons regarding the operation of the CPT more generally. What follows is principally devoted to aspects of the visits and the CPT appraisal, but I shall attempt to use the example of the Netherlands visit to make wider observations, though it has to be conceded that the empirical basis for these observations is slender.

---

[1] The Dutch Government's response was published initially in Dutch: an English translation was published on 1 September 1994.

[2] *Ad hoc* visits were made to both territories in June/July 1994, and a *follow-up* visit was made to the Netherlands Antilles in December 1997. The reports arising from the 1994 visits were published, together with the Dutch Government's responses, in 1996.

[3] On 10 September 1998.

2. THE CPT IN THE NETHERLANDS

Given that the CPT reports arising out of the first and second *periodic* visits to The Netherlands were for the most part not critical, I will concentrate on the more contentious aspects of the reports.

(a) Access to medical files: a conflict of values

At the Demersluis Prison in Amsterdam in 1992 the medical staff refused the CPT's medical specialists access to the medical files of prisoners. The CPT considered this to be a breach of Article 3 of the Convention, which requires that the national authorities of state parties co-operate with the Committee.[4] The reason for the denial of access is to be found in Dutch privacy legislation. According to Dutch law access to patients' medical files can be obtained only with patients' written consent and the Dutch statute is grounded on the ECHR Article 8. The Demersluis medical staff deemed it their duty to protect the privacy of prisoners' medical dossiers. The CPT neither accepted the denial of access or its reasoning nor did the delegation seek the assistance of the prison administration's medical inspector. The conflict was quickly resolved because the prisoners concerned gave their written consent. But the CPT nevertheless complained that the incident represented a breach of Article 3 and though the CPT's reasoning appears solid so also does that of the Dutch Government.[5] Certainly for the Demersluis medical staff the practical immediacy of the national legislation was more concrete and specific than Article 3 of the ECPT, which is directed primarily at states and governments, and required them to co-operate in general terms. But the incident illustrates the fact that the two European Conventions contain potentially conflicting values and rules. The two obligations cannot simultaneously be fulfilled in the manner in which they were interpreted on this occasion.

This issue was raised by the Dutch and other CPT liaison officers with the CPT Bureau and Secretariat at a general meeting for liaison officers in Strasbourg in March 1994. The CPT insisted that ECPT Article 8(2)(d) provided that 'A Party shall provide the Committee . . . with other information . . . which is necessary for the Committee to carry out its task' and that it was for the Committee to determine what information it needed to carry out its task. However, it was also noted that Article 8(2)(d) provides that 'in seeking such information, the Committee shall have regard to applicable rules of national law and professional ethics'. It was decided that this potential conflict should be resolved on a 'case by case' basis in the spirit of mutual understanding and co-operation on which the ECPT rests.[6] It is

---

[4] Netherlands 1, para 9.   [5] Netherlands 1 R 1, para 10.
[6] See Gen Rep 5, paras 12 and 14.

notable that no difficulties regarding this issue appear to have arisen during the second *periodic* visit.

(b) Police custody: remand prisoners

The CPT found that in The Netherlands remand prisoners may remain for a few days in police cells considered unsuited for stays longer than a few days.[7] The CPT was informed that the Dutch authorities were considering measures designed to remedy this situation and the Committee asked that these measures be given a high priority and that they be informed of their implementation.

Measures have since been taken and the matter resolved. Remand prisoners are no longer held in Dutch police cells, something the CPT largely confirmed during its visit in 1997.[8] The cost of ensuring that this is the case has been immense: new remand prisons have been built and the number of prison personnel increased. The cause of the problem was the significant rise in the Dutch prison population and the fact that, for want of accommodation for sentenced prisoners, convicted and sentenced prisoners were backed up in remand prisons. The prison system was overcrowded as a result of the increasing numbers of committals ordered by the courts. There was a time lag in solving the problem. This is clearly a problem which the CPT will encounter in many countries, not all of them so well blessed as The Netherlands with the resources necessary to solve it. The CPT appears currently to address this issue with what Evans and Morgan term a *variable geometry* approach: a common standard the achievement of which is taken necessarily to be variable depending on the resources.[9] I take this to be necessary, for otherwise the CPT's common standards are no more than symbolic. But recognition of this fact raises a question: Are the CPT's standards the *minimum* standards for preventing torture and ill-treatment?; Or are they medium or high, which is to say *aspirational*, standards?

(c) Police custody: access to lawyers

The CPT was critical that the Committee's fundamental safeguard that suspects should have right of access to legal advice from the *outset* of police detention was not satisfied in The Netherlands. There is no such right in The Netherlands.[10] The Dutch police notify legal advisers only when suspects are detained for more than six hours—access to a lawyer during the first

---

[7] Netherlands 1, paras 31–33.
[8] Netherlands 2, para 29—'the practice . . . had now *almost* been brought to an end' (emphasis added).
[9] Evans and Morgan (1998), 349.   [10] Netherlands 1, paras 41–43.

six hours is not a right—and this is normally done only after six hours have elapsed. Moreover, lawyers are often in no hurry to attend, which means that suspects may not see their lawyers for one or two days. Furthermore, there is no right in The Netherlands for suspects to have their lawyers with them during police interrogations. Some police districts have a policy of allowing lawyers to be present, and have formulated their own regulations for this purpose, but most do not.

The response of the Dutch Government to the CPT stressed two aspects of Dutch practice. First, it was asserted that to allow lawyers to be present during interrogations during the first six hours would reduce the effectiveness of interrogations: there would be fewer confessions.[11] And were that the case, then the police would have to rely on other means of criminal investigation, some of them technical and most of them intrusive: telephone taps, use of informers, covert surveillance, undercover operations, and so on. The argument sought to balance the intrusiveness and cost of investigations against the CPT's safeguards. Secondly, it was emphasized that there are in The Netherlands, as the CPT had established, many and effective ways of complaining about the behaviour of the police and the conditions of arrest and imprisonment. Moreover, the Dutch police are well trained in the use of non-oppressive interrogation techniques. Since it was not suggested that the Dutch police did ill-treat their charges the Dutch authorities could not see, therefore, why their procedures should be altered.[12]

The CPT has not responded to this answer from the Dutch Government and one concludes from this that the answers of the Dutch authorities are considered satisfactory. It is noticeable, for example, that although in its second *periodic* report the Committee reiterates its recommendation that access to lawyers be assured from the outset of custody, it does so in formulaic terms without adducing any evidence that there is particular need for the safeguard in The Netherlands.[13] This suggests that the CPT takes a balanced view when implementation of its safeguards is concerned: there are very few complaints against the behaviour of the police in The Netherlands. On the other hand, research regarding the presence of lawyers during police interrogations in The Netherlands has shown that it makes little difference to the outcome of interviews.[14] Professional criminals scarcely ever confess, so the police have to use more intrusive methods of investigation in such cases no matter how interrogations are conducted. Moreover, research on the presence of lawyers during interrogations in other countries suggests that though the proportion of suspects refusing to answer any or all questions may increase marginally, the police have not been greatly

---

[11] Netherlands 1 R 1, 23–24.   [12] Ibid, 23–25.   [13] Netherlands 2, paras 33–34.
[14] Fynaut, C (1988) *De Raadsman bij het Politieverhoor* (The Lawyer Present during Police Interrogation) (Den Haag: Ministerie can Justitie) (unpublished).

disadvantaged by the development.[15] The CPT would have been able to deploy good arguments had it chosen to press the Dutch authorities on this issue, but the Committee chose not to do so.

(d) High security prison units: the 1994 CPT request for information

Like most other countries, the Netherlands prison system includes high security units. The CPT visited one of them—the EBI Unit (*Evaluatiecommissie Beveiligingsbeleid Gevangeniswezen*) at De Schie Prison—and made a number of critical recommendations regarding it.[16] The Committee considered aspects of the regime in the unit to be oppressive. Of great interest, therefore, is the exchange of letters which occurred between the Dutch authorities and the CPT, following publication of the CPT report and the Dutch response, concerning the use of handcuffs in the EBI units subsequent to the CPT visit in 1992. When some prisoners are removed from their cells in EBI units they are now required by the prison officers to be handcuffed.[17] The CPT learned about this rule in 1994 and asked for information regarding it. The Dutch authorities confirmed the practice and explained that its use had improved communication between prisoners and officers, the poor quality of which had led to CPT complaints in 1992. Prison officers now felt safer and their attitudes had improved. This conclusion was based, they claimed, on an independent evaluation of the handcuffing procedure. Thus, contrary to the view implicit in the CPT's request for information, handcuffing did not signify a more restrictive regime: on the contrary, the atmosphere was said now to be more relaxed.

There are several issues worth pointing to here. First, the CPT received information regarding the practice of handcuffing subsequent to a visit. The CPT made an isolated request for information outside the context of a visit, albeit the request arguably involved a follow-up to a visit. This appears to point to broad monitoring effort by the CPT. But it may also be seen as a merely incidental reaction. If the CPT is engaged in broad monitoring, why did the Committee request information regarding only one issue, there had been a good many other changes to Dutch penal policy since 1992? If the request was merely incidental—stimulated probably by intelligence being sent to Strasbourg by some individual or organization in The Netherlands—it seems to have involved a waste of energy, because when the Dutch authorities replied with the relevant information, there was no reply from the CPT. That appeared to be the end of the matter. Once again, silence could be interpreted to indicate CPT satisfaction with the answer. There was no discussion of the issue. No pressure was applied by the CPT seeking

---

[15] See, regarding England and Wales, Sanders, A and Young, R (1994) *Criminal Justice* (London: Butterworths), Chapter Four.
[16] Netherlands 1, paras 69–95. [17] See Netherlands 2, paras 7–9 and 76–77.

clarification or challenging the interpretation of the evidence. Whether this was because the CPT had not gathered comparative data on the use of such practices in other high security settings is not known.

The manner in which this issue was dealt with by the Committee in the report arising from the second *periodic* visit is of particular interest. First, for the first time, as far as this observer is aware, in any visit which has been the subject of a published report, the CPT was presented by the prison authorities with restrictions on the manner in which delegation members were to interview prisoners which the Committee found unacceptable and, instead of pressing their case and prevailing, the delegation retreated and declined to interview the prisoner in the manner prescribed (though see the 1992 'incident' described below). The Dutch authorities stipulated that a prisoner subject to the 'handcuff regime' in the EBI unit at Nieuw Vosseveld Prison could be interviewed only if he remained handcuffed, with officers present, or with a glass screen separating him and the CPT interviewer. The Committee did not find either of these arrangements acceptable because they would have meant that the interview was not private. They were of the opinion that they should have been permitted to interview the prisoner by using less intrusive security safeguards.[18] Secondly, the Committee came to the conclusion in 1997 that the regime for all prisoners in the EBI units visited 'could be considered to amount to inhuman treatment'. The Committee noted that the unit psychologist was of the opinion that the regime had no 'harmful effects on prisoners' but they observed that his assessment had not been made subject to any external professional review, that not all specialist advisers were of the same opinion, and that there was some evidence that former EBI prisoners did appear to be suffering 'persistent psychological sequelae'. The Committee called on the Dutch authorities to commission an independent study.

The conclusion to be drawn from this sequence is as follows. Had the Committee closely monitored what was happening in The Netherlands from 1994 onwards the Committee might at that stage have drawn the conclusion that the 'independent evaluation' of the EBI regime was not independent as far as the Committee was concerned and they might then have pressed for an evaluation that they could have regarded as independent. Had those steps been taken then, to the extent that the EBI regime is shown to have had damaging psychological effects, the Committee might more effectively have prevented them.

(e) Monitoring police custody: the value of perseverance

The CPT noted with approval an initiative in Amsterdam for the external monitoring of police cells. The Committee invited the Dutch authorities to

---

[18] See Netherlands 2, paras 7–9.

consider extending the system to all police and gendarmerie stations.[19] To this invitation the Dutch authorities made a procedural or constitutional response: this was not a matter for the Dutch Government but the municipal authorities.[20] This is technically true, but few municipal authorities have set up such systems and the Government could have taken the initiative by making provision for such supervisory systems in police legislation being prepared at the time. The timing of the CPT report represented an excellent opportunity to mount such an initiative but the Dutch Government failed to take it and the CPT, possibly not being aware of police reforms being undertaken in The Netherlands, failed to react to the procedural response of the Dutch Government. This was a lost opportunity which illustrates the value of CPT–state party dialogue being pursued assiduously and promptly. Had the CPT pressed home their suggestion we might well have a national supervisory system for police stations in place today.

Perseverance is an essential aspect of an inspection system which has confidentiality and dialogue as its main tools. The success of the CPT depends on it. This is not just a matter of CPT resources to maintain perseverance. The Committee must also have the means to gather local intelligence so that the Strasbourg-based Secretariat and Committee knows what opportunities are being presented by developments on the ground. In order to harness this intelligence capacity, the CPT needs to stimulate dialogue with agencies other than the state authorities.

(f) Incidents

Though not among the first group of countries to be visited, The Netherlands was visited relatively early on in the history of the CPT. As in most other countries, the visit was not entirely smooth. There were incidents which are illustrative of more general problems.

The CPT delegation was refused entry at one police station.[21] Access problems, particularly at police stations, have been encountered from time to time by the CPT.[22] Police officers appear sometimes not to have been informed about the Committee and to the extent that that is true then officers are correct not to permit delegations entry. In 1992, at Almelo Police Station, there was another factor at work. Several Turkish national Kurds were in custody on suspicion of having committed a serious crime and were not permitted to have contact with each other in order to prevent collusion. There was a suspicion that the prisoners had terrorist connections. A judge had ordered the isolation of the suspects and thus, when the police contacted the public prosecutor about the arrival of the CPT delegation, the public prosecutor was not prepared to authorize their entry either. At this

---

[19] Netherlands 1, para 52.   [20] Netherlands 1 R 1, 26–27.
[21] Netherlands 1, para 8.   [22] See Evans and Morgan (1998), 338–339.

point, somewhat unusually given CPT accounts of the Committee's persistence when faced with such obstructions in other places, the delegation then departed, only to return the following morning.[23] In the interval the Ministry of Foreign Affairs was contacted and access guaranteed. It is clear that the CPT had an absolute right of access and that the Dutch authorities had done insufficient to inform the police and other officials about the nature of the visit and the obligations of the Dutch authorities arising from the Convention. Similar problems were encountered in 1997.[24] But this example illustrates a broader point. The Dutch Government is highly supportive of the ECPT and this incident of apparent non-co-operation was therefore highly embarrassing to the Dutch authorities. The fact that the CPT was denied access to a police station in The Netherlands of all countries is indicative of the general lack of knowledge about the CPT among criminal justice personnel generally.

A second incident is if anything even more embarrassing because it indicates the lack of control exercised by the authorities over their own personnel. The prison officers in a special unit at Demersluis Prison refused to co-operate with the CPT and continued their oppositional stance even after intervention by officials from the Ministry of Foreign Affairs. The officers hindered the CPT's work by not meeting appointments. The CPT inspection continued and was completed, but took longer than was intended.[25] This example is interesting because it occurred in a recently established special unit catering for difficult-to-handle prisoners. Staff working conditions were bad. Staff–prisoner relationships were problematic and the staff were irritated with their situation. Following the CPT visit senior staff were replaced, new and experienced personnel brought in, and more support (including a psychologist) and training for prison officers provided.

Such incidents are likely to continue to occur irrespective of the knowledge which custodial staff have of the CPT. Many custodial environments are inherently tense and in many countries—of which The Netherlands would not generally be thought to be an example—there is no tradition of control and external oversight over the police and criticism of the police has not been tolerated, with the consequence that they (and probably prisons personnel) are used to being masters of the situation, expecting to be deferred to if not obeyed. In such circumstances it is to be expected that the CPT will be met with non-co-operation, hostility, and sabotage. Lack of co-operation may stem from several causes. The custodial institutions may be the direct responsibility of regional or municipal authorities as opposed to central government ministries and the relationship between the local authorities and the centre may not be of the best. Disciplinary

---

[23] Netherlands 1, para 8.   [24] Netherlands 2, para 6.   [25] Ibid, para 9.

control among custodial personnel may be poor. An adequate budget and effective management may be lacking. It is likely that the CPT will continue to encounter such situations which the Committee will have to criticize as unacceptable.

3. CONCLUSION: RECEPTIVITY REGARDING HUMAN RIGHTS AND CPT EFFECTIVENESS

A single CPT report is no more than an incident and can be dealt with as such by the government concerned. The impact of the CPT is very much dependent on the general receptivity of a human rights perspective within member states and this varies greatly. The Dutch Government is keen to set the highest possible standards regarding human rights and wishes to promote human rights internationally. It follows that the Dutch Government is inclined generally to implement whatever the CPT recommends: it has supported the creation of the CPT and would not wish to undermine the Committee's operation and credibility. This means, *inter alia*, that if the Ministry of Justice is uncertain about an aspect of policy falling within the CPT's mandate, the Secretariat in Strasbourg is consulted. In 1996 when new cellular accommodation in police stations was being built, Strasbourg was consulted about the appropriate size of cells.[26] Within the Ministries of Justice and Foreign Affairs the standards of the CPT and the jurisprudence of the European Commission and Court are studied closely to examine their relevance for policy in The Netherlands. Moreover, within the Dutch Parliament members are liable to ask ministers questions regarding the implementation of CPT standards.[27] This does not mean, as we have seen, that support for CPT standards is unconditional: where the Dutch Government believe Dutch arrangements to be defensible and to work satisfactorily, they resist change. Nevertheless, there is a high level of support for the CPT and for a human rights perspective both within the upper echelons of the Dutch civil service and among Dutch politicians.

The converse is arguably the case within other member states and it has to be recognized that both positive and negative cultures regarding human rights are deep-seated and difficult to change. The CPT's capacity to change local cultures is limited. The Committee, as I have emphasized, visits only occasionally and then sees few institutions and meets with only a small proportion of custodial personnel. All of which reinforces the need for

---

[26] The CPT Secretariat replied in April 1996 with 'Some standards developed by the CPT concerning conditions of detention in police stations'.
[27] See, for example, questions asked on 10 July 1997 by member Marijnisse (SP) regarding the new High Security Unit at Vught (Tweede Kamer (Second Chamber) 1996–1997, 1668).

building as much support and pressure as possible locally through human rights activists and NGOs. It was argued above that the CPT needs a local intelligence base so that, by means of the continuous dialogue through which the CPT will ideally press home its recommendations, the Committee can grasp opportunities for legislative, administrative, and organizational change. Achieving cultural change regarding human rights will require no less of a community-based infrastructure, particularly in the former Warsaw Pact states now undergoing a vital period of transition.

4. POSTSCRIPT: ACCREDITED INSTITUTIONS, MONITORED INSTITUTIONS

The Netherlands mainland has been visited only twice in nine years of CPT operation and this is roughly the average interval between visits which the CPT now concedes is feasible.[28] As the number of state parties to the ECPT has increased and the number of custodial establishments available to be visited grows enormously in scale—with over one million prisoners the prospect of inspecting the Russian Federation is truly daunting, for example—the question urgently arises as to how the CPT should use its limited inspectoral resources.

The editors of this volume have assembled, both in this text and previously,[29] the 'jurisprudence' of the CPT—the standards that the Committee routinely applies to the custodial institutions that the Committee inspects. These standards include those in respect of what might be termed the institutional 'hardware'—the cells, exercise yards, and so on—and the institutional 'software'—the manner in which detainees are arrested, interrogated, generally treated, or cared for and the administrative procedures, safeguards, and supervisory systems which cover those processes.

Let us, for the moment, put on one side the fact that the CPT deals with a variety of custodial institutions—police stations, prisons, psychiatric hospitals, and so on. All such institutions can be conceived in a more abstract vein as processing systems through which people pass and all processing systems can be broken down into their component subsystems which contribute to the whole. These subsystems and their linked control mechanisms can be thought of as needing to employ certain management devices in common. We can decide whether certain subsystems require light or onerous control devices, or single or double safeguards, depending on their importance for some aspect of the functioning of the whole. Such an approach, a systems approach, is used in what are called 'quality control

---

[28] Evans and Morgan (1998), 166–167.   [29] Ibid, Chapters Six to Eight.

systems'.[30] Most large companies have quality control systems. These meticulously describe all the processes, related to production and decision making, which are vital to the success of the company, establish minimum standards of performance, put in place means to measure that performance, and establish procedures for correcting shortfalls in performance. Most factories would perish if they did not have such systems. Moreover, if their systems meet certain standards—for instance, ISO standards[31]—they can be certified or accredited. The outside world then knows that the company meets certain minimum standards regarding public health, worker safety, and so on.

Such systems of control, systems of self-assessment and control to be precise, are used not only in chemical plants or car factories. In a number of countries such systems are also used for the purposes of state control and inspection. Enforcement and inspection agencies thereafter do not inspect factories with regard to given regulations—some requirements regarding the environment, for example—but rather inspect with a view to seeing that a quality control system, which the government has approved, is in place and is functioning. In systems theory terms, the inspection becomes a second order inspection. This approach to inspection can be much more cost-effective than a system based on incidental inspections by government officials. The idea is being taken up within, for example, policing.[32]

These considerations give new relevance to the CPT jurisprudence collected by the editors of this volume. If made comprehensive, standardized, and organized, a compendium of CPT standards could be used as the starting point for an initiative in which state parties to the ECPT could be encouraged, to put it modestly, to develop domestic quality control approaches to the various categories of custodial institutions falling within the CPT mandate. Were that to happen, the task of the CPT would be made that much easier. This is a less utopian suggestion than might be thought. Quality control and institutional accreditation systems are already in place in some countries. In the USA there are well-developed and documented systems of accreditation for prisons and police stations operated by the American Corrections Association. In the UK aspirational

---

[30] See, for example, Sashkin, M and Kiser, KJ (1992) *Total Quality Management* (Seabrook, Maryland); and Boland, T and Silvecrbcrg, D (1996) 'Managing for Quality', 62 (3) *International Review of Administrative Sciences* 352.

[31] The International Standardisation Organisation has produced a series of organizational standards for procedures, processes, and internal controls and the ISO certifies organizations that have adopted such standards. Certification is on the basis of periodic inspection.

[32] See Waters, I (1998) 'The Pursuit of Quality', *The Police Journal* LXXI, 1, 55; and Younis, T, Bailey, SJ and Younis, CD (1996) 'The Application of Total Quality Management to the Public Sector', 62 *International Journal of Administrative Sciences* 369.

operational standards have been published by the Prison Service for prison facilities and regimes which are used as the basis for managerial self-assessment and prisons accreditation.[33] Within The Netherlands one police district[34] has already obtained an ISO certificate and a quality control system is being developed for prisons.

This way of looking at the work of the CPT may be slightly unusual and may be regarded by lawyers as unorthodox. The proposal may meet formal objections. The ECPT, for example, does not refer to self-assessment and the domestic accreditation of institutions. Moreover, the value of accreditation has been questioned in those countries where it is well advanced.[35] Conversely, the CPT is free to choose the manner in which it carries out its inspections and may rely to the extent that the Committee considers it appropriate on whatever domestic documentation and information systems it wishes. Whatever the formal limitations of accreditation systems and the CPT's use of them, they should nevertheless be of interest to the Committee. The CPT could express that interest by: generally gathering and exchanging information on accreditation systems; encouraging self-assessment and accreditation in those jurisdictions where interest is shown; formulating a complete set of working standards which could be used as a basis for accreditation within member states; and sponsoring pilot projects to test the value of accreditation. Were domestic self-assessment and accreditation based on CPT jurisprudence put in place, the CPT's task might then be to monitor the integrity of the domestic system and test the relationship between the Committee's standards and the incidence of torture and ill-treatment generally.

REFERENCES

Boland, T and Silveerberg, D (1996) 'Managing for Quality', 62 (3) *International Review of Administrative Sciences* 352

Branham, LS (1993) 'Accreditation: Making a Good Process Better', 57 (2) *Federal Probation* 11–16

Evans, MD and Morgan, R (1998) *Preventing Torture* (Oxford: Clarendon Press)

Fynaut, C (1988) *De Raadsman bij het Politieverhoor* (Den Haag: Ministerie can Justitie) (unpublished)

Prison Service (1994) *Operating Standards* (London: Prison Service)

Sanders, A and Young, R (1994) *Criminal Justice* (London: Butterworths)

Sashkin, M and Kiser, KJ (1991) *Total Quality Management* (Seabrook, Maryland: Ducochon Press)

[33] Prison Service (1994) *Operating Standards* (London: Prison Service).
[34] Rotterdam-Rijnmond Police District.
[35] See Branham, LS (1993) 'Accreditation: Making a Good Process Better', 57 (2) *Federal Probation* 11–16.

Waters, I (1998) 'The Pursuit of Quality', *The Police Journal*, LXXI, 1, 55

Younis, T, Bailey, SJ and Younis, CD (1996) 'The Application of Total Quality Management to the Public Sector', 62 *International Journal of Administrative Sciences* 369

11

The CPT and Turkey

SEMIH GEMALMAZ

1. THE TURKISH LEGAL SYSTEM AND INTERNATIONAL HUMAN RIGHTS

According to the 1982 Turkish Constitution,[1] duly enacted international agreements have the authority of law and are not subject to challenge before the Constitutional Court on the ground that they are unconstitutional. The position was the same under the 1961 Constitution.[2] This has two consequences. First, since international conventions ratified by Turkey automatically become an integral part of Turkish law, all relevant domestic authorities must apply them as if they were domestic legislation. In other words, by ratifying an international instrument, the Turkish Parliament incorporates that instrument into Turkish law and, where relevant, its provisions become self-executing.[3] Secondly, although applied as if they were domestic legislation, the inability to challenge the constitutionality of duly ratified international instruments endows them with a special status: whilst they are not constitutional norms from a legal-positivist perspective, they have at least a kind of semi-constitutional status. This means that, in general terms, when there is a clash between international and domestic norms supremacy has to be given to duly enacted international norms. This is based not just on a teleological interpretation: it also flows from the fact that the nature of the resolution of the conflict between the national and international norms will be subject to international control mechanisms.

It should be stressed, however, that even if an international instrument has been ratified and the Law on the Approval of the Ratification has been promulgated, that promulgation does not necessarily entail publication of the international instrument (in either its original or official Turkish translation texts). This is a serious problem because it is only possible to invoke those laws which have been published in the Official Gazette, this being the only valid legal text. This may be a source of delay.[4] Moreover, in

---

[1] Article 90, para 5.   [2] Article 65, para 5.

[3] It is important, however, to remember that only those norms which are intended to be directly applicable can be self-executing.

[4] For instance, the official Turkish translation of the texts of the 2nd and 3rd Protocols to the ECHR were published in the Official Gazette on 6 February 1968, some seven months after the promulgation of the two separate but identically dated Laws on the Approval of the

some cases, the official Turkish translations published in the Official Gazette contain serious errors.

Turkey has not shown a great deal of enthusiasm for participating in and ensuring the domestic applicability of international and regional human rights instruments. Out of 25 basic human rights instruments sponsored by the United Nations, Turkey has ratified only 11 and the list does not include either of the International Covenants of 1966.[5] At the regional level, Turkey ratified the European Convention on Human Rights (ECHR) and its First Protocol as long ago as 1954.[6] However, it was another thirty-three years before Turkey

Ratification regarding the 2nd and 3rd Protocols of the ECHR (Law No 900, 13 July 1967; Official Gazette, 24 July 1967, no 12655) and Law on the Approval of the Ratification of the 3rd Protocol of the ECHR (Law No 901, 13 July 1967; Official Gazette, 24 July 1967, no 12655). Similarly, there was a delay of nearly five months between the promulgation of Law on the Approval of the Ratification of the 8th Protocol of the ECHR (Law No 3526, 12 April 1989; Official Gazette, 20 April 1989, no 20145) and the publication of the text in the Official Gazette (29 August 1989, no 20267). Cf the delay of two months in the case of the 5th Protocol of the ECHR, between taking the Decision and its publication simultaneously with the text in the Official Gazette: the Council of Ministers Decision on the Approval of the Ratification of the 5th Protocol of the ECHR (Decision No 7/3211, 29 September 1971; Official Gazette, 30 November 1971, no 140285).

[5] As at 31 December 1997 the UN Conventions signed and ratified by Turkey were: Convention on the Prevention and Punishment of the Crime of Genocide (accession, 31 July 1950; enacted by Law No 5630, 23 March 1950; Official Gazette, 29 March 1950, no 7469); Convention on the Rights of the Child (signed, 14 September 1990; ratified, 4 April 1995; enacted by Law No 4058, 9 December 1994; Official Gazette, 27 January 1995, no 22184: Turkey ratified this Convention with the reservation: 'The Republic of Turkey reserves the right to interpret and to apply the provisions of Articles 17, 29 and 30 of the United Nations Convention on the Rights of the Child in conformity with the word and spirit of the Constitution of the Republic of Turkey and of the Treaty of Lausanne of 24 June 1923'); Convention on the Elimination of All Forms of Discrimination against Women (accession, 20 December 1985); Convention on the Political Rights of Women (signed, 12 January 1954; ratified, 26 January 1960; enacted by Law No 7288, dated 25 May 1959; Official Gazette, 2 June 1959, no 10220); Convention against Torture and other Cruel, Inhuman or Degrading Treatment or Punishment (signed, 25 January 1988; ratified, 2 August 1988; enacted by Law No 3441, dated 21 April 1988; Official Gazette, 29 April 1988, no 19799); Slavery Convention of 1926 (accession, 24 July 1933) as amended by the Protocol of 7 December 1953 (signed, 14 January 1955); Supplementary Convention on the Abolition of Slavery, the Slave Trade and Institutions and Practices Similar to Slavery (signed, 28 June 1957; ratified, 17 July 1964; enacted by Law No 361, dated 27 December 1963; Official Gazette, 6 January 1964, no 11599 and 4 April 1964, no 11674); Convention relating to the Status of Refugees (signed, 24 August 1951; ratified, 30 March 1962); Protocol relating to the Status of Refugees (accession, 31 July 1968); International Convention on the Elimination of All Forms of Racial Discrimination (signed, 13 October 1972).

[6] Turkey signed the ECHR on 4 November 1950, and the 1st Additional Protocol on 20 May 1952. Following the deposit of the instruments of ratification, the ECHR and the 1st Additional Protocol came into effect on 18 May 1954. Domestically, the Convention and Protocol were enacted by the Law on the Approval of the Ratification of the ECHR and its Additional Protocol (Law No 6366, 10 March 1954; Official Gazette, 19 March 1954, no 8662). The texts of the ECHR and its Additional Protocol were published in the same Official Gazette, attached to Law No 6366. As of November 1997, Turkey had not become a party to ECHR Protocols Nos 4, 6, 7, 9, and 10. As regards Protocol No 4, Turkey has signed it and promulgated the Law on the Approval of the Ratification of the 4th Protocol of the ECHR

recognized the right of individual petition to the European Commission of Human Rights.[7] Even then, the Turkish Government attached five conditions to its acceptance which it characterized as 'interpretative declarations' and which have been whittled away over time. Some commentators argued at the outset that these amounted to 'reservations' and so were null and void.[8] When the declaration under Article 25 was prolonged for another three years as from 28 January 1990, the fifth of the conditions was omitted.[9] In the wake of further criticism, and in light of the admissibility decision in *Chrysostomos and others v Turkey*[10] which held these conditions to be null and void but recognition of the jurisdiction of the Commission remained valid, a revised declaration was deposited on 15 June 1992, valid until 27 January 1993.[11] This retained only the first of the conditions. When this revised declaration was itself renewed in 1993[12] for a period of three years this first condition was still maintained and continues to provide that Turkey accepts responsibility 'as far as acts or omissions have been performed within the boundaries of the national territory of the Republic of Turkey', even though this is invalid, following the decision in

(Law No 3975, 23 February 1994; Official Gazette, 26 February 1994, no 21861). The text was published (following the Turkish Council of Ministers Decision No 94/5749, 9 June 1994) in Official Gazette, 14 July 1994, no 21990 but the instrument of ratification has not been deposited with the Secretary General of the Council of Europe. Rumpf, C (1993) 'The Protection of Human Rights in Turkey and the Significance of International Human Rights Instruments', 14 *HRLJ* 394, 403 has claimed that Turkey was a party to the 9th Protocol but, though this Protocol was signed on 6 November 1992, the Law on the Approval of the Ratification of the 9th Protocol has not been enacted nor has an instrument of ratification been deposited. Turkey neither signed nor ratified the 10th Protocol. Of course, the substance of both the 9th and 10th Protocols are incorporated in the 11th Protocol which Turkey has ratified and which entered into force on 1 November 1998. (See Note 18 below.)

[7] Turkey's first declaration was deposited on 28 January 1987 and was valid for a period of three years (as have subsequent declarations). This first declaration was published in the Turkish Official Gazette (21 April 1987, no 19438). See also Council of Europe, Information Sheet No 21, 3–12. On the status of the ECHR in domestic law see Soysal, M (1989) 'The effect of international convention on the domestic law in Turkey' in *The Implementation in National Law of the ECHR, Proceedings of the Fourth Copenhagen Conference on Human Rights, 28–29/10/1988*, 48–49; Polakiewicza, J and Jacob-Foltzer, V (1991) 'The European Human Rights Convention in domestic law: The Impact of the Strasbourg case-law where direct effect is given to the Convention (second part)', 12 *HRLJ* 140–141.

[8] eg Cameron, I (1988) 'Turkey and Article 25 of the European Convention on Human Rights', 37 *ICLQ* 887.

[9] See the Turkish Council of Ministers Decision No 90/82, 24 January 1990. Neither this Decision nor the text of the second declaration was published in the Official Gazette. For the text see Council of Europe, Information Sheet No 26.

[10] *Chrysostomos and others v Turkey*, App Nos 15299/89, 15300/89, and 15318/89, Comm Dec, 4 March 1991, 68 *DR* 216.

[11] See the Turkish Council of Ministers Decision No 92/2982, 27 April 1992. This new version of the declaration was published in the Official Gazette, dated 21 May 1992, no 21234. See also Council of Europe, Information Sheet No 30, 7.

[12] This has not been published in the Official Gazette. For the text see Council of Europe, Information Sheet No 33, 2.

Chrysostomos.[13] A fourth declaration was made, also for a three-year period, with effect from 28 January 1996.

The instrument recognizing the compulsory jurisdiction of the European Court of Human Rights under Article 46 of the ECHR was deposited on 22 January 1990 for a period of three years.[14] This also contained conditions which have been objected to on the grounds that they were in fact 'limitations' and 'reservations', and so were null and void.[15] Turkey's acceptance of the Court's jurisdiction was prolonged for another three years on 22 January 1993[16] and consecutively on 22 January 1996.[17] With the entry into force of the Eleventh Protocol, the need for acceptance of jurisdiction in this fashion ceases.[18]

Turkey has tended to become a party to both regional and international human rights instruments during periods when the Government has faced serious international pressure over allegations of human rights violations. Following the 12 September 1980 *coup d'état*, for example, the so-called '12 September Regime' was established, resulting in massive violations of human rights. The considerable international reaction included demands

[13] Indeed, in recognizing the responsibility for acts carried out in Northern Cyprus by the Turkish authorities this confirms the Commission jurisprudence in *Cyprus v Turkey*, App Nos 6780/74, 6950/75, and 8007/77, the report of which was made public by virtue of Council of Europe Committee of Ministers Resolution DH (92) 12 of 1 April 1992 and is published in (1992) 13 *HRLJ* 154. Turkey claimed that 'Turkey had no jurisdiction over the territory of the Turkish Federated State of Cyprus—the area where the alleged acts were claimed to have been committed'. In its decision of 10 July 1978 on the admissibility of the application the Commission found that 'Turkey's jurisdiction in the north of the Republic of Cyprus, existing by reason of the presence of her armed forces there, which prevents exercise of jurisdiction by the applicant Government, could not be excluded on the ground that jurisdiction in that area was allegedly exercised by the Turkish Federated State of Cyprus.'

[14] On the domestic level, recognition of the jurisdiction of the European Court of Human Rights was first decided by the Council of Ministers of Turkey on 25 September 1989, Decision No 89/14563, on the basis of reciprocity and for a period of three years (Official Gazette, 27 September 1989, no 20295). But this Decision was not immediately transmitted to the Council of Europe. The Turkish Council of Ministers later decided that the instrument of recognition had to be deposited with the Secretary General of the Council of Europe (Decision No 89/14866, 12 December 1989; Official Gazette, 26 December 1989, no 20384). It was deposited on 22 January 1990. Thus the period between the Decision taken by the Turkish Council of Ministers on the recognition of the jurisdiction of the European Court and its submission to the Council of Europe was almost four months.

[15] See, eg, Council of Europe, Information Sheet No 27, 4–5.

[16] See Turkish Council of Ministers Decision No 93/3987, 8 January 1993 (Official Gazette, 30 January 1993, no 21481) and Council of Europe, Information Sheet No 32, 3–4.

[17] See (1996) 17 *HRLJ* 234.

[18] Turkey signed Protocol No 11 on 11 May 1994. The Turkish Council of Ministers Decision on the Ratification of the Protocol No 11 was submitted to the Turkish Parliament on 10 March 1997 and unanimously accepted by the Foreign Affairs Commission of the Turkish Parliament. This was followed by the promulgation of the Law on the Approval of the Ratification of the Protocol No 11 (Law No 4255, 14 May 1997). Following the Turkish Council of Ministers Decision, Decision No 97/95/6, 30 May 1997, the English text of Protocol No 11 and the official Turkish translation were published in the Official Gazette, 20 June 1997, no 23025. The Turkish Government deposited the instrument of ratification of Protocol No 11 on 11 July 1997.

for normalization or democratization.[19] In response the Turkish Government became more active in ratifying human rights instruments.[20] Moreover, Turkey's application for full membership of the European Community/Union had a certain impact on the Turkish Government's human rights policies.[21] Turkey applied for full membership in April 1987 and, both before and after this application, concrete measures were taken both at the national and international level. They included the ratification of a number of human rights instruments[22] and recognition of the jurisdiction of the European Commission and Court of Human Rights.[23] It is against this background that Turkey signed and ratified the ECPT. The ECPT was opened for signature on 26 November 1987. Although Turkey did not sign until 11 January 1988, it was the first state to deposit an instrument of ratification, on 26 February 1988. The Grand National Assembly of Turkey (GNAT, the Turkish Parliament) had promulgated the Law on the Approval of the Ratification of the Convention[24] and the official Turkish translation of the Convention and the English original text were published in the Official Gazette on 27 February 1988.[25]

Turkey also signed the First and Second Protocols to the ECPT on 10 May 1995 and promulgated the Law on the Approval of the Ratification of the First and Second Protocols of the European Convention Against Torture of 4 April 1997.[26] The official Turkish translations of the texts were published in the Official Gazette on 23 June 1997[27] and the instruments of ratification deposited with the Council of Europe on 17 September 1997.[28]

At the time of writing, the CPT has visited Turkey eight times, more than any other state party. These visits can be grouped into three distinct periods: 1990–1992, 1993–1994, and 1996 onwards. Uniquely among state parties that have been visited more than once, Turkey has yet to authorize

---

[19] See Gemalmaz, MS (1989) *The Institutionalization Process of the Turkish Type of Democracy: A Politico-Juridical Analysis of Human Rights* (Istanbul), 28–35.

[20] At the time of ratification of the ECPT, the President of Turkey was the former General Kenan Evren, the leader of the military junta of the 12 September 1980 *coup d'état*. The Prime Minister was Mr Turgut Özal, a former Minister in the military government during the *de facto* regime of 12 September 1980 and subsequently leader of the newly established Motherland Party.

[21] Rumpf (1993), 403.

[22] See above, Notes 4 and 5.

[23] See above, Notes 7 and 14.

[24] No 3411, 25 February 1988; Official Gazette, 26 February 1988, no 19737 bis.

[25] This being a rare example of the publication of a Law of Ratification being swiftly followed by the publication of the convention text in the Official Gazette.

[26] Law No 4237, Official Gazette, 4 April 1997, no 22960. For the ratification of these Protocols, also see Turkish press, for instance, *Demokrasi*, 9 April 1997.

[27] Following the promulgation of Law No 4237 and the Turkish Council of Ministers Decision No 97/9455, 7 May 1997, the texts of the Protocol No 1 and No 2 of the ECPT were published in the Official Gazette, 23 June 1997, no 23028.

[28] Council of Europe, Press Release, 17 September 1997, ref 510a97.

the publication of any of the materials arising out of CPT visits.[29] Turkey is also the only state in respect of which the CPT has issued a Public Statement under Article 10(2). It has done so twice, on 15 December 1992[30] and on 6 December 1996.

2. THE CPT'S VISITS TO TURKEY: THE FIRST PERIOD (1990–1992) AND ITS CONSEQUENCES

(a) The first three visits (1990–1992)

The CPT visited Turkey on 9–21 September 1990, 20 September to 7 October 1991, and 22 November to 3 December 1992. The first two of these visits were *ad hoc* in nature, the third was *periodic*.[31]

During these three visits the number of places of detention visited was increased from eight, to twelve, to twenty[32] and the geographical spread of sites inspected was also increased from three provinces during the first and second visits to four in the third visit.[33] A number of facilities in Ankara and Diyarbakır were visited on each occasion, thereby enabling the Committee to follow up its observations. In Turkey the CPT's attention was chiefly focused on civil security and police establishments.

There are many places of detention in different provinces throughout Turkey and many allegations of torture and ill-treatment are made regarding them. The CPT is constrained by financial and staffing considerations and, in combination, these factors mean that the on-site investigations conducted by the CPT in Turkey are insufficient, too infrequent, and inefficient. Few provinces have been visited. It is arguable that, under such circumstances, and at a comparatively early stage in its work, the pressure on the CPT to issue a Public Statement was more of a psychological nature than of a legal nature or necessity under the terms of the Convention.

---

[29] The CPT has stressed the fact 'that publication of the CPT's visit reports has become the norm, non-publication the exception'. CPT, Gen Rep 5, para 11.

[30] CPT, Gen Rep 3, paras 9–11 and Appendix 4, 30–39. For an analysis of the Convention, the CPT, and the first Public Statement and its consequences from the perspective of Turkish law, see Gemalmaz, MS (1994) *Right to Life and Prevention of Torture* (Istanbul), 351–399 (in Turkish).

[31] See ECPT Articles 2 and 7(1) and Rules of Procedure, Rule 31. In its early years, the order of *periodic* visits was determined by lot—and Turkey came towards the end of the list. This doubtless explains why the first visits to Turkey were described as *ad hoc*, thus permitting visits which were otherwise virtually indistinguishable from *periodic* visits to take place earlier than would otherwise have been possible.

[32] For details of the places of custody visited see: Gen Rep 1, Appendix 3, 35; Gen Rep 2, Appendix 3, 25; and Gen Rep 3, Appendix 3, 29.

[33] The provinces visited during the first and second visits were Ankara, Diyarbakır, and Malatya, and Ankara, Diyarbakır, and İstanbul respectively. During the third visit Adana, Ankara, Diyarbakır, and Istanbul provinces were visited.

(b) The 1992 Public Statement on Turkey

The first Public Statement on Turkey of December 1992[34] set out details of the CPT's findings in the course of its first three visits. During its 1990 visit the CPT delegation formed the view that both physical and psychological torture and other forms of severe ill-treatment were frequently applied by detectives of the Anti-Terror Departments of the Ankara and Diyarbakır Police when holding and questioning suspects. The allegations were consistent in nature. They were made both by persons suspected or convicted of offences under the Anti-Terror Law and persons suspected or convicted of ordinary criminal offences. As regards the latter, the number was especially high among persons detained for drug-related, property, and sex offences. Many forms of serious physical ill-treatment were alleged.[35] The medical members in the CPT's visiting delegation examined the detained persons and observed physical marks or conditions consistent with their allegations of torture or ill-treatment by the police. Furthermore, particularly at Ankara Police Headquarters, the CPT's visiting delegation was subjected to a series of delays and diversions and on several occasions given false information. A number of detainees were removed in order to prevent the delegation from meeting them. The CPT transmitted its observations to the Turkish authorities and recommended that a series of immediate and efficient measures be taken to combat the problem of torture and other forms of ill-treatment.

At the end of its second visit to Turkey in the autumn of 1991, the CPT found that no progress had been made by the police in eliminating torture and ill-treatment. The pattern and number of allegations was much the same except that more beatings with a stick or truncheon were recorded. The evidence suggested that there remained a problem in the Anti-Terror Departments of the Ankara and Diyarbakır Police. In its report on its second visit to Turkey the CPT recommended that a body composed of independent persons be set up immediately to carry out an investigation of the methods used by police officers when questioning suspects.[36] The reports and recommendations prepared by the CPT following these two visits were submitted to the Turkish authorities but the CPT concluded that in the more than two years following the CPT's first visit, almost nothing had been achieved as regards the prevention of, and strengthening the legal safeguards against, torture and ill-treatment by the police in Ankara and

---

[34] PS 1, Gen Rep 3, Appendix 4, 30–39.

[35] Most frequently: Palestinian hanging; electric shocks to sensitive parts of the body including the genitals; squeezing of the testicles; beating of the soles of the feet (*falaka*); hosing with pressurized cold water; incarceration for lengthy periods in very small, dark, and unventilated cells; threats of torture or other forms of ill-treatment to the person detained or against others and severe psychological humiliation (Turkey PS 1, paras 4–9; Gen Rep 3, 31–32).

[36] Turkey PS 1, paras 10–11; Gen Rep 3, 32.

Diyarbakır. Moreover, reports of torture and ill-treatment continued to be received from other parts of the country.[37]

The situation remained the same at the time of the third visit in 1992. The CPT observed that when it had come to power late in 1991 the new Turkish Government undertook to stop such practices,[38] but noted that the problem had not been resolved. In the course of this visit, the medical members of the delegation found marks of torture and ill-treatment on the bodies of persons examined and material evidence of the use of such practices as had been alleged. Torture equipment was found in police stations.[39]

Based on its first three visits the CPT's conclusions were that: the practice of torture and other forms of severe ill-treatment of persons in police custody remains widespread in Turkey, though there was no evidence of such treatment in the prisons and hospitals visited; both ordinary criminal suspects and persons held under anti-terrorism provisions were victims; both the police and to a lesser extent gendarmerie were involved in the ill-treatment. The Committee recommended that a number of measures be taken: legal safeguards against torture and other forms of ill-treatment needed to be reinforced and new safeguards introduced; education on human rights law matters and professional training for law enforcement officials had to be intensified; public prosecutors had to react expeditiously when confronted with complaints of torture and ill-treatment; the medical examinations of persons in police and gendarmerie custody carried out by the Forensic Institutes had to be broadened in scope and steps taken to guarantee the independence of both Forensic Institute doctors and other doctors who perform forensic tasks; there had to be specialized training and proper managerial control and supervision of law enforcement officials, including, *inter alia*, the institution of effective independent monitoring mechanisms; the maximum periods of detention had to be reduced; and access to an independent lawyer (though not necessarily a suspect's own lawyer), as well as a doctor other than one selected by the police, established as rights; suspects for whom extensions of custody were being sought should have to be physically brought before the court.

The Committee found that many existing legislative safeguards against torture were little more than dead letters. Torture and ill-treatment problems would not be eradicated, the CPT concluded, 'by legislative fiat alone': mentalities had to be transformed and the whole of the criminal justice system had to be involved.[40]

[37] Turkey PS 1, paras 12–16, Gen Rep 3, 33–34.

[38] At the time of the first visit a coalition government of the True Path Party (DYP), led by Mr Süleyman Demirel (who was to become President of the country following the death of former President Mr Turgut Özal), and the Social Democrat People's Party (SHP), led by Prof Dr Erdal İnönü, was in power.

[39] Turkey PS 1, paras 17–20; Gen Rep 3, Appendix 4, 34–35.

[40] Turkey PS 1, paras 26–37; Gen Rep 3, 36–39.

(c) National and international background and the consequences of the 1992 Public Statement

The findings of the CPT were consistent with what had already been observed and declared by Turkish non-governmental human rights organizations. The two main domestic NGOs are the Human Rights Association of Turkey (HRAT) and the Human Rights Foundation of Turkey (HRFT). The HRFT produces well documented annual reports which receive considerable attention in national and international human rights circles.[41] A summary of the information presented under the heading of 'torture' in the 1991 Annual Report reveals that 168 separate reports containing allegations of torture were received by the HRFT in 1991 and for 218 of the 552 people involved these allegations were supported by official medical reports. In addition, 23 people lost their lives under suspicious circumstances whilst in police custody or prison. The same Report also records that 152 deaths occurred under suspicious circumstances as a result of torture, extrajudicial executions, and unnecessary force used by security forces.[42] Subsequent annual reports paint a similar picture.[43]

The work of international organizations also illustrates Turkey's record regarding torture and ill-treatment. For example, the CAT has brought its heaviest sanction to bear against Turkey.[44] Article 20 of the UNCAT authorizes the CAT to determine whether there are well-founded indications that torture is being systematically practised in the territory of a state party and, if so, to request an on-site inquiry. In its first use of this procedure, the CAT requested permission to visit Turkey. The Turkish Government initially refused but in November 1991 permission was given for two CAT members and their staff to visit Turkey and a visit of nearly

---

[41] The HRAT also publishes many reports both on a monthly and an annual basis mostly in Turkish. Statistical information given in the HRAT reports generally confirms the numbers given in the HRFT reports.

[42] HRFT (1992) *Turkey Human Rights Report 1991* (Ankara: HRFT).

[43] The 1992 Report records 17 deaths in custody, 8 disappearances after detention, and 594 known cases of torture. The 1993 Report records 29 deaths in detention and prisons, 13 disappearances after detention, and 827 known cases of torture. The 1994 Report records 34 deaths in detention or in prison, 49 disappearances after detention, and 1,128 known cases of torture. The 1995 Report records 19 deaths in detention and prisons, 94 disappearances after detention, and 1,232 known cases of torture. During 1995 a total of 713 persons received medical treatment from the Rehabilitation Centres for the Victims of Torture established by the HRFT.

[44] Turkey signed the UN Convention against Torture on 25 January 1988 and promulgated the Law on the Approval of the Ratification of the UN Convention Against Torture, Law No 3441, 21 April 1988 (Official Gazette, 29 April 1988, no 19799). The official Turkish translation of the Convention was published in the Official Gazette, 10 July 1988, no 19895. This text also covered the 'declaration' made by the Government of the recognition of the competence of the CAT under Articles 21 and 22 of the Convention. The instrument of ratification was deposited on 2 July 1988. The Convention entered into force with regard to Turkey on 1 September 1988.

two weeks took place in June 1992. The visiting delegation reported to the full CAT and the CAT adopted their report, which was subsequently transmitted to the Turkish Government. The Government objected to the publication of the report but, acting in accordance with Article 20(5), the CAT adopted a *Summary account of the results of the proceedings concerning the inquiry on Turkey* on 9 November 1993. This was published in the CAT's Annual Report to the UN General Assembly.[45] The Report clearly underlines the prevalence of torture in Turkey.

... torture is practised systematically when it is apparent that the torture cases reported have not occurred fortuitously in a particular place or at a particular time, but are seen to be habitual, widespread and deliberate in at least a considerable part of the territory of the country in question. Torture may in fact be of a systematic character without resulting from the direct intention of a Government. It may be the consequence of factors which the Government has difficulty in controlling, and its existence may indicate a discrepancy between policy as determined by the central Government and its implementation by the local administration. Inadequate legislation which in practice allows room for the use of torture may also add to the systematic nature of this practice.[46]

The Turkish authorities who ... have publicly condemned torture as a crime against humanity, should take measures that such a provision [Article 2(2) of the Convention] is implemented strictly by all State authorities. Particular attention should be paid to implementation of this provision in the provinces under a state of emergency.[47]

In this connection, efforts should be made to prevent certain departments within the Ministry of Interior in particular from becoming as it were, a State within a State and appearing to escape control by senior authorities, (para 43); Although the Turkish Government has taken initiatives to combat torture, the current situation is still one in which torture is systematically practised in various premises under the authority of the Ministry of Interior. There is an obvious discrepancy between, on the one hand, the measures taken and the intentions expressed by the authorities with regard to action to combat torture, and on the other, the practice followed in Ministry of Interior premises.[48]

The Turkish Government's reaction to the CAT's published summary account was made public in a statement made in Geneva on 24 November 1993[49] and in a letter dated 29 November 1993 addressed to the Secretary General in New York.[50] The former focused particularly on the confidential

---

[45] UNGA Off Rec A/48/44/Add.1, 1–11. The summary account is also reproduced in 14 *HRLJ* 426–430. For comment see Gemalmaz, MS (1997) 'The Activities of the CAT: November 1991–April 1994 Era and the summary account of the results of the proceedings concerning the inquiry on Turkey' (in Turkish), 17–18 *İnsan Hakları Yıllığı* (Yearbook of Human Rights), 121–147.

[46] UNGA Off Rec A/48/44/Add.1, para 39.   [47] Ibid, para 42.   [48] Ibid, para 51.

[49] For this statement, made by the Permanent Representative of Turkey in Geneva, Ambassador Mr Gündüz Aktan, see 14 *HRLJ* 430–432.

[50] Made by the Permanent Representative of Turkey to the UN, Ambassador Mr Ünal Batu

report prepared by the two members of the CAT rather than the content of the summary account. Although the statement criticized the CAT it conceded that:

The Turkish Government has never denied the fact that sporadic cases of torture may occur in Turkey. Besides, it is almost impossible to completely eliminate torture in a struggle against a savage terrorism. Therefore, we admit that governments should be extremely vigilant in their combat against torture . . . There are a set of recommendations in the report with which we are already familiar. The core of them is reduction of the detention period. The existence of a relatively long detention period in state of emergency areas is taken as a priori evidence to the existence of torture. This is wrong. Moreover, the length of detention is of crucial importance for the combat of terrorism. That was why even in some European countries there existed a practice of precautionary detention until not long ago. The Turkish Government, at this stage, is not prepared to reduce the detention period in order to satisfy the authors of the organized torture allegations, whose main objective is fatally to curb the efficiency of the fight with terrorism. The murder of an innocent child is more important than all the allegations put together . . .[51]

In short, the CAT's conclusions as stated in the *Summary Account* of 1993 were consistent with those of the CPT in its 1992 Public Statement.

3. THE CPT'S VISITS TO TURKEY: THE SECOND PERIOD (1993–1994) AND ITS CONSEQUENCES

In this second period the CPT visited Turkey twice, in 1993 and 1994. Both visits took a different form from those in the previous period.

(a) The December 1993 visit

From 7 to 9 December 1993, a year after the Public Statement had been issued, a delegation of the CPT held talks with Ministers and senior officials in Ankara. These talks formed part of the 'on-going dialogue' between the Turkish authorities and the CPT and no places of detention were visited.[52] The timing, duration, and form of this visit suggests that its purpose was to re-establish mutual confidence and co-operation rather than to determine

(see UNGA Off Rec A/C.3/48/21, 1 December 1993). Mr Batu stated that, 'the text of the letter and its annex were circulated as a document of the General Assembly under agenda item 114(a)'. The annex of the letter was entitled 'The views of the Government of Turkey with regard to the *Summary account of the results of the proceedings concerning the inquiry on Turkey* of the Committee against Torture'.

[51] The Turkish translation of the text of the statement made by Ambassador Mr Gündüz Aktan was published in one of the Turkish dailies as a series of articles. See Gemalmaz, MS, *Cumhuriyet*, 18–21 September 1997, 4.

[52] Gen Rep 4, para 3.

whether there was any improvement in the incidence of torture and ill-treatment. The visit attracted little attention in the Turkish press. A short notice in *Hürriyet* noted:

Turkey is once again inspected for human rights. The CPT established by the Council of Europe is continuing its contacts in Ankara. It is noted that, this visit is the continuation of the CPT's visit held on 22 November 1992 in Turkey. The Deputy Spokesman of the Ministry of Foreign Affairs, Mr. Ferhat Ataman, stated that 'Turkey publicizes its political will to prevent torture'. The Spokesman stated that, 'Turkey has already taken concrete steps directed to this end; Turkey maintains the rule of law despite the existence of terrorism'. The CPT also visited State Ministers Concerning Human Rights, the Minister of Internal Affairs and the Minister of Justice.[53]

As this report shows, there is little knowledge of the Convention and the CPT within the Turkish media and, like the Turkish authorities, the media are not overly keen to publicize its work.

(b) The October 1994 visit

The CPT carried out a *follow-up* visit to Turkey from 16 to 28 October 1994 to examine developments since the 1992 Public Statement.[54]

This was a more wide-ranging visit than those undertaken previously: a total of nine locations involving twenty-four separate establishments (eleven police stations, five gendarmerie stations, seven prisons, and the Hac Camp) were visited, embracing five provinces and four districts. Moreover, most of the places visited—20 of the total of 24—were in the south-east region of Turkey which is subject to a state of emergency (the remaining four being in Ankara and İstanbul).[55] This visit, then, marked an upturn in CPT activity in Turkey. It also suggested that, despite the 1992 Public Statement and the reaction of the Turkish authorities, the relationship between the parties remained stable. It indicates that the CPT has continued to focus its attention on the south-east of the country and this parallels the work of other intergovernmental and non-governmental human rights organizations.

The visit nevertheless failed to attract much attention in the national press, which neither follows up the activities of the CPT, nor disseminates any official information on the subject provided by the Turkish authorities. There was some coverage in *Özgür Ülke*, according to which the military security unit known as 'Jitem' in Diyarbakır province was evacuated and detainees were transferred to other places and its building painted in

---

[53] *Hürriyet*, 9 December 1993 (all newspaper quotations are translations from the Turkish by the author).
[54] Gen Rep 5, para 1.
[55] For details of the custodial sites visited see Gen Rep 5, Appendix 3, 21–22.

preparation for a possible visit by the CPT delegation.[56] According to another article in the same paper, the CPT delegation met with the HRAT and the HRFT. The Secretary General of the HRAT, Mr Hüsnü Öndül, is reported to have informed Mr Jan Malinowski, a member of the delegation,[57] of incidents of torture occurring during the previous two years, of the recent disappearance of Mr Kenan Bilgin, and to have presented a file on the situation in Diyarbakır prison. It was also reported in the press that the CPT visited the Deep Research and Examination Laboratory unit (the *Derin Araştırmalar ve İncelemeler Laboratuarı* or *DAL*) in the Ankara Police Headquarters, where it was alleged the police were hiding three detainees about to be taken before the State Security Court (SSC). Whilst in the SSC Prosecutor's office, these detainees were examined by medical members of the delegation who observed signs of torture on their bodies. The police reportedly threatened the detainees in order to ensure that they would not say that they had been ill-treated.[58] A few days later it was reported that one of the three detainees, Mr İ Özçelik, was again detained by the police soon after the CPT delegation left the country.[59] Clearly, the Turkish security authorities tend to hide torture and forms of ill-treatment and its victims rather than strive to eliminate such abuses of power.

Though the CPT did not visit Turkey in 1995 the Committee continued to receive reports of torture and ill-treatment by Turkish law enforcement officials.

4. THE CPT'S VISITS TO TURKEY: THE THIRD PERIOD (1996) AND ITS CONSEQUENCES

During the course of 1996 the CPT visited Turkey three times and the year closed with the issuing of a second Public Statement. It was a year of controversy in which the visits of the CPT attracted considerably greater attention internally than had previously been the case.

(a) The May 1996 visit

The first visit was carried out in May 1996[60] when the coalition government of the Motherland Party (ANAP) and True Path Party (DYP) was in power. The first report of this visit occurred on 8 May and the scope and possible international and internal consequences, as well as the reaction of the Turkish press to this visit, were examined in a series of six articles published

---

[56] *Özgür Ülke*, 22 October 1994, 8.
[57] In fact, Mr Malinowski is a member of the CPT Secretariat.
[58] *Özgür Ülke*, 19 October 1994, 8.   [59] *Özgür Ülke*, 24 October 1994, 7.
[60] Gen Rep 7, para 4.

in the national press.[61] It is instructive to consider the CPT's visit on the basis of this reportage. *Cumhuriyet* reported that a CPT delegation comprising the CPT President, Mr Claude Nicolay, Vice-President Ms Ingrid Lycke Ellingsen, and Secretary Ms Mayer had a meeting with the Prime Minister Mr Mesut Yılmaz (leader of the Motherland Party) for one and a half hours at the İstanbul Swiss Hotel on 7 May. A press communiqué was handed to reporters after the meeting which indicated that the delegation would continue its visit until 10 May.[62] Another newspaper, *Evrensel*, wrote as follows:

The CPT President stated that he did not have power to make a statement. He invited journalists to put their questions to the Prime Minister. On the insistence of the journalists, he declared that, 'They had not been able to find adequate grounds for the exchange of views'.[63]

Hürriyet published a different account of events:

The members of the European Human Rights Commission centred in Helsinki carried out investigations in the İstanbul Police Headquarters. It is reported that members of the Commission inspected in particular the Anti-Terror Section, the Security Department and the Foreigners' Bureaus and especially examined interrogation rooms and custody cells. After the investigations, which would take a few more days, the members of the Commission would go to Ankara for further meetings.[64]

Although the CPT did indeed visit the İstanbul Police Headquarters this inaccurate report (the CPT has nothing to do with the European Commission on Human Rights and neither are based in Helsinki) was not attributed to any source, but were it to have stemmed from the police or other authorities it would suggest that even they were ill-informed.

Press coverage continued. According to *Cumhuriyet*, the CPT visit to İzmir province:

... has alarmed the Police Headquarters of İzmir. Over the radios of the police and Gendarmerie, there was a call to arrange the detention rooms. The delegation, following the investigations in İstanbul and Ankara and a meeting with Prime Minister Mr. Yılmaz, will continue its activities in İzmir today. The preparations commenced before the arrival of the CPT members to İzmir. By means of police and Gendarmerie radio announcements, officials were warned to be attentive at visiting sites. Moreover, by drawing attention to the expectation that the visit of the delegation would not be limited to a particular institution, it has been ordered that detention rooms be scrutinized and reorganized to see that they are in order.[65]

---

[61] See Gemalmaz, MS, 'Avrupa İşkenceyi Önleme Komitesi Yeniden Türkiye'de: 1–6' ('The CPT is once again in Turkey: 1–6'), *Bizim Gazette*, 30 May, 6, 13, 20, and 27 June, and 4 July 1996. The articles were reproduced in *Evrensel* between 20 May and 24 June.
[62] *Cumhuriyet*, 8 May 1996, 7.   [63] *Evrensel*, 8 May 1996, 3.
[64] *Hürriyet*, 8 May 1996, 25.   [65] *Cumhuriyet*, 9 May 1996, 7.

This suggests, first, that the detention and interrogation rooms in İzmir security departments did not bear scrutiny. Secondly, that officials were alerted to make temporary and possibly misleading arrangements in order to prevent the delegation discovering the true situation. *Hürriyet* now reported the meeting between the delegation and the Prime Minister:

The delegation, composed of five members, met Mr. Yılmaz in İstanbul yesterday. The members of the Committee directed searching questions to Mr. Yılmaz on the subject of torture. In response to members asking 'Why is torture still practised in Turkey?' Mr. Yılmaz stated that, 'Even though we pay great attention, because of our struggle against terror, cases of torture unfortunately still occur. However, a cessation of the state of emergency regime will decrease torture cases'. Mr. Yılmaz responded to the question 'Why is there no Ministry of Human Rights?' as follows: 'Each minister of our government is responsible for human rights'. According to information *Hürriyet* has received from governmental circles, the detention periods which may be increased up to one month in cases of crimes falling within the jurisdiction of State Security Courts (SSCs) will be decreased to a period of ten days by an amendment in the Turkish Penal Procedure Code. Consistent with this news, 'Prime Minister Mr. Yılmaz promised the CPT to decrease the detention period applicable for terrorist offences and the offences falling within the jurisdiction of the SSCs'.[66]

Evrensel noted that the delegation:

met the Minister of Internal Affairs, Mr. Ülkü Güney and the Minister of Health, Mr. Yıldırım Aktuna on 8 May and also carried out an investigation in detention and interrogation rooms of Ankara Police Headquarters. The Directorate of Police was aware of the visit, so cells were generally kept vacant and the investigations were made in the absence of the press.[67]

Finally, *Bizim Gazette* reported on the meeting held between the delegation and Minister of Health. It reported that after a one and a half hour meeting Mr Aktuna stated:

It could have been easier if there was no terrorism in Turkey. Obstacles arise from the current terrorism and the activities of the extreme leftist organizations in relation to it. However, we struggle against these and endeavour to prevent torture and protect human rights . . . the doctors of the health care units examining persons kept under detention will be trained on 4–5 June 1996 and informed on how to perform their duties.

The newspaper indicated that the meeting was good-humoured and that the Minister had made a joke during the course of it:

One of the members of the delegation was smoking and I wanted to make a joke. I said, 'Human rights has become an ideal, but some circles may turn this ideal into an obsession. They may go so far as to take action against those smoking within the

---

[66] *Hürriyet*, 9 May 1996, 31.   [67] *Evrensel*, 9 May 1996, 11.

community and harming others'. The delegate said that there existed an ash-tray. I said this was a trap and that the interdiction was posted on the wall. Everybody laughed. It was an intelligent and witty exchange.[68]

These press reports give an insight into the nature and scope of the CPT's mission in Turkey. First, the comments attributed to the Prime Minister concerning a decrease in the detention period for crimes falling within the jurisdiction of SSCs appears to have been an important and unheralded statement on which one might expect the press to focus. This was not the case: the press probably considered the comment to be of little significance. The relevant law[69] had been heavily criticized in both national and international human rights circles and if the national administration circles had been ready for such an amendment much greater political capital would have been made of it. The Prime Minister's comments are best seen as an attempt to divert the CPT which did not fool the press. It was not a sensible strategy to follow since the CPT is likely to criticize the authorities for the non-fulfilment of promises.

Secondly, the argument, allegedly made to the CPT both by the Prime Minister and Minister of Health, that there is a relationship between the struggle against terrorism and the phenomenon of torture implies that attempts to combat terrorism can justify torture and other forms of ill-treatment. It also suggests that the absence of terrorism would lead to the elimination of torture. However, the CPT and other national and international NGOs and intergovernmental human rights organizations have found that the practice of torture and other forms of ill-treatment are systematic and widespread in Turkey and that almost any suspect—male or female, children or adult, the suspects of ordinary crimes or terrorism—is vulnerable. Whatever one's views on this question, the very use of the argument by ministers is tantamount to confessing to state terrorism. Thirdly, the Prime Minister's argument that were the state of emergency to cease, the incidence of torture would decrease, implies that there is a direct relationship between the two phenomena. It suggests that torture and ill-treatment are inevitable under a state of emergency and cannot be prevented. From a legal perspective, domestic law does not permit the suspension of the right not to be subjected to torture and ill-treatment in a state of emergency. The problem stems from the frequent abuse of power by law enforcement officials and the indirect and direct toleration of such abuses by political, administrative, and judicial figures.

States of emergency have been so common in Turkey that they have become the norm. The south-east of the country has been subject to either martial law or a state of emergency continuously since 1978. Moreover, since the establishment of the Turkish Republic in 1923, the entire country

---

[68] *Bizim Gazette*, 9 May 1996, 3.   [69] No 3842 of 18 November 1992.

has been governed with exceptional regimes for approximately half of its seventy-five years.[70] This does much to explain the deep-rooted and complicated nature of the problems posed by torture and ill-treatment in Turkey today. Once again, to link torture and states of emergency is tantamount to confessing to a breach of Turkey's international human rights obligations. The UNCAT, Article 2(2), provides that 'no exceptional circumstances whatsoever, whether a state of war or a threat of war, internal political instability or any other public emergency may be invoked as a justification of torture'.

Fourthly, the manner in which the Minister of Health, who is by training a psychiatrist, is reported to have made a joke relating the prohibition of smoking and the prohibition of torture is extraordinary. It is unusual for someone to boast about the quality of their own jokes, but to boast about a joke involving the point of view that 'some circles could turn human rights into an obsession' to an international body whose main task is the prevention of torture reflects, at the very least, an astonishing lack of sensitivity.

The final stages of this visit were also reported in the national press. Following its inspections in İstanbul and Ankara the CPT was reported to have moved on to İzmir and Manisa provinces. According to *Cumhuriyet*, the delegation:

> ... stimulated the city. The arrangements started a week before and units of the Police were inspected last night. The Governor of the city, Mr. Muzaffer Ecemiş, came to the Police Headquarters of Manisa early in the morning. The Governor and the Director of the Police, Mr. Kemal İskender inspected the detention rooms. Mr. İskender, before the arrival of the delegation to Manisa responded to the reporters' questions on torture. He said, 'there is no torture. There is nothing we can not give account of. All the detention rooms completely meet the standards'. The CPT delegation also met the Director of Police. The delegation then met the doctor and examined the medical records. Afterwards they went to the Manisa Bar Association. It has been a crowded day at the Bar Association. The delegation talked separately to M.A., Ö.Z., A.K., F.A.S., E.T., K.K., Jale Kurt, Hüseyin Kurt who alleged they had been tortured in the Police Headquarters.[71]

Evrensel wrote as follows:

The delegation arrived in Manisa in the early hours yesterday and met the Director of Police first. The Vice-President, Ingrid Lycke Ellingsen, and a member,

---

[70] See Gemalmaz, MS (1990) 'State of Emergency Rule in the Turkish Legal System: Perspectives and Texts', 11–12 *Turkish Yearbook of Human Rights* 1–42; (1991) 'Historical Roots of Martial Law within the Turkish Legal System: Perspectives and Texts', 13 *Turkish Yearbook of Human Rights* 73–145; (1992) '1920–1950 Martial Law in Turkey: Is it an Additional Measure or a Main Instrument for Repression? Perspectives and Texts', 14 *Turkish Yearbook of Human Rights* 85–115.

[71] *Cumhuriyet*, 11 May 1996, 1 and 4.

Trevor Stevens, were in the delegation. After the meeting members of the delegation made no statement to the press. Mr. İskender (Director of Police) responded to the reporters: 'Am I Don Quixote to make declarations?' The delegation went to Manisa Central Health Institution No. 2 in order to meet the doctor who gave a medical report of torture. The delegation then went to meet child torture victims, their families and a member of parliament Mr. Sabri Ergül at the Court House. The victims who met the delegation, Jale Kurt, B.S., A.A. and Ö.Z. who are still undergoing trial by the Court, stated that some of the policemen who tortured them were among the persons accompanying the delegation.[72]

According to another newspaper *Yeni Yüzyıl*:

the members of the CPT carried out investigations in İzmir and Manisa. Two of the members came to Manisa and three to İzmir. The CPT members met Director of Police in Manisa Mr. Kemal İskender and the Public Prosecutor Mr. Muzaffer Çelebi.[73]

Some general conclusions can be drawn concerning the nature of the national press coverage of this final stage of the CPT's May 1996 visit. First, only a small number of mainly left-wing Turkish daily papers followed the activities of the CPT seriously. Secondly, the content of the press reports is limited and sometimes inaccurate and contradictory. Finally, there are issues concerning the sources of the information. Newspaper reporters are rarely the source of information in Turkey. The sources are either a national semi-official news agency (the Anatolian Agency) or the Security units themselves. Although some newspapers did assign their own reporters, the errors suggest that they had not been well briefed on the CPT, its powers, and its previous activities in Turkey, and that both the items prepared by the reporters themselves or the information obtained from other sources were not subjected to serious scrutiny before publication. The coverage of the CPT's visit to Manisa province also revealed that prior to the visit the Provincial Governor inspected police establishments to see whether the interrogation rooms were in conformity with relevant standards. This raises the question as to why the Governor had not previously inspected these places as an advance preparation for the CPT.[74] The CPT was followed by National Security agents. Reporters listening to police radios found out that the delegation was also being followed by the police. Moreover, the children who met the delegation and who claimed to be the victims of torture stated that some of the officers who had tortured them were among

---

[72] *Evrensel*, 11 May 1996, 11.   [73] *Yeni Yüzyıl*, 11 May 1996, 5.

[74] Interestingly, this visit to İzmir and Manisa was not specifically referred to in the 7th General Report which merely noted that: 'The Bureau [of the CPT] also went to the Police Headquarters in four Turkish cities, in order to evaluate the implementation in practice of instructions designed to prevent torture and ill-treatment which were issued by the Prime Minister and the Minister of Interior in February 1995' (Gen Rep 7, para 4). However, it is clear that the Manisa province visit was related to the 'teenager torture victims case'.

those accompanying the delegation. This is evidence of the extent to which the authorities sought to keep both the CPT delegation, and persons alleging torture, under pressure.

The CPT met the Public Prosecutor of Manisa, some of the lawyers from the Manisa Bar Association, a doctor from the Manisa Central Health Institution, the police chief of Manisa, and individuals claiming to be victims of torture and their families. It also examined the medical records of the Health Institution and inspected the interrogation rooms of the police establishments. Given that such investigations are already within the mandate of the Committee, there would seem to be no reason not to provide similar investigative powers to relevant national bodies such as Bar Associations and the Human Rights Commission of the Turkish Parliament. Were this done—and the CPT has recommended that it should be done—this would significantly enhance the protection of detainees as well as fulfil the obligation on Turkey to bring its national legislation into line with international human rights standards.

(b) The 19–23 August 1996 visit

In the summer of 1996 twelve prisoners died while participating in hunger strikes which had broken out in prisons across the country in protest at the official response to requests from prisoners for improved prison conditions.[75] These hunger strikes put the conditions of the infamous Eskisehir province prison back on the public agenda[76] and, in the face of internal and international pressure, the Turkish Government decided to invite the CPT to visit it. This was the first time that the CPT had been invited by a state party to carry out a visit and it is interesting to note that it was not mentioned in the second Public Statement on Turkey which was issued in December 1996. In consequence, there is no published record of the CPT's findings or recommendations[77] though the Committee did take the unprecedented step of issuing a press release following the visit. This was intended to correct certain impressions which had been conveyed in the Turkish media.

According to *Cumhuriyet*:

The Ministry of Foreign Affairs reports that a delegation of the CPT will come to Turkey on 19 August in order to examine the situation in the prisons.

---

[75] Political responsibility for these strikes lay with the new coalition government of the Islamic-oriented Welfare Party (RP) and the centre-right True Path Party (DYP). The Prime Minister was Mr Necmettin Erbakan (leader of the RP), the Deputy Prime Minister and Minister of Foreign Affairs Mrs Tansu Çiller (leader of the DYP), and the Minister of Justice, Mr Sevket Kazan (member of the RP).

[76] Following the 1991 general election, Eskisehir Prison was evacuated on the grounds that conditions were not compatible with accepted international standards.

[77] It was, of course, mentioned in the General Report for the year. See Gen Rep 7, para 2.

The delegation, will inspect the Eskisehir Prison. The Deputy Speaker of the Ministry of Foreign Affairs, Mr. Nurettin Nurkan, organized a press conference and said that the delegation comprising four members was invited by the Minister of Foreign Affairs Tansu Çiller. The delegation would first visit the Ministry of Justice and then go to Eskisehir Prison. It is reported that the delegation comprises one Belgian and a Norwegian independent Committee members and two experts. Following the reactions raised abroad by the death of 12 inmates during the hunger strike, the Minister of Foreign Affairs transmitted a message of invitation to the CPT in order to carry out investigations in Turkey.[78]

Bizim Gazette published a more detailed account:

The Speaker of the Ministry of Foreign Affairs Mr. Ömer Akbel stated that, following criticisms aimed at Turkey in relation to the deaths of 12 inmates as a result of the hunger strike, the CPT of the Council of Europe was invited to Turkey. Mr. Akbel said that some European authorities had sent messages of distress to the Minister of Foreign Affairs, Tansu Çiller, about the situation. Mr. Akbel added that, in her response to those persons Mrs. Çiller underlined that, 'it was observed that, Western public opinion was influenced by false information suggesting that these events were caused by prison conditions'. Mrs. Çiller, in her response also stated the following: 'There are no serious criticisms of ill-treatment applied in Turkish prisons in the reports of the CPT which is an impartial, objective institution and one of the most credible organs in the whole of Europe'. Mr. Akbel added that, 'Our Western friends would not let the situation be used against Turkey'. According to Mr. Akbel, the message also stated that, Turkey, unconstrained by criticisms addressed to her, has the will to continue improving the situation in the field of democracy and human rights. During the hunger strike, the German Minister of Foreign Affairs Mr. Klaus Kinkel, the French Minister of Foreign Affairs Mr. Herve de Charette, the Italian Minister of Foreign Affairs Mr. Lamberto Dini, the European Union Commissar Mr. Hans van den Broek and the Socialist Group President of the European Parliament Mrs. Pauline Green sent messages expressing concern and requested efforts to stop the hunger strikes.[79]

The reasoning behind the invitation to the CPT was probably that its previous visit reports had not been particularly critical of Turkish prison conditions. However, this was because during the first period of visits (1990–1992) the CPT mainly focused on the treatment of detainees in police custody.[80] Even so, the first Public Statement observed that there were

[78] *Cumhuriyet*, 8 August 1996, 7. The same story was also carried in *Hürriyet*, 8 August 1996, 28 and *Evrensel*, 8 August 1996, 11. Although it was correct in substance, the headline in *Cumhuriyet* wrongly stated: 'CPT: An Investigation in the Eskişehir Prison by the European Union'. *Evrensel* mistakenly referred to 'a Human Rights Delegation from the European Parliament . . .'. Both title and content were accurate in *Hürriyet*.

[79] *Bizim Gazette*, 30 July 1996, 1.

[80] During the 1990 visit five security establishments were visited, compared to three prisons. During the 1991 visit only three of the 12 places visited were prisons and during the 1992 visit only five out of 20 places visited were prisons. Moreover, Ankara Central Closed Prison and Diyarbakır-1 Prison were visited on each occasion and İstanbul Bayrampaşa Prison was visited twice, so that the CPT had experience of a total of only six prisons in Turkey during this period.

'problems which need to be addressed' in prisons,[81] and the number of prisons visited increased in later visits.[82] Moreover, the standards applied by the CPT were already accessible both from reports on conditions in other countries and the Committee's general reports.[83] If the relevant standards produced by the CPT and other international organs are taken into account,[84] the inadequacies of prison conditions in Turkey are clear.

At the time of the Eskisehir Prison visit further information was published in the Turkish press. *Evrensel* reported:

The CPT, visiting Turkey at the invitation of the Ministry of Justice, carried out an investigation at the Eskisehir Special Type Prison. Following the meeting with the Minister of Justice, Mr. Sevket Kazan in Ankara, the Committee members Ingrid Lycke Ellingsen, Lambert Kelchtermans, Gordon Lakes, Jean Pierre Restellini and Trevor Stevens escorted by four translators, went to the prison in three taxis in the morning. Eighty seven political prisoners and a total number of 352 detainees and prisoners and also Chief Prosecutor Süleyman Karaca were met individually by the Committee members until 7 p.m. It was observed that, the political prisoners shouted slogans such as 'freedom to prisoners', 'human dignity could beat torture' when the Committee members entered their cells. The members did not comment on their visit to the reporters waiting for them in front of the prison, but stated that their investigation would continue the following day. Eskisehir Chief Prosecutor Mr. Karaca stated that, in the course of the investigation the Committee members expected to see a terrible prison full of coffins, but were amazed at what they saw. 'We believe that the members of the delegation have a positive impression of the Prison' the Prosecutor said.[85]

According to *Cumhuriyet*:

The CPT members investigated Eskisehir Prison. They met detainees and prisoners individually for two days . . . Eskisehir Prosecutor Mustafa Can Bolat, who escorted the delegation, said that the Europeans stated that they were impressed by the prison. Mr. Bolat also added that during the visit the members of the delegation were surprised. They were of the opinion that the prison could not be classified as a coffin.[86]

---

[81] Turkey PS 1, para 22. Admittedly, this is somewhat masked by the context: the CPT underlined that, 'The Committee has heard very few allegations of ill-treatment by prison staff in the different prisons visited over the last two years, and practically none of torture. *Certainly, there are problems which need to be addressed in Turkish prisons*, but the phenomenon of torture is not one of them. As already indicated, the CPT's dialogue with the Turkish authorities on prison matters is on the whole progressing satisfactorily' (emphasis added).

[82] During the 1994 visit, seven of the 24 places visited were prisons. Of these, three had been visited previously and six, including the four visited for the first time, were in the south-east region. Thus the CPT had visited a total of ten different prisons in Turkey prior to its invitation to Eskisehir Prison.

[83] See, eg, the section on 'Health Care services in Prisons' contained in Gen Rep 3, paras 30–77.

[84] These standards, and their relationships, are set out and considered in detail elsewhere in this volume.

[85] *Evrensel*, 21 August 1996, 3.   [86] *Cumhuriyet*, 23 August 1996, 5.

Cumhuriyet later reported that:

According to the statement given by the Committee, the four day visit was carried out at the invitation of the Turkish Government and the Committee had reached a generally positive impression regarding conditions in the prisons.[87]

Bizim Gazette, however, reported that:

The members of the delegation did not comment on their visit but it was stated that they would prepare a report on it.[88]

The information published in the national press concerning the visit was generally inaccurate. According to the terms of the Convention and the operation of the principle of confidentiality, neither the CPT delegation nor the Turkish authorities were in a position to comment publicly on the visit at this stage. It is also clear that the main source of the reports which were printed was the semi-official Anatolian Agency. In the light of the nature of this press coverage, the CPT made a written official statement from Strasbourg soon after the visit in which the Committee underlined that:

The visit was organised following an invitation from the Turkish Government, which requested that the CPT visit Eskişehir Special Type Prison. . . . According to certain reports in the Turkish media, the CPT's delegation commented favourably upon the situation at Eskişehir Special Type Prison. Such reports are figments of the imagination; the CPT's delegation made no comments whatsoever concerning this prison establishment during its visit to Turkey.[89]

This official written reaction of the CPT to the dissemination of false information by the national press was published only in *Bizim Gazette* and *Evrensel*, which also published six articles concerning the August 1996 visit.[90] The remainder of the Turkish press was silent on the issue. This saga raises questions which need answering: in particular, do the national authorities bear any responsibility for the dissemination of false information on the CPT activities and could national authorities be in a position to take the initiative in declaring that information issued by the national press is incorrect?

---

[87] *Cumhuriyet*, 28 August 1996, 5.   [88] *Bizim Gazette*, 23 August 1996, 1.

[89] Council of Europe Press Release, 454(96) 27 August 1996. See also *Bizim Gazette*, 10 September 1996, 1, 'The CPT did not express any opinion on the Eskişehir Prison' (source not mentioned). Also, *Evrensel*, 10 September 1996, 3, 'The CPT: No Opinion Stated (source, Anatolian Agency).

[90] Gemalmaz, MS, 'Türkiye'nin Avrupa İşkenceyi Önleme Komitesi'ni davet etmesi:1–6' ('Turkey's invitation to the CPT for a visit: 1–6'), *Bizim Gazette*, 5, 12, 19, and 26 September, and 3 and 10 October 1996. The articles were reproduced in *Evrensel between* 12 August and 16 September 1996.

(c) The 18–20 September 1996 visit

The CPT again visited in September 1996.[91] Bursa and Sakarya provinces were visited for the first time. As with all the previous visits, the Turkish press paid little attention to this visit. In contrast to all previous visits, not even the national TV reported the fact. Although the CPT does not seek publicity, the manner in which the press responded to this visit suggests that there might be some explanation other than mere lack of information.

(d) The second Public Statement on Turkey (6 December 1996)

On 6 December 1996 the CPT issued its second Public Statement.[92] Two aspects will be considered: the content of the Statement and the response to it within Turkey.

(i) The contents of the second Public Statement

The Statement summarized the facts found during the CPT visits to Turkey between 1990 and 1992 and recorded that in the course of its subsequent visits in 1994 and 1996 the CPT had 'once again found clear evidence of the practices of torture and other forms of severe ill-treatment by the Turkish police'.[93] During the visits the CPT's forensic doctors examined a considerable number of persons and found marks or conditions consistent with allegations of recent ill-treatment by the police. The delegation once again found material evidence of resort to ill-treatment in the İstanbul Police Headquarters. These findings were transmitted to the Turkish authorities, but, according to the CPT, a reply received from the Turkish authorities on 22 November 1996 'failed to acknowledge the gravity of the situation'.[94] The CPT also listed many circulars issued by the Prime Minister, Minister of Interior, and Minister of Health to ensure that persons taken into custody are not ill-treated and to set out the required content of forensic certificates. The CPT concluded that, 'the need is not for more circulars, but rather for effective control and supervision of the activities of law enforcement agencies'.[95]

The Statement stressed again the ineffective judicial reaction to torture and ill-treatment and highlighted two important problems. First, although public prosecutors receive allegations from detained persons complaining of ill-treatment at the hands of police, they do not pay them serious attention: public prosecutors had 'a tendency to seek to defend the police rather than to view objectively the matter under consideration'.[96] Secondly, the

---

[91] For details of the places visited see Gen Rep 7, Appendix 3, 29.
[92] Turkey PS 2, issued on 6 December 1996. See also Gen Rep 7, paras 10–11.
[93] Turkey PS 2, para 2.   [94] Ibid, para 3.   [95] Ibid, paras 4–6.
[96] Ibid, para 7.

provisions of the Turkish Penal Code,[97] and the policy of the Turkish courts in relation to them, do not 'correspond to the seriousness of the offences involved'.[98] The CPT also underlined the need to reduce the maximum permitted periods of detention in police custody, particularly for suspects falling under the jurisdiction of SSCs. According to information provided to the CPT, the period of police custody for offences falling under the jurisdiction of the SSC was to be reduced to four days, with a possible extension to seven days by a decision of a judge. Under the state of emergency, the maximum period would be reduced to seven days, with a possible extension to ten days. The CPT concluded that 'such provisions, if enacted, would obviously represent a significant step in the right direction'.[99] However, the Committee also noted that:

The CPT has been informed that the Bill provides for a right of access to a lawyer after 4 days. In other words, access to a lawyer shall continue to be denied for 4 days; this is not acceptable ... The CPT recognizes that in order to protect the interests of justice, it may exceptionally be necessary to delay access by detained persons to a particular lawyer of their choice for a certain period. However, this should not result in the right of access to a lawyer being totally denied during the period in question. In such cases, access to another independent lawyer who can be trusted not to jeopardize the legitimate interests of the police investigation should be arranged ... The CPT wishes to reiterate that all persons detained by the police—irrespective of the offence of which they are suspected—should be granted, as from the outset of their custody, the right of access to an independent lawyer (although not necessarily their own lawyer) and to a doctor other than one selected by the police. Further, they should in principle have the right immediately to notify their next of kin of their situation; any possibility exceptionally to delay the exercise of that right should be clearly defined and strictly limited in time.[100]

Finally, the CPT referred to the problem of terrorism:

The CPT has made clear that it abhors terrorism and has recognized the serious difficulties faced by the Turkish authorities in this regard. According to the CPT, Turkey is entitled to the understanding and support of others in its struggle against this destructive phenomenon. However, the Committee has also emphasized that response to terrorism must never be allowed to degenerate into acts of torture or other forms of ill-treatment by law enforcement officials. Further, the information gathered by the CPT in the course of its visits to Turkey shows clearly that torture and ill-treatment are also inflicted by law enforcement officials upon ordinary criminal suspects. Consequently, it would be quite wrong to assume that the problem of torture and ill-treatment is simply an unfortunate consequence of the scale of terrorism in Turkey. The problem may well have been exacerbated by terrorism, but its roots go far deeper.[101]

---

[97] Article 243, the criminal offence of obtaining confessions by torture or inhuman treatment, and Article 245, the criminal offence of ill-treatment by law enforcement officials.
[98] Turkey PS 2, para 7.　　[99] Ibid, para 8.　　[100] Ibid, para 9.　　[101] Ibid, para 11.

One particular aspect of this Statement must be questioned. The CPT accepted that even though the right of access to a lawyer could never be denied, a person held under police custody, exceptionally and in the interests of justice, might have access not to his own lawyer but to 'another independent lawyer who [could] be trusted not to jeopardize the legitimate interests of the police investigation'. This approach may be acceptable elsewhere but is entirely unacceptable in the Turkish context. The CPT is surely aware that from time to time Turkish lawyers suffer serious persecution, including: murder, kidnapping, and death threats; office searches and confiscation of client files by the police without legal authorization; illegal interrogation by the police (according to Turkish law only the prosecutor is entitled to interrogate a suspect lawyer); and ill-treatment by the police both when taken into custody themselves and when visiting clients in custody. Both national and international non-governmental human rights organizations, and statements made by the Bar Associations, provide numerous examples of such cases.[102] Set against this background, the CPT's position opens a possible new door for the abuse of power and is arguably not compatible with the views of other intergovernmental human rights bodies. The question has to be asked: who, and under which legal and objective criteria, will determine that a particular lawyer may jeopardize the interests of justice?

(ii) The response within Turkey

The response to the second Public Statement within Turkey can be simply stated: it was virtually ignored. The national press, generally speaking, failed to note its significance. According to *Hürriyet*:

the CPT's second statement relating to Turkey accused Turkish authorities once again and stated that 'all the commitments given by the Turkish authorities were not followed'. During the visit, the CPT delegation also found some torture instruments.[103]

Cumhuriyet wrote that:

The CPT accused Turkey for a second time. The draft Bill submitted to the Turkish parliament in order to reduce the detention period was considered a positive step. But the CPT underlined the need for further measures.[104]

---

[102] In some cases before the European Commission on Human Rights, particularly in the years immediately following the recognition of the right of individual petition in January 1987, some applicants (including Turkish lawyers as well as their clients) were faced with serious threats and similar actions. Many such applications were declared admissible. See Reidy, A, Hampson, F and Boyle, K (1997) 'Gross Violations of Human Rights: Invoking the European Convention on Human Rights in the Case of Turkey', 15 *NQHR* 161–173.

[103] *Hürriyet*, 7 December 1996, 34.   [104] *Cumhuriyet*, 7 December 1996, 4.

Similar information was provided by *Yeni Yüzyıl*,[105] *Radikal*,[106] and *Bizim Gazette*.[107]

Many national human rights NGOs in Turkey remain unaware of the Public Statement and have therefore not given it publicity. Nor have the Turkish authorities, including the Ministry of Foreign Affairs, who are certainly well aware of its existence. As a consequence, and despite its importance, the second Public Statement was and is not an object of public knowledge, discussion, or concern within Turkey. It has had an impact only in the international sphere and has simply added a new item to the list of problems to be dealt with by the Turkish Foreign Ministry.

The effectiveness of this sanction by the CPT depends on the combined responses of international human rights circles, the state itself, and the people living within and under its jurisdiction. In Turkey the national human rights circles and lawyers' organizations are largely unaware of the potential for using the CPT and its Public Statements (in the absence of its Reports) to produce a demand for the elimination of torture and the restoration of the rule of law.

5. CONCLUSIONS

A few observations may now be ventured on the effectiveness of the CPT's activities in Turkey, the degree to which the Committee is taken seriously by the national authorities, and how far the Turkish public is aware of and acknowledges the functions of the Committee.

There is insufficient information concerning the ECPT and CPT in the Turkish media and there are very few publications of either an academic or generalist nature on the convention system. The policy of the national authorities is to keep information about the CPT's activities out of the public eye and this is buttressed by the principle of confidentiality since the information released by the CPT itself is insufficiently specific and not considered worth publishing.[108] Some of the national journalists apply

---

[105] *Yeni Yüzyıl*, 7 December 1996, 5.   [106] *Radikal*, 7 December 1996, 6.

[107] *Bizim Gazette*, 7 December 1996, 1. This paper also carried a series of articles by Gemalmaz, MS, 'Avrupa İşkencenin Önlenmesi Komitesi'nin Aralık 1996 Tarihli Türkiye Hakkında İkinci Kamuya Duyurusu: 1–9' ('The Second Public Statement on Turkey by the CPT of December 1996: 1–9') on 1, 8, 15, 22, and 29 May, and 5, 12, 19, and 26 June 1997.

[108] Language presents another potential problem. It is, perhaps, understandable that the Turkish authorities are not keen to translate and disseminate these Public Statements. The Council of Europe has produced an unofficial translation into Turkish of the full text of the second Public Statement (see Press Communiqué, ref 707 (96)). If the CPT Secretariat is not able to do so, there must be some organ of the Council of Europe which can also provide a full Turkish text of the first Public Statement. Although it might reasonably be argued that CPT visit reports cannot all be translated into local languages, this argument does not seem very strong in the case of shorter, infrequent, and exceptional Public Statements.

self-censorship when writing on the subject of human rights out of fear of prosecution or dismissal from their posts. In recent years the press has been subject to increasingly monopolistic control, with the consequence that trade unionism in this sector has declined. It should also be remembered that were an article or news item to give rise to legal proceedings, it could result in the imprisonment of the journalist and, if the author is anonymous, the editor being held responsible. Also in both cases it results in the imposition of heavy fines. Against this background, editorial decisions on whether to publish material on human rights issues are delicate and dangerous.

There is also a general feeling against international human rights organizations on the part of both the authorities and some sections of the national press and the public. They consider the missions and reports of many international human rights organizations to be politically rather than legally inspired. The need for state security in the face of both terrorism and religious fundamentalism weighs heavily in the public mind. In a consciously provocative atmosphere of fear, the distinction between the legal and the political has been fudged and the feeling that Turkey is surrounded by internal and international enemies has been strengthened.

If the CPT has difficulties in disseminating information about its work generally, it has particular difficulties in establishing fruitful co-operation with Turkish academic human rights circles or institutions, both with regard to exchanging and disseminating information.[109] The CPT members and Secretariat regularly declare that information within the mandate of the CPT and received in Strasbourg from individuals or institutions is welcomed, but that it is a one-way process. Experience teaches that this is not a recipe for a successful relationship and the possibility of establishing means for more efficient mutual exchange of information needs to be reconsidered as a matter of priority.

The Public Statements on Turkey have not surprisingly caused difficulties in the relationship between the CPT and the Turkish authorities. Yet it is clear that the Turkish Governments have taken some positive steps to try to restore that relationship, for example, by recently ratifying the First and Second Protocols to the ECPT. Moreover, Turkey has taken some legislative measures intended to assist in the prevention of torture and other forms of ill-treatment. These measures fall short of what is required

---

[109] Nevertheless, the then CPT President, Mr Nicolay, was invited to Turkey on two occasions to attend academic seminars. The first took place in November 1996 and was organized by İzmir Bar Association (shortly before the issuing of the second Public Statement). The second was in December 1997 and was organized by the Human Rights Centre of the İstanbul University Law Faculty. In both cases, despite the diplomatic and careful tone of his presentation, important messages could be read between the lines of his speeches. The author of this chapter gave more robust accounts of the messages sent by the work of the CPT but, once again, the Turkish press and authorities paid insufficient attention to what was being said.

to meet basic, minimum standards. For instance, the 'Law on the Amendment of Law of Penal Procedure and State Security Courts and the Law No 3842'[110] shortens detention periods. According to this Law the period of custody for ordinary crimes is twenty-four hours, which can be extended by a decision of a judge (at the request of the public prosecutor) if investigations are incomplete. For crimes committed by three or more persons and which are under the jurisdiction of the SSC, the initial period is forty-eight hours, extendable by written order of the public prosecutor for up to four days. If the investigation is still not complete, the custody period may be extended up to seven days, once again by judicial decision at the request of the public prosecutor. As regards those suspects arrested or detained under the state of emergency declared in accordance with Article 120 of the 1982 Constitution, this maximum period of seven days may be extended to ten days by judicial decision at the request of the public prosecutor. Although this is certainly an advance on the previous position, the recognized European minimum standard for the length of police custody is a maximum four days under normal circumstances and seven days under special regimes. Thus these new custody periods still fall short of accepted European standards.

The newly amended Law on State Security Courts also has a serious deficiency. Article 16 provides that suspects whose detention period in police custody has been extended to seven days shall not be permitted access to their lawyer. The corollary is that those who might be in a position to have their custody extended in this fashion cannot have access to their lawyer in the meantime. Since those under the jurisdiction of the SSC may be held for up to four days before this decision is taken, this means that during that period there is no opportunity to see a lawyer. The CPT constantly stresses that the first forty-eight hours is of vital importance for persons taken under police custody and that it is in this period that the risk of torture and other forms of ill-treatment is greatest. For a suspect to have the right of access to his or her lawyer, and also to be examined by an independent physician at the early stages of the custody, undoubtedly plays a key role in the prevention of possible abuse of power.

As these examples show, even in areas where moves have been made to accommodate and build bridges with the CPT, Turkish legislation still falls short of meeting the relevant standards. Against this background, the need for the CPT to continue its work, and for its work to gain a higher profile within Turkey, remains.

From both an internal perspective, given the existing legislation and law enforcement policies, and from an external perspective, given the considerable number of judicial and quasi-judicial decisions and Public

---

[110] Law No 4229, adopted 6 March 1997; Official Gazette, 12 March 1997.

Statements of international organs regarding torture and ill-treatment, it would not be surprising to see further condemnations in the future. However, all sides should bear in mind that whilst such practices cannot be tolerated, the overuse of the sanctions available to the international bodies threatens to undermine their effectiveness, particularly if they are not enforced or acted upon by the national authorities or are not well received by public opinion. In the light of this, the priority must be to establish and improve the quality of fruitful co-operation between the parties.

REFERENCES

Cameron, I (1988) 'Turkey and Article 25 of the European Convention on Human Rights', 37 *ICLQ* 887

Gemalmaz, MS (1989) *The Institutionalization Process of the Turkish Type of Democracy: A Politico-Juridical Analysis of Human Rights* (Istanbul)

Gemalmaz, MS (1991) 'Historical Roots of Martial Law within the Turkish Legal System: Perspectives and Texts', 13 *Turkish Yearbook of Human Rights* 73–145

Gemalmaz, MS (1992) '1920–1950 Martial Law in Turkey: Is it an Additional Measure or a Main Instrument for Repression? Perspectives and Texts', 14 *Turkish Yearbook of Human Rights* 85–115

Gemalmaz, MS (1994) *Right to Life and Prevention of Torture* (Istanbul)

Gemalmaz, MS (1997) 'The Activities of the CAT: November 1991–April 1994 Era and the summary account of the results of the proceedings concerning the inquiry on Turkey', 17–18 *Turkish Yearbook of Human Rights* 121

Polakiewicza, J and Jacob-Foltzer, V (1991) 'The European Human Rights Convention in domestic law: The Impact of the Strasbourg case-law where direct effect is given to the Convention (second part)', 12 *HRLJ* 140

Reidy, A, Hampson, F and Boyle, K (1997) 'Gross Violations of Human Rights: Invoking the European Convention on Human Rights in the Case of Turkey', 15 *NQHR* 161–173

Rumpf, C (1993) 'The Protection of Human Rights in Turkey and the Significance of International Human Rights Instruments', 14 *HRLJ* 394

Soysal, M (1989) 'The effect of international convention on the domestic law in Turkey' in *The Implementation in National Law of the ECHR, Proceedings of the Fourth Copenhagen Conference on Human Rights, 28–29/10/1988*

12

The CPT's Visits to the United Kingdom

STEPHEN SHAW

The United Kingdom offers, for two reasons in particular, an interesting viewpoint on the relevance and effectiveness of the CPT. First, because in comparison with most European states the UK is relatively well endowed with both official and unofficial monitors of almost all the institutions which come within the CPT's remit (military guardrooms being perhaps the one exception to that rule). Secondly, because the situation in Northern Ireland means the UK is one of the few European countries in which troops, intelligence agencies, and the criminal justice system are routinely engaged in a struggle to combat domestic terrorism. Four visits to the UK have been made to date—the first in 1990, the most recent (and, as yet, unreported) in 1997.

The first visit by a CPT delegation just involved England and concentrated upon five prisons: Brixton, Leeds, Wandsworth, Holloway, and Bulwood Hall. (Visits were also made to inner-city police stations in Leeds and London—including the high-security Paddington Green—all of which were given a clean bill of health.) This focus on prisons was undoubtedly part of the fallout from the riots at Strangeways and elsewhere which had occurred just four months previously (although disturbances had not, in fact, taken place at any of the five gaols visited). The CPT's visit coincided with the investigations of the Woolf Inquiry into the causes of the riots. Indeed, the publicity—which, to the CPT's displeasure, attached to its visit—added to the public view of Britain's prisons as antiquated and in need of thoroughgoing reform. The CPT repeated many of the criticisms made by Lord Woolf and his co-signatory, Stephen Tumim, although its strongly-worded report was not freely available until ten months after the Woolf Report itself had appeared.[1]

It is difficult to challenge the choice of Brixton, Leeds, and Wandsworth as prisons for the CPT to visit. At the time, they were amongst the very worst gaols in the country, suffering from what the CPT was to call a 'trinity of interrelated problems: overcrowding, lack of integral sanitation . . . and inadequate regime activities'.[2] It is not so much that the CPT had anything

---

[1] Woolf Report (1991) *Prison Disturbances April 1990*: Report of an Inquiry by the *Rt. Hon. Lord Justice Woolf (Part I and II)* and *His Honour Judge Stephen Tumim (Part II)*, Cm 1456 (London: HMSO).

[2] UK 1, para 36.

very new to say about these conditions, rather that it complemented the assessments made by Woolf and Tumim. The same is true of the CPT's equally strong criticisms of the then practice of segregating prisoners who were HIV positive.[3]

However, two issues advanced by the CPT, which were not covered by Woolf, are worthy of note. The first of these was the CPT's characterization of the body belt as 'a potentially dangerous form of restraint' and its demand for greater safeguards to govern its use.[4] Subsequently, a strengthening of procedures was put in place, although the British Government did not respond favourably to the CPT's hope that the body belt could be removed from the list of authorized restraints and the campaign to ban it completely continues.[5] The second, and of much greater impact, was its criticisms of Brixton's F Wing, then used to house prisoners with mental health problems and probably the most shameful part of the entire prison estate. Although measured in tone, the CPT's conclusion that F Wing did not have the means 'to deal in a medically appropriate way with severely mentally disturbed and violent patients' had a catalytic effect.[6] It was of particular help to the then governor in his campaign to reduce the number of mentally ill people held at Brixton and to improve facilities. Within two years of the CPT's visit, F Wing was no more and no prison unit remotely as barbaric now exists.

More generally, while finding no evidence of torture (as it has been the case on each occasion it has come to the UK), the CPT concluded that 'the cumulative effect' of overcrowding, slopping out, and lack of activity amounted to 'inhuman and degrading treatment'.[7] Perhaps predictably, this assessment was rejected by the British Government in its response to the report. Acknowledging that it is 'difficult to judge when inadequate facilities and an unpleasant environment can be said to constitute "inhuman and degrading treatment" ', the Government said that conditions needed 'considerable improvement' but 'were not so poor' as to merit the description of inhuman and degrading.[8]

Be that as it may, most of the response details ways in which the treatment of prisoners had been and was being improved. The triple use of cells in Leeds and Brixton had ended; young offenders had been transferred from Leeds to Moorland; major building works were in place; and so on. Stating that 'work is in hand or planned to address most of the other recommendations made by the Committee', the response referred explicitly to the White Paper, *Custody, Care and Justice*, issued in reply to (and repeating much of) the Woolf Report.[9]

---

[3] UK 1, paras 166–168.   [4] Ibid, paras 92–93.   [5] UK 1 R 10.
[6] UK 1, para 59.   [7] Ibid, para 57.   [8] UK 1 R 1, para 6.
[9] Home Office (1991) *Custody, Care and Justice: The Way Ahead for the Prison Service in England and Wales*, Cm 1647 (HMSO 1991).

Can it be said that the first CPT visit made a substantive difference? Probably not, given the Strangeways riot, the Woolf proposals, and the political will which then existed to implement them. But it undoubtedly contributed to a climate of opinion—and strengthened the hand of reform-minded officials and governors. British prisons needed kick-starting into the twentieth century. Through its 1990 visit, the CPT was one of the actors applying the boot.

That first visit was carried out under the CPT's *periodic* programme. In contrast, the visit to prisons (to interview prisoners as much as to inspect the facilities), police stations, and holding centres in Northern Ireland in 1993 was an *ad hoc* visit following 'a number of reports containing allegations of ill-treatment of persons suspected of offences related to terrorism by the security forces'.[10] In particular the focus was upon the three police stations known as 'holding centres' at Gough Barracks, Armagh, and Castlereagh, at which persons detained under the Prevention of Terrorism Act were then questioned.

The CPT's report, published in November 1994, said there was 'legitimate concern about the treatment of persons detained at the holding centres'.[11] A 'substantial proportion' of those detained for terrorist offences 'alleged that they had been ill-treated . . . at the time of their arrest and/or during their detention at the holding centres'.[12] Criticizing the fact that interviews with people detained under the Prevention of Terrorism Act were not tape-recorded, the CPT asserted that 'instances of physical ill-treatment have sharply decreased (although not entirely disappeared) in recent times; however, that decline has apparently not been matched by a fall in instances of psychological forms of ill-treatment'. It was implied that these psychological forms of ill-treatment—to which persons detained in Northern Ireland under the Prevention of Terrorism Act ran 'a significant risk'— included death threats and blackmail.[13] The CPT also criticized physical conditions, especially at Castlereagh (the absence of exercise facilities and the absence of natural light), and the various restrictions placed on the right of access to a lawyer.

The British Government's response is short, sharp, and less than fulsome. Allegations of ill-treatment 'are easily made and form part of the strategy of some terrorist suspects'.[14] The demand for a right of access to an independent lawyer 'does not take account of the differing situations in Northern Ireland and England and Wales'.[15] As to the electronic recording of interviews, this 'would inhibit still further the chances of lawfully obtaining information that would lead to the conviction of terrorists or to the saving of other people's lives'.[16] The Government of the United Kingdom 'cannot accept' the contention that suspects face a considerable

---

[10] UK 2, para 5.   [11] Ibid, para 35.   [12] Ibid, para 27.   [13] Ibid, para 34.
[14] UK 2 R 1, 8.   [15] Ibid, 12.   [16] Ibid, 18.

degree of psychological pressure. Furthermore, the Government 'would respectfully advise the Committee' that all RUC officers are fully aware of the law and regulations governing unacceptable and unprofessional behaviour.[17] However, the UK does accept that conditions at Castlereagh are unsatisfactory—'this has also been highlighted by the Independent Commissioner for the Holding Centres'.[18]

All in all, it is difficult to see that the visit to Northern Ireland achieved a great deal. The tone of the UK Government response is unusually terse. However, as with the first visit in 1990, it is perhaps best to regard the CPT as one of a range of individuals and organizations keeping an eye on places of detention. The authorities in Northern Ireland may not welcome the extent of international oversight of their affairs. But such oversight (whether by the US Congress, or through the European Court of Human Rights, or the International Red Cross) is one reason why the ill-treatment which has undoubtedly occurred has not gone on to spawn torture or death squads or totally to undermine the rule of law. As the CPT itself points out, on eighteen occasions between 1989 and 1992, the Northern Ireland Office paid compensation on grounds of alleged assaults in the holding centres.

In May 1994, the CPT made its third visit (its second periodic visit) to the UK. For the first time, the visit included prisons and police stations in Scotland along with Immigration Service detention facilities and Rampton Special Hospital. However, the visit was most notable for the CPT's decision (under Article 8(5) of the Convention) to make immediate observations in respect of the holding of prisoners in the Main Bridewell Police Station in Liverpool. The prisoners concerned 'were being held in grossly overcrowded conditions . . . with no outdoor exercise and almost nothing that could be called a regime. Moreover, the regulations to which they were subject failed to provide them with adequate protection against the risk of ill-treatment.'[19] The delegation 'received allegations that prisoners . . . [were] taken under restraint to a distinctive cell, where they had been punched and kicked by police officers . . . the CPT has been led to conclude that remand and convicted prisoners . . . ran a not inconsiderable risk of physical ill-treatment by police officers'.[20]

Within four days of the CPT's intervention, all Prison Service prisoners had been transferred out of the Bridewell into Liverpool Prison. As the Prison Reform Trust had expressly advised the CPT of the circumstances obtaining in the Main Bridewell, I celebrate this demonstration of the Committee's boldness and influence. To no-one's surprise, Merseyside Police's later *internal* investigation found no evidence to substantiate the allegations of maltreatment.

The CPT also reported more generally on the use of police cells as

---

[17] UK 2 R 1, 21.   [18] Ibid, 9.   [19] UK 3, para 27.   [20] Ibid, para 22.

overflow accommodation for prisoners. As temporary accommodation for those being interviewed by the police, the cells seen by the CPT provided 'acceptable conditions'. But the Committee recommended 'as a matter of urgency'[21] the ending of the use of police cells to hold Prison Service prisoners. On grounds of cost alone, the Prison Service had a strong, material interest in ending the use of police cells. By June 1995, this had occurred.

During its time in England, the CPT was able to revisit Leeds and Wandsworth prisons. Improvements were noted in a number of respects, but the Committee was worried by the pace of increase in the prison population. An end to overcrowding by the mid-1990s—which, bizarrely as it now appears, was still being predicted by the UK authorities—was no longer a valid assumption: 'the United Kingdom authorities must be prepared to make more radical efforts to address the problem of over-crowding'.[22] Moreover, 'certain areas' of Leeds, Liverpool, and Wandsworth were still blighted by the same combination of overcrowding, lack of integral sanitation, and poor regime activities which the CPT had found amounted to inhuman and degrading treatment four years earlier.

In contrast, conditions in Immigration Service detention generally received a thumbs up as did (perhaps more surprisingly) Rampton Special Hospital. However, the CPT noted that: 'Security was omnipresent and seemed to take priority over treatment.'[23] Specific shortcomings were also noted in the seclusion rooms.

In Scotland, the CPT found little to comment upon in the four police stations which were visited. On the prisons side, the Committee's report includes allegations of two serious incidents of ill-treatment by staff at Shotts and Barlinnie. On the basis of documentation seen by the delegation, the CPT concluded that 'prisoners considered to be violent and/or disruptive may on occasion be the victims of ill-treatment, especially in the aftermath of a major incident'.[24]

Unlike the dismissive response which the CPT's report on its Northern Ireland visit received, the British Government is positively effusive in its response to the 1994 CPT visit. 'The Government welcomes the Committee's recognition of the improvement in accommodation standards and prison conditions.'[25] The Committee's report of its visit to Rampton is 'a balanced account of the major areas of concern . . . the Government is pleased to note the many positive observations'.[26] The Scottish Prison Service 'has reacted in a very positive manner to the Committee's recommendations'.[27]

Did the UK get off too lightly? Certainly the comments on Scottish

[21] Ibid, para 22.   [22] Ibid, para 79.   [23] Ibid, para 258.   [24] Ibid, para 309.
[25] UK 3 R 1, para 6.   [26] Ibid, para 8.
[27] 'Custody deaths provoke European Inquiry', *Guardian*, 8 September 1997.

prisons (which in terms of physical conditions lag well behind standards in England and Wales) might suggest so. Observers of the Special Hospitals may also be surprised by the relative mildness of the comments on Rampton. However, since the primary concern of the CPT visit was the state of the prisons in England, and since English prisons were undoubtedly improving greatly (albeit from a low base), the tone of both its report and the UK Government response reflects that rare period of penal optimism. (In any case, the press did not pick up on the more critical implications of the CPT's remarks about Leeds, Liverpool, and Wandsworth. Unlike the first, second, and fourth visits, there was little media interest.) The storm clouds were to regather by the time of the Committee's fourth visit to these shores in 1997.

At the time of writing, only a short press notice about the 1997 visit has been issued although, at its commencement, I was amongst those who met with the CPT delegation. (A misleading newspaper account, focusing disproportionately on the issue of deaths in custody, also appeared—the second time the CPT's rule of confidentiality had run into trouble in the UK.) The visit was again to England, plus the Isle of Man. This leaves Wales and the Channel Islands—the Ruritanian nature of whose criminal justice procedures might be of interest to the CPT—as the only parts of the UK not to be so honoured.

Matters which we know to have been of interest to the CPT included the efficacy of existing legal remedies in cases involving allegations of ill-treatment by police officers. It is of note that the CPT visited four London police stations (Brixton, Notting Hill, Peckham, and Streatham) serving areas in which relationships between the police and the local black community have been strained. (In 1994, the Committee had visited the no less controversial Stoke Newington Police Station, although finding nothing of note.) According to the press statement issued at the end of the Committee's visit, the CPT also made use of its time in England 'to review the measures being taken ... to tackle the problem of overcrowding in prisons'. As well as raising this issue in its meetings with Home Office Ministers and officials, the delegation visited Dorchester—a small but routinely overcrowded gaol—and the 'prison ship', HM Prison The Weare, moored nearby in Portland harbour.[28] In the Isle of Man, in addition to meeting the Chief Minister, other senior politicians, and officials, the CPT visited three police stations and the Headquarters of the Isle of Man Constabulary, plus the island's one prison in Douglas.

Judged overall, what is to be made of the CPT's watchdog role in regard to the UK? The truth is that, given the infrequency of its visits, the size and number of the UK's criminal justice systems, and the many domestic

[28] 'Visit by the European Committee for the Prevention of Torture to the United Kingdom and the Isle of Man', Council of Europe Press Release, September 1997.

monitoring processes which are in place, its impact can only ever be modest. But judged against that background, then the CPT has performed rather well. The places which the Committee has visited include most of the more controversial establishments of the 1990s. (Although, in time, the Committee may wish to visit other Special Hospitals and secure units within the mental health system, one or other of the top security prisons in England, places of confinement in military barracks, and secure provision for delinquent children.) Its reports have been generally accurate, pertinent, and hard hitting. And it can also demonstrate clear examples of its influence.

I have detailed two specific occasions when the involvement of the CPT has ended human rights abuses: its criticisms of the Liverpool Main Bridewell, and in condemnation of the treatment of the mentally ill at Brixton Prison. To those should be added the more general influence which the first CPT visit exerted at a time of major reform of the prison system in England and Wales. On the other hand, with the exception of its comments on the Liverpool Bridewell, the Committee's report on its 1994 visit was excessively complimentary. And it is difficult to see what was achieved by the CPT's 1993 foray into Northern Ireland except to act as a reminder to the authorities that here was another international body with a watching brief over affairs in the Province.

What the CPT's visits have done is to show that even in a relatively stable and mature democracy like the UK, ill-treatment of people in detention can and does occur. Furthermore, that visits and reports by a pan-national body of experts can help prevent such abuses occurring. Despite the relatively open nature of criminal justice services in the UK, on two occasions in the past decade it was the involvement of the CPT, rather than a domestic institution, which was instrumental in ending systematic malpractice. This may not be an earth-shattering record of achievement, but it is not an insignificant one either.

REFERENCES

Home Office (1991) *Custody, Care and Justice: The Way Ahead for the Prison Service in England and Wales*, Cm 1647 (London: HMSO)
Woolf Report (1991) *Prison Disturbances April 1990*: Report of an Inquiry by the Rt. Hon. Lord Justice Woolf (Part I and II) and His Honour Judge Stephen Tumim (Part II), Cm 1456 (London: HMSO)

Appendix 1

Table of Signatures and Ratifications (as at 31 December 1998) of the European Convention for the Prevention of Torture and Inhuman or Degrading Treatment or Punishment

Member State	Date of Signature	Date of Ratification	Entry into Force
Albania	02.10.96	02.10.96	01.02.97
Andorra	10.09.96	06.01.97	01.05.97
Austria	26.11.87	06.01.89	01.05.89
Belgium	26.11.87	23.07.91	01.11.91
Bulgaria	30.09.93	03.05.94	01.09.94
Croatia	06.11.96	11.10.97	01.02.98
Cyprus	26.11.87	03.04.89	01.08.89
Czech Republic	23.12.92	07.09.95	01.01.96
Denmark	26.11.87	02.05.89	01.09.89
Estonia	28.06.96	06.11.96	01.03.97
Finland	16.11.89	20.12.90	01.04.91
France	26.11.87	09.01.89	01.05.89
Germany	26.11.87	21.02.90	01.06.90
Greece	26.11.87	02.08.91	01.12.91
Hungary	09.02.93	04.11.93	01.03.94
Iceland	26.11.87	19.06.90	01.10.90
Ireland	14.03.88	14.03.88	01.02.89
Italy	26.11.87	29.12.88	01.04.89
Latvia	11.09.97	10.02.98	01.06.98
Liechtenstein	26.11.87	12.09.91	01.01.92
Lithuania	14.09.95	26.11.98	01.03.99
Luxembourg	26.11.87	06.09.88	01.02.89
Malta	26.11.87	07.03.88	01.02.89
Moldova	02.05.96	02.10.97	01.02.98
Netherlands	26.11.87	12.10.88	01.02.89
Norway	26.11.87	21.04.89	01.08.89
Poland	11.07.94	10.10.94	01.02.95
Portugal	26.11.87	29.03.90	01.07.90

Member State	Date of Signature	Date of Ratification	Entry into Force
Romania	04.11.93	04.10.94	01.02.95
Russia	20.02.98	05.05.98	01.09.98
San Marino	16.11.89	31.01.90	01.05.90
Slovak Republic	23.12.92	11.05.94	01.09.94
Slovenia	04.11.93	02.02.94	01.06.94
Spain	26.11.87	02.05.89	01.09.89
Sweden	26.11.87	21.06.88	01.02.89
Switzerland	26.11.87	07.10.88	01.02.89
The 'former Yugoslav Republic of Macedonia'	14.06.96	06.06.97	01.10.97
Turkey	11.01.88	26.02.88	01.02.89
Ukraine	02.05.96	05.05.97	01.09.97
United Kingdom	26.11.87	24.06.88	01.02.89

Appendix 2

List of Visits and of Resulting Reports and Responses, 1990–1998

A: In Alphabetical Order

Country	Date of Visit	Type of Visit	Report Published	Interim Report Published	Follow-up Report Published
Albania	09.12.97–19.12.97	Periodic			
Albania	13.12.98–17.12.98	Follow-up			
Andorra	27.05.98–29.05.98	Periodic			
Austria	20.05.90–27.05.90	Periodic	03.10.91	03.10.91 (a)	
Austria	26.09.94–07.10.94	Periodic	31.10.96	31.10.96 (a)	
Belgium	14.11.93–23.11.93	Periodic	14.10.94	03.05.95	21.02.96
Belgium	31.08.97–12.09.97	Periodic	18.06.98		
Bulgaria	26.03.95–07.04.95	Periodic	06.03.97	06.03.97	06.03.97
Croatia	20.09.98–30.09.98	Periodic			
Cyprus	02.11.92–09.11.92	Periodic	22.05.97		
Cyprus	12.05.96–21.05.96	Periodic	22.05.97		
Czech Republic	16.02.97–26.02.97	Periodic			
Denmark	02.12.90–08.12.90	Periodic	06.09.91	21.03.96	21.03.96
Denmark	29.09.96–09.10.96	Periodic	24.04.97	11.12.97	28.04.98
Estonia	13.07.97–23.07.97	Periodic			

Country	Date of Visit	Type of Visit	Report Published	Interim Report Published	Follow-up Report Published
Finland	10.05.92–20.05.92	Periodic	01.04.93	26.08.93	25.02.94
Finland	07.06.98–17.06.98	Periodic			
France	27.10.91–08.11.91	Periodic	19.01.93	19.01.93	17.02.94
France (Martinique)	03.07.94–07.07.94	*Ad Hoc*	24.09.96	24.09.96	24.09.96
France	20.07.94–22.07.94	Follow-up	23.01.96	23.01.96	N/A (b)
France	06.10.96–18.10.96	Periodic	14.05.98	14.05.98	14.05.98
Germany	08.12.91–20.12.91	Periodic	19.07.93	01.03.94	
Germany	14.04.96–26.04.96	Periodic	17.07.97	17.07.97	
Germany	25.05.98–27.05.98	*Ad Hoc*			
Greece	14.03.93–26.03.93	Periodic	29.11.94	29.11.94	21.02.96
Greece	04.11.96–06.11.96	Follow-up			
Greece	25.05.97–06.06.97	Periodic			
Hungary	01.11.94–14.11.94	Periodic	01.02.96 (c)	18.04.96	
Iceland	06.07.93–12.07.93	Periodic	28.06.94	20.10.94	12.02.96
Iceland	29.03.98–06.04.98	Periodic			
Ireland	26.09.93–05.10.93	Periodic	13.12.95	13.12.95	19.09.96
Ireland	29.03.98–06.04.98	Periodic			
Italy	15.03.92–27.03.92	Periodic	31.01.95	31.05.95	
Italy	22.10.95–06.11.95	Follow-up	04.12.97	04.12.97	
Italy	25.11.96–28.11.96	*Ad Hoc*			

Country	Date of Visit	Type of Visit	Report Published	Interim Report Published	Follow-up Report Published
Liechtenstein	14.04.93–16.04.93	Periodic	23.05.95	23.05.95	
Luxembourg	17.01.93–25.01.93	Periodic	12.11.93	01.04.94	
Luxembourg	20.04.97–25.04.97	*Ad Hoc*	03.12.98	03.12.98	N/A (b)
Malta	01.07.90–09.07.90	Periodic	01.10.92		
Malta	16.07.95–21.07.95	Periodic	26.09.96	26.09.96	10.07.97
Moldova	11.10.98–21.10.98	Periodic			
Netherlands	30.08.92–08.09.92	Periodic	15.7.93	20.12.93	
Netherlands (Antilles)	26.06.94–30.06.94	*Ad Hoc*	18.01.96	18.01.96	
Netherlands (Aruba)	30.06.94–02.07.94	*Ad Hoc*	03.10.96	03.10.96	03.10.96
Netherlands	17.11.97–27.11.97	Periodic	29.09.98		
Netherlands (Antilles)	07.12.97–11.12.97	Follow-up	10.12.98	10.12.98	N/A (b)
Norway	27.06.93–06.07.93	Periodic	21.09.94	21.09.94	26.04.96
Norway	17.03.97–21.03.97	*Ad Hoc*	05.09.97	22.01.98	N/A (b)
Poland	30.06.96–12.07.96	Periodic	24.09.98	24.09.98	24.09.98
Portugal	19.01.92–27.01.92	Periodic	22.07.94	22.07.94	
Portugal	14.05.95–26.05.95	Periodic	21.11.96	21.11.96	27.11.97
Portugal	20.10.96–24.10.96	Follow-up	13.01.98	13.01.98	N/A (b)
Romania	24.09.95–06.10.95	*Ad Hoc* (d)	19.02.98	19.02.98	19.02.98
Russia	16.11.98–30.11.98	*Ad Hoc* (e)			
San Marino	25.03.92–27.03.92	Periodic	12.10.94		

Country	Date of Visit	Type of Visit	Report Published	Interim Report Published	Follow-up Report Published
Slovakia	25.05.95–07.07.95	Periodic	03.04.97	03.04.97	03.04.97
Slovenia	19.02.95–28.02.95	Periodic	27.06.96	27.06.96	
Spain	01.04.91–12.04.91	Periodic	05.03.96	05.03.96	
Spain	10.04.94–22.04.94	Periodic	05.03.96	05.03.96	
Spain	10.06.94–14.06.94	*Ad Hoc*	05.03.96	05.03.96	N/A (b)
Spain	17.01.97–18.01.97	*Ad Hoc*			
Spain	21.04.97–28.04.97	*Ad Hoc*	19.05.98	19.05.98	N/A (b)
Spain	22.11.98–04.12.98	Periodic			
Sweden	05.05.91–14.05.91	Periodic	12.03.92	01.10.92	15.03.93
Sweden	23.08.94–26.08.94	Follow-up	03.04.95	02.10.95	N/A (b)
Sweden	15.02.98–25.02.98	Periodic			
Switzerland	21.07.91–29.07.91	Periodic	27.01.93	27.01.93	08.06.94
Switzerland	11.02.96–23.02.96	Periodic	26.06.97	26.06.97	29.01.98
The 'former Yugoslav Republic of Macedonia'	17.05.98–27.05.98	Periodic			
Turkey	09.09.90–21.09.90	*Ad Hoc*			
Turkey	29.09.91–07.10.91	*Ad Hoc*			
Turkey	22.11.92–03.12.92	Periodic			
Turkey	16.10.94–28.10.94	Follow-up			
Turkey	19.08.96–23.08.96	*Ad Hoc*			

Country	Date of Visit	Type of Visit	Report Published	Interim Report Published	Follow-up Report Published
Turkey	18.09.96–20.09.96	*Ad Hoc*			
Turkey	05.10.97–17.10.97	Periodic			
Ukraine	08.02.98–24.02.98	Periodic			
UK	29.07.90–10.08.90	Periodic	26.11.91	26.11.91	15.04.93
UK (Northern Ireland)	20.07.93–29.07.93	*Ad Hoc*	17.11.94	17.11.94	
UK	15.05.94–31.05.94	Periodic	05.03.96	05.03.96 (f)	
UK/Isle of Man	08.09.97–17.09.97	*Ad Hoc*			

(a) Published as 'Comments', but forming the Interim Response.

(b) No Follow-up Report requested.

(c) Published with 'Comments'.

(d) The ECPT entered into force for Romania on 1.02.95. Although the visit undertaken resembled a periodic visit in form and substance, it was not conducted within the scheduled periodic visit programme for 1995 and so is classified as an *ad hoc* visit.

(e) The ECPT entered into force for Russia on 1.09.98. Although the visit undertaken resembled a periodic visit in form and substance, it was not conducted within the scheduled periodic visit programme for 1998 and so is classified as an *ad hoc* visit. A periodic visit is scheduled to take place to Russia in 1999.

(f) Described as 'Final Response'.

B: In Date Order

[1990]

Country	Date of Visit	Type of Visit	Report Published	Interim Report Published	Follow-up Report Published
Austria	20.05–27.05	Periodic	03.10.91	03.10.91 (a)	
Malta	01.07–09.07	Periodic	01.10.92		
UK	29.07–10.08	Periodic	26.11.91	26.11.91	15.04.93
Turkey	09.09–21.09	*Ad Hoc*			
Denmark	02.12–08.12	Periodic	06.09.91	21.03.96	21.03.96

(a) Published as 'Comments'.

[1991]

Country	Date of Visit	Type of Visit	Report Published	Interim Report Published	Follow-up Report Published
Spain	01.04–12.04	Periodic	05.03.96	05.03.96	
Sweden	05.05–14.05	Periodic	12.03.92	01.10.92	15.03.93
Switzerland	21.07–29.07	Periodic	27.01.93	27.01.93	08.06.94
Turkey	29.09–07.10	*Ad Hoc*			
France	27.10–08.11	Periodic	19.01.93	19.01.93	17.02.94
Germany	08.12–20.12	Periodic	19.07.93	01.03.94	

[1992]

Country	Date of Visit	Type of Visit	Report Published	Interim Report Published	Follow-up Report Published
Portugal	19.01–27.01	Periodic	22.07.94	22.07.94	
Italy	15.03–27.03	Periodic	31.01.95	31.05.95	
San Marino	25.03–27.03	Periodic	12.10.94		
Finland	10.05–20.05	Periodic	01.04.93	26.08.93	25.02.94
Netherlands	30.08–08.09	Periodic	15.07.93	20.12.93	
Cyprus	02.11–09.11	Periodic	22.05.97		
Turkey	22.11–03.12	Periodic			

[1993]

Country	Date of Visit	Type of Visit	Report Published	Interim Report Published	Follow-up Report Published
Luxembourg	17.01–25.01	Periodic	12.11.93	01.04.94	
Greece	14.03–26.03	Periodic	29.11.94	29.11.94	21.02.96
Liechtenstein	14.04–16.04	Periodic	23.05.95	23.05.95	
Norway	27.06–06.07	Periodic	21.09.94	21.09.94	26.04.96
Iceland	06.07–12.07	Periodic	28.06.94	20.10.94	12.02.96
UK (Northern Ireland)	20.07–29.07	*Ad Hoc*	17.11.94	17.11.94	
Ireland	26.09–05.10	Periodic	13.12.95	13.12.95	19.09.96
Belgium	14.11–23.11	Periodic	14.10.94	03.05.95	21.02.96

[1994]

Country	Date of Visit	Type of Visit	Report Published	Interim Report Published	Follow-up Report Published
Spain	10.04–22.04	Periodic	05.03.96	05.03.96	
UK	15.05–31.05	Periodic	05.03.96	05.03.96 (a)	
Spain	10.06–14.06	*Ad Hoc*	05.03.96	05.03.96	N/A (b)
Netherlands (Antilles)	26.04–30.04	*Ad Hoc*	18.01.96	18.01.96	
Netherlands (Aruba)	30.06–02.07	*Ad Hoc*	03.10.96	03.10.96	03.10.96
France (Martinique)	03.07–07.07	*Ad Hoc*	24.09.96	24.09.96	24.09.96
France	20.07–22.07	Follow-up	23.01.96	23.01.96	N/A (b)
Sweden	23.08–26.08	Follow-up	03.04.95	02.10.95	N/A (b)
Austria	26.09–07.10	Periodic	31.10.96	31.10.96 (c)	
Turkey	16.10–28.10	Follow-up			
Hungary	01.11–14.11	Periodic	01.02.96 (d)	18.04.96	

(a) Described as 'Final Response'.
(b) No Follow-up Report requested.
(c) Described as 'Comments', but forming the Interim Response.
(d) With 'Comments'.

[1995]

Country	Date of Visit	Type of Visit	Report Published	Interim Report Published	Follow-up Report Published
Slovenia	19.02–28.02	Periodic	27.06.96	27.06.96	
Bulgaria	26.03–07.04	Periodic	06.03.97	06.03.97	06.03.97
Portugal	14.05–26.05	Periodic	21.11.96	21.11.96	27.11.97
Slovakia	25.05–07.07	Periodic	03.04.97	03.04.97	03.04.97
Malta	16.07–21.07	Periodic	26.09.96	26.09.96	10.07.97
Romania	24.09–06.10	*Ad Hoc* (a)	19.02.98	19.02.98	19.02.98
Italy	22.10–06.11	Periodic	04.12.97	04.12.97	

(a) The ECPT entered into force for Romania on 1.02.95. Although the visit undertaken resembled a periodic visit in form and substance, it was not conducted within the scheduled periodic visit programme for 1995 and so is classified as an *ad hoc* visit.

[1996]

Country	Date of Visit	Type of Visit	Report Published	Interim Report Published	Follow-up Report Published
Switzerland	11.02–23.02	Periodic	26.06.97	26.06.97	29.01.98
Germany	14.04–26.04	Periodic	17.07.97	17.07.97	
Cyprus	12.05–21.05	Periodic	22.05.97		
Poland	30.06–12.07	Periodic	24.09.98	24.09.98	24.09.98
Turkey	19.08–23.08	*Ad Hoc*			
Turkey	18.09–20.09	*Ad Hoc*			
Denmark	29.09–09.10	Periodic	24.04.97	11.12.97	28.04.98
France	06.10–18.10	Periodic	14.05.98	14.05.98	14.05.98
Portugal	20.10–24.10	Follow-up	13.01.98	13.01.98	N/A (a)
Greece	04.11–06.11	Follow-up			
Italy	25.11–28.11	Follow-up			

(a) No Follow-up Report requested.

[1997]

Country	Date of Visit	Type of Visit	Report Published	Interim Report Published	Follow-up Report Published
Spain	17.01–18.01	*Ad Hoc*			
Czech Republic	16.02–26.02	Periodic			
Norway	17.03–21.03	*Ad Hoc*	05.09.97	22.01.98	N/A (a)
Luxembourg	20.04–25.04	*Ad Hoc*	03.12.98	03.12.98	N/A (a)
Spain	21.04–28.04	*Ad Hoc*	19.05.98	19.05.98	N/A (a)
Greece	25.05–06.06	Periodic			
Estonia	13.07–23.07	Periodic			
Belgium	31.08–12.09	Periodic	18.06.98		
UK/Isle of Man	08.09–17.09	*Ad Hoc*			
Turkey	05.10–17.10	Periodic			
Netherlands	17.11–27.11	Periodic	29.09.98		
Netherlands (Antilles)	07.12–11.12	Follow-up	10.12.98	10.12.98	N/A (a)
Albania	09.12–19.12	Periodic			

(a) No Follow-up Report requested.

[1998]

Country	Date of Visit	Type of Visit	Report Published	Interim Report Published	Follow-up Report Published
Ukraine	08.02.98–24.02.98	Periodic			
Sweden	15.02.98–25.02.98	Periodic			
Iceland	29.03.98–06.04.98	Periodic			
The 'former Yugoslav Republic of Macedonia'	17.05.98–27.05.98	Periodic			
Germany	25.05.98–27.05.98	*Ad Hoc*			
Andorra	27.05.98–29.05.98	Periodic			
Finland	07.06.98–17.06.98	Periodic			
Ireland	31.08.98–09.09.98	Periodic			
Croatia	20.09.98–30.09.98	Periodic			
Moldova	11.10.98–21.10.98	Periodic			
Russia	16.11.98–30.11.98	*Ad Hoc* (a)			
Spain	22.11.98–04.12.98	Periodic			
Albania	13.12.98–17.12.98	Follow-up			

(a) The ECPT entered into force for Russia on 1.09.98. Although the visit undertaken resembled a periodic visit in form and substance, it was not conducted within the scheduled periodic visit programme for 1998 and so is classified as an *ad hoc* visit. A periodic visit is scheduled to take place to Russia in 1999.

Appendix 3

CPT Document Citation

A: Table of CPT Visit Reports and State Responses

Country	Visit	Nature of Document	CPT Ref	Our Citation
Austria	20.05.90– 27.05.90	Report Comments	CPT/Inf (91) 10 CPT/Inf (91) 11	Austria 1 Austria 1 R 1
	26.09.94– 07.10.94	Report Comments	CPT/Inf (96) 28 CPT/Inf (96) 29	Austria 2 Austria 2 R 1
Belgium	14.11.93– 23.11.93	Report Interim Report Follow-up Report	CPT/Inf (94) 15 CPT/Inf (95) 6 CPT/Inf (96) 7	Belgium 1 Belgium 1 R 1 Belgium 1 R 2
	31.08.97– 12.09.97	Report	CPT/Inf (98) 11	Belgium 2
Bulgaria	26.03.95– 07.04.95	Report Interim Report Follow-up Report	CPT/Inf (97) 1 CPT/Inf (97) 1 CPT/Inf (97) 1	Bulgaria 1 Bulgaria 1 R 1 Bulgaria 1 R 2
Cyprus	02.11.92– 09.11.92	Report	CPT/Inf (97) 5	Cyprus 1
	12.05.96– 21.05.96	Report	CPT/Inf (97) 5	Cyprus 2
Denmark	02.12.90– 08.12.90	Report Interim Report Follow-up Report	CPT/Inf (91) 12 CPT/Inf (96) 14 CPT/Inf (96) 14	Denmark 1 Denmark 1 R 1 Denmark 1 R 2
	29.09.96– 09.10.96	Report Interim Report Follow-up Report	CPT/Inf (97) 4 CPT/Inf (97) 14 CPT/Inf (98) 6	Denmark 2 Denmark 2 R 1 Denmark 2 R 2
Finland	10.05.92– 20.05.92	Report Interim Report Follow-up Report	CPT/Inf (93) 8 CPT/Inf (93) 16 CPT/Inf (94) 3	Finland 1 Finland 1 R 1 Finland 1 R 2
France	27.10.91– 08.11.91	Report Interim Report Follow-up Report	CPT/Inf (93) 2 CPT/Inf (93) 2 CPT/Inf (94) 1	France 1 France 1 R 1 France 1 R 2

Country	Visit	Nature of Document	CPT Ref	Our Citation
France (Martinique)	03.07.94–07.07.94	Report	CPT/Inf (96) 24	France (Martinique) 1
		Interim Report	CPT/Inf (96) 24	France (Martinique) 1 R 1
		Follow-up Report	CPT/Inf (96) 24	France (Martinique) 1 R 2
France	20.07.94–22.07.94	Report	CPT/Inf (96) 2	France 2
		Response	CPT/Inf (96) 2	France 2 R
France	06.10.96–18.10.96	Report	CPT/Inf (98) 7	France 3
		Observations	CPT/Inf (98) 8	France 3 R 1
		Follow-up Report	CPT/Inf (98) 8	France 3 R 2
Germany	08.12.91–26.04.96	Report	CPT/Inf (93) 13	Germany 1
		Interim Report	CPT/Inf (93) 14	Germany 1 R 1
	14.04.96–26.04.96	Report	CPT/Inf (97) 9	Germany 2
		Interim Report	CPT/Inf (97) 9	Germany 2 R 1
Greece	14.03.93–26.03.93	Report	CPT/Inf (94) 20	Greece 1
		Interim Report	CPT/Inf (94) 21	Greece 1 R 1
		Follow-up Report	CPT/Inf (96) 8	Greece 1 R 2
Hungary	01.11.94–14.11.94	Report	CPT/Inf (96) 5	Hungary 1
		Interim Report	CPT/Inf (96) 15	Hungary 1 R 1
Iceland	06.07.93–12.07.93	Report	CPT/Inf (94) 8	Iceland 1
		Interim Report	CPT/Inf (94) 16	Iceland 1 R 1
		Follow-up Report	CPT/Inf (96) 26	Iceland 1 R 2
Ireland	26.09.93–05.10.93	Report	CPT/Inf (95) 14	Ireland 1
		Interim Report	CPT/Inf (95) 15	Ireland 1 R 1
		Follow-up Report	CPT/Inf (96) 23	Ireland 1 R 2
Italy	15.03.92–27.03.95	Report	CPT/Inf (95) 1	Italy 1
		Interim Report	CPT/Inf (95) 2	Italy 1 R 1
	15.03.92	Report	CPT/Inf (97) 12	Italy 2
		Interim Report	CPT/Inf (97) 12	Italy 2 R 1
Liechtenstein	14.04.93–16.04.93	Report	CPT/Inf (95) 7	Liechtenstein 1
		Interim Report	CPT/Inf (95) 8	Liechtenstein 1 R 1
Luxembourg	17.01.93–25.01.93	Report	CPT/Inf (93) 19	Luxembourg 1
		Interim Report	CPT/Inf (94) 5	Luxembourg 1 R 1
	20.04.97–25.04.97	Report	CPT/Inf (98) 16	Luxembourg 2
		Response	CPT/Inf (98) 16	Luxembourg 2 R
Malta	01.07.90–09.07.90	Report	CPT/Inf (92) 5	Malta 1
	16.07.95–21.07.95	Report	CPT/Inf (96) 25	Malta 2
		Interim Report	CPT/Inf (96) 26	Malta 2 R 1
		Follow-up Report	CPT/Inf (97) 8	Malta 2 R 2

Country	Visit	Nature of Document	CPT Ref	Our Citation
Netherlands	30.08.92– 08.09.92	Report Interim Report	CPT/Inf (93) 15 CPT/Inf (93) 20	Netherlands 1 Netherlands 1 R 1
Netherlands Antilles	26.06.94– 30.06.94	Report Response	CPT/Inf (96) 1 CPT/Inf (96) 1	Netherlands Antilles 1 Netherlands Antilles 1 R 1
Netherlands Aruba	30.06.94– 02.07.94	Report Interim Report Follow-up Report	CPT/Inf (96) 27 CPT/Inf (96) 27 CPT/Inf (96) 27	Netherlands Aruba 1 Netherlands Aruba 1 R 1 Netherlands Aruba 1 R 2
Netherlands	17.11.97– 27.11.97	Report	CPT/Inf (98) 15	Netherlands 2
Netherlands Antilles	07.12.97– 11.12.97	Report Response	CPT/Inf (98) 17 CPT/Inf (98) 17	Netherlands Antilles 2 Netherlands Antilles 2 R
Norway	27.06.93– 06.07.93	Report Interim Report Follow-up Report	CPT/Inf (94) 11 CPT/Inf (94) 12 CPT/Inf (96) 16	Norway 1 Norway 1 R 1 Norway 1 R 2
	17.03.97– 21.03.97	Report Response	CPT/Inf (97) 11 CPT/Inf (98) 3	Norway 2 Norway 2 R
Poland	30.06.96– 12.07.96	Report Interim Report Follow-up Report	CPT/Inf (98) 13 CPT/Inf (98) 14 CPT/Inf (98) 14	Poland 1 Poland 1 R 1 Poland 1 R 2
Portugal	19.01.92– 27.01.92	Report Interim Report	CPT/Inf (94) 9 CPT/Inf (94) 9	Portugal 1 Portugal 1 R 1
	14.05.95– 26.05.95	Report Interim Report Follow-up Report	CPT/Inf (96) 31 CPT/Inf (96) 32 CPT/Inf (97) 13	Portugal 2 Portugal 2 R 1 Portugal 2 R 2
	20.10.96– 24.10.96	Report Response	CPT/Inf (98) 1 CPT/Inf (98) 2	Portugal 3 Portugal 3 R
Romania	24.09.95– 06.10.95	Report Interim Report Follow-up Report	CPT/Inf (98) 5 CPT/Inf (98) 5 CPT/Inf (98) 5	Romania 1 Romania 1 R 1 Romania 1 R 2
San Marino	25.03.92– 27.03.92	Report	CPT/Inf (94) 13	San Marino 1
Slovakia	25.03.95– 07.07.95	Report Interim Report Follow-up Report	CPT/Inf (97) 2 CPT/Inf (97) 3 CPT/Inf (97) 3	Slovakia 1 Slovakia 1 R 1 Slovakia 1 R 2

Country	Visit	Nature of Document	CPT Ref	Our Citation
Slovenia	19.02.95– 28.02.95	Report Interim Report	CPT/Inf (96) 18 CPT/Inf (96) 19	Slovenia 1 Slovenia 1 R 1
Spain	01.04.91– 12.04.91	Report Interim Report	CPT/Inf (96) 9 (a)	Spain 1 Spain 1 R 1
	10.04.94– 22.04.94	Report Interim Report	CPT/Inf (96) 9 CPT/Inf (96) 10	Spain 2 Spain 2 R 1
	10.06.94– 14.06.94	Report Response	CPT/Inf (96) 9 CPT/Inf (96) 10	Spain 3 Spain 3 R
	21.04.97– 28.04.97	Report Response	CPT/Inf (98) 9 CPT/Inf (98) 10	Spain 4 Spain 4 R
Sweden	05.05.91– 14.05.91	Report Interim Report Follow-up Report	CPT/Inf (92) 4 CPT/Inf (92) 6 CPT/Inf (93) 7	Sweden 1 Sweden 1 R 1 Sweden 1 R 2
	23.08.94– 26.08.94	Report Response	CPT/Inf (95) 5 CPT/Inf (95) 12	Sweden 2 Sweden 2 R
Switzerland	21.07.91– 29.07.91	Report Interim Report Follow-up Report	CPT/Inf (93) 3 CPT/Inf (93) 4 CPT/Inf (94) 7	Switzerland 1 Switzerland 1 R 1 Switzerland 1 R 2
	11.01.96– 23.02.96	Report Interim Report Follow-up Report	CPT/Inf (97) 7 CPT/Inf (97) 7 CPT/Inf (98) 4	Switzerland 2 Switzerland 2 R 1 Switzerland 2 R 2
UK	29.07.90– 10.08.90	Report Interim Report Follow-up Report	CPT/Inf (91) 15 CPT/Inf (91) 16 CPT/Inf (93) 9	UK 1 UK 1 R 1 UK 1 R 2
	20.07.93– 29.07.93	Report Response	CPT/Inf (94) 17 CPT/Inf (94) 18	UK 2 UK 2 R 1
	15.05.94– 31.05.94	Report Response	CPT/Inf (96) 11 CPT/Inf (96) 12	UK 3 UK 3 R

(a) Not published as a CPT/Inf document but available, in Spanish, from the CPT Secretariat on request. See CPT/Inf (96) 10.

B: CPT General Reports

General Report No	Calendar Year	CPT Ref	Our Citation
1	1990	CPT/Inf (91) 3	Gen Rep 1
2	1991	CPT/Inf (92) 3	Gen Rep 2
3	1992	CPT/Inf (93) 12	Gen Rep 3
4	1993	CPT/Inf (94) 10	Gen Rep 4
5	1994	CPT/Inf (95) 10	Gen Rep 5
6	1995	CPT/Inf (96) 21	Gen Rep 6
7	1996	CPT/Inf (97) 10	Gen Rep 7
8	1997	CPT/Inf (98) 12	Gen Rep 8

Index